The advent of modern
in France, 1770-

	DATE DUE	
JAN 02 1996 S		

THE ADVENT OF MODERN
CAPITALISM IN FRANCE,
1770–1840

THE ADVENT OF MODERN CAPITALISM IN FRANCE, 1770–1840

The Contribution of Pierre-François Tubeuf

GWYNNE LEWIS

CLARENDON PRESS · OXFORD
1993

Oxford University Press, Walton Street, Oxford OX2 6DP
Oxford New York Toronto
Delhi Bombay Calcutta Madras Karachi
Petaling Jaya Singapore Hong Kong Tokyo
Nairobi Dar es Salaam Cape Town
Melbourne Auckland
and associated companies in
Berlin Ibadan

Oxford is a trade mark of Oxford University Press

Published in the United States
by Oxford University Press, New York

British Library Cataloguing in Publication Data
Data available

Library of Congress Cataloging in Publication Data
Lewis Gwynne.
Pierre-François Tubeuf and the advent of capitalism in France, 1770–1840 / Gwynne Lewis.
p. cm.
Includes bibliographical references and index.
1. Tubeuf, Pierre-François. 2. Businessmen—France—Cévennes Mountains Region—Biography.
3. Coal mines and mining—France—Cévennes Mountains Region—History—18th century.
4. Coal mines and mining—France—Cévennes Mountains Region—History—19th century.
5. Castries, Armand-Charles-Augustin de la Croix, duc de, 1756–1842. 6. Cévennes
Mountains Region (France)—Industries—History—18th century. 7. Cévennes Mountains Region
(France)—Industries—History—19th century. 8. Capitalism—France—Cévennes Mountains
Region (France—History—18th century. 9. Capitalism—France—Cévennes Mountains Region
(France)—History—19th century. I. Title.
HD9552.5.T83L49 1992 338.7′622334′092—dc20 [B] 92–12455
ISBN 0–19–822895–3

Typeset by Pure Tech Corporation, Pondicherry, India
Printed and bound in Great Britain by Bookcraft Ltd.,
Midsomer Norton, Bath

PREFACE

A DECADE ago, Professor Pierre Deyon provided an agenda for future research on the development of modern French capitalism suggesting, *inter alia*, that it might be appropriate to examine, in far greater detail than had hitherto been the case, 'the relationship between protoindustrialisation and the old feudal–seigneurial society, defining it as a phase which was typical of the transition towards modern bourgeois, capitalist society'.[1] More recently, Professor John Davis, assessing the work already completed by a number of social and economic historians over the past couple of decades, particularly at the local level, commented on the growing consensus which prefers 'to think of "proto-industry" as a frame of reference rather than a theory', adding that once this is accepted,

then the important common feature is the emphasis these studies place on the ways in which economic growth has been influenced by social, institutional, and other non-economic factors. Although the region or the locality is the preferred focus of 'proto-industrial' studies, they make no attempt to portray the region as an economic unit or to draw a rigid distinction between regional and national economies. Indeed, through the light that is thrown on changing institutional structures and on the impact of administrative and political innovations at a local level, local studies of this sort are often particularly valuable in offering insights into the complex economic and political relationships that existed between the periphery and the centre, the region and state.[2]

The present work is focused upon the relationship between seigneurial, protoindustrial, and modern forms of capitalism, and, whilst it is grounded, geographically, in the Cévennes region of south-eastern France, its political and economic boundaries extend to the corridors of power at Versailles, the coal-mines of Anzin and Littry, and the commercial and manufacturing trade routes of central Europe, the east coast of America, Saint-Domingue, and the ports of Latin

---

[1] P. Deyon, 'Premier bilan et perspectives pour un congrès', *Revue du Nord*, 63 (248) (1981), 6.

[2] 'Industrialization in Britain and Europe before 1850: New Perspectives and Old Problems', in P. Mathias and J. Davis, *The First Industrial Revolutions* (Oxford, 1989), 63.

America. In eighteenth-century France, protoindustrialization was an international, not a local or regional, phenomenon. Hence its vulnerability to economic recession, changing markets, and fashions. A cévenol weaver could be making silk stockings for Peruvian ladies one winter, but making sacks for his farming neighbours the next. Hence, also, the bitter and prolonged resistance to capitalist entrepreneurs whose plans to create a 'modern' coal-mining industry in the Basses-Cévennes threatened to disrupt traditional patterns of economic and social relationships.

If 'protoindustrial studies' have proved the pace-setter in establishing an agenda for research into eighteenth- and nineteenth-century French history, the study of the French Revolution, whether as the harbinger of modern totalitarian regimes, or as a barrier to the expansion of the French economy at a crucial phase of the economic history of modern Europe, has come a close second. Revisionist historians have denounced the Revolution as the cradle of modern political barbarism and the source of France's relative economic stagnation after 1815.[3] Our own conclusions are far less dramatic and ideologically supercharged. The history of the Revolution, especially when one is dealing with the long-term economic and social evolution of modern France, must surely be placed within the overall context of French history, at the very least from the reign of Louis XVI to that of Louis Philippe. The roots of the economic stagnation which affected most areas of French industry and manufacture during the turbulent 1790s were deeply embedded in the *ancien régime*, thus providing us with a partial explanation of the outbreak of the Revolution itself. However, there can be no doubt that the political uncertainty of the Revolutionary and Napoleonic period, the consequence of the drastic restructuring of French government and society accompanied by over twenty years of war, seriously exacerbated the problem. In this study, a great deal of emphasis is placed on the decentralization of French government after 1789, which gave to the tens of thousands of municipalities in France the power to resist, *on an economic as well as on a political level*, the introduction of modern, and possibly risky, forms of industrial capitalism. It is equally certain that the cold embrace of modern forms of capitalism by the restored Bourbons between 1814 and 1830 served to protect the more traditional forms of commercial and protoindustrial production.

[3] Typical of the genre is the best-seller *Citizens* by Simon Schama (London, 1989).

Although this study seeks to unravel the complex problems associated with the impact of the Revolution upon the processes of modern French capitalism by examining the contemporary responses of provincial politicians and property-owners, urban lawyers and *gens d'affaires*, textile workers, coal-heavers, and colliers, the actions of two men—the maréchal de Castries, friend of Marie Antoinette, and Pierre-François Tubeuf, friend of many of Louis XVI's ministers—dominate the scene. Their private papers provide a fascinating insight into a truly epic struggle for control of the rich coal-mines situated in south-eastern France, culminating in the emigration of both men at the beginning of the Revolution. Their heirs continued the bitter fight throughout the Revolution and Bourbon Restoration. In a sense, the prize was the future shape of French capitalism, at least in the Bas-Languedoc region. Few men fought with more courage and foresight than one of the great entrepreneurs of eighteenth-century France, Pierre-François Tubeuf. History appears to have left him by the archival wayside. This study is, in part, a contribution towards his rediscovery.

G. L.

January 1991

CONTENTS

MAPS

FIGURES

TABLES

ABBREVIATIONS

AC Alès	*archives communales d'Alès* (in *AG*)
AC Anduze	*archives communales d'Anduze* (in *AG*)
AG	*archives du Gard*
AH	*archives de l'Hérault* (in *AG*)
AHC	*archives des Houillères des Cévennes*
AN	*Archives nationales*
B. de N.	Bibliothèque de Nîmes

INTRODUCTION: THE BASSES-CÉVENNES IN THE MID-EIGHTEENTH CENTURY

IT seems incongruous today that the streamlined Paris–Marseille express—*le Corail*—should stop at the rather depressed and drab town of the Grand-Combe. And so it is; unless, of course, one is familiar with the history of the Alès coal-basin, with the fact that one of the first railways in France was transporting coal from the Grand-Combe to Alès and Beaucaire in the 1840s, ultimately to compete with coals from Newcastle and South Wales in Marseille and other Mediterranean ports. If one has time to alight at the village and walk a few yards outside the station, a simple glance at the architecture of the town will reveal its history—Louis Philippe and Second Empire buildings around the colliery; mid-Third Republican higher up the hillsides; high-rise tower blocks, constructed during France's post-Second World War boom, representing the final tier. The sight of derelict miners' terraced houses, rusting railway lines and coal-wagons, silent pit-head winding-gear is familiar enough to someone raised in the Rhondda valley of South Wales, whose history offers so many instructive comparisons with that of the Grand-Combe. For the coal valleys of South Wales and those of the south-east of France, the time when 'coal was king' is long over.[1] Depressing contemporary images should not be allowed to obscure the fact, however, that two centuries ago coal from the Abilon, Grand-Combe, and Rochebelle mines helped to fuel a potential 'industrial revolution' in the Basses-Cévennes, one that was eventually to be halted by the inadequate response of a government concerned with national growth but hamstrung by aristocratic vested-interest groups, the structures of a protoindustrial socio-economy, and, subsequently, by the damaging effects of the Revolution of 1789. Under Napoleon Bonaparte, a new, rather hesitant, *étatiste* 'political economy' would emerge, only for its evolution to be arrested by the debilitating effects of successive economic and

---

[1] The nearby Aubin coal-basin has experienced the same pattern of decline: 'Daily life in Decazeville is no longer structured around shifts at the mine; the soot which every visitor to the town remarks upon may soon be a thing of the past.' D. Reid, *The Miners of Decazeville: A Genealogy of Deindustrialization* (Cambridge, Mass., 1985), 1.

political crises, and the even more hesitant action of Restoration governments. The 'take-off' in the coal industry would be delayed until after the Revolution of 1830.

The Alès coal-basin is situated in the Basses-Cévennes in south-eastern France. The region we shall be studying includes the coal-basin itself as well as the towns and villages which were economically linked to it. We may describe it as a (very rough) circle, having Alès at its base then, travelling in a clockwise direction, the manufacturing and trading towns of Anduze, Lasalle, Saint-Jean-du-Gard, Saint-André-de-Valborgne, Saint-Germain-de-Calberte, Bessèges, and Saint-Ambroix

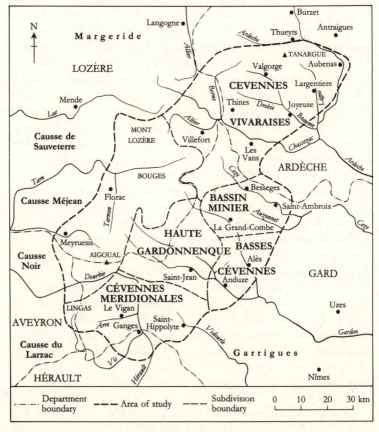

MAP I.1. The Cévennes region of south-eastern France. Taken from Philippe Joutard, *Les Cévennes de la montagne à l'homme* (Toulouse, 1979)

as points on the circumference. The coal-mines of the Alès basin—as we shall discuss more fully in the following chapter—all lay within this circle with, appropriately enough, the richest mine of all, the Grand-Combe, at its centre. In other words, we shall be concentrating, in the main, on the manufacturing and trading towns of the *ancien régime* dioceses of Alès and Uzès, which were to constitute the northern part of what was to become the department of the Gard after 1790. However, these coal-mines served a much wider community including lime-burners, silk-spinners, small forge-masters, and distillers operating within a circuit of exchange identified by Michael Sonenscher as stretching as far as Mende in the Gévaudan to the north, as well as to Uzès, then, eastwards, to les Vans, Joyeuse, and Aubenas in the Bas-Vivarais (the southern Ardèche after 1790), and to the international port of Beaucaire on the river Rhône.[2] To the south-east, the trade routes ran through Saint-Hippolyte-du-Fort and Ganges to Lunel, thence to Montpellier and Nîmes. From a manufacturing and commercial standpoint, the latter city dominated the entire region. It was the second largest silk-manufacturing city in France; its commercial contacts linked Europe to the Americas.[3] Our study, then, will be focused on the Basses-Cévennes, but will encompass much of Bas-Languedoc.

Alès, still known today as 'the capital of the Cévennes', itself boasts a long and honourable commercial and historical pedigree. A Roman colony—called Alestum—has been documented for the period around the year 26 BC,[4] and anyone acquainted with the present-day department of the Gard can hardly be ignorant of its classical heritage. Nîmes, situated just 44 kilometres to the south-east of Alès, with its remarkably well-preserved amphitheatre and the classical jewel of the Maison Carrée around the corner, has been called the 'Rome of France', whilst the Pont-du-Gard, the aqueduct constructed by the Romans to solve one of the major problems besetting Nîmes as a manufacturing city—shortage of water—has been acknowledged as one of the marvels of European civilization. Alès has very few physical memorials to its Roman past. It has derived its strength from the

---

[2] M. Sonenscher, 'Royalists and Patriots: Nîmes and its Hinterland in the Late-Eighteenth Century', Ph.D. thesis, Warwick, 1975, 257–8.

[3] See Map I. 1.

[4] M. Bruyère, *Alès, capitale des Cévennes: vie politique, religieuse, intellectuelle, économique et sociale* (Nîmes, 1948), 10–11. From 1694 to 1926, the town was referred to as 'Alais'. I have used this form when quoting from documents of the period, but the modern form of 'Alès' throughout the main body of the text.

range of rugged hills and mountains of the Cévennes stretching in an arc from north-west to north-east and shielding Catholic and Protestant communities, a few of whom affronted the sensibilities of Arthur Young.[5]

If it could not compete with Nîmes in terms of its classical heritage, Alès was fiercely proud of its tradition of muncipal liberties. As early as the year 1200, the *commune d'Alais* had been granted a charter from the local nobility permitting the election of four *consuls* to head its administration, the *premier consul* acting as mayor. Even at this date, the town was a thriving trading and commercial centre, as it had been since Roman times.[6] In the eighteenth and nineteenth centuries, families like the Dhombres and Firmas-Périès produced a succession of mayors and municipal councillors destined to play a formative role in the transformation of an economy based on wool and silk to one based on coal and iron. Such families were conscious, and proud, of the municipal independence of their town. They well understood the elaborate and complicated procedures by which, from the fourteenth century on, the town had selected eighty *conseillers* from 'les nobles, bourgeois, marchands, laboureurs et artisans, partagés en dix échelles', these ten rungs (*échelles*) subsequently being divided into four ranks (*rangs*), 'suivant l'ordre des dignités'.[7] They would have regretted the attempts by a centralizing and (perhaps more important) impoverished monarchy to curtail their freedoms, by the legislation of 1692 and 1772, for example, which forced municipal taxpayers throughout France to purchase the right to choose their own magistrates, from mayors to *sergents-trompettes*. Louis Dhombres, fulfilling a key role in the decades immediately preceding the Revolution as *sub-délégué* of the

[5] A. Young, *Travels in France during the Years 1787, 1788 and 1789* (Cambridge, 1950), 46: 'To Montdardier (near Ganges), over a rough mountain covered with box and lavender; it is a beggarly village, with an *auberge* that almost made me shrink. Some cut-throat figures were eating black bread, whose visages had so much of the galleys that I thought I heard their chains rattle.'

[6] M. Rivière-Dejean, 'De l'émancipation de la bourgeoisie et des fonctions consulaires d'Alais', *Société scientifique et littéraire d'Alais*, 24 (1893), 90. See also M. A. Gros, 'Étude sur la ville d'Alais', *Société scientifique et littéraire d'Alais*, 26 (1891), 86.

[7] *Recherches historiques sur la ville d'Alais* (Alès, 1860), 508–23. An Act passed in 1294 laid down the procedures for the choice of *conseillers*, including the stipulation that the *premier consul* had to be chosen from the *échelle* of 'gentilshommes, docteurs et licenciés en droit ou en médicine, bourgeois et autres notables . . . n'exerçant aucun négoce ou art mécanique'. After 1689, the *consuls* of Alès were confirmed, from a list provided by the *corps municipal*, first by the Intendant and subsequently by the comte d'Alais, who, at least during the period when the Contis were the local seigneurs, usually accepted the names proposed without too much fuss.

Intendant as well as *receveur des tailles* for the diocese of Alès, was in the vanguard of the struggle by the Estates of Languedoc to retain their 'historic liberties' against 'despotic' ministers and intendants. This political struggle between Versailles and the Estates was to determine much of the agenda for the economic debate in the decades immediately preceding the Revolution.

Of more immediate concern to the leading families of Alès and neighbouring cévenol towns was religion. The mountains of the Cévennes had provided a refuge for 'heresy' since the Cathar movement of the thirteenth century: it had been the scene of some of the bloodiest conflicts in French history since the visit of Calvin to Nîmes in the mid-sixteenth century.[8] During my first prolonged spell of research in the region, I well remember finding myself—as if it were the most natural thing in the world—in an apartment block in Montpellier, attending a service conducted by an octogenarian pastor for ageing Protestant refugees from Franco's Spain. From the thirteenth to the twentieth century, as Le Roy Ladurie's *Montaillou* confirms,[9] heresy was the constant companion of shepherds and commercial travellers who traversed the Franco-Spanish border. For Protestants, given their exclusion from public office, were deeply involved in the world of finance, manufacture, and commerce: Geneva doubled up as a spiritual and financial home for the wealthiest of them. Michael Sonenscher notes that 'In all the cévenol towns, running from le Vigan to les Vans, Protestants controlled the largest proportion of property and revenue.' In 1767, the list of those eligible for municipal office in Alès contained not a single *négociant*, no tanner, and only two *marchands de soie*, Protestants, of course, being amongst the ineligible.[10] Anduze and Saint-Jean-du-Gard, just 13 and 27 kilometres respectively from Alès, were predominantly Protestant manufacturing and trading *bourgs*, dominated numerically and economically by *les huguenots*. Like Alès, these, and other, mainly Protestant towns and villages had lived through the excesses of the Wars of Religion, which often spread like a contagion from Nîmes, like la Michelade of 30 September 1567, in which dozens of Catholics were killed. Five years later, an even bloodier revenge was enacted during the Massacre

[8] P. Joutard, 'Les Cévennes entrent dans l'histoire', in Joutard, P. (ed.), *Les Cévennes de la montagne à l'homme* (Toulouse, 1979).

[9] E. Le Roy Ladurie, *Montaillou: The Promised Land of Error* (New York, 1979).

[10] Sonenscher, 'Royalists and Patriots', 275.

of St Bartholomew.[11] From the late sixteenth century to the siege of Alès by royalist troops in 1629, Protestants had dominated the administrative and political life of the region, the last time they were to do so until the Revolution of 1789.[12]

The reign of the Sun King, Louis XIV, was to stamp an indelible mark upon the physical and administrative life of Alès. The *fort d'Alais*, which still dominates the town, was built in the late 1680s to deal with potential Protestant rebellions. In 1694, the diocese of Alès was created by Pope Innocent XII, mainly to facilitate the Catholic repression of the Protestant community following the Revocation of the Edict of Nantes. The Revocation, and its brutal enforcement by the Intendant, Bâville, was bitterly resented and resisted in the Cévennes, giving birth to the evangelical *prédicateur*, the spiritual descendant of *les Bonshommes* of the Cathar faith.[13] Deeply rooted, and well fortified, in their cévenol *bourgs* and hamlets, Protestants, particularly the poorer peasants and artisans, were loath to take the road to exile; the majority of young men preferred to take to the hills to join the armed bands led by Jean Cavalier. The Guerre des Camisards, which erupted during the mid 1700s, proved to be the most ferocious of all eighteenth-century Protestant–Catholic conflicts, reinforcing the existence of two bitterly divided communities.[14] Sporadic, and occasionally ferocious, repression of Protestants during the first half of the century, including breaking on the wheel and imprisonment in the galleys, eroded class differences in their communities, the manufacturing and financial élites achieving greater control over their work-force by highlighting the very real threat of persecution. The tacit toleration of Protestantism in France during the latter half of the century could never really heal the wounds inflicted by two centuries of intermittent religious fanaticism. Certainly events during the Revolution would support this contention. Throughout the second half of the eighteenth century there was increasing resentment of Catholic domination of the political and administrative life of the region amongst leading Protestants,

---

[11] J. Hood, 'Permanence des conflits traditionnels sous la Révolution: l'exemple du Gard', *Revue d'histoire moderne et contemporaine*, 24 (1977), 604–5.

[12] Bruyère, *Alès, capitale des Cévennes*, 208.

[13] Joutard, 'Les Cévennes entrent dans l'histoire', 136–40.

[14] See P. Joutard, *Les Camisards* (Paris, 1976); J. Armogathe, and P. Joutard, 'Bâville et la guerre des Camisards', *Revue d'histoire moderne et contemporaine*, 19 (1972); J. Cavalier, *Mémoires sur la guerre des Camisards* (Paris, 1979). Philippe Wolff estimates that, between 1680 and 1720, around 15,000–18,000 Protestants emigrated from Bas-Languedoc as a result of the religious conflict. *Histoire du Languedoc* (Toulouse, 1967), 372–3.

conscious of their vastly superior financial resources. In Alès, this domination had been underlined by the creation of new *collèges*, the establishment of ten religious orders and *confréries*, as well as a considerable expansion in the activities of the *frères des écoles chrétiennes* who maintained their school in the place Saint-Nicolas up to 1789.[15]

It is clear that the exile of some of the wealthier Protestants, either to safer havens in France or to Switzerland, should not be entered too thoughtlessly on the debit side of the balance-sheet relating to the Revocation. The Protestant diaspora, linking Nîmes to Lyon and thence to Geneva, was to be extremely important in oiling the financial wheels of the mid-eighteenth-century boom in the textile industry.[16] None the less, the troubled years between 1680 and 1720 undoubtedly left an unenviable legacy in the economic sphere. It was not until the mid-eighteenth century, for example, that pre-Camisard patterns of trading had been fully reactivated. In 1751, the municipalities of Alès and Saint-Hippolyte petitioned the government for the re-establishment of their annual fairs 'qu'ils disent n'avoir été interrompus que par les ,guerres civiles'.[17] By this time the cévenol region was feeling the benefit of the expansion of the silk industry, which had been registered in Nîmes during the 1730s.

For the better part of the seventeenth and well into the eighteenth century, it had been the woollen industry which had created the manufacturing base of the Languedoc economy, the cévenol hill-towns possessing 'the sort of advantages which economic historians now consider to be of primary significance in explaining the location of 'protoindustrialization'.[18] At the beginning of the eighteenth century, Languedoc was already enjoying the benefits of the biggest textile industry in France. However, although the woollen industry was to maintain its domination in and around towns like Clermont-de-Lodève until the mid-eighteenth century, it was the silk stocking and silk fabrics industry which had begun to assume pride of place in Nîmes by the 1730s, spreading northwards to Alès, Uzès, les Vans, and their satellite towns and villages over the next two or three decades. The

---

[15] *Recherches historiques sur la ville d'Alais*, 528–9.

[16] Wolff, *Histoire du Languedoc*, 373–4.

[17] *AN* F12 1228, letter of the Intendant, Saint-Priest, 15 Mar. 1751. Saint-Priest stressed that the reopening of the fair would be good 'pour le commerce des manufactures et des tanneries qui est assez considérables dans les villes d'Alais et de St. Hippolyte'.

[18] See e.g. J. Thomson, *Clermont-de-Lodève, 1633–1789: Fluctuations in the Prosperity of a Languedocian Cloth-Making town* (Cambridge, 1982), 38.

silk *organsins*, *trames*, *burats*, and *fleurets* of Nîmes and Uzès began to replace the poor-quality *molletons* of Sommières, the *cadis* of Saint-Mamert, and the *serges* associated with Alès.[19] By 1789, only the towns of Sommières, Anduze, Lasalle, Saint-Jean-du-Gard, and Saint-Hippolyte-du-Fort were still producing woollen goods on any substantial scale, and in Anduze production was only one-eighth of what it had been in 1750. Overall, the woollen industry was employing a quarter of its 1668 figure.[20]

Undoubtedly one of the major factors explaining the decline of woollens, particularly in the colonies, was the rise of the cotton industry: cotton thread was increasingly used in Nîmes and the Cévennes, often mixed with silk or wool. The *jurés-gardes* of Marvéjols, bemoaning the decline of their woollen industry, complained in 1775: 'No sooner had cotton goods appeared than, either because of cost or because of their novelty, every woman started to wear them, and weavers were forced to take jobs in those workshops in Nîmes and Montpellier which had begun to work on cotton goods.'[21] However, raw cotton had to be imported and transported at considerable cost to the remote *bourgs* of the Cévennes: raw silk could be produced, literally, at home. Throughout the eighteenth century, and increasingly after 1750 thanks to government encouragement,[22] the mulberry tree, upon whose leaves the voracious silkworms fed, began to compete for space with olive trees, chestnuts, and the vine along the ribbed cévenol hillsides. By 1759, three-quarters of all the mulberry trees in Languedoc were growing in the dioceses of Alès, Uzès, and the Bas-Vivarais.[23] Tens of thousands of peasant-artisans devoted themselves and their families, from April to August, to the delicate business of feeding the silkworms, producing the cocoons, then winding, reeling, and spinning the raw silk. A consequence of the international

---

[19] Sonenscher, 'Royalists and Patriots', 259–62.

[20] Joutard, 'Les Cévennes entrent dans l'histoire', 156–7.

[21] P. Wolff, *Documents de l'histoire du Languedoc* (Toulouse, 1969), 268.

[22] The French government, copying the success of the Italian silk industry, gave sizeable bounties to silk workers and manufacturers who were prepared to bring their skills to France. Also, by the 1750s, the Intendant of Languedoc was offering 25 *livres* for every 100 feet of land devoted to the planting of mulberry trees. F. Taillefer, 'La Cévenne ou les Cévennes', in Joutard (ed.), *Les Cévennes de la montagne à l'homme*, 27. For a comparison of the French and Italian silk industries and their relationship to the German market see S. Ciriacono, 'Esquisse d'une histoire tripolaire: les soieries franco-italiennes et le marché allemand à l'époque moderne', *Études réunies en l'honneur du Doyen Georges Livet* (Strasbourg, 1986), 317–26.

[23] Sonenscher, 'Royalists and Patriots', 293–4.

division of labour relating to textiles, the lower Cévennes region, despite the continued diversity of its economy—tanning, sheep-rearing, manufacturing stockings and hats, etc.—was being transformed into a colony producing the raw materials for the manufacturing cities of Saint-Étienne, Lyon, Tours, and Paris.

The rise of the silk industry would involve increased dependence upon Nîmes, with important economic and political consequences for the entire region. On the eve of the Revolution, Alès and its immediate hinterland would be producing around 6,000 *quintaux* of silk-cocoons a year, Anduze and Saint-Jean-du-Gard 5,000, and Saint-Ambroix 4,000, representing in all 15 per cent of total French production. The manufacture of cheap silk stockings began to consume a higher percentage of a family's annual work time, particularly through the autumn and winter months. Many more local *marchands-fabricants* were acting as *commissionnaires* for the international Protestant commercial houses in Nîmes and Montpellier.[24] By the 1780s, the last Intendant of Languedoc, Ballainvilliers, would describe the province as 'pleine de manufactures',[25] its most obvious structural feature being 'l'extrême diversité de la fabrique à travers bourgs et villages'.[26] However, the city of Nîmes would attract the lion's share of the hosiery industry during the second half of the century. In 1750, just 500 stocking-frames were operating in the city; in 1768, that figure would rise to 1,900 and, five years later, to 3,000. By this time, the commercial houses of Nîmes and Montpellier had well-established branches in Germany, Russia, Switzerland, Italy, and—by far the most important outlet of all—Cadiz in Spain.[27]

National and regional, as well as international, competition, was increasingly exerting pressure on the nîmois and cévenol textile industry by the mid-eighteenth century. This competition was forcing it to concentrate on the 'popular' end of the market. Never really in the same league, so far as high-quality textiles were concerned, with their counterparts in Lyon, the *négociants* of Nîmes fell back increasingly on cheap and shoddy goods produced by semi-skilled 'proto-industrial' workers. One consequence of this was the ferocious

---

[24] Joutard, 'Les Cévennes entrent dans l'histoire', 155.

[25] E. Tarlé, *L'Industrie dans les campagnes en France à la fin de l'ancien régime* (Paris, 1910), 11. It should be noted, however, that Ballainvilliers, like Pierre-François Tubeuf, whom he supported, favoured the concentration of production.

[26] R. Dugrand, *Villes et campagnes en Bas-Languedoc* (Paris, 1963), 383.

[27] F. de la, Farelle, *Étude historique sur le consulat et les institutions municipales de la ville de Nîmes, suivie d'un mémoire sur son passé industriel* (Nîmes, 1841), 240.

opposition to the Colbertian system of quality control beloved of seventeenth-century royal bureaucrats. James Thomson has argued persuasively that there was a general loss of faith in 'interventionism' during the second half of the eighteenth century as the political economy of the likes of Turgot and Adam Smith, buttressed by the undoubted supremacy of the English industrial machine, shook the complacency of government officials.[28] This was possibly the first, though by no means the last, disservice that Smith's doctrines—based on the needs of commerce rather than those of heavy industry—was to perform for mankind in general, and the interests of the French coal industry in particular. One of the most revolutionary consequences of this change in official attitudes, which, in truth, was founded more upon French than British economic theory, was the decree of 7 September 1762 which allowed country-dwellers to work without joining the *corporations de métier*, although they were still bound to observe the *règlements* of their particular industry.[29] In the Alès region, the edict of 1762 was to be extremely important in pushing the *fabrique de Nîmes* further in the direction of cheap mass-produced goods, increasing the antagonism which already existed between urban master-craftsmen and the *négociants* and *marchands-fabricants* who were eager to satisfy the demands of an international market. Given that the great majority of the latter were of the Protestant faith, and that a sizeable proportion of the former were Catholics, the seeds of the violent conflict which was to manifest itself during the Revolution were being sown.

An expanding, yet extremely vulnerable, economy exerted its impact upon population growth in the lower Cévennes, a region which had experienced a long period of demographic stability. The population of the Bas-Vivarais did not increase appreciably between 1640 and 1715; that of the woollen town of Clermont-de-Lodève appears to have remained reasonably stable, at around 5,000 inhabitants, between

---

[28] Thomson, *Clermont-de-Lodève*, 358–9.

[29] The last Intendant of Languedoc, Ballainvilliers, notes, however, that the *règlements* were more often honoured in the breach than the observance. See Tarlé, *L'Industrie dans les campagnes en France*, 75. The local authorities did their best. As late as 12 Feb. 1771 the *jurés gardes de la ville d'Anduze* paid a surprise visit to a domestic weaver living a few kilometres out of the town 'pour veiller à la manutention de la fabrique'. They found that Baux was not using the weights on his loom appropriate for the production of the *molletons d'Anduze*. He was taken to the *hôtel de ville* 'afin d'y faire prononcer . . . les peines portées par le règlement'. *AC* Anduze HH 15–16, report by Berbiguier and Saltet.

1347 and 1769.[30] Nineteenth-century chroniclers suggest an even more static pattern for the town of Alès: 930 households in 1393 increasing to only 1,098 as late as 1858![31] We appear to be in the territory of Ladurie's *histoire immobile*, of Braudel's *longue durée*.[32] However, even if we ignore the increasing impact of the State upon individual lives, the human cost of protracted and bloody wars and civil strife, as well as major changes in the structure of the economy, and stick narrowly to statistics, we discover that the cévenols were, in fact, experiencing considerable change. In an increasingly commercial and manufacturing society, however, population growth was occurring outside the city walls rather than within them. The population of Alès *ville* increased from 5,300 in 1690 to 5,800 in 1721. However, the total population of Alès, including its rapidly expanding suburbs, had jumped to 6,400.[33] As we shall see, the population continued to rise throughout the region at a higher rate than the national average throughout the eighteenth century. Many eighteenth-century manufacturing towns were bursting at the medieval walls, producing spasms of apprehension amongst the real bourgeois, terrified at the prospect of having to mingle with the 'unwashed' outside. In Nîmes, a scheme to pull down part of the ancient walls in the 1780s provoked fierce resistance from many inhabitants, anxious that if the plans went ahead 'the city would be at the mercy of the *peuple des faubourgs*, five-eighths of whom are inclined towards theft, pillage, murder and immorality'.[34]

Changing patterns of work and trade, the increasing influx of people to the town, led to a physical reshaping of Alès in the mid-eighteenth century. A major new road—the rue d'Avéjan—linked the *route de Nîmes* to the *route d'Auvergne*. The Grand'rue was taken over by merchants and market stall-holders.[35] New houses were being built for wealthy Protestant merchants. During the 1740s, builders began work in the heart of the city on a new *hôtel de ville*, which eventually

---

[30] A. Molinier, 'En Vivarais au XVIIIe siècle: une croissance démographique sans révolution agricole', *Annales du Midi*, 92 (1980), 304; Thomson, *Clermont-de-Lodève*, 47.

[31] *Recherches historiques sur la ville d'Alais*, 20. The author concludes that Alès 'slept' for three centuries!

[32] Ladurie, Le Roy E. 'History that Stands Still', in *The Mind and Method of the Historian* (Chicago, ILL., 1981), 1–27.

[33] Bruyère, *Alès, capitale des Cévennes*, 269 and 310. The figures for 1690 and 1721 are fairly accurate since a detailed investigation of population movements was undertaken at the time of the last outbreak of plague in the region.

[34] F. Rouvière, *Mercredis révolutionnaires* (Nîmes, 1901), 42–3.

[35] Gros, 'Étude sur la ville d'Alais', 88–90.

opened its doors to the local dignitaries in 1752.[36] Who were these local dignitaries? What kind and condition of people, living and working in the eighty parishes which comprised the diocese of Alès, did they represent? Fortunately, we are able to make a fairly accurate assessment of cévenol society from the tax-rolls of the period—the detailed *capitation* rolls covering the diocese for 1736, together with the 1754 *vingtième d'industrie* for Anduze.[37]

The documentation on the diocese of Alès covers no fewer than 19,709 individuals. They are divisible (excluding at this stage domestic servants, widows, etc.) into the socio-economic categories shown in Table I.1. If we break down the figures in terms of the average amount of tax paid by each *classe*, we arrive at Table I.2. Perhaps the most striking fact to emerge from these figures is the apparently modest position—in economic terms—of the nobility. But we know that the nobility escaped the lion's share of the *taille* and the *capitation*, whilst the clergy escaped altogether. The modest profilé of the nobility, however, is confirmed by Philippe Joutard: 'The first characteristic to strike one is the relative weakness of the cévenol nobility . . . The great noble families which one discovers in the Haut-Gévaudan and on the periphery did not exist in the Cévennes', adding that the majority of nobles enjoyed an income of less than 3,000 *livres* a year in *rentes*.[38] The Intendant Bâville in his memoirs named only two noble houses of distinction in the diocese of Alès—the La Fares and the Bérard de Montalets, both truly *noblesse de l'épée*. He concluded: 'One can say that, with the exception of a few *grands seigneurs* who live at Court, the nobles (*gentilshommes*) of Languedoc are not wealthy . . . Those who live in the towns, mainly in Bas-Languedoc, do not possess carriages, avoid costly commitments, and make a profession of saving.'[39] The real value of annual incomes is difficult to assess unless related to the cost of living. Arthur Young was informed that he, and his family, could live in the region very comfortably 'for 100 *louis* [2,400 *livres*] a year; that there were many families of noblesse, who subsisted on 50, and even on 25 (*louis*) a year'.[40] It is also clear from the figures

[36] *Recherches historiques*, 271–7.

[37] *AG* C512, *état des capitables du diocèse d'Allais (sic)*; *AG* C512, *état des contribuables sujets à payment du vingtième de l'industrie.*

[38] Joutard, 'Les Cévennes entrent dans l'histoire', 101.

[39] *Recherches historiques*, 613–14. Bâville added that out of 4,486 *familles de gentilshommes* in the province of Languedoc, only 15 had more than 20,000 *livres de rente.*

[40] Young, *Travels in France*, 47. Young was actually in Millau.

TABLE I.1. *Distribution of socio-economic categories in the diocese of Alès, 1736*

Social category	Number	Percentage
Nobility		
(*Gentilshommes* or *gens vivant noblement*)	196	1.0
Bourgeoisie		
Rentiers	381	2.0
Avocats, médicins	73	0.4
Procureurs, notaires	83	0.4
Négociants	155	0.8
Marchands-fabricants, marchands de détail	769	4.0
Apothicaires, chirurgiens	122	0.6
Agricultural sector		
Ménagers	1,043	5.2
Fermiers, métayers	768	3.9
Travailleurs de terre, journalites	5,509	27.9
Industrial sector		
Artisans et ouvriers	5,228	26.5
Compagnons et apprentis	324	1.6

TABLE I.2. *Average tax paid by each social category, Alès, 1736*

Social category	Average tax paid	
	L.	s.
Nobles	38	8
Négociants	29	10
Bourgeois (rentiers)	18	5
Procureurs, notaires	13	15
Ménagers	12	5
Marchands	9	6
Fermiers, métayers	5	2
Artisans et ouvriers	4	18
Travailleurs, journaliers	3	2

that, as early as the 1730s, no great disparity of wealth separated a 'noble' from a 'négociant'. James Thomson makes the point, referring to the province as a whole, that in some cases the roles could be combined.[41] Indeed, it is now established that the majority of 'nobles'

[41] 'Many of Languedoc's noble families, if not actually owing their origin to industrial

in Languedoc had bought their way into the aristocracy via commerce, the classic example being the Airebeaudouze brothers of Anduze, rich merchants who, in the second half of the sixteenth century, had purchased the *seigneurie d'Anduze*.[42]

The records relating to the levy of the *vingtième de l'industrie* for Anduze list eight *négociants* who bought and sold raw silk, cloth, grain, chestnuts, and mules, and who were estimated to have made a modest annual profit of around 1,800 *livres* a year.[43] These figures are almost certainly underestimates,[44] reinforcing the conclusion drawn above for the diocese as a whole concerning the narrow financial band separating nobles from *négociants*. One should not, however, leap to the facile conclusion, based after all upon averages, that certain nobles, particularly the La Fares and the Montalets, did not regard themselves as being in a different *classe* from the *négociants*, as indeed did the official responsible for drawing up the tax lists. This applies with even greater force to the noble who will figure prominently in this work—the maréchal de Castries—who lived at Court and enjoyed the favours of Marie Antoinette. It should also be noted that the great majority of *négociants* and *marchands-fabricants* in Alès, Anduze, and Saint-Jean-du-Gard were, if not in a different *classe*, then certainly in a different financial bracket from many of their counterparts in Nîmes and Montpellier, who operated on a national and international level, and for whom they frequently acted as *commissionnaires*.

A more detailed enquiry into the social structure of the region will follow in a subsequent chapter. It is important from the outset, however, to emphasize the size and numerical wealth of the legal and professional bourgeoisie. Omitted from Table I.1—since their numbers were not statistically significant—were the three *receveurs de taille*. One of them was the local notable we have already mentioned as

production, had been reinforced at some stage by intermarriage with the children or grandchildren of clothiers.' Thomson, *Clermont-de-Lodève*, 40.

[42] J.-C. Hélas, 'Avant la soie, avant Calvin: une pré-histoire', in Joutard (ed.), *Les Cévennes de la montagne à l'homme*, 94.

[43] Anduze was typical of the larger cévenol towns surrounding Alès. The totals collected for the *vingtième de l'industrie* were: Alès 2,276 *livres*, Saint-Hippolyte-du-Fort 2,074, Anduze 1,939. Saint-Jean-du-Gard paid 930, Sauve 844, Sumène 834, Lasalle 819, Valleraugue 790, and le Vigan 740.

[44] *AG* C512, *état des contribuables*. The document makes it very clear that it was extremely difficult to make realistic estimates of manufacturing wealth. The figures relating to profit margins were acquired as a result of talking to people in the town and trying to estimate the value of goods merchants had in their windows! This is why tax-returns, throughout the period we are studying, must be treated with great caution.

destined to play a key role in the transition of Alès from a commercial and textile-manufacturing town to an industrial city, Louis Dhombres. Their average *capitation* payment of 48 *livres* 8 *sols* was significantly higher than the average for the nobility. Almost as wealthy, and actually listed at the head of the tax-roll as dispensers of the king's justice, were the nineteen *officiers de justice*, paying, on average, 32 *livres* 9 *sols*. These, along with the *avocats*, *procureurs*, and *notaires* (the twenty-two *huissiers* and *sergents* were small fry, paying an average tax of 2 *livres* 11 *sols*), were possibly the most hated group so far as the *petit peuple* of the region were concerned.

In the agricultural sphere, the *ménagers* (relatively well-to-do farmers, counterparts of the *laboureurs* of more northern regions), who farmed their own land as well as leasing farms from others, were both wealthier and more numerous than the *fermiers* and the far more impoverished *métayers* or sharecroppers. One should also note the balance between the number of agricultural and industrial workers, giving the 'rural lobby' a considerable voice in the attack on unbridled commercial and manufacturing growth. The significance of this point is reinforced by Maurice Agulhon's analysis of provençal society: 'We see, behind these abstractions, which social forces were really in conflict . . . industry and agriculture. Competitors for water, competitors for wood, competitors, finally, for labour. . . . such were the jealous sisters.'[45] The relationship between these 'jealous sisters', the way in which the agricultural lobby, linked to a protoindustrial form of production, obstructed the development of heavy industrialization in particular, will form one of the main themes of this study. Staying in the agricultural sector, the high figure of 118 *maîtres bergers* is worth isolating, stressing as it does the importance of sheep-rearing and tanning in the region. Their average tax payment of 3 *livres* 3 *sols* places them above the *travailleurs de terre*.

To complete our survey we should also emphasize the high percentage of widows in the region—7.8 per cent—as well as the 341 *filles sans qualité*. However, the most numerous and in fact the poorest single category were the 2,974 *valets et servantes*, representing 15 per cent of the total and paying an average of just 1 *livre* 1 *sol* tax. We are reminded of Jean Gutton's statement that 'la domesticité forme un groupe important dans la société de l'ancien régime'.[46] It is clear

---

[45] M. Agulhon, *La Vie sociale en Provence intérieure* (Paris, 1970), 40.

[46] J.-P. Gutton, *Domestiques et serviteurs dans la France de l'ancien régime* (Paris, 1981), 7.

from the more detailed returns for the *vigueries d'Alais et d'Anduze* on the eve of the Revolution that few wealthy nobles or bourgeois in the lower Cévennes employed more than 1 or, at most, 2 servants. Gutton notes that the wealthiest lawyer attached to the Parlement de Toulouse in 1789 had 9 servants; the oldest noble family in the Alès region—the Montalets—had only 5, whilst another distinguished family—the Suffrens—had 4. The vast majority of *négociants* and *marchands* had only 1.[47] Again, we are confronted with the picture of a small, *property-owning* society without the extremes of wealth and poverty common in many other regions of France. This was the overall impression derived by Young during his travels throughout the region: 'Such a knot of active husbandmen, who turn their rocks into scenes of fertility, because I suppose THEIR OWN, would do the same by the wastes, if animated by the same omnipotent principle.'[48] The importance, in socio-economic and political terms, of private property in our region was to represent one of the rocks upon which the audacious and disruptive plans of Pierre-François Tubeuf were to founder.

A final comment. The 122 *apothicaires et chirurgiens* on the *capitation* roll of 1736 paid an average amount of 7 *livres* 18 *sols*, but it is clear from other documentation that many were quite poor. The two 'appoticaires' (*sic*) serving Anduze in 1754 had virtually empty shops and could not live off their professional earnings: 'people go to the grocers (*épiciers*) . . . when they are obliged to purchase drugs'. However, since the names of the two apothecaries were Isaac Dassand and Abraham Bousquet, could it be that their shops were 'fronts' for the more lucrative business of money-lending? The reality of social life during the *ancien régime* was often masked by such 'shop-front' façades. The wig-makers of Alès, for example, doubled up as barbers and did a few shaves on Saturdays and Sundays.[49] On the other hand, *maîtres-perruquiers* were the only commoners entitled to wear swords, enjoying a social prestige well above their meagre income.

The average tax figures obviously conceal significant variations in the wages and conditions of *valets et servantes*.

[47] Gutton, *Domestiques et serviteurs*, 45. In 1789, the Montalets had 1 *femme de chambre*, 1 *cuisinier*, 1 *fille de cuisine*, 1 *laquais*, and 1 *cocher*. The Suffrens 2 *laquais*, 1 *palefrenier*, and 1 *femme de chambre*. *AG* C1846, *rôle de répartition de la capitation des vigueries d'Alais et d'Anduze, année 1789*.

[48] Young *Travels in France*, 47.

[49] *AG* C512, *état des contribuables*. The clerk noted that 'leur profession seule' would not have provided enough income for them to live on.

As they went into the second half of the eighteenth century, the inhabitants of the Basses-Cévennes could look ahead with some degree of optimism. True, religious hatreds lay just beneath the surface despite the fact that intellectuals told them that they were entering upon a more tolerant age, but so far as the economy was concerned, they had rarely had it so good. This was their 'âge d'or', with the city of Nîmes representing the hub of an expanding wheel of manufacture and trade, and towns like Alès, Uzès, and Bagnols benefiting from the increased volume of trade. By the 1760s, the cévenols had more money in their pockets, slightly less hatred in their hearts, and, unbeknown to the majority of them, some of the richest seams of coal in Europe under their feet. Everything seemed set for a new phase of industrialization, particularly when one of the most dynamic entrepreneurs in France, Pierre-François Tubeuf, armed with the wholehearted support of the government, decided to move his sphere of operations from the Rouergue and the Comtat-Venaissin to the Alès coal-basin.

PIERRE-FRANÇOIS TUBEUF AND THE FOUNDATIONS OF A MODERN COAL-MINING INDUSTRY

'DURING a voyage which I have just made with my wife, I saw, passing through Languedoc and the Comtat d'Avignon, several coal-mines which were being very badly worked. On our return to Paris, I made a point of speaking to M. Bertin, government minister, who asked me if I would be prepared to return to the region to examine these mines more thoroughly and then report back to him'.[1] This is the first entry, dated 12 March 1770, in Pierre-François Tubeuf's hand-written Journals which provide a rich and fascinating account of the activities of one of the most remarkable, but largely forgotten, figures in eighteenth-century French economic history.[2] For Tubeuf was to lay the foundations for the development of heavy industrialization in the Alès coal-basin, as well as opening up new coalfields in Normandy and the outskirts of Paris. One local study of the Alès region refers to him as 'le premier grand mineur de notre pays'.[3] His correspondence with Bertin and other government officials reveals the nature of the relationship which existed during the *ancien régime* between various administrations and individual entrepreneurs, as well as between a 'centralizing' State and provincial bodies like the Estates

---

[1] It took some time to track down one of the main sources of documentation used in this study. The invaluable Journals of Pierre-François Tubeuf were eventually discovered—where I always suspected they were—in the archives of the Houillères des Cévennes, although, without the assistance of Monsieur Y. Chassin du Guerny at the *archives départementales du Gard*, I doubt whether my mission would have been accomplished. The Journals have now been deposited in the *archives du Gard*. They are listed in the Bibliography.

[2] Two early works did, however, point to the significance of Tubeuf's achievements: A. Bardon, *L'Exploitation du bassin houiller d'Alais sous l'ancien régime* (Nîmes, 1898) and M. Rouff, *Tubeuf: un grand industriel français du XVIIIᵉ siècle* (Paris, 1922). Both works are important, but Bardon's suffers from presentational faults and errors of omission, whilst Rouff's short work was only intended as the first stage of a more thorough account of Tubeuf's life and work.

[3] Bruyère, *Alès, capitale des Cévennes*, 743.

of Languedoc. Tubeuf represented the forces of monopoly capitalism and his frequently tactless efforts to defeat local representatives of traditional market economics was to pose problems for the State and the Estates alike. The dialectic between economic and political issues will be one of the central concerns of this study.

In a letter to the marquis de Lafayette, Tubeuf decribed himself as 'issu des premiers propriétaires de la baronnie de Tubeuf'.[4] However, if there had been any blue blood coursing through the Tubeuf veins, it had lost its coloration a long time ago. Pierre-François Tubeuf was a 'bourgeois' so far as his immediate origins, family ties, and marriage were concerned. His *mentalité* was very much that of a capitalist bourgeois, the kind of man revisionist historians find it so difficult to track down. In his general correspondence (when not trying to impress internationally known aristocrats) he describes himself as 'Pierre-François Tubeuf, Bourgeois'.[5] He had been raised in that part of Normandy which was to become the department of the Orne. His brother was Directeur du couvent des Bénédictines in the beautiful old cathedral town of Bayeux. In 1768, he married Marie-Margueritte Brochet, daughter of a Lyon *tireur d'or*, who not only blessed him with two sons and a daughter (sadly, she died in infancy), but was to contribute, in no small measure, to the remarkable history of the Tubeuf family. Marie-Margueritte brought her husband a modest dowry of 10,000 *livres*.[6] Both husband and wife were Catholic: the latter's sister was a nun to whom the Tubeufs paid an irregular gift of money.[7]

The two boys, Pierre-François, born on 14 February 1774, and Pierre-Jean-Alexandre, born on 8 November 1779 and baptized the same day in the Church of Saint-Paul in Paris, were to involve

---

[4] *AG* 58J 5, 1 May 1791. Tubeuf added that the *baronnie* could be traced back to 1350 through the Parachas de Biron and Bardouville families, *noblesse de robe*. There was also 'à Versailles dans les Galeries du 2ᵉ étage (no.4100) la portrait de Jacques Tubeuf, président de la chambre des comptes, mort en 1670'.

[5] See e.g. the copy of a letter dated 23 May 1780 headed 'Le sieur Tubeuf, Bourgeois, demeurant rue des Barres, maison de monsieur de Saint-Sauveur'. *AG* 58J 4.

[6] *AG* 8S 95, Marie was the daughter of Antoine Brochet, *négociant de Lyon*. The marriage contract was signed on 21 Apr. 1768. All goods were to be held in common 'suivant la coutûme de Paris'. Marie's goods 'avec la portion que lui appartient dans la succession de la dite feu de sa mère et 3000 livres d'habits, linges et hardes', plus the inheritance of 10,000 *livres* originally bequeathed to her by her uncle Étienne Alexandre Pillourchery Davenay, former cavalry captain and a *chevalier de l'ordre royal*. See also Rouff, *Tubeuf*, 12–13.

[7] e.g. *AG* 58J 2, 13 Sept. 1781.

themselves not only in the family coal-mining business but in trading and commercial ventures which took them to most parts of Europe, North America, and the Caribbean.[8] Correspondence between the Tubeuf trading company and Toussaint L'Ouverture, the great black leader of Haiti, has survived. It will be argued that the move away from heavy industrialization on the part of Tubeuf's sons to glass-making and international commerce in the 1800s reflects the failure of successive regimes under the monarchy, the Revolution, and Napoleon—at least until 1810—to defeat the powerful vested-interest groups of small property-owners and raw-silk producers, represented by local municipalities, the Estates of Languedoc, and, under the *ancien régime*, one of the most powerful nobles in France, the maréchal de Castries. However, despite this shift away from the industrial vision of their father, the second generation of Tubeufs played their part in expanding the family's fortunes, and they did so through the most dramatic and difficult years in the history of France, only withdrawing from their interests in coal-mines on the eve of the 1830 Revolution.

In 1770, Tubeuf embarked upon his return journey to the coalfields of the Basses-Cévennes. As we have noted, his quest reflected the keen interest which the more far-sighted of the king's ministers, particularly Bertin, were beginning to take in the coal industry. It is important to note that in these early days, when the scope of Tubeuf's plans were still unknown, the Estates of Languedoc seemed anxious to encourage the Norman interloper, as indeed the Estates encouraged other proposals which might bring economic prosperity to the province, actively investing in major public works.[9] In January 1774, Tubeuf went to Montpellier and was considerably cheered by the reception he was given by the officials of the Estates, 'who expressed their strong approval of my establishments, whilst encouraging me to pursue my work with the greatest possible activity; they even went so far as to indicate that they might support me themselves'.[10] A year later, Tubeuf made another of his frequent visits to Montpellier, this time to collar the Archbishop of Narbonne (president of

[8] Some of Pierre-Alexandre Tubeuf's correspondence is also now housed in the *archives départementales du Gard*—58J 7–11.

[9] Arthur Young was most impressed by the roads constructed by the Estates: 'We have not in England a conception of such exertions; they are splendid and superb'. *Travels in France*, 43.

[10] *AG* 58J 2, Jan. 1774.

the Estates of Languedoc) and the Archbishop of Toulouse. Political and economic power in eighteenth-century France was often found under a mitre. In Tubeuf's words, both men 'expressed considerable satisfaction in my work and hoped very much that it would succeed'.[11]

It is not surprising that coal should have become an important topic of conversation amongst the population at large in Languedoc given the rapidly dwindling reserves of wood available to fuel the economic boom which had taken place over the last four or five decades. The Estates of Languedoc had recognized the dangers of a fuel crisis as early as 1722.[12] The *capitouls* of Toulouse periodically expressed worries about dwindling supplies of wood in the mid-eighteenth century. By 1780, their concern had changed to a state of alarm as figures were produced which showed that the diocese was burning three times as much wood annually as it produced.[13] In 1766, the Estates of Languedoc had commissioned a local expert named Gensanne to prepare a report on the location and extent of the coal reserves in the province.[14] The report (which took over ten years to publish) emphasized the increasing demand for coal, revealing for the first time the extent to which coal was now being bought for domestic heating: 'the people living in the diocese of Alès began using coal for all their domestic heating needs. A few distinguished households in the capital of this diocese began using it in their apartments throughout the winter of 1777, without the least inconvenience, by making simple and cheap rearrangements to their chimneys.'[15] A recent study, stressing the importance of the fuel crisis in Languedoc, laid particular emphasis on the increased use of coal by silkworm rearers and the consequences of the government's edict of 5 July 1770, encouraging forest clearances, which released peasants from payment of all taxes on cleared land for fifteen years.[16]

Paris had also taken a keen interest in the manufacturing potential of Languedoc since the days of Colbert, whose army of inspectors

---

[11] *AG* 58J 2, Jan. 1775.

[12] E. A. Allen, 'Deforestation and Fuel Crisis in Pre-Revolutionary Languedoc', *French Historical Studies*, 13 (1984), 462.

[13] G.-R. Galy, 'L'Exploitation des houillères en Languedoc et le marché du charbon au XVIIIᵉ siècle', *Annales du Midi*, 81 (1969), 166.

[14] See M. de Gensanne, *Histoire naturelle de la province de Languedoc, publiée par ordre de NN. SS. des États de cette province*, 4 vols. (Montpellier, 1778).

[15] Ibid. iii. 7–8.

[16] Allen, 'Deforestation and Fuel Crisis in Pre-Revolutionary Languedoc', 463.

and regulators, if they did not often penetrate the fastnesses of the Cévennes mountains, still managed to leave a legacy of State interference which, as James Thomson concludes, was to prove beneficial, at least in the early stages of the Languedocian boom in textile production.[17] A clear indication of the government's serious interest in the heavier side of industrialization came with the publication of the most important *arrêt* to govern the fledgling coal industry in the eighteenth century—Trudaine's *règlement général* of January 1744. It heralded in the modern era of coal-mining in France, rejecting previous *laissez-faire* legislation in favour of a far greater supervisory role for the State. In the words of one of the leading experts on the French mining industry: 'It marked a complete reversal of government policy on mining, an innovation of the first importance. The *arrêt* of 1744 laid down the legislative and organizational principles which still operate today.'[18] The *arrêt* had been introduced as a result of a government inquiry which revealed the lamentable state of the thousands of small coal-mines dotted throughout France.[19] In order to bring at least a semblance of order out of chaos, Article 1 of the decree insisted that no one, not even 'seigneurs dans l'étendue de leurs fiefs et justices', could legally work a mine without first obtaining the approval of the Contrôleur-général des finances. Other articles in the *arrêt* required mine-owners to provide the government with details, within six months, of the quantity of coal produced and the number of workers employed. Articles 3 to 11 covered safety and technical matters, including the width of roadways in the mines. Finally, the *arrêt* also confirmed the principle that entrepreneurs should indemnify property-owners for all damage incurred in the exploitation of a mine.[20]

The 1744 *arrêt* did indeed represent the first comprehensive and modern piece of legislation relating to coal-mining in France. So far

[17] Thomson, *Clermont-de-Lodève*, 455.

[18] M. Rouff, *Les Mines de charbon en France au XVIIIe siècle, 1744–1791* (Paris, 1922), p. xviii. It is no coincidence that Rouff begins his study in 1744.

[19] Bardon, *L'Exploitation du bassin houiller d'Alais*, 47. Also Galy, 'L'Exploitation des houillères en Languedoc', 174: 'L'arrêt du conseil du roi du 14 janvier 1744 fut pris avant tout pour substituer la surveillance de l'État à la liberté et l'anarchie des exploitations entreprises par les propriétaires du sol.'

[20] Rouff is surely right when he states that it was concern for the economic well-being of the State, rather than an attempt to replenish the king's coffers through royalties, that really prompted the decree. The attention paid to the more technical aspects of mining justifies Rouff's conclusion that the *arrêt* 'inaugure la période moderne de l'histoire des mines'. *Les Mines de charbon*, p. xviii.

as the small coal-owners and producers of the Basses-Cévennes were concerned, however, the government might never have bothered to publish it. Their passion for property-rights, based upon the written and Roman law of Languedoc, and central to an understanding of Tubeuf's problems as he set about implementing his 'grand design' for the region, led them to ignore the competing claims of the Crown, demanding that the Estates of Languedoc protect them from the 'illegal' rape of their traditional rights. In the Basses-Cévennes,

this anarchy produced disastrous results—high costs of production; lower output than should have been the case; the extraction of low-quality coal. French industry, only finding a small percentage of its needs from local and national markets, had to resort to foreign coal, which, despite all the protectionist measures taken by the government, continued to compete in France on favourable terms.[21]

Long before Great Britain undermined the power of France overseas, 'coals from Newcastle', dumped in Bordeaux and Marseille, were weakening the future industrial base of the French economy. It is a shocking indictment of the state of the French coal industry that exports from Britain, transported over a 1,000 miles, could compete favourably with coal being mined in the Cévennes less than 100 miles inland.[22] And Frenchmen knew it. Certainly this is what Pierre-François Tubeuf believed as he walked through the medieval hamlets of Meyrannes, Saint-Andéol-de-Trouilhas, and Nôtre-Dame-de-Laval, taking in the depressing sight of medieval systems of mining with half-naked miners, usually working as family units, dragging a few sacks of coal a day out of the 'foxholes' scraped into the hillsides. Achille Bardon suggests that there may have been as many as eighty small mines scattered throughout the dioceses of Alès and Uzès in the 1760s: 'Aucune n'était en règle avec l'édit de 1744.'[23]

From the beginning of his truly epic struggle to impose a modern and 'scientific' system of mining upon the cévenols, Tubeuf was under

---

[21] C. Delormeau, 'L'Arrêt du Conseil du 14 janvier 1744 sur les mines de charbon et son application dans le diocèse d'Alès', in *Mines et mineurs en Languedoc-Roussillon et régions voisines de l'Antiquité à nos jours* (Montpellier, 1977), 166.

[22] Since 1741, an import duty of thirty *sols* a *baril* had been levied on English coal landed at Cherbourg, which only led to 'dumping'. See C. Pézeril, *Ces mineurs de Littry: pionniers de l'ouest* (Bayeux, 1978), 33–4.

[23] Bardon, *L'Exploitation du bassin houiller d'Alais*, 57–8. So far as Tubeuf's concession was concerned 13 mines were to be found in the parish of Portes, 9 in Castillon-de-Courry, 9 in Saint-Jean-de-Valériscle, 8 in Saint-Andéol-de-Trouilhas, 5 in Nôtre-Dâme-de-Laval, 3 in Sénéchas, and 2 in Saint-Cécile d'Andorge.

no illusion about the technical difficulties confronting him. What he was to underestimate—with dire consequences for himself, his family, and the future of industry in the region—was the ferocious resistance of the hundreds of seigneurs and small *propriétaires*, often involved in the textile or distilling industries, supported by the *gens d'affaires* operating through the local institutions of the Estates of Languedoc—the *assiettes des diocèses*. In order to overcome this resistance, Tubeuf would lean heavily upon Bertin and fellow sympathizers in the royal Court. But this would prove a mistake in the long run. Louis XV had been prodigal with his royal prerogative, granting scores of huge mining concessions to individuals and societies, anxious to exploit the increasingly valuable coal and iron-ore reserves of France, but the implications and difficulties had never really been thought through. Like so many aspects of Bourbon government, laws were passed in the hope, more than in the expectation, that they would be observed.

In 1757, the Contrôleur-général Trudaine actually announced that, given the interminable and costly legal battles being fought between *propriétaires* and *concessionnaires*, it might be better if the former were left alone to exploit their own minerals![24] Despite this pragmatic conclusion, however, concessions were in fact granted with increasing frequency, and for longer periods, between the 1730s and the 1760s: coal played its part in the *âge d'ôr* of the Languedoc economy.[25] In Tubeuf's native Normandy, the marquis de Balleroy was given an indefinite concession of the Littry mines in November 1744.[26] The concession relating to the most productive mining complex in France at Anzin was granted a few months later. In Languedoc, the marquis de Solages's twenty-year concession of the right to mine coal on his Blajac estate—eventually to be known as the Carmaux mines—which he obtained in 1752, was extended to fifty years in 1767. The granting of these long-term concessions, which continued during the last decades of the eighteenth century,[27] covering very wide stretches of land, was bound to provoke fierce resistance from local seigneurs and

[24] Galy, 'L'Exploitation des houillères en Languedoc', 179.

[25] Ibid. 166. Galy points out that the demand for concessions started around 1730 and was associated with a greater availability of capital, a result of the economic take-off of the period. The *arrêt* of 1744, then, was a consequence, not a cause, of the demand for concessions.

[26] Pézeril, *Ces mineurs de Littry*, 23.

[27] G. Chaussinand-Nogaret provides an incomplete list of 26 concessions made to nobles during the last two decades of the *ancien régime*. *The French Nobility in the Eighteenth Century: From Feudalism to Enlightenment* (Cambridge, 1985), 106 n. 39.

roturiers, just as Trudaine feared. The case of an entrepreneur named Gibrat, forced to abandon his concession at Saint-Jean-de-Cuculles near Montpellier in 1753 following the destruction of his tools and machinery by local peasants, is typical, not exceptional.[28] Donald Reid points out that in the Aubin coal-basin—which was to be known as Decazeville in the nineteenth century—the inhabitants 'responded with violence to the nascent capitalist entreprises which attempted to work concessions granted by the crown'.[29] However, without support, small landowners and miners did not always find it easy to defeat an energetic entrepreneur if the latter enjoyed the confidence of the government and, as was the case with Tubeuf it seemed, powerful provincial institutions like the Estates of Languedoc. It was when these institutional rugs were pulled from under his feet that the entrepreneur looked vulnerable. This was to be Tubeuf's fate as we shall discover in the following chapter.

Before receiving his own concession from Louis XV—a concession which was to dominate the history of the Alès coal-basin up to the Revolution—Tubeuf had been learning his trade by opening mines and sinking pits in the nearby regions of the Rouergue and the Comtat-Venaissin. The documentary evidence for this early stage of his career is extremely sketchy, since the Tubeuf Journals do not begin until 1770. We do know, however, that Tubeuf, again with the support of the government, had been in charge of the Cransac mines in the Rouergue (future department of the Aveyron) from 1764 to 1770 and that—a harbinger of subsequent difficulties—all had not run smoothly. The lignite coal was poor in quality and difficult to mine; there were major disagreements with the shareholders of the mining company.[30] More important was the violent resistance manifested towards the entire company by small peasants and property-owners. In 1763, they wrecked mining equipment whilst 'Men armed with sticks and stones pursued Tubeuf for an hour and a half on horseback . . . calling him "robber" and "Englishman".'[31] It was to be Tubeuf's first baptism of fire as a 'foreign' entrepreneur in the Midi.

---

[28] Galy, 'L'Exploitation des houillères en Languedoc', 180.

[29] Reid, *The Miners of Decazeville*, 11.

[30] *AHC* Fonds Tubeuf. *Mémoire que Tubeuf, Directeur des mines de Cransac, a l'honneur à présenter aux messieurs les intéressés aux mines, 29 février 1768.* Apparently, the shareholders were not happy with Tubeuf's share of the profits. He rejected their criticisms, stressing that 'il a plus besoin de sa probité que d'argent', a good example of the touchy Norman's *amour-propre* and quick temper which were to be much in .evidence during his career!

[31] Reid, *The Miners of Decazeville*, 11.

Constantly seeking new opportunities to satisfy his boundless energy, Tubeuf decided to test the water across the Rhône in the Comtat-Venaissin, the region north of Avignon whose suzerainty was contested between France and the Papacy. On 25 April 1770, he was given a concession, for just one year, of the mines of 'Saint-Paulet-de-Caisson et des environs du Comtat-Venaissin'. The interaction of politics and economics resulted in a fairly brief sojourn in this historic region: over the next couple of years, Tubeuf's work in the Comtat became increasingly sporadic. In 1772, legal possession of the Comtat by the Papacy was confirmed and, following another disagreement with a local seigneur, Tubeuf began to spend far more time in the Cévennes.[32] He had already written to Bertin in December 1770 informing the minister of far better prospects for coal-mining in the dioceses of Alès and Uzès. On 19 January 1771, Tubeuf sent an official request for a concession to be granted to him covering a wide area of the Basses-Cévennes. It was to be over two years before his request was officially approved, years in which Tubeuf pursued his other interests in the Rouergue and the Comtat, as well as in a new project on the banks of the Rhône near Pont-Saint-Esprit, where he and his young wife had taken an apartment in the spring of 1770. It is clear from his Journal, however, that Tubeuf was increasingly pinning all his hopes on the Alès coal-basin.[33] The mines at Pont-Saint-Esprit turned out to be a costly and unproductive venture.

On 17 April 1773, Louis XV finally issued his *arrêt* granting Pierre-François Tubeuf a thirty-year concession to work 'the coal-mines which already exist and those which might be discovered in the region of Alès and Saint-Ambroix, as well as those situated on the land between Pont-Saint-Esprit, Laudun, Uzès, Anduze, Villefort, Aubenas, and Viviers, having Barjac as its central point'. Tubeuf was directed to observe the regulations passed in 1744 concerning safety and mining procedures; to compensate property-owners for any damage caused; and to pay 800 *livres* annually to the newly created École royale des mines. On 24 March 1774, Tubeuf's concession was

---

[32] After a visit to Paris, Tubeuf wrote that if the Comtat were to be handed back to the Papacy it 'boulverserait mon entreprise'. *AG* 58J 2, 1 Dec. 1772. Perhaps a more pressing reason for Tubeuf's disenchantment with the Comtat was yet another conflict with a seigneur, the marquis de Crochat, who fought and won a case against him for the right to mine coal on the outskirts of Avignon. *AG* 58J 2, entry for 23 Aug. 1771, which refers for the first time to the Crochat affair.

[33] *AG* 58J 2, 28 Apr. 1770, which records his decision to move into Pont-Saint-Esprit with his family.

confirmed, its geographical contours finally established in the shape of a circle, five *lieues* in diameter, with Barjac at its centre.[34] It was, by most standards, a very generous concession, complicated, however, not only by the very considerable number of landowners affected, but by the confusion which existed over the exact unit of measurement which applied to this particular decree.[35] For the moment, however, the Norman entrepreneur and engineer was only interested in one thing—making a success out of 'cette grande entreprise'.

Tubeuf's first major decision was to concentrate production at three main sites, chosen, in part, to serve local and regional markets. In July 1773, following an exhaustive tour of the entire concession, he decided that he would establish the first site at Banne, to supply the Bas-Vivarais; the second near Saint-Ambroix, to cover the diocese of Uzès; and the third, 'à la porte d'Alais', to serve the needs of the town itself, as well as those of Nîmes and Montpellier.[36] By the beginning of September, Tubeuf's handful of miners were cutting into the hillside at la Pigère near Banne; others were starting a roadway at the foot of the mountain near the village of Meyrannes, whilst a third group were fighting to drain several old workings, 'faites par les gens du pais', at the foot of the Montaud mountain outside Alès. This last venture, which came to be known as the mines of Rochebelle, was to be associated with the Tubeuf family until the later 1820s.[37] It was only a few years ago that the last tonne of coal came up the pit-shaft.

The modern industrial vision of Pierre-François Tubeuf is illustrated in the first place by his plans to concentrate all coal production on these three strategically placed sites, which implied the forced closure of the scores of small and unproductive mines which none the less

[34] *AG* 58J 2, July 1773. 'Je vais disposer cette grande entreprise et abandonner celle-ci [the mines of Pont-Saint-Esprit] qui ne soutiendrait jamais la concurrence avec les mines du comtat venaissin.'

[35] The incredible complexity of the *ancien régime* system of weights and measures was to cause—or be the excuse for—endless legal wrangling over the concession. One *lieue*, *mesure commune de France*, equalled 2,282 *toises*. Given that one *toise* equalled 1 metre 949, the *lieue* (de France) was approximately 4½ kilometres. This would have made the radius of Tubeuf's concession just over 22 km. However, one *lieue*, *mesure commune de Languedoc*, was 3,000 *toises*, which would have made the radius of Tubeuf's concession around 30 km. The crucial issue for the future was that the richest mine in the coal-basin, the Grand-Combe, lay *outside* Tubeuf's concession if the *mesure de France* was applied. Naturally, Tubeuf preferred the *mesure de Languedoc!*

[36] *AG* 58J 2.

[37] *AG* 58J 2, 9 Sept. 1773.

threatened unwelcome competition. During the first decade of his work in the region he pursued his plans with increasing determination and rigour, always falling back upon his friends in the Conseil des Mines at Versailles. His intentions were made perfectly clear in a letter he dispatched as early as October 1774. Stressing the important work he had already completed, Tubeuf concluded: 'I have only one request left to make. It is the closure of all the small, badly worked mines in the vicinity which could, whether through accidents, inexperience, or malice, cause difficulties for me.' He explained that he was thinking of about forty 'méchantes, petites mines' around Rochebelle alone, which took a sorry toll of human life.[38]

The battle between Tubeuf and the small *propriétaires* of the Alès region had been well and truly joined. In January 1777, Tubeuf solicited the support of the Intendant in his conflict with several small coal-owners, stressing that one of his major objectives was to prevent unfair competition: '*les gens du pais*, who now have no extra costs to meet [given that Tubeuf's men had drained all the old workings], are selling their coal at lower prices than I am'.[39] Three years later, Tubeuf was facing the same old problem and decided to embark upon 'the final solution'. He wrote to his mine director, Mahieu, requesting information, immediately, on the number, location, and ownership of all the mines operating in his region 'sans en exceptant une seule petite' ('including the very smallest').[40] A few months later he instructed his director at Rochebelle to 'Shut down, without distinction, every mine in the neighbourhood of Alès.' The same policy was to be followed in the Robiac and Meyrannes valley: only one pit was to be left open 'to provide for the needs of the local community'.[41]

The problem, however, was an intractable one: 'illicit' mines were to be the bane of every *concessionnaire*'s life until well into the Bourbon Restoration. Lacking the legal and repressive machinery to deal with the problem—*ancien régime* governments tended to deal with the consequences of social rebellion, not their causes—Tubeuf tried to bribe his enemies: 78 *livres* a year in 1775 to Paul Gazaix of Meyrannes,

---

[38] Rouff, *Les Mines de charbon*, 150.

[39] *AG* 58J 2, 1 Jan. 1777. Tubeuf pointed out that colliers named Drulhon, Fayeol, Girard, and Justet were extracting coal in their respective drift mines from the same seam which he had spent so much time and money on drying out. Tubeuf sought permission to close their mines, as well as those at Robiac, whose product was undercutting his at Banne.

[40] *AG* 58J 4, letter to Mahieu, 3 Aug. 1780.

[41] Ibid. Letter to Laporte, 16 Dec. 1780.

propriétaire du terrain; 18 *livres* to a certain Redaruy 'so that he closes down his mine without my having to resort to harsher measures'.[42] In 1778, Tubeuf set his sights much higher, agreeing to pay the prince de Conty the not inconsiderable sum of 2,400 *livres* a year if he agreed to supervise the closure of all the mines in the *marquisat de Portes*.[43] For the poorest villager dependent upon the local mines for his living, Tubeuf offered less glittering prizes. One of his former employees, Alles, relates the tale of one of Tubeuf's managers, accompanied by a *notaire*, driving 'in a carriage loaded with meat and wine intended as bribes for everyone in the parish [of Robiac] who had anything to do with the mines. They tried to get them to sign an agreement, saying that they would employ anyone in the parish who was presently working down the mines; but in vain, since no one had any wish to eat and drink with them, far less sell or farm out their mines.'[44]

Concentration of production was accompanied by the kind of technological innovation and management of the mines more commonly associated with the nineteenth than the eighteenth century, although technological improvements were obviously determined by geological conditions and current scientific knowledge. The 120 or so seams which made up the Alès coal field were of varying thicknesses, but they were, 'above all, very irregular in character, since they had been deformed by movements of the earth's crust, by faults and humps, one overlaying the other, all of which made exploitation difficult and costly'.[45] The Alès coalfield was really divided into two geological basins—the Grand-Combe and the Alès basin. At the higher levels, it was often extremely easy to reach the coal-seams, whilst, in between these two geological faults, the area once covered by the *ancient forêt domaniale du Rouergue*, coal broke through the surface and, as one knowledgeable observer phrased it, 'one only had to have a pair of eyes to know about it'.[46] The complicated geology of the coalfield had obviously dictated the historic pattern of mining. In general, traditional miners—'les anciens' or 'les gens du pais'—had followed outcrops of coal for 100 feet or so, at best, into the hillsides.

---

[42] *AG* 58J 2, 27 Mar. 1775.

[43] *AG* 58J 2, 23 Mar. 1778. The contract stipulated that if Tubeuf himself worked the mine, he could take the necessary timber from the *forêt de Portes*.

[44] B. de N., 496 MSS, Alles to Richard, 27 Aug. 1779.

[45] Taillefer, 'La Cévenne ou les Cévennes', in Joutard (ed.), *Les Cévennes de la montagne à l'homme*, 40–1.

[46] *AN* F14 7684, *rapport général sur les mines des environs d'Alais, Portes et Saint-Ambroix par Beaunier*, Sept. 1807.

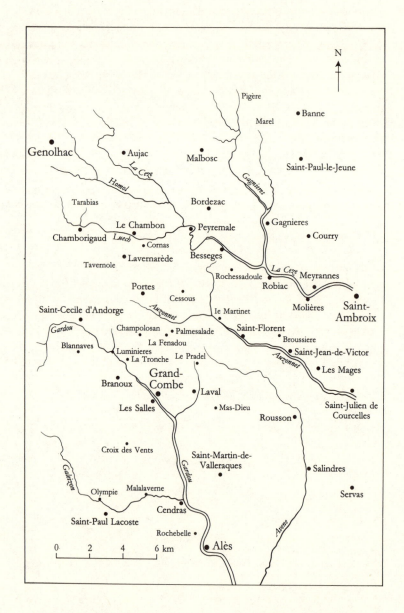

MAP 1.1. The coal-mines of the Alès basin in the late eighteenth century. Taken from A. Bardon, *L'Exploitation du bassin houiller d'Alais* (Nîmes, 1898)

Tubeuf was to attack the same seams, occasionally the deeper ones, but in a far more scientific and organized manner. Reaching the deepest seams had to await the superior geological and technological know-how of the late nineteenth century. The above generalizations also apply to the development of the Anzin coalfield and the Ruhr mines in Germany, as well as to those in the South Wales coalfield.[47]

The mines of the Alès coalfield extended northwards from Alès itself to Banne and were situated in the hills above three river valleys. The first may be subdivided into three main groups:

1. Along the river Gardon (Gardon d'Alès)
   (*a*) The mines in the immediate neighbourhood of Alès on the Montaud and la Loubière mountains. These were, eventually, to become the main concern of the Tubeufs and were to be known as Cendras and, finally, the *mines de Rochebelle*.
   (*b*) Moving up the Gardon river, the mines around the Grand-Combe (Trouilhas)—Mas-Dieu, Abilon, Trescol, Levade, Pradel, etc. All these were to become part of the *mines de la Grand-Combe*.
   (*c*) The mines to be found along the old Alès–Villefort road between the Gardon d'Alès and the Auzonnet valley, the outcrop mines of the *forêt domaniale du Rouergue*—Plusor, Fenadou, Champcloson, Portes, Saint-Cécile d'Andorge, known collectively as the *mines de Portes*.
2. Along the Auzonnet valley
   The only important mine in our period was that of Saint-Jean-de-Valériscle.
3. Along the Cèze valley
   The two most important mines in our period were those of Robiac and Meyrannes. (Eventually the mines in this valley would become *the mines de Bessèges*.)[48]

---

[47] Ignorance of basic geological principles remained widespread, however, well into the 19th century. See M. W. Flinn and D. Stoker, *The History of the British Coal Industry, 1700–1830: The Industrial Revolution* (Oxford, 1984), 69. R. Geiger, *The Anzin Coal Company, 1800–1833* (Philadelphia, Pa., 1974), 56. E. D. Lewis, *The Rhondda Valleys: A Study in Industrial Development, 1800 to the Present Day* (London, 1959), 9–11. The geological faults which characterized the Alès coal-basin bore many similarities to those of South Wales. It is not surprising, therefore, that productive mining in both regions should have ended about the same time.

[48] There were, of course, many other mines in the coal-basin. Those listed above are the most important from the standpoint of Tubeuf's activities and the future of the coalfield.

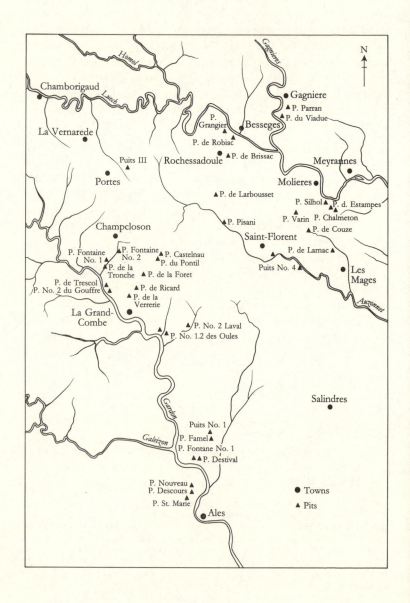

MAP 1.2. The coal-mines of the Alès basin in 1946. *Source*: Houillères des Cévennes

Although Tubeuf started work at la Pigère near Banne, and continued to work it for almost a decade, technical, financial, and transport problems would eventually force him to abandon it in the early 1780s. The mines of Robiac and Meyrannes would also be abandoned to the locals, enabling Tubeuf to concentrate his attention on Rochebelle and, although he never succeeded in acquiring actual control of it, the richest prize of all in the Alès coalfield, the Grand-Combe. He never interfered with the Saint-Jean-de-Valériscle mine, which was controlled by the Gilly family.

Before Tubeuf's arrival, traditional methods of mining coal in the Cévennes had not really diverged from medieval times. A contemporary account in Gensanne's *Histoire naturelle* may be taken as typical: 'The workers begin by making an opening in the hillside, like a foxhole, and then extract all the coal they can until the mine floods. They then abandon it and dig another opening a short distance away'.[49] The Cévennes hills were littered with mines dug into the hillsides until they flooded or the roofs collapsed. The same procedures characterized mining in many other parts of Europe.[50] Tubeuf was the first entrepreneur in the history of the Alès coalfield to engage skilled men to dig research pits and blast out drainage canals and ventilation shafts. His *puits de recherche* at Carsan had been 200 feet deep; those he was to dig at la Pigère and Rochebelle went even deeper.[51] Although greater depths had been plumbed elsewhere in Europe, nothing like it had ever been seen in the Cévennes.[52]

---

[49] Gensanne, *Histoire naturelle de la province de Languedoc*, iii. 215. See also a report commissioned by Monsieur, the king's brother, in 1786 concerning the potential of the *mines de Portes*. Coal is extracted, the report explains, 'par des paysans à leur manière . . . tant qu'on en a eu la facilité sans étayer. Mais dès qu'il a été question d'ouvrir une galerie en règle, ils ont tout abandonné'. *AN* F14 4240, *rapport sur les mines de charbon à la vicomté de Portes, par Faujas de Saint-Fonds.*

[50] Compare, for example, the Forest of Dean in Gloucestershire: 'Where they could, the miners took advantage of the slope of the seams to help with drainage, driving their levels upwards into the hillsides to meet the crop. When the water in the pits (which were sunk where levels were not practicable and which rarely went below 25 yards) became uncontrollable, the miners abandoned the work and started another.' C. Fisher, *Custom, Work and Market Capitalism: The Forest of Dean Colliers, 1788–1888* (London, 1981), 8.

[51] Letter to the Conseil des mines in which Tubeuf explains that whereas 'les gens du pais' had scraped holes into the hillsides, he had dug 'puits de deux, trois et quatre cents pieds de profondeur'. *AG* 58J 4, 20 Feb. 1780.

[52] By the end of the 18th century, the average depth of a shaft in the Anzin mines was 450 feet. Geiger, *The Anzin Coal Company*, 59. In the north-eastern coalfields of Britain, depths of up to 600 feet had been attained by the late 1770s. Flinn and Stoker, *History of the British Coal Industry*, 74–80.

Sinking pits and blasting rock obviously required men with particular skills who were in great demand—an 'aristocracy of labour' so far as eighteenth-century mining was concerned. As Michael Flinn has observed, 'Boring was a highly-skilled craft invariably undertaken by specialised teams'.[53] John Harris has rightly placed some emphasis on the importance of these skills in promoting the industrial revolution which occurred in Britain, skills which were not readily available in France.[54] The result was that Tubeuf was obliged to recruit his skilled labour from outside France, particularly from Germany. A cursory glance through his Journal will reveal the importance he attached to attracting the right people for the job: 21 April 1770, six German *mineurs* and two *commis* brought from mines in Brittany; 1 August 1770, a special payment of 24 *livres* for one of his German miners; 1 August 1773, payments to Haoul and Hulker, 'bons mineurs allemands'.[55] German workers were usually placed in charge of mining operations (*maîtres-mineurs*) by Tubeuf in the 1770s—Gantzler at Banne, George Forster at Rochebelle.[56]

Even experienced foreign workers, however, had to work within the technological limits established in Europe by the second half of the eighteenth century. There was no 'technological revolution' at Anzin, where 'Techniques of exploitation and the organization of work . . . were essentially the same in 1833 as in 1789.'[57] It was to be some time before the inventions of Savary and Newcomen were widely adapted to the lifting of coal and the draining of pits. Human beings and horses found, excavated, and hauled minerals almost everywhere in the eighteenth century.[58] Tubeuf, who hailed from Normandy and who was to open mines there in the 1780s, must have been aware that a Newcomen engine had been tried at Littry in the 1750s, with disastrous results. James Watt's adaptation of Newcomen's work would eventually provide the Périer brothers with the foundations for

---

[53] Flinn and Stoker, *History of the British Coal Industry*, 72.

[54] J. Harris, 'Skills, Coal and British Industry in the Eighteenth Century', *History*, 52 (1967). Also, J. Harris, 'The Diffusion of English Metallurgical Methods to Eighteenth-Century France', *French History*, 2 (1988).

[55] *AG* 58J 2.

[56] Ibid. Gantzler appointed as *maître-mineur* at la Pigère in Jan. 1776; Forster at Cendras (Rochebelle) on 30 Sept. 1777.

[57] Geiger, *The Anzin Coal Company*, 49.

[58] The first introduction of steam-power—a Newcomen pump—to the mining industry in France was at Anzin (the Fresnes pit) in 1736. It was supervised by English workers. Rouff, *Les Mines de charbon*, 348–50.

their work on steam-engines at their Chaillot works near Paris, but it was not to be until 1798 that one of their *machines à vapeur* was to be installed at Littry.[59] If Tubeuf did not mechanize the back-breaking, and time-consuming, business of extracting coal and water from his pits, therefore, he was not unique: for him, as for the majority of mine-owners in the 1770s, it was a case of all hands, or hooves, to the pumps.

We do know, however, that Tubeuf was anxious to avail himself of every opportunity to improve and accelerate production methods. In the pit which he sank near Pont-Saint-Esprit, the men who worked the water-pumps in shifts, 'de quatre heures en quatre heures, jour et nuit', were only asked to do so 'jusqu'à ce que j'y établiserai une machine'.[60] When one of his managers in Normandy asked for assistance in dealing with flooding, Tubeuf replied immediately: 'I am sending you the sketch of *la machine hydraulique du sieur Vérac* which will be of great use to you in the pits you are sinking', adding that he had tried it out himself in Normandy 'where it proved most successful'.[61] In the mines which Tubeuf was to open near Paris in the 1780s, he would immediately turn to the Périer brothers for expert advice.[62]

The issue of technological change was obviously related to cost. The existing mines in the Alès coalfield included seams which were easily accessible from the bottom, or the sides, of the Cévennes hills, and it was easier, and cheaper, even in the medium term, to dig drainage canals and ventilation shafts than to spend time and money on pumping equipment which, to say the least, was often suspect. The marquis de Solages in Carmaux was the only mine-owner in the province of Languedoc to use a steam-pump until the nineteenth century.[63] When one of Tubeuf's most respected and experienced *directeurs* asked for a steam-pump in 1788, he was told by Tubeuf that

[59] Pézeril, *Ces mineurs de Littry*, 58–9. The Newcomen engine had, in fact, blown itself up in 1755. 'All the pumping engines at Anzin until 1800 were of the Newcomen type.' Geiger, *The Anzin Coal Company*, 87.

[60] *AG* 58J 2, 23 Oct. 1770. Tubeuf was probably thinking of a *machine à molettes*, which represented an intermediate stage between a hand-pump and a steam pump. Rouff, *Les Mines de charbon*, 347.

[61] Rouff, *Tubeuf*, 96. It seems that the pumping carried out in such mines was comparable to the procedures adopted in Lancashire mines in the 1750s, one pit requiring four horses and two men, working around the clock, to clear the workings. Flinn and Stoker, *History of the British Coal Industry*, 113–14.

[62] See p. 157.

[63] Rouff, *Les Mines de charbon*, 352.

such a piece of equipment simply was not necessary to work the Alès mines.[64] The key to successful mining for Tubeuf was to work with, not against, the forces of gravity. The development of the Rochebelle mines provide us with an excellent example of how Tubeuf adjusted his plans to cope with the natural advantages and disadvantages of the terrain.

His early work in the hills around Alès had been seriously hampered by the thin and faulty seams as well as by the sudden and torrential downpours which characterized the climate in the Cévennes region. Tubeuf finally moved his centre of operations to the foot of the mas de Bouat mountain near Cendras, just above the flood level of the Gardon river. From here, his men excavated a roadway into the hillside, sloping upwards at an angle of 25° to meet, at right angles, all the known seams, draining water away from the old workings 'which forced the *gens de pais* to abandon the numerous excavations which they had made'. This main roadway, which also had a drainage canal allowing water to flow away into the Gardon river, was blasted with gunpowder from earth and solid rock for an original length of some 700 feet. 'These works are going to be lengthy and costly,' Tubeuf noted in his diary in 1775, adding, however, that 'they will provide us with the possibility of working every seam which will eventually produce an immense amount of coal'.[65] It was not until 1782 that Tubeuf was to reach 'la grande veine de Cendras' through a roadway cut for 210 feet through the rock.[66] On 7 September 1788, Tubeuf's Journal records that his miners had broken through to 'la grande veine de Rochebelle', the rich fifth seam which was to be worked well into the nineteenth century. Achille Bardon, writing a century ago, concludes 'Evidently, this project alone [at Rochebelle] heralded the beginning of a new era in the history of coal-mining.'[67]

The same application of long-term planning and skilled labour characterized the actual methods employed by Tubeuf to extract coal

---

[64] *AG* 58J 5, letter to Renaux, 22 July 1788.

[65] *AG* 58J 2, 2 Feb. 1775. Tubeuf also constructed a number of *galeries de traverse*, again starting from just above the flood level of the river bed, at Meyrannes, marking the real beginning of modern mining methods for what was to become the Bessèges Coal Company. Ibid., 9 Sept. 1773.

[66] *AG* 58J 2, 9 Oct. By the summer of the following year, Tubeuf's men had traced the richer seams, in what was to become the Rochebelle mines, for over two-thirds of a mile. His miners were now able to attack the seams 'par les deux bouts ce qui donnera une superbe exploitation'. Ibid., 28 June 1783.

[67] Bardon, *L'Exploitation du bassin houiller d'Alais*, 87.

from his mines. Having tackled the basic problems of constructing outlets for water and foul air, his mine managers were instructed to make all the workings as safe as possible. Roofs had to be properly secured by propping with oak timbers, particularly at the entrance of the mines.[68] The roadways leading to the *tailles* or *chambres* (the 'stalls' where the coal was actually cut from the seam) had to be 12 feet wide to facilitate access and the haulage of coal from the face.[69] The 'pillar and stall' method of excavation, which left pillars of coal on either side of the stall to sustain the roof, was the most common form of excavation in most coalfields until well into the nineteenth century.[70] It was copied in all Tubeuf's mines. What was not copied was the highly dangerous and destructive procedure employed by the *gens du pais* of pulling down the pillars as they retreated to the mine entrance after following the seam for just 100 feet or so, thus ruining future working of the mine. Since there were few tramlines in eighteenth-century mines, coal had to be hauled in tubs over logs laid side by side or pushed to the surface in barrows.[71]

No technological 'revolution', then, but certainly we are dealing with an entrepreneur interested in large-scale production (*l'industrie en grand*), itself a revolution in the Cévennes. At the beginning, Tubeuf worked with German and Flemish miners, appointing the most experienced, like Gantzler and Forster, as his *maître-mineurs*. Despite their experience, however, it was Tubeuf who constantly exhorted them to work 'en suivant les règles'. Tubeuf's Journals contain scores of letters which reveal his determination to ensure that work in his mines was

---

[68] See entries in Tubeuf's Journal for 15 July 1770 recording the payment of 449 *livres* for 28 oak trees; 27 Apr. 1771, 63 oaks bought from the *forêt de Chartreux* for 20 *livres* each; 9 Oct. 1773, 371 *livres* to *maître-mineur* for wood 'pour assurer l'entrée des galleries [*sic*]'. *AG* 58J 2.

[69] See letter to Renaux, 29 June 1789. *AG* 58J 5. A typical example of the method of excavation in the Cévennes is given by Faujas de Saint-Fonds in his report on the *mines de Portes*, *AN* F14 4240. 'Les filons ont souvent jusqu'à quatorze pieds d'épaisseur et des pilliers [*sic*] de charbon qu'on a soin de laisser de distance en distance à chaque côté servent de support aux galeries.'

[70] For details of working at Anzin, see Geiger, *The Anzin Coal Company*, 60–1; at Littry, Pézeril, *Ces mineuss de Littry*, 61–2. Differing practices were adopted in British mines, but the 'pillar and stall' method 'was universally used in the North-east and in many other coal-fields'. Flinn and Stoker, *History of the British Coal Industry*, 82–3.

[71] At the Grand-Combe mine, coal was brought to the mine-entrance and then lowered down the hillside by sliding large wooden boxes (*coffres*), controlled by a simple system of pulleys, over planks to waiting coal-wagons.

conducted with long-term considerations in mind. One to Gantzler himself, for example, in which he warned his mine manager that if he was to continue in his employ he would have to 'suivre les travaux avec plus d'exactitude'.[72] Bribery was frequently employed. A letter to his *maitre-mineur* at la Pigère: 'I am very happy with your work. On my first trip to see you I will bring the watch that I promised you.'[73] A gift, or a hint about time and work discipline?

By the late 1770s, the organization of work and the management structure was well established, with a clear distinction evident between 'general managers' (*directeurs*) and 'works managers' or 'foremen' (*maître-mineurs*). In his Normandy pits, Tubeuf would also introduce an overseer (*contrôleur*). Normally the administrative and financial aspects of running a mine were fused. Cajon, his *directeur* for a time at la Pigère, was appointed initially as 'Directeur et receveur des mines'; the same title was bestowed upon the *directeurs* of the Robiac and Cendras mines. In a letter to Cajon, Tubeuf explained that a sharp distinction would have to be drawn between his own functions and those of his *maître-mineur*, Gantzler, who, in Tubeuf's words, was an excellent chap and all that, but it was essential that Cajon took responsibility for 'all the detailed accounts, even the smallest items of expenditure and receipt, relating to the mine. Gantzler's job is to supervise the actual work of extracting the coal with every possible measure of intelligence and safety . . . my confidence in him does not extend any further than this.'[74] The relative values of *directeurs* and *maîtres-mineurs* may be assessed from the salaries they obtained. Louis Alles, *directeur* in 1775, was paid 1,320 *livres* a year, including his lodgings. François-Joseph Renaux, Tubeuf's most gifted and loyal *directeur*, was getting 1,500 *livres* in the mid-1780s, but later requested, and received, 2,400 to cover the expenses of his family and one servant. Forster, *maître-mineur* in Cendras for a time, was paid 600 *livres* year in 1786, but, having played the field and obtained a position in the Grand-Combe mine, was receiving 1,000 *livres* by February 1787. Clerks (*commis*) were normally paid around 500 *livres* a year; a black-smith received 480 *livres* in 1777, a weigh-man, 432.[75]

---

[72] *AG* 58J 2, 1 Aug. 1772. See also letters to his *directeurs* at Banne and Alès, written on the same day, exhorting them to be more precise and professional. *AG* 58J 4, 1 Feb. 1780.

[73] Bardon, *L'Exploitation du bassin houiller d'Alais*, 98.

[74] *AG* 58J 4, 17 Dec. 1779.

[75] *AN* 306AP 487, agent to maréchal de Castries, 11 Feb. 1787; *AG* 58J 2 Jan. 1777.

The heaviest pressure exerted by Tubeuf upon his *directeurs* was related, as indeed is the case today, to the question of raising productivity and lowering wage-rates. In a letter to his brother-in-law Laporte, whom he appointed for a time *directeur et receveur des mines d'Alès* (Rochebelle), he expressed some disappointment that the one *toise* of the coal-face then being worked was only producing 116 *quintaux* of coal at the pit-head, 'qui n'est pas profitable'. According to Tubeuf, Laporte and his men should be aiming at the production of between 140 and 160 *quintaux* of coal from one *toise* of face.[76] Tubeuf had no qualms about sacking those workers, or managers, who did not reach his exacting standards. Louis Alles, another German brought in to oversee the Cendras–Rochebelle complex in 1776, was dismissed within a year; Forster was eventually sacked in favour of his son Adam.[77] Excellence was finally achieved with the arrival, in May 1783, of a graduate of the École royale des mines de Paris, François-Joseph Renaux, a man who not only supervised the remarkable transformation of the Rochebelle mines near Alès, but who became the Tubeuf family's *ingénieur-en-chef* for the whole of the Alès coal-basin throughout the period of this study. Renaux was to become the most widely recognized and respected of all the mining engineers in Languedoc by the nineteenth century.[78]

Like any modern capitalist employer, control over the work-force, in terms of wages and conditions of service, was also of cardinal importance to Tubeuf. Breaking the mould of traditional attitudes towards industrial work was one of the hallmarks of early capitalist employers, as E. P. Thompson has shown for England.[79] So far as the Alès coalfield in the last decades of the eighteenth century is concerned, of course, we are dealing with a total work-force of a few hundred at most (not counting the scores of 'illicit' mining families). At Carmaux, the marquis de Solages was employing around 100 men at this time.[80] It is, of course, very difficult to produce exact figures

[76] *AG* 58J 4, 15 Dec. 1779.

[77] *AG* 58J 2. Alles was officially appointed *maître-mineur* on 1 Jan. 1777. His subsequent dismissal made him a cautious, but important, enemy of Tubeuf since he became the local agent for the Richard et Carouges coking company, of which more later.

[78] *AG* 58J 2, 2 May 1783, a date which marks Renaux's arrival in Alès. He was to spend the rest of his working life there, to the great advantage of the Alèsiens.

[79] E. P. Thompson, *The Making of the English Working Class* (London, 1970), 268–71 for wages and the impact of 'rapid technical innovation'. Also, E. P. Thompson, 'Time, Work-Discipline, and Industrial Capitalism', *Past and Present*, 38 (1967).

[80] Galy, 'L'Exploitation des houillères en Languedoc', 182.

since, for the majority of unskilled and semi-skilled men, women, and children, the work was largely seasonal.[81] This posed major headaches for Tubeuf and other mine-owners. The local work-force had been raised, with a few notable exceptions, in the hills of the Cévennes and the Auvergne, mainly illiterate peasants who were used to working by the sun and season not the clock. Even those local families which had made a profession out of mining—and there were the Puechs, the Larguiers, and the Drulhons, whose families had been *charbonniers* and *charbonnières* for generations—preferred to work for themselves or for local landowners or manufacturers whose work patterns fitted into essentially agricultural rhythms of work. As we shall see in the following chapter, this is why the production of wine, and of raw and reeled silk, attracted the cévenols, who retained a passion for their *lopin de terre*.

The time-honoured rituals associated with planting and harvesting the chestnuts, grapes, rye, and, in particular, the silk-cocoons, had to be respected. Early mining entrepreneurs were thus confronted by 'independent colliers'[82] who strongly resented attempts to disfranchise them of their traditional working practices, or by unskilled peasants who, in the 'dead seasons' were prepared to earn a few *sous* digging out coal, just as they always dug out ditches to plant the twin sisters of the cévenol economy, the *vigne* and the *mûrier*. In the Alès coalfield 'the miners, who were practically all peasants from the surrounding countryside, simply did not know how to dig coal out in blocks. They did not even possess the right tools for the job, with the result that they reduced everything to small coal.'[83] Coal from the Mas-Dieu mine was only fit for lime-burners, on account of its poor quality and because it was only worked by 'peasants who, when there is no more agricultural work available, find themselves at a loose end and, as a result, happy to be able to earn three or four *livres* a day digging to right and left in a coal level', and this was as late as 1817![84]

[81] For example, we know that Tubeuf had 23 *regular* workers in his Cendras (Rochebelle) mine in 1783 (Bardon, *L'Exploitation du bassin houiller d'Alais*, 276), and that there were 26 men employed in the Grand-Combe in Apr. 1785 (*AN* 306AP 485, agent to Castries). Yet, on 5 Mar. 1787, when flooding had prevented work in the mines, approximately 100 workers were employed, by Castries, on repairing, or building new, roads to the mines (ibid. 489, agent to Castries). It seems evident, from these and other sources, that mine-owners employed a regular body of men, but kept a much larger number of men, women, and children as 'casual' workers.

[82] See, Fisher, *Custom, Work and Market Capitalism*, 130–46; R. Harrison (ed.), *The Independent Collier* (London, 1977).

[83] Bardon, *L'Exploitation du bassin houiller d'Alais*, 138.

[84] *AN* 306AP 502, Lefebvre to Castries, 19 May. In Oct. 1789, the maréchal de Castries' agent explained that the Grand-Combe had been closed down for almost a

We have noted how the relative absence of skills associated with sinking pits and working seams methodically had forced Tubeuf to import experienced foreign workers, and these included even coal-face workers like the *piqueurs*, who actually cut the coal, and the *sorteurs*, who put it in sacks and hauled it to the mine-entrance. Since the number of workers in large mining concerns was so small in the eighteenth century, and reliable figures almost impossible to obtain, at least for Languedoc, it is extremely difficult to present a convincing breakdown of eighteenth-century work-forces. However, the following has been included because it suggests a pattern which was to be reproduced, on a far larger scale, in the nineteenth century. Of the 16 *regular* workers employed at the Rochebelle mine in 1795, 6 came from the Alès region. The *directeur* came from Roubaix (Nord), the *maître-mineur* from the Limousin, 3 workers came from the Lozère department, and 4 others from equally poor mountainous regions to the north and east of the lower Cévennes. One worker came from Piedmont.[85]

It is almost certain that none of these men were Protestants, although Philippe Joutard's conclusion is only partly true: 'The mining companies distrusted the Protestant population of the Cévennes, "more disputatious" and politically more to the Left. They preferred to recruit amongst the Ardéchois and the Lozériens, regarded as more docile.'[86] Only partly true because the roots of the aversion Protestants felt about mining lay in the fact that they were far more deeply involved in the cévenol textile industry than their Catholic neighbours. Attitudes towards work were conditioned as much by socio-economic and cultural factors as by politics, although the leading role played in the Revolution by Protestants in the south-east during the 1790s certainly made them suspect to some nineteenth-century employers.[87] As for the lone Piedmontais, he was to be the precursor of hundreds

fortnight, partly as a result of bad weather, but also because of 'des vendanges et des semences qui occupent actuellement la majeure partie des ouvriers'. Ibid. 492, 21 Oct.

[85] *AN* F14 4240. *Noms et professions des agents et ouvriers employés aux mines nationales d'Alais*, n.d. (but almost certainly the Year III). Again, one suspects that these lists almost invariably omit the names of women, children, and unskilled male surface workers.

[86] P. Joutard, 'La Cévenne en difficulté', in Joutard (ed.), *Les Cévennes de la montagne à l'homme*, 274.

[87] Marcel Rouff makes the point that in the Montcenis mine only 10 of the 289 strong work-force were not Catholic. He goes on to divide the workers into four categories: dispossessed small property-owners, poor peasants, industrial workers from foundries and glassworks, and foreign workers. This categorization is a fair reflection

more of his compatriots who would flood into the mines of the Alès coalfield in the nineteenth century, leaving 'their mountain villages each year for periods of six to nine months in search of employment elsewhere in Italy and France as miners, masons . . . unskilled casual labourers'.[88] There was to be a Mediterranean flavour to the social composition of mining in the nineteenth century, just as the silk industry would increasingly become part of the Mediterranean world. Also, whether we are dealing with Piedmontais, Lozèriens, or Ardèchois, 'seasonality' of one kind or another would continue to characterize the nature of their labour.[89]

It is hardly surprising that mine-owners found it difficult to recruit any but the poorer members of society, whether from inside or outside the region. Coal-mining was the dirtiest and most dangerous civil occupation known to eighteenth-century man, woman, and child. As one eighteenth-century observer noted: 'We are dealing with the most miserable kind of life. Workers suddenly confronted with yawning chasms in the ground, with tortuous shafts, some so low overhead that they had to crawl on their knees, dragging sacks of coal along in their teeth, sweating profusely, gasping for air . . . feeling their way along in the dark like drunken men.'[90] A shade melodramatic perhaps but, given that the extract makes no mention of poisonous gases, rock falls, or flooding, there is no reason to question its general message. The agent for the Grand-Combe mine reported in 1787 that many miners were complaining about conditions in the number 2 seam, which had three feet of very hard coal: 'This causes difficulties for the *piqueurs* working in the stalls as well as for the *sorteurs*, who are forced to bend very low to accommodate the leather sacks on their backs.'[91] A month later, the back-breaking job of dragging out sacks of coal on one's hands and knees was somewhat eased when the German *maître-mineur* introduced *chieurs*, tubs of coal which could be harnessed to a man, or mule, and hauled out over a log floor.[92] One

---

of the composition of miners in the Gard, particularly after 1800. *Les Mines de charbon*, 282–5.

[88] S. Woolf, *The Poor in Western Europe in the Eighteenth and Nineteenth Centuries* (London, 1986), 57.

[89] Rouff notes that miners from the Limousin and the Auvergne were 'ouvriers intermittents'. *Les Mines de charbon*, 288.

[90] The chevalier de Grignon, referring to the Saint-Étienne mines, quoted by Rouff, ibid. 43.

[91] *AN* 306AP 489, agent to Castries, 15 Sept. 1787.

[92] Ibid. 490, 8 Oct. 1787.

hardly requires a historical imagination to appreciate the problems caused by dust and its consequent impact upon the lives of miners, nor of the danger inherent in being handed, as one entered the mine, gunpowder, candles, and oil for blasting and lighting in the pre-Davy lamp age.[93] In most mines, it was the custom, before work began, to send in a man with a naked flame, protected only by a mask and coat, soaked in water, to explode pockets of gas. As Marcel Rouff concludes, 'The fact that there were no frightful slaughters can only be explained by the shallow depth of the mines.'[94]

The recourse to foreign labour to minimize the costly errors of an indigenous, untrained work-force brought its own group of problems. It was usually necessary to pay 'foreign' workers higher wages in order to attract them, and then to keep them in a not always friendly environment. The marquis de Solages paid his Flemish workers 27 *sols* a day, plus wine; the less skilled local workers, 17 *sols*, although, probably to prevent jealousy exploding into violence, wine was also free.[95] When one of Tubeuf's German *maître-mineurs* left him to join the maréchal de Castries's work-force, no one was in any doubt about the man's mining ability, but there were problems concerning his relationship with his fellow workers: 'I fear', Castries's agent wrote, 'that it may well be a matter of jealousy, since the miners here cannot stand foreigners.'[96] A few of the latter, like Samuel Pichet, could not take the strain. He was paid off by Tubeuf's *directeur* in Banne, who explained that he 'is sorry that he has to leave us, but as one says in his *pais, sa femme et son enfant languissaient beaucoup*'.[97] The human face of an inhuman business.

It would have been strange if Tubeuf had not empathized with men like Pichet, hailing as he did from far-off Normandy and suffering, as he and his family did, from the increasing animosity of the local population. Perhaps this was why the case of a fellow Norman called

[93] Sir Humphrey Davy's famous lamp was being widely used in Britain after 1816 but 'was almost untried in France before the Anzin catastrophe of 1823'. Geiger, *The Anzin Coal Company*, 96.

[94] Rouff, *Les Mines de charbon*, 367. A government decree, passed on 19 Mar. 1783, reflected the deteriorating situation in the mines by laying particular emphasis on safety provisions.

[95] Ibid. 304.

[96] *AN* 306AP 487, agent to Castries, 1 Aug. 1786. The local 'independent collier' Soleiret, having been replaced as *maître-mineur* by Forster, absolutely refused to acquaint the German miner with any of the particular problems of the Grand-Combe mine!

[97] *AHC*, Fonds Tubeuf. Cajon to Tubeuf, 3 Oct. 1778.

Barthélemy posed so many potential problems. Barthélemy was apparently 'fort attaché' to Tubeuf (fellow Normans after all) and was an excellent worker. His dissatisfaction sprang from the conditions of his employment and, in particular, the system of payment *à la journée*. Since he was engaged upon the arduous business of opening up new seams, he wanted to be paid on a piece-work basis (*à prix fait ou à toise*). He was told that 'He will have to wait until production is taking place on a large-scale (*production en grand*), which will make it possible for each worker to be paid on the same basis and thus avoid any jealousy.'[98] In fact, Tubeuf was quite keen to introduce piece-work and did so whenever and wherever it proved feasible, despite the fact that 'le travail à la tâche est l'exception'.[99] The marquis de Solages appears to have observed the traditional, perhaps agricultural, practice of paying day-rates,[100] as indeed did the maréchal de Castries. In this again, Tubeuf proved to be something of a pioneer.

Tubeuf's determination to mould his men into a nineteenth-century work-force can be seen in the strict regulations first introduced in his du Plessis mine in lower Normandy. Considerable authority was given to the *maître-mineur*, who was instructed to be 'juste et sévère' with his workers. He could impose a fine of 6 *livres* for drunken or disorderly conduct and even dismiss someone for repeated, or more serious, offences, so long as he informed the mine's *directeur* of his decision. 'Les appels', marking the beginning of a twelve-hour shift, went at 3.45 a.m. and if any miner arrived after the powder, candles, and oil had been handed out, he would be obliged to lose his shift—a good example of 'time and work-discipline'. Article 9 of the work regulations imposed further constraints upon the 'independence' of the traditional collier: 'It is expressly forbidden for *mineurs*, *manœuvres*, and *sorteurs* to play cards underground, to sleep, smoke, or defecate in the mine.' Article 10 stipulated that no worker would be allowed to leave his work-place unless absolutely necessary, and then only after securing permission to do so.[101] These regulations must have appeared

---

[98] Ibid. In the same letter from Cajon, there is a reference to the perennial problem of drunkenness. A worker called Joseph, threatened with dismissal, 'a promit de modérer ses propos et de prendre moins de vin'.

[99] Rouff, *Les Mines de charbon*, 300.

[100] Galy, 'L'Exploitation des houillères en Languedoc', 181–2.

[101] *AG* 58J 6, *règlement concernant l'exploitation des mines du Plessis en basse-Normandie*, 4 Oct. 1781. The regulations make it absolutely clear that, as was the case with the highly skilled *souffleur* in the glass-making industry, it was the *maître-mineur* who 'hired and fired' workers ('prendre comme de chasser un ouvrier').

as draconian to the old 'independent collier' as they did to the untutored peasant.

An even more radical attack upon traditional work-practices was Tubeuf's attempt to keep mines open seven days a week, including some of the *jours de fêtes*. It was, of course, often imperative, for safety reasons, that a few workers were released from the obligation 'to keep the sabbath holy'.[102] Tubeuf's final assault upon the independence of his workers was his extraordinary scheme, submitted to the Intendant of Normandy, that miners should be seconded to the army in times of war, returning to their civil duties once hostilities had ceased: 'This could be accomplished quite easily,' Tubeuf explained, with scant regard for the horror of conscription amongst the vast majority of eighteenth-century Frenchmen: 'All that is needed is the authorization for *concessionnaires des mines* to submit the miners they employ to military discipline in their works, obliging them to sign an agreement with the management (*l'administration*), who will then supply them with a distinctive uniform'. When these miners were called up, the mine-owners would recruit more labour, who would also, of course, be liable to 'la discipline militaire'.[103] The scheme was one of Tubeuf's more fanciful brainwaves, of which there were many! The attraction for employers was obvious: at a stroke—or possibly a lash—it would have dealt with the perennial problem of 'work indiscipline', creating a more submissive work-force out of the early amalgam of 'independent colliers' and 'seasonal' peasants. It was an eighteenth-century solution to an eighteenth-century problem.

It is not easy to establish precisely how much Tubeuf was prepared to pay to attract local workers, partly because he preferred to sign individual contracts with small groups of workers. He did have the reputation in some quarters of being a rather mean employer. The available evidence suggests that he wanted to get the most from his workers, but that he was prepared to pay top wages for top men. We have noted that Tubeuf was obliged to pay over the odds to attract

---

[102] *AG* 58J 6 29 July 1778. The mayor of Montebourg had written to Tubeuf to say how pleased he was to have a mine opened in his parish and that 'comme il est très important que les travaux ne soient pas interrompus, je vous permet d'y employer les ouvriers les jours de fêtes et de dimanches'. Tubeuf was asked to take the mayor's letter to the local *curé*, who would deal with the formalities. If only things had been this easy in the Alès region!

[103] *AG* 58J 4, 29 Oct. 1782. The advantage for the government, according to Tubeuf, was that the king would always have a detachment of 'sappers' trained to the peak of perfection and costing him nothing in peacetime.

the best foreign workers. For those willing and able to work around the clock, the rewards could also be reasonable. Let us take a typical example—a *convention* drawn up on 3 August 1773 by which Tubeuf agreed to pay two German miners 567 *livres* for 3,780 *quintaux* of coal brought to the mine-entrance. Since, according to the times recorded in his Journal, they must have extracted the agreed amount of coal in under 100 days and that the agreement provided for the payment of exactly three *sols* for each *quintal*, then each miner must have received the equivalent of 57 *sols* a day.[104] This was double the amount the marquis de Solages was paying his Flemish miners at Carmaux, but then averages can be very misleading.[105]

As we have seen, the policy of paying good money for the best men can also be verified by examining the salaries paid to his *directeurs*. Although Louis Alles had to pay for his own accommodation,[106] François Renaux was given a roof over his head plus the additional perk that 'my garden will provide him with fruit and vegetables'.[107] So far as 'average' wages for 'average' workers is concerned, Tubeuf bears favourable comparison with his peers—20 *sols* (occasionally 25 at peak times) a day for *piqueurs*; 10–20 *sols* for *sorteurs*.[108] In December 1779, he rapped his *directeur* at Banne on the knuckles for paying over the odds: 'Thirty *sols* a day is excessive. Reduce it, at most, to twenty-five.'[109] At Rochebelle, the majority of his workers were paid 18 *sols* a day in winter; up to 24 *sols* in summer.[110] The conclusions to be drawn are obvious: work in the mines was bearable, perhaps vital, in the winter months when it was difficult to obtain agricultural work, but far less so in the summer and autumn when there was grain, chestnuts, silk, and grapes to be harvested. Finally, when

---

[104] *AG* 58J 2. Details of the payment were recorded in the Journal on 8 Nov. 1773. Given that the miners extracted an average of 37.8 *quintaux* a day and were paid 3 *sols le quintal*, this amounted to 114 *sols* a day for the two men, which obviously involved 'double shifts', a not uncommon practice in the mining industry.

[105] Solages paid 27 *sols* for a 12-hour *journée*. Rouff, *Les Mines de charbon*, 306.

[106] *AG* 58J 2, 1 Jan. 1777. Alles, and other German miners employed at the beginning of January, 'se logeraient sur leurs appointments et sur leurs journées'.

[107] *AG* 58J 2, 1 May 1783.

[108] In Carmaux, for example, the rate was 20 *sols* for *piqueurs* and 15 for *sorteurs*, plus free wine. Galy, 'L'Exploitation des houillères en Languedoc', 181–2. In the Littry mines, it was 20 *sols* for *piqueurs* and between 10 and 20 for other workers. Rouff, *Les Mines de charbon*, 300–5. Such figures can only be estimates since, as we have seen, payments varied according to the job, the season, or the *convention* agreed with the *maître-mineur*.

[109] *AG* 58J 4, 17 Dec.

[110] *Recherches historiques de la ville d'Alès*, 628.

discussing wage-rates, we clearly need to keep in mind Michael Sonenscher's conclusion that, almost everywhere in the eighteenth century, wages were usually a matter of personal, not national or even local, bargaining.[111]

For employers like Tubeuf, however, custom and practice had, on occasions, to be observed—which never prevented Tubeuf from trying to undermine them. Tubeuf's attempt to introduce work on Sundays and feast-days in his Normandy mines is a case in point. Alès was not in Normandy, however, and given the traditional enmity between Catholics and Protestants, flags and *fêtes* carried more than symbolic significance: they were vital to the cohesive force of Catholic culture. There are frequent references in Tubeuf's Journal to the sums of money allocated to his workers for 'une messe en honneur de Saint-Barbe et pour leur dîner'.[112] Saint-Barbe was the patron saint of miners and, galling as it may have been to most mine-owners, they were obliged to dig fairly deeply into their pockets to subsidize celebrations in his honour. It is also fair to add, in order to soften images of Tubeuf as a Dickensian employer, that he paid the not inconsiderable sum of 600 *livres* a year to the *hôpital d'Alès* for the care of miners injured in his employ.[113]

In an increasingly accident-prone industry, it was the cost of treating the sick and the injured that led Tubeuf to introduce an early form of 'medical insurance', paid by his employees of course. In his *Règlement concernant l'exploitation des mines du Plessis en Basse-Normandie*, a document which lays some emphasis on the control and care of workers, Tubeuf made detailed provisions for a sickness scheme. Beginning with a preamble which stressed the considerable sums he was already paying for the care of his workers, the section then decreed that 'To cover the medicines and the advances which have been paid out, it is decreed that, from 1 October, six *deniers* in every *livre* will be set aside from the salaries of '*M. les officiers, gagistes, mineurs et journaliers,* and that the sum provided will be put on one side to pay for the care of the sick and the injured'. The precise sums to be withdrawn from the fund would be determined by the miners themselves,

---

[111] M. Sonenscher, 'Work and Wages in Paris in the Eighteenth Century', in M. Berg *et al.* (eds.), *Manufacture in Town and Country before the Factory Age* (Cambridge, 1983).

[112] *AG* 58J 2, 4 Dec. 1770. The same payment, 72 *livres*, was made in Oct. 1773.

[113] On medical services generally in French mines, see Rouff, *Les Mines de charbon*, 309–11.

although overall control would be in the hands of the *directeur*.[114] As Flinn and Stoker point out in their *History of the British Coal Industry*, 'From the latter years of the eighteenth century it became more common for miners to make provision for these contingencies [accident and sickness] by means of friendly societies.'[115] But what was true of Britain was not always true of France. Tubeuf's scheme clearly places him in the forefront of those who were creating the conditions for a modern mining industry. It is not that dissimilar from one introduced in Decazeville fifty years later.[116]

New methods of concentrating and organizing industry, new techniques of 'man management', all this was clearly of great importance in accelerating the pace of capitalist change, but, without the injection of huge sums of money, the foundations of a modern industrial complex could never have been achieved. Compared with the small sums invested in coal-mining by locals, Tubeuf's investments were truly massive. One of the major difficulties confronting early entrepreneurs in heavy industry was the long delay before investments could be transformed into profits. The marquis de Solages only began to see positive results—from a financial standpoint—in 1780, more than two decades after his Flemish miners had first arrived in the Carmaux region.[117] In 1782, Tubeuf asked one of his Norman friends to visit the *puits d'Alais* (Rochebelle) and judge the scale of his undertaking: 'You will begin to appreciate its importance and the enormous expense involved.'[118] Tubeuf was not a wealthy man: throughout his turbulent career he was never really solvent. His original investment appears to have been not more than 22,000 *livres*, which included the 10,000 *livres* dowry from his wife. After a decade working in Cransac and the Comtat-Venaissin, Tubeuf estimated that he had already spent 100,000 *livres* (of other people's money). He was, however, reimbursed by the government for the loss of his concession in the Comtat-Venaissin. It seems that he was paid enough to cover his debts and little else, since, according to his own accounts, he was down to his last *livre* in Alès by 1773.[119]

---

[114] *AG* 58J 6, *règlement concernant l'exploitation des mines*.

[115] Flinn and Stoker, *History of the British Coal Industry*, 426.

[116] Reid, *The Miners of Decazeville*, 34–5.

[117] Galy, 'L'Exploitation des houillères en Languedoc', 182.

[118] *AG* 58J 2, letter to Cautionnement, 4 May 1782.

[119] Bardon, *L'Exploitation du bassin houiller d'Alais*, 65, who suggests that Tubeuf 'manipulated' the accounts in his Journal in order to provide ammunition for his many

The confirmation of his huge concession gave him the credibility he required to seek further loans. The complicated and tortuous procedures which he was obliged to adopt in order to secure financial backing, however, illustrates another major theme in this present study—that it was far easier to find coal than credit in Bas-Languedoc. His first request for a loan of 20,000 *livres*, repayable over four years at 5 per cent per annum interest, was rejected by the Estates of Languedoc. Tubeuf then turned to the Archbishop of Narbonne, who put him in touch with leading industrialists and *négociants* in Montpellier, who agreed to a loan on condition that Tubeuf supplied them with 120,000 *quintaux* of coal per annum, which they would sell for him, over a five-year period, at 30 *sols le quintal*, thus making a sizeable little profit.[120] Unfortunately, Tubeuf, at this early stage of his venture, could not have hoped to produce the amount of coal demanded. His next move was to push him further into debt; the securing of a loan from a Jewish money-lender in Nîmes named Cavaillon, who charged him 8 per cent interest per annum. By March 1776, he could not find the cash to pay the interest on the loan and was therefore driven, like so many entrepreneurs in eighteenth-century Languedoc, to accept loans at even higher rates of interest to pay off his earlier creditors. On this occasion his 'benefactor' was a wholesale wine merchant named Ode. Ode lived at Condoulet, but was known as the seigneur de Chusclan after the estate he had purchased, a not untypical example of Protestant upward mobility from commerce and money-lending into a measure of landed gentility. The good seigneur promised to pay off Tubeuf's debts to Cavaillon and to provide him with enough cash for the next stage of his expansionist mining schemes. The cost of the loan was high: 8 per cent per annum interest plus one *sol le quintal* on all the coal Tubeuf would sell to Nîmes, Lunel, and Montpellier for seven years. Tubeuf recorded rather ruefully in his Journal: 'Having no more money at my disposal, I was forced to accept these conditions.'[121]

legal battles. Marcel Rouff, who reproduces the details of Tubeuf's expenses for Cransac and the Comtat Venaissin mines, disagrees. See *Tubeuf* 15–18. My own impression is that the round figures which Tubeuf introduces from time to time in the Journal are suspicious, and are not supported by detailed accounts. This does not call into question the scale of his achievements in the Alès coal-basin, which, from a financial standpoint, are supported by the reliable figures relating to his loans from the Chaulieus.

[120] *AG* 58J 2, 23 Oct. 1774. Ordinarily, Tubeuf sold coal in Montpellier for 25 *sous le quintal*.

[121] *AG* 58J 2. His troubles appear to have begun with the refusal of financial assistance from the Estates of Languedoc, 29 Jan. 1776.

The spiralling costs of his 'grand design', added to the high interest charges he was paying on his loans,[122] meant that by the end of 1777 Tubeuf was obliged to point his berline in the direction of Paris to secure the kind of financial backing vital to the success of his plans. Ode, in fact, had encouraged him to draw upon the deeper financial wells of the capital by telling him that if he were successful he could forget about the extra interest charged on the volume of coal sold by Tubeuf.[123] It was in this way that Tubeuf was put in touch with the Chaulieu family, which was to exhaust most of its immense wealth in financing his schemes.[124] Over the next two decades, the fortunes of the Chaulieus and the Tubeufs were to become inextricably linked. Following the deaths of Pierre-François Tubeuf and Jacques-Abraham Aufric, marquis de Chaulieu, their two widows would live together in the same apartment in what is now the fourth *arrondissement* of the city. Thus, private lives were to be interwoven—tragically in Tubeuf's case—with public finance and industry.

In November 1777, Tubeuf received the first loan of 50,000 *livres* in cash from the marquis de Chaulieu, out of which he settled his debts with Ode. The price of this deliverance from the clutches of local and regional financiers was a high one. Tubeuf promised to repay the loan over five years at no less than 12 per cent per annum interest. The social and legal constraints under which nobles like Chaulieu were obliged to operate is well illustrated by the terms of a fourth loan of 35,000 *livres* drawn up on 8 October 1778, which added to the capital 'at the moment of signing the contract, interest in such a way that the promissory notes would not appear usurious'.[125] This precaution was indeed wise. A year later, an arrest warrant was issued against the marquis de Gamaches for money-lending. Commenting on the fact that Gamaches and his wife had been forced to go into hiding, the *syndic-général* of the Estates of Languedoc wrote: 'What a disaster for

---

[122] Loans were not only costly, they were extremely complex. In May 1776, Tubeuf had received 13,189 *livres* from Ode in *lettres de change*, plus 3,600 in cash, with the promise of another *lettre de change* of 4,400 *livres* which could be cashed at the *foire de Pézenas*. On 18 Dec. 1776, following another loan of 25,400 *livres*, a new contract had to be drawn up by which the repayment period was extended to 12 years, still at 8% interest p.a., but now with an additional payment of 9 *deniers* on each *quintal* of coal sold in Tubeuf's Alès coal depot. *AG* 58J 2, 18 Dec. 1776.

[123] *AG* 58J 2, Oct. 1777.

[124] Galy refers to 'la grosse fortune des Chaulieu'. 'L'Exploitation des houillères en Languedoc', 181.

[125] Bardon, *L'Exploitation du bassin houiller d'Alais*, 148–9.

a man of note . . . Thus, wherever he is, he is lost for ever.'[126] These constraints are conveniently ignored or underplayed by those who make little distinction between the operations of capitalism before and after 1789. Altogether, between December 1777 and August 1781, the Chaulieus, marquis and marquise, were to loan Tubeuf over a quarter of a million *livres*.[127] This sum represents one of the biggest investments by a single family in the history of eighteenth-century mining.

Given that Tubeuf was not a man of great personal wealth, how can we explain the scale of his technical and financial operations. Why did he place himself in such financial peril? Certainly there was his boundless energy and enthusiasm, attributes essential to the successful Languedocian entrepreneur. But this alone would not have been enough for him to sell his plans successfully to financiers, *négociants*, and archbishops. The answer in one word, as Arthur Young realized, was 'GOVERNMENT'.[128] Eighteenth-century royal concessions bore some comparisons with today's government contracts, and Tubeuf had been granted one of the biggest mining concessions in France, signed, sealed, and delivered by two kings, guaranteed by royal ministers and officials. As John Harris has noted, 'It is not so much the names of firms and business-men but those of great officials like Trudaine and Tolozan, their important minions like Holker and Jars, of Controller Generals whose interest could readily be aroused like Turgot and Calonne, which dominate the record.'[129] In Tubeuf's case, the key figures linking Versailles to Alès were the Intendant des mines, Bertin, and his first secretary, Jérôme-Thomas de La Barbérie. It was La Barbérie who had originally bought the Cransac mine from Douin de Cransac, inviting Tubeuf to become its *directeur*.[130] By 1773, Bertin's first secretary had become intimately involved in the success or failure of the mines of the Alès coal-basin by accepting Tubeuf's offer of becoming 'un associé secret'. The deal included a provision for La Barbérie to be paid one-quarter of the profits on all coal sales: the price of government support in the eighteenth-century was high.[131]

---

[126] Ibid. 126.

[127] For a detailed breakdown of this global sum see *AHC*, Fonds Tubeuf, *état des fonds que j'ai employé pour mon entreprise d'Alais*. The marquis de Chaulieu made 10 loans amounting to 189,070 *livres*; the marquise, 5 totalling 37,447 *livres*. Rouff, *Les Mines de charbon*, 28–30 analyses the significance of these loans.

[128] Young, *Travels in France*, 255: 'Everything in this world depends on government.'

[129] Harris, 'The Diffusion of English Metallurgical Methods', 43.

[130] Rouff, *Les Mines de charbon*, 61.

[131] Rouff, *Tubeuf*, 14. It is clear that Jérôme-Thomas de La Barbérie was much more than an official contact. Not only was he a secret shareholder, he was the godfather to

What with high-interest loans and 'kick-backs' for government officials, it is little wonder that Tubeuf was never solvent!

Not only was La Barbérie a shareholder in Tubeuf's mining venture,
he was also the principal guarantor for the latter's huge loans. The
favour and patronage of the Bertins and the Neckers represented the
'gold standard' for eighteenth-century entrepreneurs. In 1776, when
local pressure was being exerted upon Tubeuf to limit his concession,
the first thing he did was to write to La Barbérie asking the latter to
press Bertin for 'une lettre de recommandation'. It duly arrived, and
Tubeuf used it in an attempt to win over the Estates of Languedoc
from the clutches of local seigneurs and property-owners.[132] La Barbérie was also used as a 'guarantor' of Tubeuf's loans with local
money-lenders like Ode and Cavaillon. Indeed, it seems that Tubeuf's
fateful decision to accept the fairly onerous terms exacted by the
Chaulieus was partly due to the fact that he had embroiled La Barbérie
too deeply—and too openly—in his financial machinations and had
to find a quick financial escape route in order to retain his credibility
at Versailles, without which he was just another mine director.[133] Like
any modern entrepreneur, Tubeuf was not above providing the
occasional 'sweetener' to keep the favour of the great and the good,
like the two crates of Côtes-du-Rhône sent to La Barbérie at Bertin's
private address.[134]

It is clear, however, that ministers like Bertin did not have to be
bribed to support *capitalistes* like Tubeuf. The influence wielded at
Court by the former Contrôleur-général became the strongest card in
Tubeuf's hand, one which he was ever eager to play. In March 1780,
when it seemed, yet again, that the local opposition to his plans would
overwhelm him, he wrote a personal letter to Bertin explaining that

Tubeuf's elder son. Also, Tubeuf's Journal records in Dec. 1778 'J'ai prêté à M. de la
Barbérie, premier commis de M. Bertin, 720 *livres*.' *AG* 58J 3. Tubeuf also drew other
officials in the Conseil des mines into his net. When, on 1 Aug. 1777, he created a
société to fund his new mining ventures in lower Normandy, two names on the list of
sociétaires are particularly interesting: 'Louis Morin, commis de M. Bertin', and 'M. Parent,
premier commis de M. Bertin'. *AG* 58J 6, *traité de société des mines de Saint-Sauveur-le-
Vicomte*.

[132] *AG* 58J 4, 22 Jan. 1776.

[133] On 25 Jan. 1776, Tubeuf wrote to Ode, who was pressing him for the repayment
of part of his loan, asking if it would be possible to keep La Barbérie's name out of
things. Presumably, Tubeuf had not told his friend at Versailles that he had used his
name as 'guarantor'. *AG* 58J 4.

[134] Bardon, *'L'Exploitation du bassin houiller d'Alais*, 105.

he found himself 'dans une cruelle situation'.[135] There can be no shadow of doubt that it was the support of Bertin and La Barbérie which saw him through that immediate crisis. His concession was confirmed and his enemies, who now counted amongst their number the maréchal de Castries, were forced, temporarily, to withdraw.[136] Once Bertin had fallen from favour, Tubeuf lost no time in knocking on Necker's door. In June 1780, he sent him a *mémoire* which included a potted history of his concession. A month later he had an audience with Necker at Versailles, using the occasion to convince him that the famous *arrêt* of 1744, favouring *concessionnaires* over *propriétaires*, should be implemented.[137]

All to little avail. If the 1770s marked the high tide of his fortunes in Alès, the 1780s, which would also see him active in Normandy and around Paris, would bring increasing and, ultimately, insoluble problems. On 7 September 1783, Pierre-François Tubeuf could have been found sitting in his *notaire*'s office in the rue Saint-Paul in Paris signing away 'my works in Alais to monsieur l'abbé Bréard, complete with tools and machinery, for one million *livres*'.[138] Crippling debts, years of struggle against local colliers, lime-burners, small landowners, lawyers, and seigneurs; his failure to take control of the richest mine in the coal-basin, the Grand-Combe; the eclipse of his great patron Bertin; all of this, plus his restless energy, had forced him to move the focus of his operations, first back to his native Normandy, then to the outskirts of Paris. And although the sale to Bréard turned out to be a temporary expedient enabling him to turn the creditors from his door, he was never to recapture the hopes that he and his wife had harboured as they toured the lower Cévennes for the first time in that spring of 1770. When he returned to Alès in the mid-1780s he was to find the resistance to his plans more fierce than ever, led this time by one of the most powerful men in France, Charles-Eugène-Gabriel, marquis de Castries, maréchal de France. Behind the maréchal

---

[135] *AG* 58J 4, 7 Mar. 1780. A week earlier, Tubeuf had written to Bertin asking him to use his influence to obtain the reconfirmation of his huge concession! *AG* 58J 4, 18 Feb. 1780.

[136] See entry in Journals for 21 June and 13 July 1780. *AG* 58J 4.

[137] *AG* 58J 4, 21 June. Tubeuf was desperate to use every ounce of influence he could muster at Versailles to offset the power at Court of the maréchal de Castries. He told Necker 'Voici le moment que mon affaire va vous être mise sous les yeux et que mon sort va être déterminé.' It was a critical battle for the Norman entrepreneur, but although he won the battle he was to lose the war.

[138] *AG* 58J 2, 7 Sept. 1783, before M. Morin, *notaire* of the Saint-Paul district.

lay the force of a 'protoindustrial' socio-economy, linked to the anticentralist Estates of Languedoc.

Pierre-François Tubeuf, supported by a constant policy at Court, would doubtless have defeated *les petits gens* of the Cévennes. He may have fought a draw with the Estates of Languedoc, which was never deaf to the appeal of economic modernization. His chances of defeating as powerful an adversary as the maréchal de Castries were remote, at least unless the Court of Louis XVI, like the Court of St James, was prepared to throw its weight unequivocally behind those who, *au fond*, had an industrial and 'capitalist', as opposed to an agrarian and 'feudal', vision of France. At the end of the day, the Court chose not to do so. It is time to turn to the maréchal de Castries and the society which gave him its (at times guarded) blessing.

2

THE MARÉCHAL DE CASTRIES:
ARISTOCRATS AND PROTOINDUSTRIALIZERS

IF Pierre-François Tubeuf's fortunes were waning—at least in the Alès region—by the early 1780s, so were those of the cévenol textile manufacturing and commercial élites. It is tempting to see a direct relationship between the two—empty pits matching silent looms. It is equally tempting to analyse the problems involved through bio-graphical lenses—the modern 'capitalist' David felled by the 'feudal' Goliath, the maréchal de Castries. There was, unquestionably, an indirect relationship between Tubeuf's failure and the dead weight of a contracting textile economy, just as the personal enmity between Tubeuf and Castries merits serious examination. Underlying every-thing, however, we find complex socio-economic and political issues and interrelationships which take us from the cévenol mountains to the corridors of power at Versailles and along the major shipping lanes of the eighteenth-century commercial world. Before we focus on the personal intervention of the maréchal de Castries we must examine the society which he entered after 1777, for it was to be the structure of this 'protoindustrialized' society, experiencing a major recession, which was to weigh most heavily upon Tubeuf.

In order to appreciate the scale of the recession which hit the Languedoc textile industry during the latter decades of the eighteenth century, let us first of all look, in Table 2.1, at cloth exports to the Levant, traditionally the most significant indicator of the province's economic performance.

It is not difficult to understand why economic historians have called the period from the 1730s to the 1770s Languedoc's 'âge d'or', followed as it was by a deepening recession which affected, in different degrees, every major textile centre in France.[1] The figures for cloth production in the region around the Alès coalfield reflect the prov-incial and national scene. In 1761, 15,000 pieces of the light woollen

---

[1] F. Crouzet, 'Angleterre et France au XVIIIe siècle: essai d'analyse comparée de deux croissances', *Annales, Économie, Société, Civilisation*, 21 (1966), 269.

TABLE 2.1. *Cloth exports from Languedoc
to the Levant, 1763–1787*

Year	Number of half-pieces
1763[a]	115,200
1767	94,530
1771	77,600
1775	102,120
1779	75,135
1783	72,763
1784	52,887[b]
1787	57,160

[a] Year of peak production.
[b] Worst figure since 1744.

Source: M. Morineau and C. Carrière 'Draps de
Languedoc et commerce du Levant au XVIII[e]
siècle', *Revue d'Histoire Economique et Sociale*, 56
(1968), cited by Thomson, *Clermont-de-Lodève*, 375.

–worsted cloths were stamped in the *bureaux* of the diocese of Uzès
alone. By 1783—the year in which we find Pierre-François Tubeuf
sitting in his *notaire*'s Parisian office temporarily signing away his
interests in the Alès coalfield—the dioceses of Uzès and Alès combined could only produce 8,000 pieces.[2]

It was, however, silk, not wool, which distinguished the cévenol
textile industry by the second half of the eighteenth century. Alès,
and the neighbouring *bourgs* of Anduze and Saint-Jean-du-Gard, were
to be pulled increasingly during the 1760s and 1770s into the commercial and manufacturing orbit of Nîmes, destined to become—with
more than a few dissenting voices raised in Alès—the *chef-lieu* of the
department of the Gard. The smaller *marchands-fabricants* in the Cévennes would be obliged to dance to the commercial tunes of their
masters in Nîmes and Montpellier. Expanding geographically from the
1720s, the number of looms employed by workers in the stocking
industry (*fabrique de bas*) had increased from 1,000 in the 1740s to
between 5,000 and 6,000 by the 1770s.[3] Of the 4,500 stocking-looms

[2] L. Dutil, *L'État économique de Languedoc à la fin de l'ancien régime, 1750–1789* (Paris,
1911), 429. Dugrand provides figures of 70,000 *serges, cadis, impériales*, and *pessots* (*la petite
draperie*), leaving cévenol towns like Saint-Hippolyte, Lasalle, Anduze, Vézénobres, and
Valleraugues in the 1760s, only half of which were being dispatched by 1789, *Villes et
campagnes en Bas-Languedoc*, 377.
[3] *AG* IVE 23, *mémoire présenté sur les règlements du commerce*, 1780. The great majority
were to be found in Nîmes, although Anduze alone had 120 silk-stocking looms as late

in Nîmes and the surrounding countryside by the beginning of that decade, four-fifths were engaged in the production of silk stockings.[4] In 1774, the Inspecteur des manufactures de Nîmes was as optimistic about the industry's prospects as Tubeuf was about his coal-mines: 'All the manufacturing concerns based in Nîmes . . . are working non-stop, and everyone involved on the commercial side is rich and satisfied with this happy state of affairs.'[5] By the eve of the Revolution, however, half of the stocking-looms in Nîmes and in most of its satellite towns lay idle, the poorer weavers forced to beg for bread in the streets.[6] The same rise and fall of commercial fortunes charac- terized the history of the silk fabrics sector (*étoffes de soie*), which was more highly concentrated in Nîmes than the stocking industry, ob- taining its silk thread from abroad and, increasingly, from cévenol towns like Alès, Anduze, and Saint-Jean-du-Gard. Starting with a few hundred looms in the 1750s, and rising to 6,000 two decades later, Rivoire estimates that only 2,500 were still operating by 1789.[7]

In his detailed study of the woollen-cloth-manufacturing town of Clermont-de-Lodève, James Thomson accepts, in part, Landes' thesis concerning the failure of entrepreneurial dynamism in precipitating economic decline: 'A priori, given this centrality of the entrepreneur, we would argue that the failure of Clermont's industry in the second half of the eighteenth century was a consequence of entrepreneurial weakness.'[8] There can be little doubt—as we shall discover when we relate the activities of Alèsian *négociants* to the conflict between Tubeuf and Castries—that there was a certain lack of commitment to the sustained growth of industrial, as opposed to commercial and agricul- tural, concerns in the cévenol region. However, the reasons for the

as the 1780s. *AG.* 9M 6, *état des fabriques et manufactures dans la commune d'Anduze, Vendémiaire, an VI.*

[4] *AG* IVE 23, *mémoire à l'Intendant*, 24, Feb. 1780. The actual figures are 3,500 silk stockings, 500 woollen stockings, and 500 *filoselle*. See also Dugrand, *Villes et campagnes en Bas-Languedoc*, 379.

[5] *AN* F12 780, letter to the *Garde des Sceaux*, 4 Apr. 1774. In the second half of the 18th century, Languedoc had 8 *Inspecteurs des manufactures*, 1 *Inspecteur principal*, 1 *Inspecteur spécial de Montpellier* (until 1767), and 6 other *Inspecteurs*. See Dutil, *L'État économique de Languedoc*, 301–2.

[6] *AG* IVE 23, letter to Vergennes, 25 Jan. 1787. The *syndic de la fabrique de bas de Nîmes* refers to 'un coup mortel' having been delivered to the industry by the 1780s, particularly to the silk-stocking industry in Nîmes, which was 'presque entièrement occupée à la fabrique de ces sortes de bas'.

[7] J. N. Rivoire, *Statistique du département du Gard* (Nîmes, 1842), i. 15–16.

[8] Thomson, *Clermont-de-Lodève*, 388.

recession in the textile, particularly the silk, industry in Nîmes and the cévenol region are more complex and varied than those which explain why Clermont's clothiers sold out in favour of the odd *seigneurie*.[9] Not surprising, given the fact that Clermont's entrepreneurial élite had been concerned during the first half of the eighteenth century with the 'monopoly' production of a single product—the *draps de Levant*. The wealthy, almost exclusively, Protestant *négociants* of Nîmes, on the other hand, managed an industry which produced a great variety of goods for rapidly changing fashions and markets.

This fact alone moves one in the direction of theses preferred by historians as dissimilar in time and methodology as Léon Dutil and Charles Carrière, who focus upon fluctuations in international trade, upon the instability and consequent fall in demand from within the Ottoman Empire, as well as upon the pivotal role played by Marseille in determining the flow of commodities and capital.[10] In addition, the conclusions of such historians are linked more closely to recent debates on 'protoindustrialization', enabling us to relate international and 'external' factors to the 'internal' socio-economic and political forces which were to prove, in our opinion, as crucial in determining the fortunes of the silk industry as they were in explaining the fate of Pierre-François Tubeuf's attempt to establish *l'industrie en grand* in the Alès coalfield. As Peter Kriedte has noted: 'Protoindustrialisation stands between two worlds, the narrow world of the village and the world of trade that crosses all boundaries, between the agrarian economy and merchant capitalism.'[11] Our argument will rest upon a sequential relationship between changing, and closing, international markets, the recession in the textile industry, and the defensive reflex action of a protoindustrial society, whose *mentalité* was far more agrarian and rural than industrial and urban.

It should be noted at the outset that, unlike the cloth industry of Clermont-de-Lodève and some other major Languedocian textile centres, the silk industry in Nîmes and the Cévennes only reached its peak production levels in the 1760s and 1770s, precisely the period

---

[9] Like the wealthy Clermont clothier Denis Flottes, who 'may well have regarded producing in the capacity of a normal clothier as beneath his dignity; he referred to himself now as the "seigneur" of Pouzols'. Ibid. 412.

[10] Morineau and Carrière, 'Draps de Languedoc'. For Thomson's assessment of Dutil, Dermigny, and Carrière, see *Clermont-de-Lodève*, 380–5.

[11] See P. Kriedte, 'The Origins, the Agrarian Economy and the World Market', in *Industrialization before Industrialization* (Cambridge, 1981), 37.

when the problems arising from instability in the Levant were being aggravated by industrial development and protectionist policies in France's traditional markets—Spain and her colonies, Prussia, Austria, and Russia—as well as by rapidly growing competition from that monarch of the British industrial revolution, 'King Cotton'. Between the late 1760s and 1782, the number of masters entering the *jurande* of the *fabrique de bas de Nîmes* tripled.[12] It was also during the second half of the eighteenth century that the cotton industry was establishing itself in the diocese of le Vigan with over 600 looms making cotton hats and stockings in Sauve and Saint-Hippolyte.[13] In the diocese of Uzès, a *négociant* named Marsial, whose father had established a workshop for the production of raw silk near Bagnols in 1728, was seeking official recognition of his works as a *manufacture royale* by 1764, and—with equal lack of success it must be admitted—again in 1786.[14] It was in the 1780s that an English hat-maker named Rose moved from Lyon to Anduze, employing forty workers on the manufacture of *chapeaux fins à la façon anglaise*, marking a small, but significant, advance in the technology of hat-making in the region.[15] And, finally, in Alès itself, one of the wealthiest *négociants* in the town, named Bénezet, was pressing the government in 1780 to pass on to him the secret behind a new machine for drawing out silk thread invented by a Lyon manufacturer and allegedly an improvement on the widely used Vaucanson wheel.[16] Just three examples of 'entrepreneurial dynamism', but chosen to illustrate the concern for technological improvements as well as the importance of Lyon in anything pertaining to the silk industry.[17]

Some cévenol entrepreneurs were clearly alive and kicking long after the mid-eighteenth century crisis; some, as we shall see, were not; all were to be adversely affected by changing patterns of foreign trade and changing policies on the part of governments controlling

---

[12] *AG* IVE 139, letter to the Intendant, 6 May 1782.

[13] Dugrand, *Villes et campagnes en Bas-Languedoc*, 379.

[14] *AN* F12 1437, *requête de M. Marsial, négociant à Bagnols*, 28 Sept. 1764. Marsial had eight machines designed for drawing and twisting silk thread 'qui la rivière Cèze fait tourner pendant toute l'année', as well as a spinning-jenny with 60 spindles.

[15] See his wife's petition to the government, which stressed the fact that Rose had never 'cessé de former des ouvriers supérieurs à ceux qui se trouvait alors à la tête des fabriques de chapeaux'.

[16] *AN* F12 1437, *mémoire du sieur Bénezet, négociant de la ville d'Alais*, 7 Sept. 1780.

[17] For the dependence of the hatting trade in the Cévennes upon Lyon, see M. Sonenscher, *The Hatters of Eighteenth Century France* (London, 1987), 36.

traditional markets. The silk industry was peculiarly susceptible to external pressures, not only so far as markets were concerned but also in terms of fashion. It is appropriate here to stress the negative aspect of Nîmes's close relationship with Lyon. In the main, Lyon produced the high-quality goods for the aristocratic and *haute bourgeois* end of the market; Nîmes met the requirements of the ordinary bourgeois or *colon* in the boulevard. Part of the problem concerned the very different markets captured by the *négociants* of Nîmes. Apart from the Levant, which took a decreasing share even of woollen goods, the textile products of Nîmes, Alès, Anduze, and Saint-Jean-du-Gard could be found adorning the heads, hands, and legs of men and women from the Urals to the Andes. If their gloves, hats, and white silk stockings could be seen in Saint Petersburg, Vienna, and Madrid, the colonial ladies of Saint-Domingue and Peru, desperate to be seen and not just heard as 'European', found the coloured, embroidered stockings and ribbons of Nîmes 'le dernier cri'.[18]

Not only were markets scattered all around the commercial globe but outlets at home, as well as frequently changing fashions, created headaches for commercial houses. Daniel Roche has shown how *le peuple de Paris* had begun to respond to a growing consumer market.[19] There was nothing inherently élitist about commercial capitalism in the eighteenth century. The Inspecteur des manufactures de Nîmes, commenting on the causes of the recession of the 1780s, informed the government that he had counted no fewer than 120 articles sold by the *négociants* of Nîmes in markets all over the world, and that many of these markets had their particular needs and peculiarities.[20] Take the ladies of Peru, whose taste for scarlet stockings had obviously changed in favour of more sober colours and less complicated embroidery by 1780.[21]

In his report of 17 March 1783, the Inspecteur des manufactures explained that it was the great variety of markets and changes of

---

[18] *AG* IVE 23, *mémoire présenté sur les règlements du commerce*, 1780, which states that the export of stockings in significant quantities started in 1743, destined increasingly for Germany, Russia, Italy, and Spain and her colonies.

[19] D. Roche, *The People of Paris: An Essay in Popular Culture in the Eighteenth Century* (Leamington Spa, 1987), 193: 'In the eighteenth century in Paris the popular classes underwent a sartorial revolution, they passed from the days of the durable and the dependable, handed down many times, to those of change and renewal; they displayed a new sensibility.'

[20] *AN* F12 780, letters of Lansel to the *Garde des Sceaux*, 17 and 20 Mar. 1783.

[21] *AG* IVE 23, *tableau de l'état annuel de la fabrique de bonneterie de Nîmes*, 24 Feb. 1780.

fashion which had dictated a 'free trade' policy upon textile producers and exporters in Bas-Languedoc. Whereas the 'monopoly' clothiers of Clermont-de-Lodève and Carcassonne may well have benefited in the first half of the eighteenth century from the Colbertian model of a regulated economy, at a time when high-quality goods were required for a fairly limited range of markets,[22] government intervention became increasingly anathema to the silk producers and exporters of Nîmes and the Cévennes. From the inception of the industry, they had peppered government officials with statistics and arguments all intended to convey the message that, however appropriate Colbert's model may have been for the first half of the century, it had no place in the second. As early as 1754, for example, they stressed that 'regulations governing manufacturing industry, which become necessary in certain countries, are impracticable and obstructive in others'.[23] In 1780, when rumours (not without foundation) were spreading about the government's intention to reimpose 'des règlements de 1754' on the *fabrique de bas*, they denounced such moves as 'un désastre', going on, quite perceptively, to point out that if regulations were needed to protect infant industries and the luxury trade, they were quite inappropriate for the kinds of product they were manufacturing. Just one practical point—revealing the distinction which had to be made between an 'élite' and a 'mass' market—how could merchants be expected to put the government's stamp of approval on every pair of stockings and gloves they produced? They would never be stamped in time for shipment.[24] As the Inspecteur concluded somewhat wearily: 'Every kind of regulation drives the *fabricants* mad.'[25] Long before Adam Smith, the *négociants* of Nîmes had realized that, for an increasingly commercial society, the 'Wealth of Nations' depended above all on the most rapid circulation of goods and capital.

They would not have been so keen on the competitive emphasis in Smith's most moral economy, however. Exchange yes, so long as the exchange was English coal for French silks and brandies. Unfortunately, the second half of the eighteenth century witnessed a period not only of increasing competition in the textile industry, but of increasing protectionism on the part of continental 'late-comers' to the Industrial Revolution. By the 1780s, English textiles, benefiting

---

[22] Thomson, *Clermont-de-Lodève*, 457–8.

[23] *AG* IVE 22, *syndic de la fabrique de bas au Garde des Sceaux*, Jan. 1754.

[24] *AG* IVE 23, *mémoire présenté sur les règlements du commerce*, 1780.

[25] *AN* F12 780, Lansel to Saint-Priest, 20 Mar. 1783.

from more favourable duties, were making a real impact on the sales
of French goods in the Levant, as well as in two of Nîmes's traditional
markets, Russia and Portugal. It is true that the English were not
competing with cévenol silk goods; it was just that English cottons
were increasingly winning over customers who had once favoured the
silk, or part-silk, velvet, and taffeta articles of Nîmes.[26] Competition
from the English was aggravated by the closure of other traditional
markets, such as those in Austria, by governments anxious to favour
their own nascent manufacturing sector. Salvatore Ciriacono has
explained how the Viennese silk industry, which 'took off' in the
1760s as a result of demand from the Court and the Viennese nobility,
'was moving ineluctably in the direction of a stronger manufacturing
base in the capital, which continued to attract skilled workers, whether
from neighbouring provinces or, increasingly, from France and Switzerland'. By 1772, over 5,000 workers would be engaged in the silk
industry in lower Austria.[27] Alain Dewerpe, in his recent work,
L'Industrie aux champs, has described the period 1750–1820 as the
genesis of the protoindustrial silk industry in northern Italy.[28] Far
greater emphasis should be placed on the strong competition provided
by the woollen and silk industries of Switzerland, Austria, and, in
particular, northern Italy as an explanation for the economic recession
which affected Languedoc towards the end of the *ancien régime*.[29] It
was to provide one of the rationales for Napoleon's Continental
System. It is, perhaps, not irrelevant to note that the future Girondin
Minister of War, Roland de la Platière, had been an *inspecteur des
manufactures* in Lyon and Montpellier before the Revolution.

But it was the closure of the Spanish market which dealt the single
most important blow to the *fabrique de bas* in Nîmes and the surrounding countryside, stretching from the Vaunage in the west to the
Gardonnenque in the north: the *fabrique de bas de Ganges*, producing a
higher-quality product, survived these crises fairly well with 4,000
looms working as late as 1788.[30] A *mémoire* of 28 December 1778,

---

[26] According to a letter from the *syndic de la fabrique de bas de Nîmes*, English textiles
were entering Russia and Portugal at two-thirds the import levy charged on French
goods. *AG* IVE 23, letter to Vergennes, 12 Mar. 1783.

[27] Ciriacono, 'Esquisse d'une histoire tripolitaire', 321.

[28] A. Dewerpe, *L'Industrie aux champs* (Rome, 1985), 38–9.

[29] In Switzerland, 2,500 looms, as opposed to 1,000 in 1700, were producing silk
articles by 1786. Bâle was competing with Saint-Étienne and Nîmes. Ciriacono, 'Esquisse
d'une histoire tripolitaire', 319.

[30] Joutard, 'Les Cévennes à leur apogée', in Joutard, (ed.), *Les Cévennes de la montagne
à l'homme*, 155.

written just four days before the official Spanish prohibition on textile goods entering the country, stated that, taking the average of recent years, 20,000 dozen pairs of stockings had been dispatched annually to the Indies alone.[31] Providing a statistical analysis, the merchants added that the 4,500 looms operating in the Nîmes area had given work to 16,250 men, women, and children, producing a total of 83,750 dozen pairs of stockings. Just two years later, those figures had been reduced to 1,962 looms operated by 6,300 workers making only 32,160 dozen pairs of silk stockings.[32] In a letter to the government—a copy being sent to Marie Antoinette—the merchants described the 25 per cent import duty levied by Spain as a disaster: 'The manufacture of silk stockings in this city is confronted with total ruin' was their verdict.[33] Perhaps they should have noticed the writing on the wall when a *négociant* from Saint-Hippolyte received an order for forty new looms from a Spanish firm in 1778.[34]

In the winter of 1786, further legislation concerning the importation of foreign goods provoked 'une profonde consternation' amongst *négociants* and manufacturers and, although dire warnings of 'total ruin' tended to fall easily from merchants' mouths, the growth of protectionism abroad, and particularly in Spain, really did spell disaster for many of the *dévideuses, doubleuses, ovaleurs, teinturiers, couturiers*, and *brodeuses* representing the skilled and semi-skilled textile workers of Nîmes. Of course, goods could always be smuggled along the time-honoured border routes. One report explains how hats and stockings reached Piedmont and Spain despite the new laws, with traders waiting on the frontiers to purchase them in order to market them in Spain under their own 'brand-name'.[35] However, the determination of governments in the Iberian peninsular, and elsewhere, to protect their developing industries—the cotton industry in Catalonia providing a good example[36]—undoubtedly represented a major set-back for the textile industries of Bas-Languedoc in general and the silk industry (heavily dependent upon the Spanish colonies) in particular. By the

---

[31] *AG* IVE 23, *mémoire à M. Sartine* (copy sent to Marie Antoinette), 28 Dec. 1778.

[32] Ibid., *tableau de l'état annuel*, 24 Feb. 1780.

[33] Ibid., *mémoire à M. Sartine.*

[34] Ibid., *syndic* to Intendant, 8 Feb. 1779.

[35] *AG* 9 M6, *réponse aux diverses questions sur les manufactures*, 1790.

[36] 'Only in the 1780s were Catalonian merchants allowed to own an unrestricted number of looms . . . the share of goods of Spanish origin in the total imports of the Spanish colonies rose from about one-eighth in 1700 to over one-half by 1789.' A. Milward and S. B. Saul, *The Economic Development of Continental Europe, 1780–1870* (London, 1973), 104.

time the Bastille had fallen in Paris, the textile industry in Nîmes was 'suffering from a general recession. Agriculture provides little work, and the price of essential food-supplies has risen to exorbitant levels. These calamities have plunged not only the majority of workers in our *corps* but the entire industry, as well as other citizens of this city, into a state of abject misery. Everyone is deprived of money and work'.[37] If the rise of capitalism in France does not explain the immediate outbreak of the Revolution in 1789, the fall of manufacturing production in the 1780s in most areas of Languedoc certainly did exercise a major impact upon the outbreak and course of the Revolution in this ancient province, as we shall see in the following chapter.

Producing cheap and often shoddy goods, confronted with increasing competition from other countries, the manufacturers and merchants of the Cévennes reacted by pursuing policies designed to weaken and 'de-skill' the small, independent master-craftsman and the skilled worker. At the beginning of the eighteenth century, it was still possible to distinguish between the *marchand faisant fabriquer* (*négociant*), who provided the raw material to the craftsman and distributed the end-product; the *marchand-fabricant*, working for himself assisted by one or two *compagnons*, and usually using material he had bought himself; and the *maître-ouvrier à façon*, working perhaps with one or two apprentices for the *négociant* at a contracted price. By the 1780s, the *négociant* had successfully weeded out many of the smaller merchants (many of whom were Catholic) and had launched a frontal attack on the protective organizations and customs of the craftsman, 'whom they proposed to reduce to the position of an ordinary worker'.[38] Christopher Johnson and Michael Sonenscher have both shown— albeit with different emphases—how the changing culture and requirements of capitalism affected public perceptions and the juridical position of weavers and journeymen by the end of the *ancien régime*.[39] Understandably, the workers fought back through their guilds, and

---

[37] *AG* IVE 139, *mémoire des marchands-cardeurs de filoselle*, 31 Oct. 1789. The *mémoire* was supported by 226 people, 86 of whom could not sign their names.

[38] *AN* F12, 780, *mémoire des maîtres-ouvriers au intendant*, 3 Mar. 1783. Also Rivoire, *Statistique du département du Gard*, ii. 15, who writes 'ainsi naquit au sein de la fabrique un corps riche et puissant qu'arrive rapidement à la fortune et laisse bien derrière lui le simple et modeste artisan'.

[39] Christopher Johnson, referring to the weavers of Lodève and Bédarieux, stresses how 'Master pareurs treated as virtual equals with the fabricants by the parlement of Toulouse in 1719 were now identified as mere *ouvriers*.' 'Artisans versus Fabricants: Urban Protoindustrialisation and the Evolution of Work Culture in Lodève and Bédarieux, 1740–1830', *European University Institute (Florence) Working Paper, No. 85/137*, n.d.,

through legal precedent, continually dragging their masters to the courts for alleged breaches of custom and practice, thus accelerating the financial ruin of their organizations by the 1770s. To little avail. So far as *négociants* were concerned the workers had to be disciplined. Capitalism was capitalism: international competition had to be combated. Craftsmen could not even pay the dues of their own *communauté*:[40] such workers should not 'rebel against a subordination established by the natural order of things'. After all, it should have been clear, even to the small independent manufacturer, that 'it is this latter class [the *négociants*] who possess all the necessary capital', so that any attempt to equate the authority and power of *négociants* and small independent workshop owners was nothing more than 'cette vanité mal fondée'.[41]

The tensions and struggles between *négociants*, the larger manufacturers, and their work-force increased during the last decades of the *ancien régime* as the factors referred to above—the international pressure for cheap, mass-produced goods, the internal competition from Lyon, and the external threat from industrial 'late-comers'—drove the merchants to introduce a low-wage economy as their profit margins became narrower and more precarious. As the merchants explained to the Intendant: the worker 'realizes that a permanent job and an assured, but modest, wage, is preferable . . . to higher paid work which is rendered precarious by the very fact that one has to pay too much for the job'. In other words, workers should not 'price themselves out of the market'. It was, and remains, the classic and inevitable capitalist response to increased international competition. In the opinion of the merchants, when they had won greater control over their work-force, whether in terms of wages or 'hiring and firing', the latter 'would be more interested in retaining their jobs by exhibiting a more docile attitude than is ordinarily the case'.[42]

---

9. Michael Sonenscher writes: 'The distinctive claims of journeymen in Paris, Lyon, and Marseille to determine with whom they worked, how they worked, and how they should be paid—claims that both echoed and were echoed by the prescriptions of the law—were by the last decade of the Old Regime no longer part of the discourse and practice of either corporate statutes or the courts themselves.' *The Hatters of Eighteenth Century France*, 159.

[40] *AN* F12 780, *mémoire des maîtres-ouvriers au intendant*, 3 Mar. 1783, which includes the statement that their *corps* was being ruined by the cost of trials held in the 1770s and early 1780s.

[41] *AN* F12 780, *mémoire des négociants au intendant*, Mar. 1783.

[42] Ibid. Also J. Rule, *The Experience of Labour in Eighteenth-Century Industry* (London, 1981), 31.

'De-skilling' involved destroying, or at least weakening, the power of the guilds, and the merchants and manufacturers waged a continual campaign against the relatively high entrance fees and lengthy apprenticeships which the guilds defended. The fee of 30 *livres* to become an apprentice ('which only gives us the title of *maître-ouvrier*'), for the stipulated period of five years, had been set in 1723. It cost 150 *livres* to obtain the *maîtrise* itself. The *négociants* argued, somewhat hypocritically, that many workers could not afford such sums and that they should be reduced to 5 and 50 *livres* respectively, the term of an apprenticeship being cut to three years.[43] In reply, the small master-craftsman argued that the quality of workmanship (not the primary consideration for the *négociants*) would be bound to decline if such changes were made; that all they were being offered was 'the humiliating prospect of remaining a simple worker (*ouvrier*) for life'.[44] As Peter Kriedte has put it, 'the trend in protoindustrialization, although slow and irregular, is clearly recognisable. Capital increasingly penetrated into the sphere of production and relatively independent petty producers who owned the means of their production were transformed into dependent wage-slavery'.[45] The action of textile manufacturers in Nîmes and the Cévennes had its counterpart in the introduction by Pierre-François Tubeuf of new 'man management' techniques and working practices during the same period.

The threat from the competition posed by foreign governments who were introducing their own industries may be seen very clearly in the demands made by textile manufacturers for legislation banning the export of both looms and workers.[46] They also sought more severe penalties to deal with workers caught stealing some of the raw material they used (*piquage d'once*) to run up a few items for themselves and their families, or to sell. In the opinion of the very wealthy merchants of Nîmes, hanging was not necessarily the answer, not because that punishment did not fit the crime but because it would be impossible to get juries to convict offenders: 'the whip and detention in chains'

---

[43] In Yorkshire, seven-year apprenticeships were being blamed for the decline in the worsted industry by the 1790s. P. Hudson, 'Protoindustrialisation: The Case of the West Riding Wool Textile Industry in the Eighteenth and Nineteenth Century', *History Workshop*, 12 (1981), 45.

[44] *AN* F12 780, *mémoire des maîtres-ouvriers au intendant*, 3 Mar. 1783.

[45] Kriedte, *Industrialization before Industrialization*, 110. Also C. Tilly, 'Flows of Capital and Forms of Industry in Europe, 1500–1800', *Theory and Society*, 12 (1983), 123–4.

[46] Dutil, *L'État économique de Languedoc*, 294–5.

was deemed most appropriate.[47] It is interesting that, in the process of these debates, anti-Semitism should have raised its ugly head.[48]

These industrial disputes and emerging class tensions were to provide a backcloth to the bloody events of the early years of the Revolution, the Terror providing the small craftsman, his *compagnons*, and apprentices with a Robespierre-sent opportunity of exacting their revenge upon the hated *négociant*.

Roland Aminzade has explained the growing indebtedness of master weavers and the increasing control by merchants over the preparatory and finishing processes of the manufacture of silk ribbons in Saint-Étienne as one aspect of the transition to capitalism.[49] Like Charles Tilly, Aminzade lays considerable emphasis on the evolution of a protoindustrial economy within urban, as opposed to rural, centres of textile manufacture. Whatever the validity of this further gloss on the protoindustrialization debate, the importance of the *bourg* as a commercial and trading centre in Bas-Languedoc, acting as a relay for the extension of merchant capitalism into the countryside, is obvious. Tarlé, in his short, but pioneering, study of 'cottage industry' written almost a century ago and relying heavily on the *mémoire* of the Intendant, Ballainvilliers, offers important insights into the relationship between international markets, towns, and hamlets in Languedoc. Tarlé stressed the importance of the *commissionnaire*:

These were men empowered by rich commercial houses to buy manufactured articles wholesale from peasants and who, in order to accomplish this task, visited the towns and villages of the region. They did not always buy merchandise to sell directly to the public. Often they sold them to dyers who turned the plain white articles into coloured ones, and it was these dyers who finally sold the goods to the consumer.

More often than not *marchands-fabricants* and *commissionnaires* were employed by internationally famous *négociants* from Marseille, Montpellier, and Nîmes.[50] *Marchands-fabricants* in Sommières employed 6,000 workers scattered throughout the Vaunage manufacturing the heavy

---

[47] *AG* IVE 23, *mémoire des négociants de Nîmes au intendant*, 31 Jan. 1784.

[48] *AN* F12 780, *observations et avis sur les contestations qui se sont élevées contre les frères Vidal, marchands juifs*, Feb. 1785.

[49] R. Aminzade, 'Re-interpreting Capital Industrialization: A Study of Nineteenth-Century France', *Social History*, 9 (1984), 339. Also Tilly, 'Flows of Capital and Forms of Industry in Europe', 132–3.

[50] Tarlé, *L'Industrie dans les campagnes*, 47–8.

woollen *molletons*. Thirty-six *marchands-fabricants* in Ganges supervised the work produced on 400 stocking-looms by protoindustrial workers scattered over a radius of 15 kilometres.[51] The same concentration of outwork production around small commercial and trading *bourgs* characterized the geography of the silk industry in northern Italy.[52]

Fortunately, using the fiscal records for the collection of the *vingtième de l'industrie*, we can focus in more detail on one such cévenol *bourg*, Anduze. Although the tax-rolls relate to 1760, we can discern quite clearly the modest condition and dependency of Anduze's merchant and manufacturing élite. The *marchands* were divided into three *classes*. In the first we find the *négociants*; in the second and third, the 'drapiers, toilliers et détailliers'. The town could boast of only 8 *négociants*, who were mainly engaged in buying and selling grain, chestnuts, and mules, and whose annual profits of 1,800 *livres* placed them, as we have seen, in a different category from their counterparts in Nîmes, or even from silk merchants like Louis Rocheblave in Alès.[53] The 26 'facturiers' making the light woollen *cadis* or *tramiers* clearly worked for *marchands-fabricants*, *à la journée*. Not one of the 13 master-weavers, who made a fairly miserable average profit of around 100 *livres* a year, owned more than three looms.[54] The 65 *tisserands*—'of all our *corps* . . . the most numerous and the most miserable'—were taxed on the basis of just 25 *livres* a year profit. A key indicator of the lack of a wide industrial base were the small number of dyers—just four of them— eliciting the comment from the clerk responsible for drawing up the records that 'one can easily appreciate the small-scale nature of industry in this town'. Most cloth was sold, as Ballainvilliers had noted, in its natural white condition, leaving the bulk of it to be dyed by 'foreign' merchants. The majority of the town's craftsmen—*menuisiers, charpentiers, tonneliers*—'parait très misérable et peu occupé'.[55]

We have already touched upon two of the most important characteristics identified by Professor Clarkson in his recent résumé of the

---

[51] Dugrand, *Villes et campagnes en Bas-Languedoc*, 348.

[52] 'C'est autour des petits centres urbains qui s'agrègent les nébuleuses proto-industrielles.' Dewerpe, *L'Industrie au champs*, 86.

[53] In 1789, Louis Rocheblave paid 18 *livres taille*. *AG* C1846, *rôle de répartition de la capitation des vigueries d'Alais et d'Anduze, année 1789*.

[54] In Nîmes, several master-weavers employed *compagnons* and apprentices using 7 or more looms. *AG* IVE 31, *visite des syndics*, 1786. Castor Moustardidier owned 13. *AG* IVE 31, *visite des syndics*, 1786.

[55] *AG* C511, *état des contribuables sujets au payement du vingtième de l'industrie*, 1760. The preamble to this document notes, significantly, that 'sous le nom des marchands sont confondus les négociants de cette ville'. At this time, before the arrival of the English

protoindustrialization debate: that 'towns located in manufacturing zones were principally centres of trade and commerce', and that 'protoindustrial craftsmen produced goods for merchants beyond the regions where they lived; often these markets were overseas and the products of one region competed with the products of another'. We have seen that many cévenol *bourgs* increasingly became 'collection points', through the intermediary of local merchants and *commission-naires*, for the urban *négociants* of Nîmes and Montpellier, whilst overseas markets and regional competition, whether from Lyon inside France, or from northern Italy and Austria abroad, dictated the rhythm of the silk industry in Bas-Languedoc. It is appropriate at this point to consider briefly the two other features of the protoindustrialization debate: that 'the industrial products were made by peasant manufac-turers who combined, say, weaving and stocking-knitting with farm-ing', and that 'rural manufacturing stimulated commercial farming by creating a market for food'.[56] This will enable us to focus more sharply on the socio-economic, cultural, and political forces which helped seal the fate of Pierre-François Tubeuf's 'grande entreprise'.

Protoindustrial rural workers provided the elasticity in the labour market which was peculiarly appropriate to an industry vulnerable to changes in fashions and international markets. In periods of recession, *négociants* and *marchands-fabricants* could respond by lowering wages in the towns, and by attacking the restrictive power of the guilds; urban workers could either look for work elsewhere or tide themselves over on the meagre charity provided by the Church and the merchants. The *bureaux de bienfaisance* set up in the major manufacturing centres of Languedoc on the eve of the Revolution were the eighteenth-century equivalents of the 'dole offices' of the twentieth century: they were favoured by the merchants since they represented an extra dimension to the control which they exercised over their work-force.[57] When pressed about the consequences of a prolonged recession by

hat manufacturer Rose, the eight *chapelliers* bought the majority of their hats from Marseille and Lyon to resell in the Cévennes.

[56] Clarkson, *Proto-industrialization*, 16. Also P. Deyon and F. Mendels, 'La Proto-industrialisation: théorie et réalité', *Revue du Nord*, 63 (1981), 13. The authors stress the linkages between external markets, rural industry, and the regional development of commercial agriculture.

[57] On 19 Apr. 1788, the *syndics de la communauté des cardeurs de la filoselle de Nîmes* reported that the terrible plight of workers in Nîmes had led to the 'établissement d'une association patriotique pour le soulagement de ces misérables individus'. *AG* IVE 139, letter to the Intendant.

the Intendant—worried that Protestant workers at least might emigrate—the *marchands-fabricants* of Nîmes replied that not many workers would do so given the charity they organized in the city. Significantly, however, they did suggest that textile workers in the towns of Alès, Uzès, Aubenas, Anduze, Sommières, and Génolhac might well emigrate since neither work nor organized charity was available in these towns.[58] An insight into the suffering of workers in such towns may be derived from the fact that out of the 150 looms which had been operating in Génolhac—just 27 kilometres from the mines of the Grand-Combe—at the beginning of 1778, only two were still working in February of the following year, just a month after the embargo on French goods entering Spain.[59] How many of the thousands of textile workers dependent, directly or indirectly, upon the *négociants* of Nîmes and Montpellier could fall back upon family charity or the benevolence of their employers for their survival? The answer is almost certainly not many, given that in 1760 the sixty-five *tisserands* of Anduze could barely make a profit for their masters working ten hours a day, with the result that 'their *maîtres* had to cut back on their food and general upkeep'.[60]

It is also unlikely that there would have been a welcome in the cévenol hillsides for returning urban craftsmen given the relationship between protoindustrialization and the poor, infertile soil which encouraged its growth. Many economic historians have stressed that 'domestic industry' and pastoral, or poor agricultural, production are closely linked.[61] The Inspecteur des manufactures de Lyon recognized the relationship for Languedoc over two centuries ago: 'Everyone agrees that, above all, it is in places upon which nature has not smiled that useful undertakings like manufacturing should be established.'[62]

---

[58] *AG* IVE 23, *mémoire à l'intendant*, 15 Feb. 1779. The last Intendant of Languedoc, Ballainvilliers, drew a distinction between the 'regions fertiles du Languedoc (comme, par exemple, le Gévaudan et le Haut-Vivarais) où la population partage son temps entre la manufacture et le travail des champs' and the less fertile, which included *bourgs* like Sommières, Anduze, and those in the Bas-Vivarais, whose workers had been more thoroughly 'urbanised'. Tarlé, *L'Industrie dans les campagnes*, 47.

[59] *AG* IVE 23, *mémoire à l'intendant*, 15 Feb. 1779.

[60] *AG* C511, *état des contribuables*, 1760.

[61] E. L. Jones, 'The Agricultural Origins of Industry', *Past and Present*, 40 (1968), 61. More recently Pat Hudson has shown how 'Around Halifax one finds the earliest evidence of the inability of agriculture to supply even the barest of subsistence needs and the spur to proto-industrial activity which this created.' 'Proto-industrialisation: The Case of the West Riding', 41. Also Kriedte, *Industrialization before Industrialization*, 14.

[62] Tarlé, *L'Industrie dans les campagnes*, 6 n. 1.

Anyone who travels along the tortuous roads between Alès, Anduze, and Saint-Jean-du-Gard today will appreciate what the Inspecteur meant, although he would have been unaware of the link between rugged scenic beauty and tourism. Shallow-rooted trees still cling to hillsides thinly covered with stony soil. Roger Dugrand noted that the chief characteristic of the silk industry was 'its wide dispersion throughout the *bourgs* and villages' of this infertile countryside.[63] In Piedmont also, 'The principal characteristic of the silk industry is its very wide dispersion and deconcentration along the heartlands of the protoindustrial zones.'[64]

Add to the poverty of the soil a marked rise in population during the eighteenth century and we have the recipe for acute hardship in times of economic depression. Although not the only factor, several studies have established 'that rural industry encouraged the growth of population'.[65] Alain Molinier has produced detailed statistics for the Bas-Vivarais region. Like that of Alès, the population of the region was much the same in 1715 as it had been in 1644. Beginning during the first half of the century, however, then gaining momentum after the 1750s, the number of inhabitants rose from 226,769 in 1759 to 273,598 by 1793. It is important to note that the biggest annual rate of increase—6.6 per cent—occurred during the 1780s. And this substantial rise in population was not matched by any 'revolution' in the agricultural sphere.[66] Guichard's study of the Andance region of the Vivarais, one of small, scattered peasant properties, their owners earning between 700 and 1,500 *livres* a year, shows that, by the 1780s, we are witnessing 'A move towards pauperization at the bottom of the social scale and a concentration of wealth at the top'.[67] Most studies of protoindustrialization have concentrated on the link

---

[63] Dugrand, *Villes et campagnes en Bas-Languedoc*, 383.

[64] Dewerpe, *L'Industrie aux champs*, 97. Students interested in the evolution of the protoindustrial worker should perhaps look more closely at old industries like tanning. In Anduze in 1760, 'les ouvriers ne s'y attachent que pour remplir le vide du temps que la culture de leurs champs et de leurs vignes leur laisse'. The tanners in this small town, however, treated around 1,200 cow skins a year; other cévenol towns, including Alès, could boast similar or more productive tanning works. The international element was also evident, with skins being imported through the port of Marseille from as far away as Buenos Aries. *AG* C511, *état des contribuables*, 1760.

[65] Clarkson, *Proto-industrialization*, 46.

[66] Molinier, 'En Vivarais au XVIIIᵉ siècle', 316.

[67] P. Guichard, 'D'une société repliée à une société ouverte: l'évolution socio-économique de la région d'Andance de la fin du XVIIᵉ siècle à la Révolution', in P. Léon, *Structures économiques et problèmes sociaux du monde rural dans la France du sud-est* (Paris, 1966), 208.

between these poor, over-populated regions and textile manufacturing. But, given that the coal was present, mining was just as important as an additional source of income to poor peasants as manufacturing. In what was to become the Decazeville mining complex, coal-mining 'prevented some people from dying of hunger, as one priest claimed, and played a role in the lives of everyone in the Basin, whether they dug coal on their own property or "share-crop mined" on their neighbour's, transported coal on land or down the Lot, or simply benefited from low coal prices in supplying their personal needs'.[68] Coal was just as vital to the lives—not just the livelihoods—of the inhabitants of the Cévennes, and without a full appreciation of this fact it is difficult to understand why Tubeuf's grandiose schemes were to fail.

Despite the considerable pressure to escape the precarious existence of a protoindustrial livelihood, few cévenols sought permanent work in the towns where, if anything, conditions were far worse. Even today, the worker in Nîmes or Alès rejoices in the ownership of his little plot in the hills, his *mazet*, to which he and his family can retreat on weekends and in the holiday season.[69] Protoindustrialization was based on the family economy. The ideal, and romanticized, picture is that painted by the Intendant Ballanvilliers: the peasant bending low over his loom, which 'occupies his time when work in the fields is no longer available. His wife and children card, spin and prepare the wool, usually during the winter months. A feeble glow from the lamp falls over the various items of clothing, made, often, in the early hours of the morning.'[70] According to an enquiry covering the canton of Sauve in 1790, the 620 looms in and around Sauve and Saint-Hippolyte provided work for '2,000 women and children', whilst 300 women were engaged upon sewing and embroidering the famous *bas de Ganges*, very popular in Saint Petersburg, by 1788.[71] In the Alès and Saint-Ambroix region, the late spring marked the beginning of feverish activity entirely confided to feminine hands which were plunged into bowls of near-boiling water to tease out and string together the delicate threads from the silk cocoons.[72] When the Intendant asked

[68]   Reid, *The Miners of Decazeville*, 10.
[69]   Dugrand, *Villes et campagnes en Bas-Languedoc*, 83.
[70]   Tarlé, *L'Industrie dans les campagnes*, 12.
[71]   Joutard, 'Les Cévennes à leur apogée', 155.
[72]   Dugrand, *Villes et campagnes en Bas-Languedoc*, 378. In northern Italy also the drawing and twisting of the silk thread was an occupation traditionally reserved for unmarried

why such peasants did not choose to move to the towns, one merchant ventured the opinion that it was because of their 'natural attachment to their place of birth', added to the fact that families were worried about 'The cost of setting up a workshop in the big cities, where the lowest-paid worker wants to boast about an apartment which was the envy of his fellow-worker.'[73] Urban living involved an entirely different way of life with very different pressures. It was customary for widows and married female *cardeurs de la filoselle* in Nîmes to work at home in neighbouring villages rather than in their master's workshops, in part 'because of the infirmity and misery of these workers, crippled by the very fine dust', but also because, at home, 'all they had to put up with were their own kids'.[74]

There is also some evidence to suggest that salaries in the countryside could be as high as those in the towns, not necessarily in *per capita* terms, but based upon the premiss that, for the merchant, the 'unit cost' covered the entire family. According to one Inspecteur des manufactures, wages in Languedoc during the 1780s tended to be higher than those in the north of France. Weavers could earn between 20 and 26 *sous* a day, although female spinners only 5 to 8 *sous*. However, the Inspecteur, stressing the importance of the family unit, went on to say that 'it should be noted that these workers set aside a part of their time for their own work, and that the women occupy themselves with their household duties. They seem happy enough; they make a living.'[75] The records of the *corps et métiers* in Nîmes offer some support to the conclusion that earnings in the countryside could compare favourably with those in the towns.[76] In 1783, the Intendant was even told that silk-stocking weavers could earn anything from 30 to 60 *sous* a day, according to demand.[77] Clearly, as with Tubeuf's miners, there was no set pattern for wages; they depended on the condition of the worker, the relationship with the merchant, and, most important of all, the nature of the job. However, despite notable exceptions to the rule, there seems no reason to quarrel with

girls. As late as 1876, 'femmes et enfants constituent 69.8% de la force de travail industriel du Piémont, 84.8% celle de la Lombardie'. Dewerpe, *L'Industrie aux champs*, 342–3.

[73] *AG* IVE 23, *mémoire à l'intendant*, 15 Feb. 1779.

[74] Ibid.

[75] *AG* IVE 139, *mémoire des syndics de la communauté des cardeurs de la filoselle*, 17 Jan. 1785.

[76] Tarlé, *L'Industrie dans les campagnes*, 34.

[77] *AN* F12 780, *mémoire des négociants à l'intendant*, 28 Feb. 1783.

Dewerpe's conclusion concerning the protoindustrial workers of Piedmont: 'The protoindustrial worker is badly paid because of his link
with the land.'[78]

And the 'link with the land' was the main concern of the cévenol
protoindustrial worker. Given that, in periods of recession, there was
absolutely no point in moving one's family to the city, the alternative
was to grow the produce that commanded a market and which allowed
one to live off the land. The ecology of the Cévennes and the
sociology of protoindustrial communities combined to produce the
near-perfect answer—*le mûrier et la vigne*. Mulberry trees to produce
the tons of leaves needed to feed the silkworm; grapes, whose juices
could be distilled to produce the *eaux-de-vie de Languedoc*. For Alain
Dewerpe, the rearing of silkworms and the consequent production of
the raw and spun silk was 'la branche protoindustrielle par excellence'.[79] The cévenol climate was well suited to the growth of the
mulberry tree; its cultivation also dovetailed neatly into a system of
land tenure based on small peasant properties and sharecropping, one
in which thousands of peasants could produce the millions of leaves
needed to feed the silkworm, whilst, with the indispensable assistance
of their wives and daughters, the silk-cocoons could be lovingly tended
to produce the silk which was then drawn, spun, and reeled.[80]
Viticulture competed with sericulture as a protoindustrial activity.
Again, the terrain and climate suited the development of the sturdy
variety of vine which produced poor-quality wine but good *eaux-de-vie*.
According to Léon Dutil, few cévenol peasants had neither vines nor
mulberry trees on their properties, and the majority of *petits propriétaires*
had both. Indeed, cultivating both 'crops' fitted very neatly into the
protoindustrial worker's calendar. The delicate process of rearing the
silkworms, then producing the spun silk, took up most of the summer
months, whilst the grapes were harvested in the autumn. Spinning and
weaving, as Dutil noted, could take up much of the winter.[81] If the
manufacturing industry was enjoying good times and the weather was
kind to mulberry trees and vines then the living could be fairly easy;

[78] Dewerpe, *L'Industrie aux champs*, 376.
[79] Ibid. 478.
[80] One merchant estimated that to make 15 pairs of silk stockings one needed 2½
pounds of silk, which in turn required 30 pounds of silk cocoons produced by silkworms
eating their way through 20 *quintaux* of mulberry leaves! *AG* IVE 23, *mémoire à M.
Sartine*, 28 Dec. 1778.
[81] Dutil, *L'État économique de Languedoc*, 70–2.

if there was a recession and the weather turned nasty, as indeed it did in the late 1780s, then starvation or increased indebtedness, or both, were the inevitable consequence.

The plantation of mulberry trees in significant numbers can be traced back to the terrible winter of 1709, which decimated the olive trees, although their expansion was clearly linked to the evolution of the silk industry. Landowners were encouraged by the government to plant mulberry trees in 1752, receiving a payment of 25 *livres* for every 100 trees planted. By 1789, the production of mulberry trees had become the most important branch of agriculture in the diocese of Alès.[82] 1,500 *tonnes* of silk-cocoons were being produced annually in the region covered by Tubeuf's mining concession; 600 in the hills around Alès, 500 in the Anduze—Saint-Jean-du-Gard area, and 400 around Saint-Ambroix. The number of silk-spinning machines increased in proportion to the production of the raw material—from 91 for the diocese of Alès in 1750 to 2,000 by the time of the Revolution, 'une croissance étonnante' as Philippe Joutard notes.[83] The lower Cévennes was experiencing its own revolution precipitated by competition from abroad, with England, Prussia, Austria, Switzerland, and Italy all producing their own manufactured articles. Internally, there was the competition from Lyon, Paris, and Tours. An international division of labour was taking place during the period covered by this study—increasingly, the raw and spun material would be produced in the Cévennes (and Provence); the manufactured articles would be produced in urban centres inside and outside France. As Dugrand concludes: 'The mulberry tree therefore became the fulcrum of the economic equilibrium in the Cévennes and the Gardonnenque.'[84]

The expansion of the vine could not quite keep pace with that of *le mûrier* or with its dramatic growth, after 1750, in what was to become the neighbouring department of the Hérault.[85] In the Bas-Vivarais, the increase in wine production during the eighteenth century was small—from 195,000 to 205,000 *hectolitres* a year. However, wine production did develop more rapidly further south, around Alès and

---

[82] Joutard, 'Les Cévennes à leur apogée', 153–4.

[83] Ibid. 154.

[84] Dugrand, *Villes et campagnes en Bas-Languedoc*, 378.

[85] Thomson, *Clermont-de-Lodève*, 439. It is also significant that wine-growing in the Beaujolais region developed out of a protoindustrial socio-economy. Tarlé, *L'Industrie dans les campagnes*, 6 n. 1.

in the plain around Nîmes, and it is noticeable that production increased during periods of recession in manufacturing industry. For example, although the distilling trade had been developing since the mid-seventeenth century, with its geographic centre of gravity between Nîmes and Lunel, it is noticeable that 22 distilling boilers were installed in Nîmes after 1775, and 28 in Saint-Gilles after 1778, the year of the Spanish embargo on French manufactured goods.[86] In 1780, Tubeuf's former *directeur*, Alles, wrote that the wine harvest that year 'has all the appearance of being the most abundant people have seen for twenty years', adding that 'if peace (in the American colonies) comes, the production of *eaux-de-vie* will quadruple. . . . There seems to be no end to the number of vines being planted in lower Languedoc.'[87] The comment underlines the relationship between war, politics, and the economy of the region. There can be little doubt that, confronted with an economic recession in the 1780s, the proto-industrial peasants of the Gard, and the Hérault, sought their salvation not in the factory, but in the soil. Those two 'enfants gâtés' of the Cévennes, the mulberry tree and the vine, rooted them to the land, providing an increasingly important source of revenue as the spinning and manufacture of silk began to be concentrated more heavily in Aubenas, Alès, Anduze, Saint-Jean-du-Gard, and Nîmes. It is vital to an understanding of the attack on Tubeuf's 'monopolistic' designs that we realize how the 'protoindustrial' production of coal dovetailed into the protoindustrial socio-economy of the region.

If the move towards the production of raw silk and wine was convenient for the cévenol peasantry, it was equally welcome to the landed and professional bourgeoisie. The silkworm fed off the mulberry leaf, the protoindustrial worker off the silk-cocoons, the bourgeoisie off the protoindustrial worker. As James Thomson has remarked: 'Throughout the long history of Languedoc's industry, it would seem, production was looked upon as a means rather than an end, a means whereby the greater security and status of landed income

---

[86] Many small property-owners agreed to distil wine into the local brandies during the winter months for *négociants*. 'On voit suffisament par là que la distillation était une petite industrie, annexe de l'agriculture, repartie entre un grand nombre de fabricants besogneux et, par suite, livrée à l'autorité des gros négociants.' Dutil, *L'État économique de Languedoc*, 182. Yet another example of the relationship between the big urban merchants and protoindustrial forms of production.

[87] B. de N. 496, Alles to Richard, 9 June 1780.

and rent from office could be obtained.'[88] From the late medieval period, the commercial and professional bourgeoisie had seized an increasing share of the available land. The landed domination secured by urban bourgeois in Nîmes, Alès, and Anduze reflected the economic stranglehold which *négociants* and successful *marchands-fabricants* exercised over *maîtres-ouvriers* and *tisserands* in the towns and protoindustrial families in the countryside. Roger Dugrand's convincing study of Bas-Languedoc published in 1963 laid particular emphasis on the fact that 'la domination de la ville sur la campagne est en Bas-Languedoc un phénomène très ancienne', this domination reaching a peak by the beginning of the nineteenth century.[89] The attraction of land, founded as it was upon secure forms of investment, the rising profits to be made out of the production of raw silk, the considerable lift up the social ladder which the purchase of a *seigneurie* or, after 1789, *biens nationaux* entailed, all this was to make it extremely difficult for entrepreneurs in heavy industry to attract the capital they needed at reasonable rates of interest. As Dugrand explains, 'Throughout the eighteenth century, urban capital launched a general offensive against the land.'[90]

It is noticeable, however, that not all Protestant *négociants* from Nîmes and Alès invested in land, many preferring to plough back their profits into the international business of commerce. It was the Catholic *petite noblesse* like the Calvières, the Ginestoux, and the La Fares who, throughout our period, were to be the most vocal defenders of the Catholic and royalist landed interest against the allegedly predatory and unethical moves of the Protestant commercial interest. The La Fares were to be involved in the traditional polyculture of Bas-Languedoc, owning 180 *hectares* near Cendras, well into the twentieth century.[91] This differing perception of the political and 'moral economy' of the region underpinned the bloody clashes between Catholics and Protestants from 1780 to 1830.

---

[88] Thomson, *Clermont-de-Lodève*, 40.

[89] Dugrand, *Villes et campagnes en Bas-Languedoc*, 343–6.

[90] Ibid. 346. The inhabitants of Clermont-de-Lodève, following its manufacturing collapse, paid more attention to land 'all the more so in so far as agricultural activities were favoured by the steady rise in agricultural prices noted throughout France in this period. The agricultural revival was given a further boost by the physiocrat-inspired edict of 5 July 1770 which granted tax exemption for a period of fifteen years on abandoned land brought back into cultivation'. Thomson, *Clermont-de-Lodève*, 439.

[91] Dugrand, *Villes et campagnes en Bas-Languedoc*, 116.

How was the domination over smallholders and sharecroppers exercised? In general, through a seigneurial system whose laws and customs were interpreted by a horde of financial, administrative, and legal *officiers*—stewards, bailiffs, *procureurs*, *avocats*, *juges seigneuriaux*, etc.—often on behalf of absentee owners, as was the case with the vicomtes de Portes and the comtes d'Alais. Until 1777, the *comté d'Alais* was owned by François-Louis de Bourbon-Conty, who was succeeded by the maréchal de Castries. As in every French province, the burden of the seigneurial system upon the inhabitants of Languedoc varied. According to Thomson, the 'feudal' system was relatively light around Clermont-de-Lodève;[92] on the other hand, Peter Jones's more detailed study of the agrarian economy concludes that the southern Massif Central region 'remained a bastion of vigorous seigneurialism on a par with Brittany at the end of the *ancien régime*. Of this there can be little doubt. . . . It was intense in the Haute-Auvergne around St. Flour, in the Brivadois, in the Bas-Vivarais and the Cévennes.'[93] Even 'revisionist' historians have now conceded the reality of a 'seigneurial reaction' in the second half of the eighteenth century, differing in kind and intensity from region to region.[94] We shall see that such a reaction was clearly operating on the Conty and Castries estates in the 1770s and 1780s.

Although, theoretically, almost all land in France was owned by a seigneur, in no part of France were the actual rights of property defended by individuals with more vigour and success than in Languedoc. Also, in no other French province was the system of leasing out land to *fermiers* more common, although Hilton Roots, resting his argument upon the encroachment of the State through the Intendant at the cost of the seigneur, notes that in Burgundy 'contact between

---

[92] Thomson, *Clermont-de-Lodève*, 73.

[93] P. Jones, *Politics and Rural Society: The Southern Massif Central, 1750–1880* (Cambridge, 1985), 162.

[94] D. Sutherland, *France, 1789–1815: Revolution and Counterrevolution* (London, 1985) is extremely cautious but admits that 'there are signs of a "reaction" here and there', 70. W. Doyle, *Origins of the French Revolution* (Oxford, 1980) is equally cautious. Whilst admitting that the feudal 'burden' falling upon the peasantry increased over the century, Doyle thinks that the notion of a 'feudal reaction . . . may be an illusion. Its reality has yet to be demonstrated,' 197. Hilton Root in his recent work on Burgundy appears to agree that Pierre de Saint-Jacob had indeed proved the reality of a reaction during the 18th century, although he shifts the focus of attention to the administrative and political changes which had turned the peasant from a 'résigné' into a 'mécontent'. *Peasants and King in Burgundy: Agrarian Foundations of French Absolutism* (Berkeley, Calif., 1987), 164–5.

the village inhabitants and the seigneurie had degenerated into disputes with estate managers and the wealthy *fermiers*'. Saint-Jacob, historian of the same province, went as far as to claim that 'the great economic and social fact of the century was the power of the *fermier*'.[95] In Languedoc, great seigneurs like the Contys and the Castries farmed out all their rights to wealthy individuals who often sublet them on annual leases to smallholders and sharecroppers. François-Louis de Bourbon-Conty farmed out his lands every nine years to 'his *fermiers directs* who then leased to this man *le leude, le pain des quatre fêtes*, then sub-let to another *les pieds de porc, les langues de boeuf*, someone else got the right to collect the tolls, yet another fees from the seigneurial courts of justice'.[96] Similarly, on the Castries estate, everything was auctioned off to the highest bidder—fields, meadows, mills, orchards, buildings, tolls, judicial charges, etc.

Let us take the example of the land covering the Grand-Combe mines. Like Gaul, it had been divided into three parts. A sieur Aquier, who leased one part from a M. de Labruyère, *propriétaire de la domaine de Plusor*, which belonged ultimately to the *commanderie de Saint-Christol*, farmed out the rights of coal-mining on the mountain to Jean Arbousset, a silk manufacturer. Sieur Favède rented his piece from the seigneur de Trouilhas, who was the vassal of the comte d'Alais. The third piece was owned directly by the comte d'Alais himself, who also exercised his seigneurial authority over many other pieces of land in the region.[97] This complicated set of legal relationships was typical of much of the land in the *comté d'Alais*: landownership was an interlocking chain of human and financial dependency from the great seigneur in the metropolitan or provincial capitals, through the wealthy *propriétaires* and/or *fermiers*, to the *sous-fermiers* and ordinary peasants, artisans, or coal-miners. No wonder Tubeuf spent as much time at Court or chasing the coat-tails of seigneurs in Versailles as he did in his mines! Usually, land in the Cévennes was leased out either for cash or for payments in kind—meat, poultry, grain, chestnuts,

---

[95] Root, *Peasants and King in Burgundy*, 174.

[96] Bardon, *L'Exploitation du bassin houiller d'Alais*, 58.

[97] *AN* 306AP 482, *observations de P. Crozade sur le mémoire de M. Monge*, 1783. Castries, in the middle of his battle with Tubeuf at this time, was trying to acquire more control over the Grand-Combe area. Crozade suggested that he might use his powers as seigneur to get Favède out of his land since the latter was behind in the payment of his *rente foncière*. Such a move would have been fiercely contested. After all, local property-owners were looking to Castries to protect them from Tubeuf's attack upon their property rights. The suggestion was never acted upon!

mulberry leaves, or even raw silk. *Négociants* and landowners alike preferred the sharecropping system with the owner, or *fermier*, providing land, tools, or raw material, as well as credit, in return for the finished manufacturing or agricultural product. *Négociants* even gave loans to peasants to encourage them to engage in the distilling business, whilst 'share-cropping, under different names, dominated the province from one end to the other'.[98] Much of the income from the *comté d'Alais* was received in the form of mulberry leaves or chestnuts. In 1783, Castries's agent suggested that the maréchal should farm out parcels of land directly to individuals, bypassing the traditional *fermier*—an indication of the agent wishing to increase the income of the estate by becoming more directly involved in the raw-silk business. As the agent remarked, 'mulberry leaves provide the major source of income from our *métairies*, with the exception of Leyrolle, which is devoted to the cultivation of chestnuts'.[99]

This complicated, but increasingly commercialized, set of relationships and property-rights formed one of the most difficult obstacles to the development of heavy industry in the Alès region. For minerals beneath the soil were treated by the Alèsians in exactly the same way as the crops and trees which grew above it. Coal was, after all, *charbon de terre*, or, as one of Castries's lawyers phrased it, 'Every mine is a part of the land which encompasses it; it is as inseparable from it as the vine is from the soil in which it has been planted.' Furthermore, crops, mulberry leaves, vines, coal, all formed part of the *complexum feodal*, hallowed by time and the feudal charter, irrevocably integrated into the fiscality of the seigneurial system:

From time immemorial, colliers have worked for certain landowners, or for their *censitaires* or *fermiers*. It forms one of their principle sources of revenue as well as providing a living for local inhabitants who are employed in the mines. One can test the ancient proof of this kind of ownership in every provincial document and, more precisely, in the land-deeds (*titres*) relating to the *comté d'Alais* which have been produced by the maréchal de Castries, tracing the history of this great fief back for over three centuries.[100]

When Tubeuf's onslaught on the mines in the Alès coalfield reached as far as the Grand-Combe—or the *mines de Trouilhas* as they were then known—the seigneur de Trouilhas recruited the weighty services

---

[98] Dutil, *L'État économique de Languedoc*, 70–6.
[99] *AN* 306AP 490, letter to Castries, 25 Sept. 1788.
[100] B. de N. 496, *Mémoire pour le duc de Castries*.

of the Archbishop of Narbonne in the defence of his property. During his visit to establish the true facts, the Archbishop was confronted with a scene reminiscent of a Sir Walter Scott novel: 'M. Deleuze-Trouilhas, accompanied by his two brothers, chevaliers de Saint Louis, as well as by other relatives and friends, was bent under the weight of a huge load—enormous and endless tomes containing bundles of title-deeds and parchments.'[101]

The Archbishop was suitably impressed, getting the message loud and clear that Tubeuf's plans represented nothing less than an attack on the sanctity of property, hallowed by time and hundreds of parchments. If wagon-loads of medieval charters could not legitimize a seigneur's right to his coal, then what could? After all, the origins of Tubeuf's mines at Rochebelle could be traced back to 1240, whilst the first recorded mention of the Mas-Dieu and Abilon mines appear in a charter, dated 7 June 1344, by which the king of France ceded the property to Humbert II.[102] If the answer to the question about ownership was to be the fiat of the king then what about the sanctity of property-rights in general, with or without mines? Coal, unlike textiles, was central to the eighteenth-century explosive debate on property-rights, and the way it had traditionally been mined fitted into a seigneurial, small property-owning society. As Marcel Rouff concluded:

The coal industry was indissolubly linked with the land. The land was the essential condition for its existence, its *raison d'être*, and this land was already subdivided in France into the hands of peasants and petits bourgeois who worked it themselves. These property-owners, therefore, had to be dispossessed before heavy industrialization could advance. This was the key to the entire conflict.[103]

It was into this protoindustrial society, about to be confronted with its worst period of manufacturing recession, reacting to this recession by becoming more heavily dependent upon land than the loom, that Charles-Eugène-Gabriel La Croix Castries made his official entry on 27 March 1777 with the purchase of the *comté d'Alais* for the princely sum of 770,000 *livres*. The *comté d'Alais* was the premier fief in Languedoc and one of the oldest in France, its recorded history dating back to Raymond Pelet, who embarked on the first crusade in 1095.

---

[101] Ibid. Alles to Richard, 21 June 1780.
[102] Bardon, *L'Exploitation du bassin houiller d'Alais*, 3–5.
[103] Rouff, *Les Mines de charbon*, 63.

The original *château d'Alais* was built in the tenth century.[104] Geographically, the fief covered about half of the present-day department of the Gard including most of Tubeuf's coal concession from the king. Its purchase gave Castries the legal right to levy feudal dues in fifty parishes; it also conferred upon its new owner important political responsibilities—president of the *assiette du diocèse d'Uzès*; a seat, as *premier baron-né* on the Estates of Languedoc, which itself attracted a *rente* of 5,000 *livres*. Excluding this, and the dues from Castries's fifty parishes, 'the *comté d'Alais* was composed of various pieces of land, farmed out to sieur Joseph Pugnière, bourgeois de la ville, a water-mill which had three grinding-wheels, one for grain, the others for oil, tolls levied on the bridges over the river Gardon, fees relating to the sale of meat,' as well as 'a levy of a tenth on all new mines which were opened in the *comté*'.[105]

It appears that the increasing interest at Court in the possibility of obtaining substantial profits from mining may have been the decisive factor prompting Castries to purchase the *comté*. One of his close friends at Versailles was the duc de Croy, who, in 1756, had obtained the effective ownership of part of the Anzin coalfield, originally discovered by the Desandrouins, but legally linked to Croy's *seigneuries* of Fresnes and Vieux-Condé.[106] There can be little doubt that the success achieved at Anzin must have whetted Castries's financial appetite, particularly since Tubeuf had done all the hard work and the coveted post of Minister of War had gone to a rival in 1775. Castries's attention turned southwards, to his estate near Montpellier[107] where the family name was widely respected long before the *comté d'Alais* appeared on the market. But whatever combination of reasons prompted the purchase of the ancien fief, Pierre-François Tubeuf was henceforth to be confronted with an opponent whose own marriage had netted him 465,000 *livres* and whose only son's marriage ceremony had been graced by the presence of Louis XVI and Marie Antoinette.

---

[104] duc de Castries, *Papiers de famille* (Paris, 1977), 296–8.

[105] Ibid. 299.

[106] Ibid. 116–17. Geiger, *The Anzin Coal Company*, 18.

[107] Castries was also a close friend of Necker, leaning heavily on the latter when he needed advice in his capacity as président de la Compagnie des Indes. The maréchal was one of the richest nobles in France at this time, at least on paper. Five years after the purchase of the *comté d'Alais*, he bought the *château d'Ollainville et la terre d'Egly*, near Arpajon, from the Archbishop of Cambrai for 460,000 *livres*.
The family seat near Montpellier had been given to Castries's son, Armand-Charles, comte de Charlus, in 1756. Castries, *Papiers de famille*, 198.

Appointed Minister of the Navy during the American War of Independence, a grateful monarch was to elevate Castries to the title of maréchal de France in 1783.[108] 'Un Grand', in the fullest meaning of the term, then, and a lord who took his feudal responsibilities very seriously indeed: 'Determined to observe tradition, the maréchal de Castries ordered his *notaire*, Pierre Lichère, to draw up a list of all those who were supposed to pay homage to him. It appears that he was most conscientious in visiting all the parishes belonging to the *comté d'Alais*, where he received many local acts of homage.'[109]

With the purchase of the *comté*, Castries became the 'official' protector of the anti-Tubeuf faction in the Basses-Cévennes. It is important to realize, however, that this faction had begun to coalesce long before Castries's arrival. Indeed, we shall argue, in this and the following chapter, that the maréchal's interest in increasing his 'industrial' revenues from coal-mining in the late 1780s would often conflict with his position as protector and patron of his vassals, who had already been alienated by Tubeuf's activities. The first signs of local resistance to Tubeuf had surfaced during the early years of his concession. On 29 May 1771, the subdelegate of the Intendant, Daudé d'Alzon, had expressed serious reservations about the concession which was about to be granted to the Norman entrepreneur. The subdelegate's main concern was the possibility that Tubeuf's plans would interfere with the traditional operations of the coal trade in and around Alès. If Tubeuf was prepared to carry on with the established policy of stocking the warehouses in Alès before selling to 'outsiders' then his fears might prove groundless and 'everything might go on as it has done in the past'.[110] Two year's later, Tubeuf had become alarmed at the welcome—to the tune of a 30,000-*livre* loan—shown by the Estates of Languedoc towards a Languedoc nobleman and army officer named, appropriately enough, Marchand de La Houlière, who was seeking to set up 'an iron foundry using coal'. Assisted by the local metallurgist, Gensanne, La Houlière's

---

[108] Ibid. 300.

[109] *Recherches historiques sur la ville d'Alais*, 386. Castries clearly fits Guy Lemarchand's description of the 'grand seigneur': 'Sa fortune, ses terres et son prestige lui permettent d'exercer une sorte de patronage en donnant l'emploi et secours à nombre de fermiers, journaliers et indigents, en arbitrant sans frais certains conflits entre paysans, en honorant les familles qu'il veut distinguer du parrainage d'un enfant . . . '. 'La Féodalité et la Révolution: seigneurie et communauté paysanne', *Annales historiques de la Révolution française*, 52 (1980), 547.

[110] Bardon, *L'Exploitation du bassin houiller d'Alais*, 71.

preliminary researches were to prove abortive.[111] The possibility that La Houlière would receive a coal concession through the good offices of the Estates (which had refused Tubeuf a loan) provoked the Norman entrepreneur into one of his periodic, but always short-lived, bouts of depression: 'What a sense of deception. The Estates granting concessions! Poor Tubeuf, poor wife, poor children!'[112]

Tubeuf was to be rescued on this occasion, as on so many others, by the political clout of his friends at Versailles, particularly La Barbérie, together with the support of the Archbishop of Narbonne and the Bishop of Alès. His own concession was confirmed by the king on 24 March 1774. A couple of months later, he had a long interview with Richard Dillon, Archbishop of Narbonne, who, as president of the Estates of Languedoc, was crucial to the success of his plans. It was as a result of this meeting that Tubeuf agreed to concentrate his mining efforts on the three sites at Rochebelle, Meyrannes–Robiac, and Banne. The Archbishop confirmed, on this occasion at least, that 'if it so happens that I have to face opposition from anyone, I should not hesitate to press ahead. The next meeting of the Estates would give me, if needed, legal backing which would save me from having recourse to the king's council.'[113] The Intendant of the province had already given Tubeuf his blessing, whilst the Bishop of Alès, de Beauteville, 'has constantly encouraged me', even loaning money to Tubeuf on one occasion, money which the latter was wise enough to repay promptly.[114]

It was this kind of support from Paris, Montpellier, and Alès which had encouraged Tubeuf in the early days of his venture: it also gave him the confidence to become more aggressive in the realization of his plans. In late 1774, and throughout the following year, Tubeuf was busily engaged in closing down the small mines, as well as a few of the larger ones, which provided 'unfair' competition to his own. Entries in his Journal for February and March 1775 record the indemnities paid to several landowners in Banne and Meyrannes who

---

[111] Ibid. 105. Chaussinand-Nogaret cites de La Houlière's efforts as a good example of noble 'industrial capitalism', but does not reveal that they failed—at a cost to the Estates of Languedoc of 30,000 *livres*. *The French Nobility in the Eighteenth Century*, 110.

[112] Bardon, *L'Exploitation du bassin houiller d'Alais*, 80.

[113] *AG* 58J 2, Jan. 1774. Exactly one year later, Tubeuf noted in his *Journal* that the Intendant and the Archbishops of Toulouse and Narbonne had congratulated him on his early researches.

[114] Bardon, *L'Exploitation du bassin houiller d'Alais*, 101.

had agreed to close down their operations.[115] By the beginning of 1776, Tubeuf was moving against the *propriétaires* on and around his future main base at Rochebelle, again with the encouragement of the Bishop of Alès. An entry for 15 January 1776 records that the Bishop, acting with the support of the diocese of Alès, had granted him 'un lopin de terre' a couple of miles outside Alès near the domain of one Pierre Rozier, and that he was about to send his miners down there to begin excavations.[116] It was to prove a fateful move. Rozier was to become one of the rocks of resistance which Tubeuf could not blast away, typical of the many small *négociants* living in Alès but with important interests in the cévenol countryside. In a personal letter to Bertin, Rozier explained that he had recently built a *maison de campagne* a few miles from Alès, which was surrounded by 'mulberry trees, vines, olives, and a garden'. Having discovered coal on his domain he had engaged a couple of miners to bring a few sackfuls to the surface until the threat of subsidence caused him to cease operations. Now Tubeuf's more extensive undertaking was threatening his property.

The most worrying aspect of the letter for Bertin must have been its conclusion, which stated that 'It would be most unfortunate for sieur Tubeuf if the king had given him the concession to land that did not belong to him.' Here, in very personal terms, was the key to the conflict which Marcel Rouff refers to above, that between the rights of property-owners and the exigencies of heavy industrialization.[117] Rozier, having been pressurized by the Intendant, was initially obliged to settle for an indemnity of just 200 *livres*, but the damage had been done. Other resisters began to follow Rozier's lead. In a letter to one of Bertin's secretaries, Tubeuf referred to Rozier as nothing more than 'an instrument of the cabal which is working to secure the destruction of my enterprise'.[118]

The cabal eventually came to consist of forty-nine protesters, all of whom claimed to have been adversely affected by Tubeuf's concession. Rouff describes the group as 'petits industriels combinés'.[119]

---

[115] e.g. 1 Feb. 1775, 120 *livres* paid to Dumas de Pigère for the closure of his mine near Banne: 27 Mar. 1775, 78 *livres* paid to Paul Gazay of Meyrannes. *AG* 58J 2.

[116] Ibid.

[117] According to a letter written by Tubeuf to Bertin, Rozier was typical of those relatively small property-owners who opened up coal-mines only to abandon them at the first indication of flooding. *AN* F14 7682, 20 Feb. 1776.

[118] Letter to Advenier de Breuilly. Bardon, *L'Exploitation du bassin houiller d'Alais*, 106.

[119] Rouff, *Tubeuf*, 51.

Apart from Rozier, it included the noble owner of a glassworks near Saint-Jean-de-Valériscle, Pierre Gilly, as well as small property-owners like Jean Larguier, whose pottery and creamery concerns were allegedly affected by the closure of the small mines which supplied him and a couple of his friends with coal. The secretary was Gilles-François Verdun, a *maître-perruquier* living in Alès but the owner of a small piece of land near Tubeuf's Rochebelle mine. The forty-nine immediately decided to arouse the support of the local coal-miners and lime-burners, as well as the clergy and the members of the diocese.[120] In the very month that the maréchal de Castries bought the *comté d'Alais*, Tubeuf wrote rather disconsolately to La Barbérie 'The miserable cabal which is persecuting me has now changed tack. They want to drag me before the king's council in order to secure the revocation of my concession. They are trying to get the prince de Conty to intervene.'[121] The prince de Conty, of course, was the previous owner of the *comté d'Alais* and it is quite possible that the conflict in Alès played some part in moving Castries towards the purchase of the fief. Marcel Rouff was certainly of the opinion that it was Castries who now began to co-ordinate the various strands of opposition to Tubeuf.[122] On 11 August 1777, the lime-burners of Alès marched to the town hall to complain about the recent rise in the price of coal, occasioned, they said, by Tubeuf's closure of the mines around Alès. A month later, the *assiette du diocèse d'Alais* agreed to support their demands for a reduction in the price of coal, passing the case on to the Estates of Languedoc.[123] At its meeting in January 1778, the Estates demanded the revocation of Tubeuf's concession.

By the summer of that fateful year—which also marked the embargo on textile goods entering Spain—the threat to his concession, coupled with the suspicion that his own life was in danger, induced Tubeuf to move himself and his young family to Paris.[124] The struggle had

---

[120] *AHC, ordonnance de M. l'Intendant*, 15 July 1776. In this document Larguier is described as a *ménager* living at the mas de Bouat employing just two coal-miners, typical of many small property-owners.

[121] Bardon, *L'Exploitation du bassin houiller d'Alais*, 114–15.

[122] Rouff, *Tubeuf*, 51.

[123] Bardon, *L'Exploitation du bassin houiller d'Alais*, 131. The *diocèse d'Alais* was responsible for 95 communes, including most of the Grand-Combe, Portes, and Bessèges valleys. Robiac fell under the jurisdiction of the *diocèse d'Uzès*.

[124] It is evident that, apart from the very real danger to life and limb, Tubeuf was anxious to be nearer Versailles: 'Il parait que le manière dont les Etats de la Province attaquent mon arrêt de concession, cette affaire aura de longue suite et qu'il est très essentiel que je la suive de près.' *AG* 58J 2, 31 July 1777.

moved into a second phase, one which was to pit a Court favourite against the *protégé des bureaux*. Before examining the reasons for Castries's ultimate victory we need to analyse in greater depth the reasons for the widespread opposition to Tubeuf's plans. Tubeuf himself thought that it was really a question of jealousy over the success he had achieved since the early 1770s.[125] Clearly, landowners, from *grands seigneurs* like Castries to *maître-perruquiers* like Verdun, were anxious to share in the increasing profits to be made from the sales of coal. But what united aristocrats, provincial seigneurs, small land-owners, and mine-owners, indeed the majority of the cévenol people, against Tubeuf was the particular fear on the part of property-owners concerning their legal rights and the general fear that Tubeuf's 'mo-nopolistic' concession might undermine a traditional market economy based upon the exchange of raw silk, wine, chestnuts, and coal coming from the Cévennes for the grain, salt, and other basic commodities arriving from the plains of Languedoc or the Gévaudan, something which we may discuss under Professor Clarkson's fourth heading—that rural manufacture stimulated commercial farming by creating a market for food. Unless we understand the close relationship between coal and grain, raw silk and salt, we will never fully appreciate the reasons for Tubeuf's flight to the capital.[126]

In his study of the relationship between agriculture and industry E. L. Jones has noted that 'the early modern European countryside did gradually separate out into broad categories of regions with two sorts of eco-systems and economy, one agricultural, the other protoindus-trial linked by trade'.[127] In broad terms, this clearly applied to the Cévennes with food and basic commodities being imported from the Gévaudan and the plains of Languedoc into the protoindustrial regions around Alès. However, Pat Hudson is surely right to stress the great diversity and variety to be found within protoindustrial regions.[128] What is peculiar to the Cévennes is not only the stubborn determi-nation to retain links with the land through the cultivation of the

---

[125] Bardon, *L'Exploitation du bassin houiller d'Alais*, 140.

[126] Franklin Mendels' later work on protoindustrialization stressed the importance of the relationship between agricultural and commercial regions. See 'Seasons and Regions in Agriculture and Industry during the Process of Industrialization', in S. Pollard (ed.), *Region und Industrialisierung* (Göttingen, 1980).

[127] E. L. Jones, 'Environment, Agriculture and Industrialization', *Agricultural History*, 51 (1977), 494.

[128] 'Proto-industrialization: The Case of the West Riding', 37.

mulberry tree and the vine but the way in which the inhabitants supplemented grain supplies with the traditional chestnut and the 'new' potato. Alain Molinier's study of the Bas-Vivarais is based upon the premiss that the region experienced pronounced population growth in the eighteenth century without an 'agricultural revolution'. There was a kind of revolution, however, with a spectacular increase in the amount of chestnuts and potatoes produced. Whereas grain production only rose from 350,000 to 385,590 *quintaux* between 1690 and 1789, the amount of chestnuts produced increased from 68,000 *quintaux* in 1731 to 130,240 *quintaux* by 1811. In addition, 192,360 *quintaux* of potatoes were being grown, mainly in the Bourg-Saint-Andéol region.[129]

This move towards self-sufficiency, however, could never bridge the 'grain and salt' gap which separated the inhabitants of the Cévennes from their compatriots around Nîmes: indeed, most of the increased chestnut production was exported to pay for incoming goods. It was this balance of trade which Tubeuf threatened to undermine. He was the 'monopolist' upsetting the traditional market economy of the region. Although in the beginning he was obliged to placate local lime-burners, distillers, and silk-spinners, Pierre-François Tubeuf's industrial horizons had always been bounded by national and international, not local, boundaries. The necessary financial returns on his massive investments could never have been obtained from satisfying the Alèsian silk-spinner or forge-master; they depended ultimately on defeating competition from the English in Bordeaux and Marseille. One of the earliest entries in Tubeuf's Journal, long before his concession in the Alès region had been confirmed, refers to a visit he had made to Marseille in order to discover new markets for his coal.[130] We also know that, as early as 1770, he was complaining to the government about the prohibitive toll charges being levied on goods transported down the Rhône, which, when coupled with Marseille's advantage as a free port, meant that English coal could easily undercut coal coming a few score miles from the French interior.[131]

Denied—temporarily he believed—major markets in Marseille and other Mediterranean ports, Tubeuf satisfied himself with opening up

---

[129] Molinier, 'En Vivarais au XVIIIᵉ siècle', 312.

[130] *AG* 58J 2, 21 Apr. 1770.

[131] Similar complaints were voiced by the marquis de Solages, who accused the English of dumping coal at Bordeaux to undercut the coal produced at Carmaux. Rouff, *Les Mines de charbon*, 387; Galy, 'L'Exploitation des houillères en Languedoc', 172.

new markets in Provence and Languedoc. In the summer of 1773, we find that Tubeuf was delivering coal to Ricard et Cie, *négociant* of Sète (one of the biggest distillers in the province), Boulabe, an important public works contractor in Montpellier, distillers and forge-masters in Lunel, Beaucaire, and, crossing the Rhône, Tarascon and Marseille.[132] Imitating the practice of the *négociants* of Nîmes and Montpellier, he placed *commissionnaires* in the major cities to ply for trade on his behalf whilst retaining strong national links with the capital. It was in Paris that he made the decision, one which was to unite the various groups opposed to him in Alès into a formidable opposition party, to sign a contract with the largest coke-producing company in France, Richard, Carouges et Cie. Finally agreed on 4 July 1778, the contract stipulated that Tubeuf would have to supply the company with 400,000 *quintaux* of coal a year for a period of twenty-four years, commencing deliveries, ominously enough, on April Fool's Day 1779.

Tubeuf's Journal records that the company gave 'trois mille livres de pot de vin à ma femme' the very day the contract was signed.[133] It was a substantial 'business gift', but one which the company could easily afford since it was potentially one of the most important industrial concerns in Europe with centres in Normandy, Dauphiné, Provence, and Languedoc. It had capital reserves of 1,200,000 *livres*.[134] Typical of Tubeuf that he should have hitched his own coal-wagon to this rising star. Again, the vision was international. If only he could persuade the local authorities to make the river Cèze navigable 'the Company would be rolling in gold. The desulphurated coal from Robiac transported down this river and then down the Rhône could be shipped to the Mediterranean and beyond.'[135] The English would have been confronted, at last, with serious competition.

But why should all this produce a sense of panic amongst the small producers of the Cévennes? Basically because the closure of small mines, any large-scale concentration of production, threatened not just the livelihood of the local population—there would be hundreds of jobs for miners in the Grand-Combe during the nineteenth century— but the protoindustrial system of production and exchange. Let us take the example of the relationship between coal and the silk-spinning industry since the latter consumed more coal than any other

---

[132] See entries in his *Journal* for 3 May and 2 June 1773, for example, *AG* 58J 2.
[133] *AG* 58J 2, 31 July 1778.
[134] Chaussinand-Nogaret, 107.
[135] B. de N. 496, Alles to Richard, 22 Sept. 1779.

industry in the Cévennes.[136] Jacques Aubrespin of Alès described himself in official documents as a *propriétaire foncier*, which masked the fact that, in addition to producing mulberry leaves, he owned a small spinning-mill. In order to obtain the coal he needed, he had leased a 'mine de charbon' at Malpertuis for nine years from Aquier of the Grand-Combe at the incredibly low cost of 40 *livres* per annum. He also paid 150 *livres* per annum for a mine on the land of sieur Favède. When, in 1777, a society of coal producers was created in the *comté d'Alais* with the intention of preventing too much competition, Aubrespin agreed to transfer the lease he had acquired from Favède to the new society on condition that 'all the coal he needed was supplied to him for his spinning-mill at four *sols le quintal* instead of at the old price of eight *sols*'.[137] If Tubeuf were allowed to get away with the closure of mines supplying small manufacturers like Aubrespin then fuel costs would rise to unacceptable, and probably uneconomic, levels.

The same problem confronted Jean-Antoine Deleuze, although coal-mines were far more important to him since he was the seigneur de Trouilhas, owning the rich Grand-Combe mine itself which was employing fifteen to twenty miners at this time. Deleuze was not only the owner of the Grand-Combe but the supplier of top-quality coal to silk-spinners and distillers in the region. The Deleuze-Villaret *frères* also owned a sizeable spinning-mill. Little wonder that he had almost buried the Archbishop of Narbonne during his visit to the Grand-Combe under a mountain of title-deeds, or that he was constantly firing off broadsides against Tubeuf—'ce concessionnaire avide'—to the officials of the diocese of Alès.[138]

Behind the wealthier *propriétaires* and *marchands-fabricants* of the Alès region stood the thousands of cévenol colliers, coal-heavers, carters,

---

[136] As late as 1791, the maréchal de Castries's agent explained why the demand for coal was not increasing substantially; 'La teinture des soyes exige sans doute une consommation du charbon, mais c'est un objet bien mince et leur fabrication en étoffes ou en bas n'exige d'ailleurs aucunement l'emploi de ce combustible. C'est la filature des cocons qui seule en entraîne une consommation.' *AN* 306AP 496, 16 Dec. 1791.

[137] *AN* 306AP 482, *observations de Pierre Crozade sur le mémoire de M. Monge*, n.d.

[138] See e.g. *AG* C194, *supplément à la requête du syndic du diocèse d'Alais contre le sieur Tubeuf*, 16 Oct. 1777. Jean-Antoine Deleuze had obtained the concession of the Trouilhas mines in 1750, but for a period of only 10 years. It was his subsequent failure to register ownership of the mine with the government—in accordance with the legislation of 1744—which placed him in an awkward legal predicament. The Deleuze-Villaret family were typical of those Protestants who had been enriched by commerce in the 18th century, enabling them to purchase the *seigneuries* of Trouilhas and Villaret. The 'conversion' to Catholicism on the part of some members of the family was also not uncommon.

lime-burners, nail-makers, tool-makers, raw-silk producers, spinners, and distillers who felt equally threatened by Tubeuf. His plan to mine the huge amounts of coal needed to fulfil the terms of his contract with Richard, Carouges et Cie provoked alarm and despondency throughout the traditional coal-mining communities of Alès, Robiac, and Banne. His former *directeur*, Alles, who was employed by the company to act as their agent in the Cévennes, reported to Paris on 27 April 1779 that two of Tubeuf's emissaries had gone to Robiac to buy out anyone who owned or leased coal-mines, but to little avail.[139] In the summer of 1780, a *mémoire* sent to the Estates of Languedoc stated that

having dispossessed property-owners who were working mines on the Montaud mountain, he [Tubeuf] seized all the mines in the *comté d'Alais*. He then moved in to the diocese of Uzès and, like a torrent which sweeps away everything in its path, he desolated the communities of Robiac, Castilhon, Courry and several others—property-owners, *fermiers des mines*, the workers themselves were all chased out indiscriminately and without any pity.[140]

It is true that neither of the authors of the reports above could be described as objective: Alles had been sacked by Tubeuf, whilst the *mémoire* sent to the Estates was prepared by Castries's lawyers. None the less, there can be no doubt that, stripped of the emotive language, the accusations against Tubeuf were substantially true. Whenever the opportunity arose, the Norman entrepreneur was capable of acting ruthlessly. At the beginning of 1783, following another round of pit closures, a public meeting was held in Robiac during which Tubeuf was denounced as an interloper who was destroying the economy of the region. If he were allowed to continue with his plans, it was argued, then the result could only be 'the most frightening misery. Many inhabitants will have no alternative but to leave the area; the silk trade will be ruined, workshops relying on this trade will have to close; government taxes could no longer be collected.' According to the author of this petition sent to the diocese of Uzès, Tubeuf had recently asked the local inhabitants to sell or lease the mines 'which nature has given to them for nothing'. A similar petition from Saint-Ambroix focused more directly on the fragility of the protoindustrial system of production which had brought wealth, through the

---

[139] B. de N. 496, 27 Aug. 1779.

[140] Ibid., *pièces concernant le département du Gard: mémoire et consultation pour monsieur le syndic général de la Province de Languedoc, 30 Aug. 1780.*

mulberry tree, to the entire region. It pointed out that Louis Gilly de la Nougarède had first mined coal seriously in order to supply fuel for his silk-spinning works, his glassworks, 'and for several other concerns of equal importance'. The result had been prosperity for the local people, a prosperity which Tubeuf was now endangering. He had raised the price of coal,

which increases the costs of producing the raw silk from the cocoons, which in turn means that the price paid for mulberry leaves, will fall. Mulberry leaves provide the local inhabitants with their main source of revenue, and if their price falls, so will the price paid for the silk-cocoons. The main burden will fall upon the respected class of *ménagers*, the majority of whom already find themselves in difficult circumstances.

It was obvious to the petitioners that higher fuel costs meant that manufacturers would be forced to pay less for their silk-cocoons and that this would 'discourage the local inhabitants from cultivating the mulberry trees, their only real source of income, without which they would not be in a position to pay their taxes'.[141]

But is there firm evidence to show that Tubeuf's plans did involve a significant rise in the price of coal? Galy suggested that the documentary evidence is too weak to do for coal prices what Dermigny has done for wine.[142] However, by using the most reliable official source and cross-checking with the information to be gleaned from the private papers of the Tubeuf and Castries families we are able to produce Fig. 2.1. The difference in price between Grand-Combe and Rochebelle coal can be explained primarily by the cost of transporting Grand-Combe coal to the depot in Alès. It was also of far better quality.

A close examination of the production methods for the manufacture of spun silk suggests that the reputation from which Nîmes suffered as a centre for the production of second-class articles was not simply a consequence of the competition from Lyon, but arose, at least in part, from the cost-cutting exercises employed by the hard-pressed, largely female labour force which was responsible for drawing the silk threads from the cocoons. On the eve of the Revolution, the Inspecteur des manufacture de Nîmes explained that local spinners had not

[141] Rouff, *Tubeuf*, 62–3.
[142] Galy, 'L'Exploitation des houillères en Languedoc', 185. In Tubeuf's *Observations que j'ai donné à M. Roux, mon avocat*, the rise from 4 to 5 *sols* for small coal, and from 8 to 10 *sols* for large is confirmed. *AG* 58J 4, 10 May 1781.

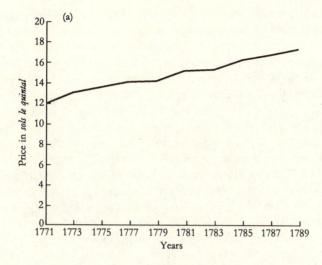

FIG 2.1 (*a*) The price of Grand-Combe large coal sold in Alès, 1771–1789

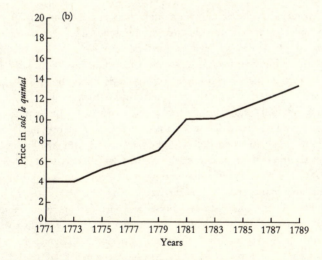

FIG 2.1 (*b*) The price of large coal sold by Tubeuf in Alès, 1771–1789

produced top-quality silk for years with the result that manufacturers producing goods for England and Italy had been forced to use inferior raw silk: 'This lack of top-quality silk', the Inspecteur explained, 'is the result of the raw material turning brown in the process of drawing out the threads from the cocoons because the *fileuses* do not bother to replace the dirty water in the basins.' The *fileuses* argued that the fuel costs would be prohibitive 'if they were obliged to empty the basins too often forcing them to reheat the clean water'. Here we have one of the direct consequences for the silk industry of Tubeuf's 'monopolistic' plans, which involved price rises. There was the additional problem for the spinner that if she took great care to produce top-quality silk then she could only produce 1 lb. 12 oz. of the raw material a day 'whilst those spinners producing the second-quality material, who are paid the same daily rate, can produce 2 lb. 8 oz.'. In a protoindustrial economy, mass production meant second-rate products.[143] Ballainvilliers was fully aware of the relationship between poor quality and protoindustrial forms of production: like Tubeuf, he was unequivocally in favour of *l'industrie en grand*. To improve the quality of the goods produced in Languedoc, he thought it essential that the government should 'encourage, either by grants, or by *privilèges*, factories (*établissements considérables*) in which one always finds a more skilled work-force than in small workshops (*les petites fabriques*)'.[144]

There was another fear which fuelled the opposition to Tubeuf's 'monopole', and that was the fear of famine. Georges Lefebvre has explained why, in many regions, peasants were opposed to too many agricultural innovations. Large-scale sheep-farming, like large-scale coal-mining, might be profitable for big landowners, but for the mass of the people 'it was just so much land which would no longer produce grain'.[145] For the cévenols, the closure of small mines ultimately involved the collapse of the silk industry, depriving them of the hard cash they needed to purchase food and salt. This fear obviously intensified during spells of bad weather as in 1782–3 and 1788–9. Bad weather meant not only poor crops but poor transport conditions, many *crises de subsistances* during the *ancien régime* being provoked by *crises de circulation*, since it was rare for climatic conditions to be common to the whole of France. The coal industry was particularly dependent upon the state of roads and rivers. Transport costs were a major factor in determining the price of coal to the consumer. There is undoubtedly a good deal of truth to the generalization that it was only with the advent of the railway in the Alès

---

[143] *AN* F12 1228, report of 5 Sept. 1788.
[144] Tarlé, *L'Industrie dans les campagnes*, 12 n. 4.
[145] *La Grande Peur de 1789* (Paris, 1932), 12.

region during the 1830s that the coal industry 'took off'.[146] The statistics appear to confirm this point. Railways obviously revolutionized the transport of bulk material like coal. However, the crude correlation between the take-off in coal production and the advent of the railway fails to explain why the English were selling coals from Newcastle almost 100 years before the railway opened up the route to the Rhône for Alèsian coal.

This is not to pretend that transport difficulties did not keep many a coal-owner awake at night before the steam-engine was put on wheels: they did. From the fastnesses of the Grand-Combe, or Robiac, or Saint-Jean-de-Valériscle, mules often provided the only feasible method of transporting coal from the mine-entrance to delivery points in the towns or on the main road.[147] It was only in the 1780s that the dioceses of Alès and Uzès began to receive serious propositions concerning transport improvements, although when new roads were opened they were frequently ignored. Old habits died hard. A new road which linked the Mas-Dieu mine to the Pradel-Alès route was often shunned by carters in favour of the quicker alternative of using the dry bed of the river Gardon.[148] Virtually all the coal being transported from the Grand-Combe before, and for a long time after, the Revolution used this time-honoured route. But this meant drastically reduced deliveries of coal during the winter months, and other periods when the Gardon was in full flow. However, given that the peak season for coal production was the late spring and summer, when the spinning industry was working full-time, this was not of major significance. Here again the relationship of coal to the protoindustrial production of silk helped to dictate transport patterns. Significantly, Tubeuf's major works at Rochebelle were on the doorstep of Alès, thus avoiding the more costly transport problems.

Transport was firmly controlled by a small group of *muletiers* and *voituriers*, whose brutality and unreliability was universally acknowledged; cheating customers by giving short measure or by mixing good

---

[146] Marcel Rouff writes: 'La prosperité des mines dépendait uniquement des transports qui leur étaient assurés', pointing out that the growth of the Rive-de-Gier coalfield owed a great deal to the existence of the canal de Givors, which facilitated transport of coal to the Rhône and to Lyon. *Les Mines de charbon*, 369.

[147] *AN* 306AP 485, Crozade to Castries, 23 May 1785, explaining why the Abilon mine was closed for most of the year.

[148] *AN* 306AP 490, 19 Sept. 1788. Castries's agent explained that the *diocèse d'Alais* had built a road linking the Mas-Dieu mine to the main route at Pradel, but that carters found it unsuitable for heavy coal loads.

coal with shale was common practice.[149] Increasingly, however, as the production of coal rose, innkeepers and general dealers began to introduce a more organized system. Some dealers, like Pierre Goirand of Alès, became coal-owners and, as we shall see, major shareholders in the big nineteenth-century Grand-Combe coal company.[150] One of the major problems was the fact that in a protoindustrial society, 'industry' often played the supporting role to 'agriculture', so that when the demand for coal from the spinning industry reached its peak in the late spring and summer carters were often booked to work for the big farmers or manufacturers who wished to transport goods to the international fair at Beaucaire. The demand for wagons often stretched into the autumn. In October 1786, the maréchal de Castries's agent explained that he had received a very good order from Montpellier but that he doubted whether he could supply the amount of coal involved because the majority of carts would be busy with the grape harvest.[151]

Transport was not only inadequate or scarce, it was costly. In September 1786, the town hall in Montpellier dispatched a request for coal to Castries's agent, who replied that he would do his best, but that the cost would be 16 *sous le quintal*, in addition to which the cost of transport would be 20 *sous le quintal*. Thus transport costs more than doubled the price of coal over a distance of just 70 kilometres from the depot in Alès. At the pit-head in the Grand-Combe, the coal could have been purchased for only 8 *sous le quintal*! When the carters demanded a rise of 1 *sous le quintal* for transporting coal from the Grand-Combe to Alès in 1786, the agent advised Castries to resist, pointing out that such a rise would increase annual costs of production by 4,000 *livres*.[152] One of the major problems was the fact that the *canal des deux mers*, which linked Bordeaux and Sète, had not yet been extended to the Rhône, so that coal destined for Montpellier and Sète had to be carted, at considerable cost, to the major distribution town of Lunel for onward shipment.[153]

[149] Rouff, *Les Mines de charbon*, 378.

[150] See pp. 286–7.

[151] *AN* 306AP 487, Crozade to Pégat, 16 Oct. 1786. In July, the agent had informed Castries that demand for coal was rising fast but that he could not hire enough carts. He decided, therefore, that, between the *foire de Beaucaire* and the harvest in Sept.–Oct., he would stockpile coal in Castries's warehouse in Alès. *AN* 306AP 487, 21 July 1786.

[152] *AN* 306AP 487, 8 Sept. 1786.

[153] Galy, 'L'Exploitation des houillères en Languedoc', 172.

Demand was never the issue in the late eighteenth century; as Louis Alles explained, 'Languedoc and the neighbouring provinces are starved of coal. It is simply a question of reducing the cost of transport.'[154] Alles, borrowing his former employer Tubeuf's ideas, had the answer. The local authorities should give grants to encourage the construction of better transport routes, a task which was not difficult since the rudimentary tracks and waterways already existed. But then Alles and Tubeuf were again thinking along national and international lines. In a report to Richard, Carouges et Cie, the latter even proposed setting up their own rapid-transit company. It would operate between Alès and Joyeuse, le Puy in the Velay and then back down to Lunel, Montpellier, and Nîmes: 'The aim would be to supply coke (*le charbon épuré*), by means of *la voiture exprès* to neighbouring provinces as well as to foreign countries.'[155]

But these radical solutions were never going to win over the support of the traditional carter, nor, indeed, the local communities which he served. It is far too simple to look at a map and list the obstacles to easy transport in mountainous and fairly inaccessible regions. We should rather enquire into the *mentalité* of the people who lived there, which is not to say, simplifying Braudel, that 'mountains maketh man', but that there were often sound and sensible reasons why such communities in the eighteenth century did not embrace 'modernization' with open arms. If, for example, Tubeuf's request to the diocese of Uzès that he be allowed, *at his own expense*, to start work on the river Cèze with a view to making it navigable had been accepted, it would have revolutionized the production and distribution of coal in that valley. The explanation by local officials for refusing Tubeuf's request is particularly revealing: 'Because this new outlet for the delivery of coal would inflict serious damage on the town of Alès and the Cévennes as a result of the rise in grain prices which would be the inevitable consequence'.[156] A similar request from Monsieur's agent to finance improved road links in the Portes region was also rejected out of hand, the reason being that the diocese of Uzès was not in favour of mining *en grand*.[157]

---

[154] B. de N. 496, 5 June 1780. It is interesting to note that Tubeuf organized his own transport system from Rochebelle, which is why he was able to sell coal in Sète for just over 20 *sols le quintal*. Rouff notes that there was fierce local opposition to Tubeuf's 'direct marketing'. *Les Mines de charbon*, 401.

[155] B. de N. 496, Alles to Richard, 19 June 1780.

[156] *AG* C194, letter of Intendant, 1 Mar. 1779.

[157] Bardon, *L'Exploitation du bassin houiller d'Alais*, 317–18.

But why should improving communications for the transport of coal increase the price of grain? The answer to this question brings us to the heart of the matter concerning the conflict between Tubeuf's 'monopolistic' plans and the functioning of a protoindustrial economy. In the first place, new transport routes threatened traditional and well-established centres of trade and commerce, and it should be recalled that Alès was one of the oldest and best-established trading and commercial centres in Languedoc. This was the point forcefully made by the maréchal de Castries when, in 1784, he sought official approval for the re-establishment of two medieval fairs. The document, annotated as it is by the Intendant Saint-Priest, provides an invaluable insight into the issues we have so far discussed in this chapter. Stressing that over recent years the fairs in Alès, traditionally held on 17 January and 24 August, had taken on a new lease of life, the document went on to emphasize the newly discovered importance of Alès as a centre for the commerce of raw silk, the 'protoindustrial' nature of its production, as well as the interlocking relationship between Alès and the *négociants* of Nîmes.

The summer fair was clearly the more important

relative to the silk trade which forms the principal form of production in the Cévennes, the Vivarais, Mende, and Montpellier. Throughout the region, the cultivation of the *mûrier*, the rearing of the silkworms and the drawing out of the silk thread occupies every family for a good part of the year, and it is from these industrious hands that the silk industry receives, directly and indirectly, most of the raw materials necessary to its operations. . . . The inhabitants of the Cévennes and the Vivarais bring this merchandise to the fair, each one bringing small amounts, and the buyers from Lyon, Tours, Nîmes, and other manufacturing towns arrive. Both sides relish the opportunity of bargaining amongst themselves over the sale and purchase price. . . . It is necessary therefore to find a meeting-place for these matters, and one could not find a better one than Alès, because it is situated almost exactly in the centre of the region which produces the silk, because much of it is produced around the town itself, and because it is close to the city of Nîmes, which is an important manufacturing centre. The *négociants* of this city represent the majority of the buyers who attend the fair. In addition, Alès always has a garrison of troops . . . to ensure public order.

The submission to the Intendant also emphasized the importance of Alès as a banking centre: 'money and banking transactions used to be rare at this fair, but they have multiplied recently as a result of our commercial progress and, above all, the rise in the silk trade. One can draw many *lettres de change* these days on the *foire d'Alais*.'[158]

Maxine Berg has stressed the importance of circulating, as opposed to fixed, capital in pre-industrial societies.[159] The *négociants* who came to Alès were extremely reluctant to place large amounts of their capital in the very risky business of heavy industry, preferring, as we have seen, to invest not just in land, but in land which flowed with silk and wine. It is significant that Tubeuf's first serious financial backer, Ode, was a wholesale wine merchant who had bought a small *seigneurie*, but just as significant that he should have backed off when the going got tough, directing Tubeuf's footsteps in the direction of Parisian capital. Roger Dugrand has rightly described this as 'the approach of a capitalism which rests more upon the old world of woollen stockings than the new one of a *laissez-faire* challenge (*affrontement*)'.[160] Tubeuf had always found it very difficult not only to obtain substantial sums for investment but even to get ready cash to pay his workers. In 1775 he wrote in his Journal: 'The difficulty of getting my *lettres de change* cashed during the course of the year in the towns around Pont-Saint-Esprit has forced me to negotiate them at Beaucaire—which has its fair at the moment—the nearest commercial centre for me to conduct my business between one fair and another.'[161] In Languedoc, as in so many other French provinces, fairs were market-places for the circulation of capital as well as for the exchange of goods.

But it was the relationship between coal and grain which proved crucial in defeating Tubeuf's *monopole*: this issue allowed the élites to play upon the concerns of the wider populace. In 1780, Alles reported that in an average year no fewer than 1,391 wagons brought in grain from the plains before loading 52,858 *quintaux* of coal for the return journey.[162] At Saint-Ambroix, the grain from the Gévaudan and the Velay was exchanged for the cheap wine of the region.[163] Tubeuf, through his association with the Richard and Carouges Company,

[158] *AN* F12 1228, letter of Saint-Priest, 26 May 1784.
[159] *Manufacture in Town and Country*, 5–6. A spinning-jenny, for example, could have been bought for just £5 in 1795. A comparable example can be found in a letter to the government from the *marchands-fabricants de Nîmes* in which the merchants deprecate the 'emigration' of looms to Spain and other countries, explaining that the problem was not so much the cost of a loom (around 300 *livres*), but the fact that in three months one loom could produce 80 pairs of stockings worth 800 *livres* in the market-place. *AG* IVE 23, *mémoire des marchands-fabricants de Nîmes*, 1778.
[160] Dugrand, *Villes et campagnes en Bas-Languedoc*, 400.
[161] *AG* 58J 2, 23 Jul. 1775.
[162] B. de N. 496, 19 June 1780.
[163] Molinier, 'En Vivarais au XVIIIᵉ siècle', 311.

threatened to undermine completely this vital and reciprocal economic relationship between the agricultural plains and the protoindustrial hills. As Achille Bardon, quoting a reply sent by Tubeuf to an official of the Estates of Languedoc who had asked him to moderate his monopolistic schemes, explained: 'Any kind of competition made it impossible for him [Tubeuf] to get back the capital he had invested, to pay back his debts, so long as consumption was restricted solely to the trade undertaken by the wagons which supplied the Céven-nes.'[164] The implication of Tubeuf's schemes were obvious to one of Castries's lawyers, who wrote that 'The importation of wheat is only possible in that part of the country around Alès thanks to the export of coal . . . in a word, it represents one of the most essential branches of commerce and the circulation of goods in the province.'[165] Cabane de Camont, *syndic* of the diocese of Alès, was equally worried, recruiting the support of his counterpart on the *assiette* of the diocese of Uzès, Alexis Trinquelaque. The latter, in a reply to one of Cabane's letters, gave what amounted to a classic description of the 'Jeffersonian democratic' or 'sansculotte' economic ideal. Resting his case upon the premiss that 'every distinction concerning property-ownership, as you know, is odious', Trinquelaque went on to sympathize with those small property-owners (who formed the majority in the Cévennes) who were already forced 'to deny themselves the advantages of large-scale production and to tailor their plans to their meagre resources without these limitations being used to deprive them completely of their property rights, which are just as respectable, just as sacred as those of any other property-owner, however rich'. Trinquelaque finished on a note which echoed the 'pre-industrial', as opposed to Tubeuf's 'monopolistic' ideal: 'In any case, divided between a greater number of property-owners, would not these mines produce more coal than if they were to be left in the hands of a single individual?'[166] For Tubeuf the answer was emphatically: No! But we would be making a very great error if we assumed for one moment that the majority of cévenols did not believe him to be mistaken.

Cabane de Camont became one of Tubeuf's bitterest opponents, and it is only when we discover that, in addition to filling the post of *syndic du diocèse d'Alais* from 1773 to 1779, he was also *juge de la*

---

[164] Bardon, *L'Exploitation du bassin houiller d'Alais*, 299.

[165] B. de N. 496, *pièces concernant le département du Gard. Mémoire et consultation.*

[166] Bardon, *L'Exploitation du bassin houiller d'Alais*, 192.

cour d'appeaux de la ville et du comté d'Alais that we can appreciate fully the reasons for his tireless efforts to destroy Tubeuf. As one of Castries's seigneurial judges, it was clearly in his personal interests to support his lord—at least until 1789!—and the traditional Grand-Combe–Alès axis against Tubeuf's plans to revolutionize not only production but transportation in the Alès coal-basin. There is also one more reason why such men, locked into the seigneurial and administrative framework of *ancien régime* France, should have opposed anyone who threatened the status quo, and that was their equal involvement in the traditional economic structures of the region, particularly the all-important grain trade. As Cabane explained, 'Many people here fear that the exclusive privileges obtained by Tubeuf and Richard et Carouges for the extraction and the sale of desulphurated and non-desulphurated coal will become, in their hands, exclusive privileges for the sale of grain.'[167] Let us remember that many a *négociant* was as involved in the sale of grain as he was the purchase of raw silk: it was one of the ways they could control the protoindustrial work-force of the Cévennes. The thought of Tubeuf gaining control of this trade sent shivers of apprehension down the spines of many *négociants* not only in Nîmes and Montpellier, but also in Alès, Anduze, Saint-Ambroix, and Aubenas.

Until 1789, however, the political battle would be fought in the town halls of Alès and Uzès, in the offices of the Estates of Languedoc in Montpellier and Paris, and, increasingly as the 1780s wore on, at Versailles, between Court favourites like the maréchal de Castries and the king's ministers, Bertin, Joly de Fleury, and Calonne. It would not be an exaggeration to claim that the battle between Pierre-François Tubeuf and the maréchal de Castries, although founded upon the realities of the socio-economic structures of the Alèsian region, were also related to the great national issues of the late eighteenth century which finally led to the collapse of absolute monarchy in France: the clash between 'industrial' and 'pre-industrial' visions of society; centralization against provincialism; the power and authority of the aristocracy; the role of the Intendant in the provinces. Marcel Rouff in his short biography of Tubeuf saw it as 'the trial of *l'homme des bureaux* against a Court favourite and against the powers of the provincial estates'.[168]

---

[167] *AG* C194, letter to Trinquelaque, 21 Jan. 1779.
[168] Rouff, *Tubeuf*, 71.

The agenda for the political and legal conflict which was to continue until the very eve of the Revolution was prepared as early as 1779 when the minister responsible for mining affairs, Bertin, castigated the Intendant Saint-Priest for not supporting Tubeuf by silencing the local opposition which had gained momentum during the late 1770s: 'I must tell you, monsieur, that the rights enjoyed by this individual must not be considered worthless simply because of the opposition which has formed against them, and that, on the contrary, he must be allowed to enjoy those rights until the Conseil des mines decides otherwise.' Saint-Priest, caught as most Intendants were between the realities of provincial politics and the demands of central government, protested that the minister had misunderstood his actions and that he was only waiting for the Conseil to give him definitive guidance on the legitimacy of Tubeuf's concession. It is, however, clear that the Intendant resented the fact that Tubeuf had an entrée to Bertin as the following suggests: 'I assure you, monsieur, that I only learn with some pain about the quite improper complaints made by this entrepreneur with the intention of getting me to accede to demands which are often ill-conceived and whose consequences he does not appreciate.'[169] It was a telling and prophetic exchange of views between a good servant of the Crown and a man who was no less loyal to the king but who lived the realities of provincial politics.

What Saint-Priest was doing was to stress the depth and the bitterness of opposition to Tubeuf. For Bertin, the issue was reasonably clear-cut. Here was a gifted entrepreneur intent upon opening up the coal reserves of the Cévennes for the greater glory of France but who was facing opposition from a tunnel-visioned group of provincial seigneurs, small property-owners, colliers, and lime-burners. And Tubeuf saw to it that the government was fed with information which supported this interpretation. During the period that the government was considering the complaints dispatched by the dioceses of Alès and Uzès, Tubeuf fired off letter after letter pressurizing Bertin to stand firm and defend the original concession of 17 April 1773 in its entirety. On 7 March 1780, he told Bertin that he found himself 'dans une cruelle situation'; a few days letter he was begging the minister to make an early and favourable decision on the affair.[170] On the thirty-first of the same month, Bertin agreed to a meeting with the

---

[169] *AN* F14 7682, letters of 7 and 20 Sept. 1779.
[170] *AG* 58J 4, 7 Mar. 1780.

representatives of the Estates of Languedoc, their deputation being led by the maréchal de Castries, the Bishop of Uzès, and the *syndic-général des États*, the marquis de Montferrier. At this meeting, the case for the Estates was put with some force, and it is not coincidental that, only a few months later, Bertin fell from power, a fall which had been engineered by Castries and his friends at Court.[171] The news was received with unfeigned joy in the Alès region and with corresponding despair by Tubeuf.[172] The fall from power of Bertin did not mark the end of Tubeuf; indeed, he was just embarking upon new schemes in Normandy and Paris. It did, however, represent a mortal blow to the more ambitious schemes which he had nurtured to bring modern industrialization to the Alès region. It cannot be overemphasized that the support of ministers of the Crown was absolutely vital to the success of early capitalist developments in eighteenth-century France.

The terms of the government's long-awaited decision concerning Tubeuf's concession which was announced on 8 August 1780, confirms the crucial role of government in promoting industry. The maréchal de Castries was awarded the Mas-Dieu and la Fôret mines; Pierre Gilly the mines of Saint-Jean-de-Valériscle; and the Contys ultimate control of the *mines de Portes*. However, Tubeuf was confirmed in his entitlement to all the remaining mines in his original concession, as well as the jewel in the Alèsian crown, the Grand-Combe. The 1780 decree was, in fact, a compromise, a compromise between the power of nobles, great and small, Tubeuf, the Estates of Languedoc, and the government. It was the victory of 'les Grands' over 'les petits'.[173]

However, if the government and 'les Grands' believed that this was to be the end of the matter they were to be disappointed. If Tubeuf had always underestimated the power of the local people, so too did his heavyweight opponents, whether in Paris or Montpellier. After all, a 'feudal' lord like Castries was only preferable to an 'industrial' entrepreneur like Tubeuf if he fulfilled his historical role as the protector of his vassals; this, after all, is why they had turned to Castries for leadership in the first place. The immediate reactions of

---

[171] Bardon, *L'Exploitation du bassin houiller d'Alais*, 182.

[172] *AG* C194, letter of Montferrier to Rome, 1 June 1780, which refers to the possibility of a new phase in the struggle against Tubeuf. See also Bardon, *L'Exploitation du bassin houiller d'Alais*, 172.

[173] Bardon, *L'Exploitation du bassin houiller d'Alais*, 182–3.

local officials made this abundantly clear. Cabane de Camont, more deeply ensconced in Castries's pocket than most, rejected every peace overture made by Tubeuf.[174] Alexis de Trinquelaque—who had always rooted for *les petits*, and who would continue to do so as leader of the counter-revolution in the Alès region after 1789—was more subtle in his approach although no less opposed to Tubeuf's long-term plans. In a *mémoire* prepared for a meeting of the Estates of Languedoc he explained why. Tubeuf had organized a meeting with all the small *propriétaires* with coal-mines on their land on 9 November 1780, during which he had offered them an indemnity based upon the average of the annual *rente* they had received over the past ten years. Trinquelaque explained that the offer had been rejected out of hand because, like everything Tubeuf did, it was a swindle. *Rentes* for coal-mines had gone up dramatically since 1776 and, even more recently, the demand for coal in the region 'has become immense and is still rising'.[175] Coal had finally become 'big business' and Tubeuf was being punished for teaching the Alèsians how to mine it!

There was also the fact that although Pierre Gilly had been temporarily pacified by the confirmation of his right to mine coal for his glassworks at Saint-Jean-de-Valériscle, his place as local leader of the small seigneurs and other property-owners in the coalfield had been taken by Jean-François-Mathieu Soustelle, seigneur of Sainte-Cécile d'Andorge, another Protestant with a commercial family background and with interests in the *mines de Portes*. Jean-François himself had entered the legal profession and acted as an agent for the vicomte de Portes. Soustelle was destined to play a leading role in the history of the Revolution in the lower Cévennes, eventually representing the department of the Gard in the National Assembly.[176] Finally, the maréchal de Castries, besieged by local *propriétaires* and municipal officials alike, was encouraging individual mine-owners to ignore the government's latest decree, which was, in any case, a provisional one.[177] By the beginning of 1781, Tubeuf was in a worse position

---

[174] On 25 Sept. 1780, Tubeuf informed the Intendant that de Camont had rejected all his offers and was now refusing to answer his letters. *AG* C194.

[175] Ibid., *mémoire pour demander aux États qu'ils forment opposition à l'arrêt du 8 août*.

[176] For Soustelle's claim to the mines on his lands see *AN* F14 7682, Soustelle to Joly de Fleury, 15 June 1782.

[177] See Tubeuf's comments, *AG* 58J 2, 31 Dec. 1780. In a letter to Tolozan, the Intendant explained that, given the opposition of the *diocèse d'Alais* and 'le très grand intérêt [*sic*] qu'à M. le marquis de Castries', he was determined to be 'très circonspect

than he had been a year earlier. The interest on his massive loans was mounting, and he had not succeeded in closing down many of the more productive small mines which were continuing to undercut the price he charged for his coal. The immediate result was the cancellation of the important contract with Richard, Carouges et Cie. It was to prove a crippling blow to his prestige and to his overall plan for the coal-basin.[178] In a lengthy document intended as the basis for a final appeal to the government, Tubeuf insisted that the farce had gone on long enough. After ten year's work, the expenditure of hundreds of thousands of *livres* in investment, with three decrees issued by two monarchs, Louis XV and Louis XVI, he was facing total ruin. Surely, Tubeuf argued, governments should not 'expose unfortunate citizens to be the playthings and the victims of illusion . . . the public interest demands that the government make decisions that are observed'.[179] It was a valid point, one that would be partly accepted by the Constituent Assembly in 1791, and more convincingly by Napoleon Bonaparte.

Left to their own devices, there can be no doubt whatsoever that the members of the Conseil des mines would have continued to supply Tubeuf with the support he so badly needed. Even after Bertin's dismissal, ministers like Joly de Fleury had no doubt of Tubeuf's value to France. In September 1782, Fleury rejected an appeal from the Estates of Languedoc demanding the revocation of Tubeuf's concession, pointing out that Tubeuf had been the first man in the region to teach the locals how to mine coal properly. As for the 'feudal' claim that the land and the mines had originally been given to 'seigneurs et autres particuliers' by the king, Fleury countered with the remark that this represented 'an abdication of property, freely undertaken, which his successors could, indeed had to, make whenever the public interest demanded it'. In other words, it was the king, not the *propriétaire des mines*, who was the real owner of the nation's mineral

---

sur la conduite que j'ai à tenir et à se marcher qu'à pas de registre'. *AN* F14 7682, 22 Jan. 1781.

[178] Tubeuf blamed the maréchal de Castries and the Estates of Languedoc for the disaster: 'Après l'opposition faite par les Etats de la province et par M. le marquis de Castries, ministre de la marine, comme seigneur d'Alais, et faisant exploiter des mines de charbon dans ma concession, à l'exécution de l'arrêt provisioire tous les particuliers ainsi que M. le marquis de Castries, ont repris leurs exploitations; à ce moyen, mon marché avec la compagnie d'Epurement est résilié.' *AG* 58J 2, 31 Dec. 1780.

[179] *AG* 58J 4, *observations que j'ai donné à mon avocat.*

wealth.[180] This was precisely the *étatiste* doctrine that the property-owners of Languedoc, and their Estates, rejected.

And it was to be the continued and fierce resistance of the Estates of Languedoc, spearheaded henceforward by the maréchal de Castries, that was, ultimately, to weaken the government's resolve. Not that the Estates were 'anti-capitalist'; its officials had often encouraged the discovery of new mines, new manufacturing techniques, the building of new roads and canals. Nor were the Estates 'anti-*laissez-faire*'. The economic philosophy of the members of the Estates, founded upon the views, and prejudices, of a small property-owning, protoindustrialized society producing for an international market, was summed up in the statement that 'Freedom is the very soul of commerce; it must be defended in the workshop.'[181] However, it should be remembered that land, not the factory, dominated the thinking of the provincial nobles, large landowners, even the *négociants* who ran the Estates, and that the concern with 'freedom' should also be construed as a defence mechanism against centralizing governments which threatened the sanctity of property, and that included clerical and aristocratic property. We are still dealing with a 'post-feudal' society, one in which there was nothing sacred (yet) or 'private' about property; at least, legal opinion was still ambivalent over the issue. The obsession with property sprang from the nervousness of property-owners, which is why every Declaration of the Rights of Man and preamble to Constitutions during the Revolution usually boiled down to a defence of the Rights of Property.[182]

It was this vexed issue, which did not conflict with the manufacturers' demands for economic 'freedom' against the government, that moved the Estates to denounce the 'monopolist' Tubeuf. This is made abundantly clear in the reaction of the *syndic-général des États de Languedoc* in Paris to the government's compromise decree of August 1780. It was denounced as a 'coup terrible', prompting the official to

---

[180] *AN* F14 7682, Fleury to the Estates of Languedoc, 8 Sept. 1782. See also Fleury's decree of 19 Mar. 1783, which marks the peak of *étatiste* legislation during the *ancien régime*. It confirmed the legislation pertaining to mining in France passed in 1744, adding that henceforth the Conseil des mines would only grant concessions 'qu'à des capitalistes sérieux ou à des grandes compagnies et qu'il exigerait des garanties aussi bien financières qu'à professionnelles'. The legislation of 1783 also improved on safety measures for miners: accidents had to be reported to the authorities. Rouff, *Les Mines de charbon*, 72–9.

[181] *AG* C374, *procès-verbal de l'assemblée de monseigneurs des États Généraux, 2 Jan. 1778.*

[182] See M. Gauchet, 'The Rights of Man', in F. Furet and M. Ozouf (eds.), *A Critical Dictionary of the French Revolution* (London, 1989), 818–28.

press for a government inquiry into the entire affair, one which would 'rest upon the most exact principles of public law, against which people are all too prone to substitute the all too fiscal and erroneous maxims of the king's Domaine'.[183] This went to the heart of the struggle between Tubeuf's 'royal' concession and Languedoc's 'provincial' rejection of it. It also posed a scarcely veiled threat to the principles of absolute monarchy—the primacy, or at least parity, of individual and provincial rights over those of the monarchy. According to Richard and Carouges's agent in Alès, the deal with Tubeuf had been torpedoed by the province's property-owners.[184]

The available documentation suggests that Alles was not exaggerating. As early as 1777, Cabane de Camont had pointed out to the government that it was Tubeuf's attack on individual property-owners which had 'caused the greatest possible sensation here, monsieur', adding that it was surely quite wrong that individuals should have been

suddenly stripped of a part of their property-rights in this way. I say the rights of *their* property, and I say it with some justification it seems to me. And here, monsieur, we come to one of the central issues which I wished to raise. This province regards the right to be administered by written law as one of its major privileges. This right confers upon owners of the surface of the land everything which that land encloses.

On the sensitive and crucial issue of who actually owned the coal-mines in the *comté d'Alais*, Cabane was certain of one thing—it was not the king, since the monarchy had sold the *comté d'Alais* to Philippe de Valois in the fifteenth century. 'Thus, if ever the rights to these mines had belonged to the king, they belong today, without fear of contradiction, to the *comté d'Alais*.' We must recall that Cabane was a seigneurial judge, and his conclusion that the land—including the coal-mines—in the *comté d'Alais* belonged to the owners of that fief, its 'vassaux et emphitéotes', reflected this fact.[185] Five years later, the *syndic-général* of the Estates of Languedoc, Rome, would elevate Cabane's thoughts to an even higher plane when he informed the

---

[183] *AG* C194, Rome to Montferrier, 11 Aug. 1780.

[184] 'On ne peut Monsieur', Alles informed his employer, Richard, 'attribuer la froideur avec laquelle la dernière assemblée des Etats à vu la mémoire de votre Compagnie . . . qu'à la jalousie des propriétaires du terrain à Alais'. The Estates had been told (correctly!) that Tubeuf and the Richard company were acting in tandem and, on the basis of 'ces raisonnements puériles', they had decided to elicit the support of the marquis de Castries. B. de N. 496, 19 June 1780.

[185] *AG* C194, letter to Joubert, 14 Aug. 1777.

government that if the concession granted to Tubeuf took precedence over Roman law and 'le droit écrit de la province', then it followed

not only that this would represent a most significant attack on the property-rights of a considerable number of families who depend for their livelihood on the possession and exploitation of their coal-mines, but also one would be destroying one of the most enduring privileges in the province of Languedoc, one which, to put it briefly, provides the foundation stones for its internal administration.[186]

In fighting to the death for his concession, Tubeuf had inadvertently opened up a constitutional can of worms.

In practice, what this alleged onslaught on the rights of the province meant was the possible incorporation of Languedoc into a centralized Bourbon State, the loss of office for judges like Cabane de Camont, and, just as frightening, a possible complete revision of the tax system which the province administered. As Rome explained, the *taille* in Languedoc was levied on land, not according to the legal status of the individual (*taille réelle*), and it was the Estates, though the *assiettes des diocèses*, which were reponsible for its collection. The tax levied on land which had coal-mines included the value of the coal produced. If Tubeuf's concession stood 'it is certain that such properties cannot continue to be assessed for the *taille* as in the past. One would have to transfer on to other goods that part which related to the mines, which would mean completely new tax-rolls, new land surveys, all of which would be extremely costly'. It was not so much the cost, however, but the implications of bringing the tax-rolls up to date during a period when a great deal of land was changing hands and many *propriétaires*, because of outdated tax-rolls, were escaping their just tax deserts that really worried the members of the Estates. As Rome concluded: 'Which of us is better placed to avoid the danger of such a revolution?'[187] If the government were not convinced of the dangers of a 'revolution' in Languedoc, in part led by landowners threatened with loss of property-rights and increases in taxation, then their doubts were quickly resolved during the winter of 1782–3 by

<hr>

[186] *AG* C194, *mémoire pour le syndic général de la Province de Languedoc*, n.d. (but probably 1782).

[187] Ibid. In 1777, the secretary of the Estates in Montpellier had warned that if Tubeuf's concession was allowed to stand, then the whole issue of property rights would be raised 'qui sont encore plus précieuse dans la Province que partout ailleurs, attendu que les fonds de terre supportent toutes les charges'. Letter of 29 Aug. 1777.

one of the most serious popular rebellions which occurred in Languedoc during the eighteenth century—*la révolte des masques armées*—and which affected the region around Banne, Saint-Ambroix, and Robiac in particular, the region where resistance to Tubeuf's plans had been most fierce.

We shall analyse the social and political significance of this revolt in the following chapter. It is important to stress here, however, that the revolt helped to convince Tubeuf that his future did not lie in Languedoc. In July 1783, he wrote to the *sub-délégué* of the Intendant, Louis Dhombres, thanking him for his past support and explaining his resolve to open up new coal-mines near Paris.[188] He had already been awarded another concession near Coutances in his home province of Normandy. On 7 September 1783, he sold his concession in Alès for a million *livres* to the abbé Bréard, but the sale included the legal proviso that if the purchaser did not fulfil the terms of the contract to the letter then the entire transaction would be declared null and void.[189] A year later, Bréard did, in fact, fail to meet his obligations, and Tubeuf decided to reclaim his concession. The Norman entrepreneur thus found himself with two major legal battles on his hands, against Bréard and against the maréchal de Castries, even more determined by this time, given the increasing demand and rising price of coal, to destroy his bourgeois enemy.[190]

In June 1783, Castries had been elevated to the position of a maréchal: his influence inside and outside Versailles had reached a new peak. Throughout the rest of the decade, Castries, supported unreservedly by the dioceses of Alès and Uzès, would block every move which Tubeuf made concerning his concession in Languedoc. Tubeuf was forced to spend considerable sums of money, which he could ill afford, preparing legal submissions and defences to the Conseil des mines and to the Comité des affaires contestataires; the major issue continued to be ownership of the rich Grand-Combe mine. In an attempt to block Tubeuf's plans, and to increase his own revenues, Castries had purchased the *terre de Trouilhas* from the Deleuze family on 17 January 1782, thus giving himself direct seigneurial rights

---

[188] *AG* 58J 4, 27 July 1783.

[189] *AG* 58J 2, 7 Sept. 1783. Tubeuf wrote that once the legal loose ends were tied up, he would settle with the Chaulieus.

[190] The legal battle with Bréard was only settled in Nov. 1787. Tubeuf was, at least, able to pay Chaulieu 36,000 *livres*, representing only the interest covering the previous three years. *AG* 58J 4, 22 Nov. 1787.

over the Grand-Combe.[191] Tubeuf's reaction was to offer Castries no less than 10,000 *livres* a year for the right to work the Grand-Combe mine; previous *fermiers* had never paid more than 1,500, but then Tubeuf knew how to mine coal! He also realized the vast potential of the Grand-Combe: 'Judge for yourself, monsieur', he wrote to La Boullaye in Versailles, 'by this sacrifice how much it means to me to keep these *mines de Trouilhas*.'[192] The Grand-Combe was, in fact, the key to all Tubeuf's plans for the future of the Alès coalfield, and Castries knew it, which is why he turned down Tubeuf's extremely generous offer. According to Tubeuf, Castries had refused to give any indication of the price he might charge for the Grand-Combe: 'He told me that it was his secret, and that, anyway, he did not feel disposed to put his affairs in the hands of someone against whom he had been waging a war.'[193]

On 19 March 1782, yet another provisional decree was issued by the government confirming Tubeuf's rights minus the Abilon and Mas-Dieu mines, which had been granted to Castries, and Saint-Jean-de-Valériscle, fief of the Gilly family. Once again, Tubeuf made himself no friends by using the decree to impose a harsh solution on the small mine-owners of the coalfield. Adopting what he termed *la voie de rigueur*, Tubeuf plastered the walls of Alès with copies of the government's decision in his favour, threatening to use armed force wherever necessary to close down 'illegal' mines.[194] As a result, opposition to his plans increased. On 27 May 1783, the *assiette du diocèse d'Alais* convened under the presidency of 'His most Illustrious and Reverend Seigneur, Pierre-Marie-Magdeleine Courtois de Balore, Bishop of Alès'. Castries was also present on this occasion, joining in Holy Mass before moving off to the town hall to vote in favour of an official denunciation to the Estates of Languedoc, based upon

---

[191] Bardon, *L'Exploitation du bassin houiller d'Alais*, 247, suggests that, originally, the purchase may have been a legal fiction designed to throw the political and social weight of the maréchal behind the property-owners of the region in their struggle against Tubeuf. The purchase price was 190,000 *livres*. On 9 Sept. 1789, Castries still owed Deleuze 50,000 *livres*. See also Castries, *Papiers de famille*, 302.

[192] *AN* F14 7682, 14 Feb. 1783.

[193] *AG* 58J 4, 14 Mar. 1782. The importance of coal is underlined by the fact that Louis Alles considered the value of the *terre de Trouilhas* to have been just 4,000 *livres* without its coal-mines, 200,000 *livres* with them! B. de N. 496, letter to Richard, 5 June 1780.

[194] On 12 Apr. 1782, Tubeuf wrote that he did not give a damn about Castries's purchase of the *terre de Trouilhas* since, according to his information, the rich Grand-Combe mine was in the neighbouring parish of Nôtre-Dame-de-Laval. *AG* 58J 4.

a statement from Cabane de Camont, concerning the evil ways of 'l'Étranger Tubeuf'.[195] Unfortunately for the latter, de Balore and his successor Monseigneur de Bausset, both Jesuit sympathizers, supported Castries and the attack on the 'protégé des bureaux' without reservation: de Bausset was to accompany Castries into exile in 1790.[196] The importance of the clergy in winning over support for the maréchal amongst the local population should not be underestimated, as Louis Alles explained to his company directors in Paris.[197]

However, as we have seen, Tubeuf was no amateur when it came to courting support for his concession. We know that he had enjoyed the confidence of leading officials in the Conseil des mines as well as that of the minister Bertin. His Journal also reveals that he was prepared to bribe his way to the throne itself through the influence of Court ladies. An entry for 16 May 1780 records his willingness to pay 3,600 *livres* (twice the annual salary of an ordinary craftsman) to Mme Hubert, *femme de chambre* to Mme Victoire, the king's aunt, 'if, through her good offices and protection, she might be able to obtain a definitive judgement in my favour from the Conseil des mines'.[198] Two years later, following the announcement of the favourable provisional decree of 19 March 1782, he wrote, in very flamboyant vein, to Mme de Fontpertuis at Versailles: 'I believe that I shall spend the rest of my life manifesting the sentiments of gratitude which I owe you for the invaluable services which you have rendered me . . . my future is safe for ever as a result of the decree which you have obtained for me.'[199] This comment proved to be a triumph of hope over good sense.

The last real chance of a compromise solution came with the intervention of Calonne early in 1784. A tentative agreement between the Intendant, the Estates of Languedoc, and Tubeuf was reached over the quantity of coal to be produced, its price, and the number of mines which should be kept open.[200] This was followed, on

---

[195] *AG* C431, *procès-verbal de l'assiette du diocèse d'Alais*. The members congregated first in the bishop's palace.

[196] According to Louis Alles, de Balore was continually 'environné des charbonniers'. B. de N. 496, letter to Richard, 24 Apr. 1780.

[197] Ibid. Alles begged the directors of his company to buttonhole the bishops of Uzès and Alès before they left Paris for the south.

[198] *AG* 58J 4, 16 May 1780.

[199] Ibid.

[200] *AN* 58J 4. The Conseil des mines worked hard to secure an agreement between the contending parties at this time. See entry for 3 Mar. 1784.

9 March, by yet another decree, which, with relatively minor amend-
ments, confirmed the decisions which had been incorporated into the
decrees of 1780 and 1782. Surely, Tubeuf had some right to believe,
this would be the end of the affair, and, to underline this point, he
took some of his workers to the Grand-Combe mine on 3 May
intending to take possession of it, as he was legally permitted to do.
Castries, through his representatives at the mine, asked for a fortnight's grace to tie up some loose ends. On 21 May, Tubeuf returned
in person, convinced that, at last, he was about to enter 'the promised
land'. Instead, according to his own version of events, he was 'assailed
by a barrage of stones thrown by Castries's workers from the mountainside above me. I sustained a severe facial injury. None the less, I
took possession of my mine and put my workers in charge.'[201] The
injury was indeed severe: Tubeuf was to be blind in one eye for the
rest of his life. Although an official complaint was drawn up, no one
was to be brought to justice for this grievous attack upon him. In
addition, his victory proved all too temporary. Castries had only asked
for a breathing-space in order to mount yet another legal onslaught
at Court, as a result of which the decree issued in March was
'temporarily' suspended. Tubeuf was forced to withdraw his workers
from the Grand-Combe to be replaced by those of the maréchal de
Castries. Tubeuf's last real hopes of controlling production in the
Alès coalfield had been dashed within sight of 'the promised land'.

The defeat inflicted by Castries's machinations at Court meant that
henceforth Tubeuf would concentrate most of his efforts on his
Rochebelle mine, as well as upon his new venture on the outskirts of
Paris. The strain under which he and his family had been operating
is clearly evident in a letter which Mme Tubeuf wrote to the Archbishop of Narbonne:

The interest on our loans rises every day, since the legal trials which have
been started against us have made it impossible for us to enjoy the full
benefits of our concession over the past eight years. We have sacrificed our
youth, my husband has lost an eye, our fortune has been eaten up, as well
as that of our friends. After all this, all we seek is to be reimbursed for our
losses. To be forced to stay in a place against the wishes of the local people
is to die a thousand times over.[202]

[201] According to Achille Bardon, François Faure, who had been involved in the
running the coal-mines of the *comté d'Alais* since the 1760s, met Tubeuf at the entrance
to the mine with the words 'Vous avez cru être enfin arrivé à la terre promise: vous
n'y entrerez pas.' *L'Exploitation du bassin houiller d'Alais*, 292.
[202] Ibid. 309.

As if to rub salt in the wound, in October 1784 the king's brother bought the *vicomté de Portes* from the Conty family, the government granting Monsieur a thirty-year concession over the *mines de Portes* which Tubeuf had originally hoped to work. It was apparently Monsieur's agents who made the simple, but daring, proposal to the king that if Tubeuf's concession were to be measured in *lieues de France*, not *lieues de Languedoc*, then the *mines de Portes* as well as the Grand-Combe would lie outside Tubeuf's grasp. It was all rather academic, however. Even the indomitable Tubeuf found it difficult to fight the maréchal de Castries *and* the king's brother.[203]

Finally, in one of the most damaging and unjust *arrêts* issued during the reign of Louis XVI, a new and definitive judgment on his concession spelled ruin for the Tubeuf family, already heavily in debt. On 29 December 1788, the Conseil du roi—apparently basing its decisions on the *lieues de France* measurement—decreed that the maréchal de Castries should be confirmed in the possession 'of the *mines de Trouilhas* [Grand-Combe], forbidding sieur Tubeuf to trouble him in this possession'. In addition, Tubeuf was asked to pay the colossal sum of 250,000 *livres* in damages to Castries, as well as the legal costs of the case. It is astonishing that even after this savage blow Tubeuf refused to withdraw completely from his interests in Languedoc. Indeed, perhaps because he was in so deep that he saw no way of getting out unscathed, he even threatened to restart court proceedings to challenge the judgment of 29 December! In a letter to his director, Renaux, he wrote: 'Stay very calm. Everything will work out fine.'[204] What is particularly interesting is that during the last face-to-face interview which Castries and Tubeuf were to arrange, the Norman entrepreneur should have offered to become Castries's *fermier*. The traditional system of leasing out property had finally triumphed. Tubeuf explained that if he could put his skilled miners in the Grand-Combe, he and the maréchal could modernize production and,

---

[203] This clever move was applauded by Castries's agent since, if it were not successful, 'non seulement M. le maréchal se trouverait privé de la grasse augmentation que les mines doit produire dans ses revenues, mais, de plus, il serait assuré de voir diminuer le produit des mines de la Forêt [d'Abilon], pour que la concurrence de celles de la Grand-Combe serait absolument ruineuse'. *AN* 306AP 483, 3 Mar. 1785. In other words, the Abilon and Mas-Dieu mines, which Castries ran legally, were only viable if there was no competition from the rich seams of the Grand-Combe.

[204] *AG* 58J 5, 1 Jan. 1789. On 26 Jan. he again told Renaux not to worry; 'vous verrez qu'elle [the decree of 1788] n'aura pas l'effet qu'on s'est promet'.

together with output from Rochebelle, they could produce over 300,000 *quintaux* a year.[205]

The maréchal refused to budge. The decree had made it clear that at the heart of the dispute was the post-feudal definition of property which still governed even the mining of coal in Languedoc. According to the terms of the decree, Castries was empowered 'to exploit directly, or indirectly, the coal-mines which exist, or which might be opened, in *les domaines utiles et directs du comté d'Alais*; to levy the *cens* which he has the right to levy from his vassals in the said *comté*, working the said mines in accordance with his titles and possessions'. As the descendant of the maréchal de Castries himself put it, the decree of 29 December 1788 confirmed the fact that, 'six months before the meeting of the Estates General, seigneurial rights took precedence over all others, even though they may have been granted by a king'.[206]

It is also clear that Castries had used, indeed, abused his authority at Versailles to obtain a favourable outcome. The council had discussed the case at a time when Tubeuf's supporters in the Conseil des mines could not attend. The *rapporteur* was the son of Castries's treasurer in the Ministry of the Navy; and, even though Tubeuf was not present, the maréchal had actually sat in on part of the proceedings.[207] There can be no doubt that both Castries and the king's brother had been determined 'to match their personal interests with those of their vassals'.[208] In Alès, the maréchal's supporters were in triumphant mood. Castries's agent wrote: 'I learned, with the greatest possible joy, the happy outcome of your trial with sieur Tubeuf.' He had gone through the town knocking on the doors of the wealthiest *propriétaires* 'so that they could profit from the advantage which the decree which you have won offers them. I left them in no doubt that they owed it all to your influence and to your unique protection.'[209] However, the political omens in that winter of 1788 were not particularly propitious for impressing Alèsians with the powers of a great noble. In just over two years both Castries and Tubeuf had decided to leave France, never to return.

---

[205] Ibid., 12 Feb. 1789.

[206] Castries, *Papiers de famille*, 306–9.

[207] Bardon, *L'Exploitation du bassin houiller d'Alais*, 325. Bardon's conclusions are corroborated by the duc de Castries himself in his *Papiers de famille*.

[208] Galy, 'L'Exploitation des houillères en Languedoc', 183.

[209] *AN* 306AP 490, 11 Jan. 1789. Castries's agent was all in favour of delivering the *coup de grâce* by moving the maréchal's miners into the small mines near Tubeuf's Rochebelle pit thus forcing the Norman entrepreneur to 'abandonner le pays' for good.

3

THE IMPACT OF A REVOLUTIONARY CRISIS

THE bicentenary of the Revolution has already provided an opportunity for yet more reappraisals of '1789'. On both sides of the Channel, and indeed the Atlantic, the accent has fallen heavily upon political and intellectual history.[1] Over the past two decades 'revisionist' historians have been beavering away, undermining the old Marxist, or Marxist–Leninist, interpretations which related political and intellectual movements to their socio-economic and class bases. The process may be said to have begun with Alfred Cobban's brief treatise *The Social Interpretation of the French Revolution*.[2] During the 1960s, however, as Norman Hampson's valuable textbook *A Social History of the French Revolution*[3] suggests, it was still widely accepted that a 'social', if not always 'socialist', approach to the interpretation of the Revolution was *de rigueur*. Recent 'revisionist' works have reneged on this gentleman's agreement, certainly on the idea that the Revolution had anything to do with 'class struggle'. 'Élites' or 'notables' are in, 'classes' are out. William Doyle's résumé of these recent trends is typical: 'Bourgeois and nobles were all part of a single propertied elite.'[4] Few—so far at least—have gone all the way with Guy Chaussinand-Nogaret, who opined that the really revolutionary class was the nobility,[5] although Donald Sutherland has summed up recent trends with the conclusion that 'the whole idea of the class origins of the Revolution with a distinct, ambitious, frustrated, capitalist bourgeoisie has collapsed, probably forever'.[6] One feels the stigma of heresy falling upon one when one claims that Pierre-François Tubeuf was a 'distinct, ambitious, frustrated, capitalist' bourgeois, but that is certainly how he saw himself and how this work interprets his career.

[1] See e.g. the proceedings of the international conference held in Chicago in Sept. 1986, K. Baker (ed.), *The French Revolution and the Creation of Modern Political Culture*, i: *The Political Culture of the Old Regime* (Oxford, 1987).

[2] A. Cobban, *The Social Interpretation of the French Revolution* (Cambridge, 1964).

[3] N. Hampson, *A Social History of the French Revolution* (London, 1963).

[4] Doyle, *Origins of the French Revolution*, 22.

[5] Chaussinand-Nogaret, *The French Nobility in the Eighteenth Century*, 85.

[6] Sutherland, *France, 1789–1815*, 12–14.

Lynn Hunt's *Politics, Culture and Class in the French Revolution*, which contains many stimulating and sophisticated lines of enquiry, appears to put the Marxist cat amongst the revisionist pigeons by agreeing that 'the revolutionary political class can be termed "bourgeois" both in terms of social position and of class consciousness'. For Professor Hunt, class must be defined as much by 'its cultural position and relationships as by its membership in occupationally defined social groups', a sociological approach which would meet with the approval of all but the most vulgar 'economistic' interpretation.[7] However, so far as the Alès region was concerned, economic change during the eighteenth century was extremely important in determining the behaviour of certain social groups and the political options they espoused. Although the conclusions he reaches are exaggerated, Chaussinand-Nogaret is right to stress that 'The world of business emerges as best-fitted to break the constraints of a socio-political structure ill-suited to the development of a modern economy, capital accumulation and the rise of large-scale industry.'[8] Indeed this statement may be taken as a fairly accurate summary of the argument pursued in this work so far, with the important qualification that it was the 'bourgeois' Tubeuf, not the 'noble' Castries who really tried 'to break the constraints' of the socio-political structures in the Alès region. It will be further argued in this chapter that the periodic bouts of violence which characterize the history of the Alès region from the *masques armés* rebellion of 1783 to the Jacobin Terror a decade later were closely linked to the trauma of a protoindustrialized population experiencing the misery of economic recession and political upheaval. Certainly geography, shared cultural values, particularly shared religious values, help to explain the confused, often contradictory, events which mark the history of the Revolution in this region, but many of these values—community solidarity, the mania for office, the frenetic defence of 'property', for example—were themselves the outcome of the uncertain economic climate of the second half of the eighteenth century.[9]

---

[7] L. Hunt, *Politics, Culture and Class in the French Revolution* (London, 1986), 150. See also p. 176: 'Was the new political class "bourgeois" in a Marxist sense? If Marxist is interpreted somewhat loosely, the answer is Yes.'

[8] Chaussinand-Nogaret, *The French Nobility in the Eighteenth Century*, 114.

[9] So far as the department of the Gard is concerned, and, indeed, much of the south-east, one can also agree with Lynn Hunt's conclusion that 'The revolutionary officials were the owners of the means of production; they were either merchants with capital, professionals with skill, artisans with their own shops, or more rarely, peasants with land.' *Politics, Culture and Class*, 177.

The impact of the Revolution upon the Nîmes and Alès regions, soon to be known as the department of the Gard, was to be immediate and extremely violent. The Counter-Revolution, as an organized Catholic royalist movement receiving encouragement and support from the *émigrés* in Turin, had its roots in the Gard; its first violent manifestation was to be the *bagarre de Nîmes* in June 1790, in the course of which several hundred Catholic workers were to be brutally slaughtered by an almost entirely Protestant crowd, recruited, in the main, from the protoindustrial villages of the Basses-Cévennes. From 1790 to 1792, Catholic royalists continued to organize resistance in their successive *camps de Jalès*, whilst, during the spring of 1792, some of the most violent episodes of a so-called 'peasant jacquerie' were to occur in the region. The Jacobin Terror was to produce further bloodshed, with 133 individuals being executed in Nîmes alone, many of them *négociants, fabricants*, and the legal bourgeoisie who had ruled in their interests since 1789. Finally, during the Directory and Napoleonic Consulate, Catholic royalist murder gangs—the infamous *égorgeurs du Midi*—found shelter and support in the Catholic regions of the Gard.

This catalogue of violence, the politics of revolution and counter-revolution, cannot possibly be understood without relating them to the socio-economic realities which had helped to shape the attitudes of the local population since the 1740s. The long-term beneficiaries of the revolutionary upheaval were to be the landed, professional, and commercial bourgeoisie who were to staff the Federalist movement of 1793, the very Protestant *gens d'affaires* against whom the *masques armés* had rebelled a decade earlier,[10] bourgeois who had often ruled, at least ostensibly, in the interests of the nobility before 1789, and in their own interests, as well as those of their local clients, after this date. Their victory did not entail the overnight triumph of 'modern industrial capitalism': the socio-economic structures and *mentalité* of a protoindustrialized population continued to impede the emergence of more modern forms of production, of technological change, whether in the textile industry or in coal-mining, well into the nineteenth century. The Revolution was to provide the opportunity for the development of modern capitalism; the entrenchment of the landed and legal bourgeoisie in office, the political experience of the 1790s,

[10] For a discussion of the historic significance of the *masques armés* affair, see G. Sabatier, 'De la révolte de Roure (1670) aux masques armés (1783): la mutation du phénomène contestataire en Vivarais', in J. Nicolas (ed.), *Mouvements populaires et conscience sociale, XVI*ᵉ*–XIX*ᵉ *siècles* (Paris, 1985), 121–47.

particularly the Counter-Revolution, the perpetuation of *ancien régime* economic structures and social attitudes was to ensure that this opportunity was only seized with one hand.

The Revolution may be said to have begun in earnest in Alès at two o'clock on 16 November 1788, when a meeting of the municipal council was convened to discuss a resolution passed by the council in Nîmes a fortnight earlier. It was decided that deputies to the forthcoming meeting of the *sénéchaussée de Nîmes* would be chosen in accordance with the regulations governing the last meeting of the Estates General in 1614. A few days earlier, a group of Alèsians had requested the convocation of a 'democratic' *assemblée générale* comprising all the tax-paying citizens of the town to debate the issues associated with the calling of the Estates General. The request was rejected, which meant, in effect, that the 'municipal revolution' in Alès had been set in motion. The *patriotes*, as they now began to call themselves, recruited support for their ideas throughout the Alèsian region, insisting that there should be no 'servile adhesion' to the decisions taken in Nîmes, influenced as they allegedly had been by the *aristocrate* mayor, baron Marguerittes. Ostracized by the Conseil politique in Alès, the *patriotes* decided to press ahead with their own *assemblée générale*, initially one of just forty members which met in the Dominican convent, rue Soubeyrane, on 23 November. Over the next fortnight, the *patriotes* widened the base of their support by appealing to like-minded souls in Anduze and Saint-Jean-du-Gard.

Decisions taken in Paris now began to influence the course of events in Alès. The rejection by the Assembly of Notables of the demand that the number of representatives for the Third Estate to the Estates General should be double those for the first two orders sharpened the resolve of the *patriotes*, and on 21 December no fewer than 380 potential supporters, now calling themselves *l'assemblée générale de la Tiers état de la ville d'Alès*, met to denounce the work of the Assembly; they also demanded the resignation of their own *aristocrate* municipal council. Confronted with growing opposition, a more representative meeting of the three orders of the town of Alès was convened to choose the deputies who were to attend a meeting of the entire diocese of Alès fixed for 8 January, at which it was decided to press for the abolition of the Estates of Languedoc.[11] According

---

[11]   Bardon, *L'Exploitation du bassin houiller d'Alais*, 326; Bruyère, *Alès, capitale des Cévennes* 389–99. See also J. P. Goirand, 'Documents historiques sur Alais pendant la Révolution',

to the terms of the king's decree of 29 January, deputies for the Third Estate were to be elected in each 'bailliage par les délégués des communautés urbaines et rurales', thus drawing all the towns and villages of the Cévennes into the political arena. Meetings to discuss *cahiers de doléances* were to be held in March. On the seventeenth of this month, the chosen deputies from the Cévennes travelled the familiar road to Nîmes for the meeting of the *Tiers état de la sénéchaussée de Nîmes*.[12] It had taken only a few months for effective power to pass from the *aristocrate* municipal council of Alès to the *patriotes*, who were destined to seize most of the influential administrative posts in the town. Reports from Castries's steward highlight the mass enthusiasm generated by the political conflict, with many worried references to 'assemblées illégales et tumultueuses'.[13]

What were the fundamental issues dividing *les patriotes de 1788* from *les aristocrates* in Alès? So far as the former were concerned the most pressing issue was the defeat of the oligarchy ensconced in the town hall, for without it their 'democratic' programme could never have been implemented. Most French cities and towns were proud of their municipal history[14] and Alès was no exception: the procedures adopted to choose its officials—*consuls* and *conseillers politiques*—dated back to the year 1200. It is important to note that, just as in Britain during the 1780s, the *patriotes* of Alès could refer back to a mythical 'âge d'or', one which pre-dated the Bourbons and the Valois rather than the Normans. Originally, the town's municipalities had been chosen from ten *échelles*, theoretically designed to reflect the entire social hierarchy from noble to impoverished artisan. During the seventeenth and eighteenth centuries, as the increasingly wealthy merchant and landed élite seized an increasing share of the economic and political cake, the ten *échelles* had been reduced to four *rangs* with the town's most important officials—the four *consuls*—being chosen from the first two *rangs*, thus excluding from the real corridors of power the smaller

---

Société scientifique et littéraire d'Alais, 19 (1887). One is inclined to query the widely accepted belief that 'municipal revolutions' were 'more common in the north than in the south' of France, although Donald Sutherland is obviously right to stress that they tended to occur 'where local institutions were particularly oligarchic and had been reluctant to show themselves "patriotic"'. *France, 1789–1815*, 69.

[12] G. Lefebvre, *La Grande Peur de 1789* (Paris, 1932), 44.

[13] According to Crozade, workers were bribed—12 *Livres* for 'facturiers et cardeurs'— to vote the right way. *AN* 306AP 490, 11 Jan. 1789.

[14] 'No two towns had quite the same constitution, customs or privileges'. Doyle, *Origins of the French Revolution*, 62.

merchants, farmers, and artisans. After 1695, the four *consuls* were chosen, again in theory, by the Intendant; in practice, they were picked by the comte d'Alais from a list of sixteen candidates drawn up by a self-perpetuating élite of wealthy landowners, merchants, and *gens d'affaires*.[15] In 1766, authority had been vested even more securely in the hands of this élite when it was decided to nullify the residual powers of the fairly representative Conseil-général extraordinaire and reduce the number of members who could sit on the Conseil politique.

Despite—or perhaps because of—the narrow social base of the town's political élite, Alès fought hard to defend its municipal rights and privileges against the venal attacks of the Bourbon monarchy, as in 1777, for example, when municipalities were required to pay for the right to elect officials to a wide range of offices. It could be argued that this legislation was simply a *fait accompli*, reflecting the domination of a rich and powerful élite. It has to be remembered, however, that the comte d'Alais still exercised considerable authority over the choice of *consuls*, and that his influence, as well as that of the local clergy, had been increased by the royal legislation of 1787 which guaranteed important roles for the seigneur and the *curé* on municipal councils whilst recognizing the narrow social base of local government.[16] The *patriotes de 1788* claimed that their demand for an assembly of taxpayers to discuss the burning issues of the day was simply a reversal to the more democratic days when the Conseil politique extraordinaire would have been convoked automatically. In their *mémoire* to the Intendant dated 17 November 1788, the *patriotes* expressed their astonishment at the undemocratic response of the *aristocrate* municipality. At their meeting of 21 December, one of their leaders, someone who knew his Montesquieu, pointed out that 'It is enough to know that, in every country, men are the products of their political systems, and that we have the misfortune to live under the influence of the most vicious municipal constitution.' The fault, it was argued, lay in the corrupt method of choosing municipal repre-

---

[15] Bruyère, *Alès, capitale des Cévennes*, 353–4. The electoral procedures were both complicated and quaint. The election of candidates for consular office were originally drawn up by the *conseil-général extraordinaire*, which met at the end of each year to choose four electors, or *pommelaires*, so-called on account of the *pommeaux*, or leather balls, used for selecting the lucky quartet, which would then decide, in secret, the list of municipal officials for the coming year. This practice was stopped after the royal edict on local government of 1766. *Recherches historiques*, 515–20.

[16] Lemarchand, 'La Féodalité et la Révolution', 552.

sentatives as well as in the nefarious influence of 'prélats et seigneurs', a criticism of the royal legislation of 1787.[17]

The influence of seigneurs like the maréchal de Castries, who, as the comte d'Alais, had the final say over the nomination of *consuls*, was by no means theoretical, as Guy Lemarchand has noted.[18] According to one local historian, the *notaire* who acted as secretary at *patriote* meetings, and whose judicial post was in Castries's gift, was summarily dismissed.[19] The ways in which the maréchal exercised his powers at local level are explained in his private correspondence; they also emphasize the influence of *gens d'affaires* like Crozade. One of the signatories to motions passed at *patriote* meetings, Chambon, was denounced to Castries by Crozade with the words 'I am of the same opinion as your *officiers*, that it would not be in your interest to choose sieur Chambon to fill the post of fourth *consul*, since he will unquestionably favour the party which has publicly announced that it wishes to attack your rights on several important fronts.'[20] The capitulation of the *aristocrate* Conseil politique at the end of December marked a very important stage in securing wider representation of opinion throughout the Cévennes, something that was vital to the success of the 'bourgeois revolution'. In Alès, as in Nîmes and many other cities and towns in the south-east of France, it was not just a matter of the 'ins' and 'outs' of local politics; it signified the overthrow of a self-perpetuating oligarchy whose decisions were strongly influenced by the clergy and the nobility and which were often uncongenial to the commercial and manufacturing élite. It was of more than symbolic importance that at the meeting of the diocese of Alais held on 8 January, nobles, bourgeois, and artisans took their seats without any observation of social rank. The 'municipal revolution' had its social as well as its political significance.

'Democratization' of government remained one of the key issues dividing *patriotes* from *aristocrates* throughout the winter of 1788–9, the 'Dauphiné model' being the preferred option for the former. At the famous meeting held at Vizille on 21 July 1788, it had been agreed that 'deputies [to the Estates General] were also to be elected, rather than to sit as of right; they were to vote by head, rather than in their

[17] Goirand, 'Documents historiques sur Alais', 35.

[18] 'Le seigneur contrôle à peu près toujours, au moins indirectement, l'administration municipale.' Lemarchand, 'La Féodalité et la Révolution', 547.

[19] Bruyère, *Alès, capitale des Cévennes*, 390.

[20] *AN* 306AP 490, Crozade to Castries, 5 Dec. 1788.

separate orders of clergy, nobility, and third estate; and the third estate
was to have as many deputies as the clergy and nobility put together'.[21]
However, the political programme outlined by the *patriotes* of Alès was
not simply a pale imitation of the Dauphiné model; it was, in fact,
far more radical, and certainly far less inhibited in its attack on the
members, and the clientele, of the first two orders.[22] At that first
pioneering meeting held on 23 November in Alès, it had been agreed
that 'nulle personne ecclésiastique, ni noble, ne sera admise dans
aucune assemblée du Tiers Etat' and that the Third Estate, said to
represent, before the famous pamphlet prepared by the abbé Siéyès,
twenty-nine-thirtieths of the population, should not just demand parity
with the first two orders of the realm but a far greater stake in the
government of the country.

But what about the working class, or the *classes laborieuses* as they
were described by the *patriotes* of Alès? It is quite clear that, although
pride of place should be given to the educated and propertied class,
the lower orders should be allowed to participate in the political
process. In an analysis that Marx would have found interesting, one
speaker expressed the opinion that the bourgeoisie had more talent
in their little fingers than clerics and nobles combined. He went on
to argue that 'The social order having created class subdivisions within
the Third Estate, and having concentrated, in certain of these subdivisions, the greatest mass of education and knowledge in the fields
of ethics, politics, public law, jurisprudence, as well as taxation,
agriculture, commerce, craftsmanship, and manufacturing', then surely
it was right that the deputies to the Third Estate should be drawn
from 'ces sortes de classes'. What did all this mean in practice so far
as the poorest 'sorte de classe' was concerned? That, 'generally
speaking, all members of the lower classes (*les classes inférieures*), who
used to be represented by their *syndics de corps* or *chefs d'échelles*, should
be allowed to vote for electors. These electors would then choose
deputies who would be required to prove that they paid 85 *livres* in
taxes, of which 50 *livres* should have been levied on landed property.[23]
What was happening in Alès provides considerable support for the

[21] Doyle, *Origins of the French Revolution*, 142. At the meeting held on 21 Dec. 1789,
one of the leaders of the *patriote* party expressly asked for the 'Dauphiné constitution'
to be implemented in Languedoc. Bruyère, *Alès, capitale des Cévennes*, 390.
[22] The 'Dauphiné constitution' had, after all, been drawn up by bourgeois and nobility,
without even consulting the rural masses. Lefebvre, *La Grande Peur*, 43.
[23] Goirand, 'Documents historiques sur Alais', 26.

thesis advanced recently by Gail Bossenga which rejects the cruder versions of both the 'orthodox' and the 'revisionist' interpretations of the origins of the Revolution in favour of a conflict between local élites (often property-owners residing outside the town limits) who had been excluded from power and corporate bodies which were filled, as at Alès, by a self-perpetuating oligarchy. Whilst emphasizing the significance of the fiscal, juridical, and historical factors which were involved in the 'municipal revolution', Bossenga also points to the importance of socio-economic divisions.[24]

These fairly radical proposals reflected the wider socio-economic realities of the Alèsian region, a region inhabited by thousands of small property-owners, *fabricants*, merchants, textile workers with varying degrees of skills, as well as by farmers and farm workers. Proof of this relationship may be detected in the propositions which implicitly attacked the historic economic stranglehold exerted by the wealthy *négociants* of Nîmes, one of which demanded that Alès, not Nîmes, should be declared the *chef-lieu* of any new 'département'. It was pointed out that Alès was the focal point for all traffic travelling through the Cévennes; that the only bridge across the Rhône in this region was at Pont-Saint-Esprit, just 60 kilometres from Alès; that the town was the centre of the coal industry; and that its annual fair, second only to that held at Beaucaire, was the focal point for the silk industry throughout the south-east.[25] At one of the last meetings of the diocese of Uzès held on 9 June 1789, Alexis Trinquelaque, one of Pierre-François Tubeuf's leading critics during the previous decade, expressed his annoyance over the fact that the *cahier de doléance d'Alais* had not included a reference to the importance of the coal industry in the region.[26] Like many of his fellow officials, Trinquelaque believed that there was a strong economic case for the creation of a 'département des Cévennes', which would have included what is now the southern Ardèche (the former Bas-Vivarais) and the northern Gard (the former dioceses of Alès and Uzès). The idea had much to recommend it. On 30 September 1789, a special deputation from Alès was sent to petition appropriate members of the National Assembly.

---

[24] G. Bossenga, 'City and State: An Urban Perspective on the Origins of the French Revolution', in Baker (ed.), *The Political Culture of the Old Regime*, 115–40.

[25] In the words of the petition sent to the National Assembly, 'Alais, le rendez-vous naturel et général de toutes les Cévennes'. Goirand, 'Documents historiques sur Alais', 273.

[26] Bardon, *L'Exploitation du bassin houiller d'Alais*, 328.

However, on 4 March 1790, it was finally announced that Nîmes had won the coveted prize, which was not entirely surprising given that, for one thing, the city had four times the population of Alès. There can be little question, however, that the defeat of the bid by the town fathers of Alès was to have serious consequences. In 1791, the town lost its bishopric. The major programme of public works which had been launched in the 1780s to save the town from the periodic flooding of the river Gardon was abandoned, to be restarted only at the end of the Napoleonic Empire.[27] Here again, we see the relationship of politics to the economic history of the Alès region.

Before going on to analyse the social composition of *patriotes* and *aristocrates* we must highlight one other important issue which was debated at length in official and unofficial meetings during the winter of 1788–9—the attack on clerical and seigneurial power. The original *Délibération de Nîmes*, which had first prompted the *patriotes* to organize in Alès, referring to the composition of the Third Estate, had made it very plain that 'seigneurial judges, their *procureurs fiscaux*, tithe-farmers, and, in general, all those who might be dependent, directly or indirectly, upon the clergy or the nobility, will be excluded'. However, the mayor of Nîmes, baron Margueritites, bestriding, somewhat uneasily, the narrow world of commerce and landed gentility, had attempted to weaken this exclusion clause by recognizing, in the first place, 'the wish expressed by those who represent commercial interests, to elect their own deputies to the said assembly [of the *sénéchaussée de Nîmes*]', but then going on to point out that the pressure to exclude clerical and seigneurial representatives 'could be seen as going too far, particularly when they might be substantial property-owners who made a major contribution to public taxation'.[28] These were revealing comments, focusing our attention on the conflict within the minds of those Frenchmen who inhabited the disputed territory between 'nobles' and 'bourgeois', particularly those public officials and *gens d'affaires* like Margueritites, or like Alexis Trinquelaque or Cabane de Camont, who had nailed their careers to a clerical or seigneurial mast.

For the *patriote* leaders in Alès, 'les officiers seigneuriaux, voilà l'ennemi!' It was the refusal on the part of the Conseil politique to eject such officials from all proposed meetings of the Third Estate

---

[27] Bruyère, *Alès, capitale des Cévennes*, 399–40. See p. 395 for a detailed résumé of the *cahier du Tiers état d'Alais*.

[28] Goirand, 'Documents historiques sur Alais', 17–18.

that had fuelled their original protest.[29] At their meeting of 23 November 1788, *patriote* leaders launched a frontal attack, not just on seigneurial *officiers*, but upon the entire feudal system. One somewhat colourful speaker put it in historic terms: 'After the anarchy of the feudal period, out of the murky waters of ignorance and superstition, the blind and deplorable habit of servitude, the unity of legitimate power emerged and, with it, almost a century of enlightenment.' In other words French modern history begins with the death of Louis XIV! The speaker went on to demand not only that all clerics and nobles should be excluded from the Third Estate but that *bourgeois* who had bought *seigneuries* with judicial powers (*les seigneuries justiciers*)— a very important qualification—should also be excluded, given that the privileges associated with such possessions 'still weigh heavily upon the public liberties of their vassals'.[30] Much has been written about the 'fusion' of nobles and bourgeois into a single élite during the eighteenth century; in the Basses-Cévennes, at least, the principal actors in the revolutionary drama drew a clear distinction between bourgeois who had purchased a *seigneurie* and those who exercised the rights and privileges, particularly judicial, associated with the nobility.

Those bourgeois who had judicial seigneurial rights were particularly vulnerable in the cévenol region given the costly and chaotic system of justice which operated until the Revolution and the history of hatred for all kinds of judicial official which stretched, at least, from the rebellion of the comte du Roure in 1670 to that of the *masques armés* in 1783. In the Alès region, half of *la justice territoriale* belonged to the comte d'Alais, the other half to the vicomte d'Alais. The former exercised his 'jurisdiction over the town as well as over a number of *justiciers*, his vassals'. Castries, wearing his cap as the comte d'Alais, could not only appoint judges to the local court of appeal (*cour d'appeaux comtal*) as well as twelve *procureurs*, but, as we have seen, he could also make the final decision concerning the choice of the four *consuls* who dominated the municipality. He could also preside over the meetings of the Conseil politique. No wonder that in towns like Alès—and there were many in France—'municipal power was perpetuated in the hands of families and the relations of seigneurial *officiers*, whether judges or *procureurs*'.[31]

[29] Bardon, *L'Exploitation du bassin houiller d'Alais*, 323.
[30] Goirand, 'Documents historiques sur Alais', 26.
[31] Ibid. 109–110.

A superficial analysis of the 'Pre-Revolution' in Alès might well depict *patriotes* and *aristocrates* as the 'ins' and 'outs' of municipal politics. Digging a little deeper, however, we find that it was far more than a thirst for local democracy which separated the two factions. Lynn Hunt is surely right to insist that 'The revolutionary political class can be termed "bourgeois" both in terms of social position and of class consciousness . . . in so far as it was distinctly anti-feudal, anti-aristocratic, and anti-absolutist.' It is more difficult to accept the conclusion that 'Revolutionary intention and meaning therefore cannot be deduced from the social composition of the new political class.'[32] Certainly, some meaning can be deduced from an analysis of the social composition and business histories of *patriotes* and *aristocrates* in the Alès region.

Before the 'November uprising' of 1788, the Conseil politique in Alès had been dominated by leading local families such as the Firmas-Périès and the Dhombres, successively first *consuls* and, therefore, mayors, the former in office at the time of the Revolution, and many *conseillers* who owed their positions, at least in part, to the maréchal de Castries. Men like Deslebres, *juge du comté d'Alais*, Cabane de Camont, *juge du cour d'appeaux de la ville et comté d'Alais*, Pierre Crozade, *notaire* and Castries's steward for the *comté d'Alais et la terre de Trouilhas*. Those who were persuaded to support the *aristocrate* cause were not men of great wealth, but it is clear from the tax-rolls for 1789 that they could mix fairly unself-consciously with the cream of Alèsian society. The tax-rolls emphasize one of the constant features of society throughout the Cévennes—the modest economic position of its élite. Whereas a great noble like Castries was by far the highest taxpayer at 500 *livres*, nobles of the two oldest and most respected local families, the vicomte d'Alais-Montalet and the marquis de La Fare-Alais, are listed as paying just 110 and 43 *livres* respectively, both employing five servants.[33] The leader of the *aristocrate* faction on the council, Cabane de Camont, was

---

[32] Hunt, *Politics, Culture and Class*, 178–9.

[33] Jacques-Alexis de La Fare had been first *consul* of Alès from 1776 to 1779. Described by Crozade as 'un bailli de Castries', the marquis de La Fare was to represent Castries in the meetings of the second order of the Estates-General in Nîmes in Mar. 1789. He married the daughter of the marquis d'Anduze. *AN* 306AP 487, Crozade to Castries, 24 Sept. 1786. The baron de Latour, a branch of the de La Fare family, paid 96 *livres*. Deslebres, employing one cook and one servant, paid 24 *livres* 15 *sols*. Pierre Crozade was clearly of more modest means, with one servant, and paying just 13 *livres* tax. *AG* C1846, *rôle de répartition de la capitation des vigueries d'Alais et d'Anduze*.

taxed at 58 *livres*. With four servants to his household, he could clearly regard himself as a member of the Alèsian élite. In addition to acting as appeal court judge for the *comté d'Alais* for over thirty years, de Camont had served as mayor of Alès in 1769 and was the *syndic du diocèse d'Alais* from 1773 to the Revolution. In 1804, he would be one of the twenty-four highest taxpayers in the town.[34] From the time of his bitter opposition to Tubeuf in the 1780s to his role in the Counter-Revolution a decade later, de Camont was to remain a loyal servant of the maréchal de Castries.

Louis Deslebres was even wealthier and stood even higher in the list of municipal dignitaries, whilst the Firmas-Périès and the Dhombres had dominated the civic life of the town for generations before the Revolution and were to do so for several generations after it.[35] Jacques-Louis Dhombres, seigneur de Saint-Paul-Lacoste, had bought the office of mayor in 1772 for the not inconsiderable sum of 36,000 *livres*.[36] As *sub-délégué de la province de Languedoc*, a *receveur des tailles*, and *procureur-fiscal du comté d'Alais* from 1783 to 1789, we are obviously dealing with one of the most influential of provincial officials, someone strategically placed to arbitrate between central and local government, which was indeed the role he played so well. His son Louis-Augustin Dhombres was to become a baron during the Napoleonic Empire, mayor of Alès in 1823, and, subsequently, a major shareholder in mining and railway companies. Interesting that the Dhombres never supported the *aristocrate* cause unreservedly, his key administrative duties making him a *politique* rather than an *aristocrate*.[37] A Firmas-Périès had been *premier-consul* in Alès as early as 1675; Jean-Louis de Firmas-Périès, born in 1750, was to be mayor of Nîmes throughout the turbulent period 1789–92. Like the Dhombres, to whom they were closely related by marriage, the Firmas-Périès family was to remain one of the most respected in Languedoc until the present day. Although Jean-Louis's brother was to be one of the leading royalists in Alès during the early 1790s, the mayor himself managed, like the Dhombres, to avoid too close an identification with

[34] Bruyère, *Alès, capitale des Cévennes*, 408 and 481.

[35] The Dhombres and Firmas-Périès families have maintained their leading positions in the social and economic life of the region to the present day. I am happy to take his opportunity of thanking M. Pierre Firmas-Périès for his most generous assistance in providing me with documents relating to the history of a branch of his family.

[36] Bardon, *L'Exploitation du bassin houiller d'Alais*, 134.

[37] R. Huard, *Les Mouvements républicains en Bas-Languedoc* (Paris, 1982), 38.

either camp.[38] Given the bloody and confused history of the Alès region, if families like the Dhombres and the Firmas-Périès had not existed it would have been necessary to have invented them. They were the 'honest brokers' between warring factions. Dhombres's role in the crisis of November 1788 is instructive. When asked what the municipal council should do about the *patriote* demand for an extra-ordinary meeting, he replied that 'he would leave the matter to the wisdom of the council'![39]

The *patriote* camp was certainly not without its relatively wealthy supporters: the Guiraudet-Laliquières and the Rocheblaves were certainly wealthier than the second rank of *aristocrates* like the Camonts.[40] Jean-Baptiste Guiraudet had been first *consul* in Alais from 1783 to 1786, but it was his Protestant relative Pierre-Marc Guiraudet-Laliquière who was to become president of the *patriote* meeting held in Alès on 23 November 1788, and who, on the last day of that momentous year, penned a letter to the Bishop of Alès attacking the unrepresentative nature of the Estates of Languedoc.[41] His son Jean-Louis Guiraudet was to become mayor of Alès in 1813. Pierre-Marc was a 'seigneur', having purchased the *seigneurie de Laliquière* as well as a half-share in the *seigneurie de Larnac*. On the face of it nothing much to distinguish him from the La Fares or the de Camonts. There are, however, very important distinctions to be made. To begin with both Louis Rocheblave and Pierre-Marc Guiraudet-Laliquière were Protestants. Also, unlike the La Fares, the latter was a 'seigneur de fraiche date', hence excluded from the Second Estate. Is this one of the reasons why, in his letter to the Bishop of Alès, he criticized the social stratification of the Estates of Languedoc, supporting instead the 'democratic' model provided by the Estates of Dauphiné? Even more important, Rocheblave and Guiraudet-Laliquière derived the major part of their income from commerce and the silk industry. By supporting the attack on *juges des seigneurs*, such men were seeking to undermine the power and influence of Catholic *officiers* like de Camont

---

[38] Bruyère, *Alès, capitale des Cévennes*, 409. See also *AG* 58J 25–33.

[39] Goirand, 'Documents historiques sur Alais', 48.

[40] Rocheblave *veuve marchand* and Paul Rocheblave together paid 75 *livres* 15 *sols capitation* in 1789. Louis Rocheblave, *marchand de soie*, paid 17 *livres*. Pierre-Marc Guiraudet Laliquière, who supported the *patriotes*, paid 96 *livres*. The Catholic branch of the family, Maximilien Guiraudet, *secrétaire du roi*, was amongst the 10 highest tax-payers in the Alès region, paying 150 *livres*. *AG* C1846, *rôle de repartition*.

[41] Goirand, 'Documents historique sur Alais', 44.

over the region's administrative affairs, and this involved a frontal attack on the maréchal de Castries.

There can be absolutely no doubt that the *patriote* campaign won the overwhelming support of the commercial and manufacturing élite of the region, the great majority being of the Protestant faith. This can be verified by examining the lists of those who voted for the *Délibération du Tiers état de la ville d'Alais* on 23 November 1788, the actual *patriote* manifesto. Of the 155 signatories whose profession can be ascertained, there were no fewer than 41 *négociants*, 13 *fabricants*, 8 *marchands* (*droguistes* etc.), 6 *marchands-tanneurs*, 6 *marchands de soie*, 4 *teinturiers*, 4 *chapeliers*—in other words over half of the signatories represented the commercial and manufacturing life of the region. Only 9 described themselves as *bourgeois*, 5 as *avocats*, and just three were listed as *propriétaires-fonciers* or *ménagers*. The remainder of the list reflected the complete spectrum of the craft and trading life of the town: 5 *perruquiers*, 4 *orfèvres*, 3 *horlogers*, 3 *passementiers*, 2 *menuisiers*, 2 *tailleurs*, 2 *boulangers*, 2 *serruriers*, 1 *molinier de soie*, 1 *maçon*, 1 *charpentier*, etc.[42] In the main, the *patriotes* represented commerce and industry; the *aristocrates*, the nobility together with the legal and landed bourgeoisie, although this élite was supported by agricultural workers and many skilled textile workers who had been adversely affected by the economic recession of the 1780s. It is significant that amongst the *patriotes* who attended the 23 November meeting there was only one *jardinier* and no *travailleur de terre*. Even more significant was the fact that François Froment, destined to become the leader of the counter-revolution in Languedoc, was the son of a disgraced municipal official in Nîmes, a supporter of the landed and legal bourgeoisie, together with the smaller Catholic *fabricants* and unemployed textile workers, a bitter enemy of the rich Protestant *négociants* and *gens d'affaires*.[43]

A brief acquaintance with the personal histories of two of the three leading figures in the *patriote* movement of 1788-9—Jean-François Soustelle and Jacques-André Sugier, Pierre-Marc Guiraudet-Laliquière being the third—will not only confirm the importance of commercial and industrial interests, it will also emphasize the relationship between the politics of the 'Pre-Revolution' and the problems of a society confronted with economic recession and the advent of industrial capitalism. We shall see how Castries's victory over Tubeuf, and his

---

[42] A complete list of signatories is one of the more precious documents unearthed by Goirand, ibid. 29–31.

[43] See Sonenscher, 'Royalists and Patriots', 54–71.

related policy of substantially increasing his own revenues from the coal-mines of the Alès basin, alienated many of his former, if fair-weather, supporters, some of whom had originally been active in the assault on 'l'Étranger' Tubeuf. The key figures in the drive to reconcile Castries's wish to maximize the increasing profits to be derived from coal-mining with the determination of his own 'vassals' to retain local control of the industry were the seigneurial judges like Cabane de Camont and, even more directly involved, stewards like Pierre Crozade in Alès and Roussel in Uzès. As the 1780s progressed, it became manifestly obvious that such men had scant regard for the smaller property-owners and coal-miners of the Grand-Combe, Meyrannes, or Portes. They may well have been useful in the initial struggles against Tubeuf, but their interests were soon relegated to second place when it became a question of defending their own interests as *gens d'affaires* against the encroachment of 'monopoly capitalism'.

To understand why Soustelle and Sugier should have assumed the direction of the *patriote* movement, the former eventually being chosen as a deputy from the Gard to the Constituent Assembly, we need to remind ourselves of the traditional attitude towards coal-mines—that they had to be 'farmed out' like any other piece of real estate. For the professional bourgeois, trained in the law, there were rich pickings to be gleaned out of farming seigneurial property and, as was originally the case with Soustelle and Sugier, from administering (in their own interests!) coal-mines belonging to the Contys and the Castries. We also need to realize that the logic of running coal-mines profitably imposed some kind of monopoly of production on whoever worked the mines. The difference between the *fermiers* whose families had traditionally exploited the coal-seams of the *comté d'Alais* and Tubeuf was, in fact, the difference between a monopoly designed to supply a local market and one aimed at international, certainly national, horizons. So far as the protoindustrial population of the Cévennes was concerned, particularly as the economic recession of the post-1778 period began to bite, it was the scale, and ultimate objectives, of Tubeuf's plans which prompted them to rebellion. Setting aside 400,000 *quintaux* a year for a generation to a 'foreign' coking company evoked the same shudder of apprehension as if 400,000 *quintaux* of grain were to be earmarked for shipment to Parisian markets. For the traditional *fermier* (or rather *sous-fermier*, since the mines were usually leased by farmers who had themselves leased land from the big landowner), however, 'monopolies' were fine so long as they involved increased profits and served the local forge-master, silk-spinner, or distiller.

It was also a question of production levels. It was Louis Alles, agent of the Richard and Carrouge company, who had first encouraged the traditional *fermiers des mines de la Grand-Combe* to buy up all the leases belonging to the small individual coal-owner in the *comté d'Alais* and the *vicomté de Portes*.[44] The *fermiers*, led by the implacable François Faure, who organized the vicious attack on Tubeuf in May 1784, did not, in fact, require much persuasion.[45] The key to success so far as coal production in the Alès region was concerned had always lain in the prevention of competition between the mines of Portes, the Grand-Combe, Abilon, and Rochebelle. Following years of legal wrangle, Faure and his associates had finally signed an agreement with the *fermiers du comté d'Alais* in December 1777, by which Faure agreed to supply their customers with coal at favourable prices if they agreed to close down the mines under their control. Faure and his friends were now in effective control of all coal-mining in the Grand-Combe valley. This 'monopolization' of production obviously increased demand but, given the cost of buying out individual leases, plus the fact that, unlike Tubeuf, Faure and his miners simply did not have the technical skills or capital to satisfy the increasing demand of the 1780s, things began to go from bad to worse. Alles depicted the plight of the traditional coal *fermier*: 'They screech like eagles; they fight amongst themselves. The ruin of the majority of them is unavoidable unless they sell out their leases.' Their only, temporary, salvation was that they were supported by the local community. Again according to Alles, the Estates of Languedoc were being hoodwinked by giving Faure grants, since the coal-mines were being ruined, but 'no one lifts a finger against these *fermiers*, because the locals are all on their side'.[46]

---

[44] B. de N. 496, Alles to Richard, 25 Oct. 1779.

[45] François Faure was the brother-in-law of Jean Larguillier, the seigneur de Trouilhas's principle *fermier*. The former was described (in his usual poor French) by Louis Alles thus: 'Un homme de plus fourbes qu'on ait jamais connu et d'un caractère très dangereux. Cet homme, dans la misère qu'il s'est meritée par son inconduite, appuyé cependant par tout ce qu'il y a de mieux à Alais, sacrifie ses associés et jous tout sort des rôles pour s'attirer la bienveillance du marquis de Castries.' B. de N. 496, Alles to Richard, 13 Mar. 1780.

[46] Ibid. Alles explained that before they produced a *quintal* of coal the *fermiers de la Grand-Combe* had to pay 6,000 *livres* to the *fermiers* of the nearby Abilon mine as compensation for ceasing production, 6,000 *livres* for the lease of the mining rights to the coal-mines of the *comté d'Alais*, and 1,500 *livres* for the rights to the lease of the Grand-Combe itself. B. de N. 496, Alles to Richard, 25 Oct. 1779. No wonder that if

The arrival of Tubeuf had compounded all their problems; hence the decision to seek the support of the maréchal de Castries. He, it was fondly imagined, would not only have the social and political clout to see the Norman entrepreneur off, but he might inject some of his own capital without interesting himself too directly in what went on down the pits. The maréchal's purchase of the *comté d'Alais et la terre de Trouilhas* fitted the bill admirably: it kept the Grand-Combe (formerly Trouilhas) out of Tubeuf's greedy hands and it solved the vexed issue of competition between the Grand-Combe and the nearby mine of Abilon. If only Castries would be satisfied with the traditional seigneur's role as protector of his vassals from outsiders like Tubeuf then Faure and his miners could happily continue to mine in the age-old fashion, thus destroying some of the best coal reserves in France. No wonder the Intendant and the more far-sighted minister like Bertin became increasingly worried about the loss of the nation's coal reserves—not that there was a 'nation' in the 1780s of course, which was precisely the problem. Which was more important, seigneurial privilege or national interest? The *ancien régime* fell, in part, because it could not provide an unequivocal reply to this question.

Unfortunately for François Faure, however, Castries, encouraged by his friend the duc de Croy, *was* interested in what went on down the Grand-Combe. Under the cloak of fulfilling his traditional role as protector of his vassals he might also fill his breeches with the profits to be made out of mining coal professionally, particularly now that Tubeuf had shown everyone the way to do it. By 1 January 1782, Castries had taken a one-eighth share in the Société des fermiers de la Grand-Combe which had recently been formed by Faure and whose financial manager was none other than the *patriote* leader of 1788, Jacques-André Sugier. On 25 April 1782, Castries placed the control of all his mining interests in Sugier's hands by appointing him *procureur-fiscal du comté d'Alais.*[47] Convinced that Castries would be far too busy as Minister of the Navy to worry his aristocratic head about coal-mines, Sugier allowed Faure to swindle not only the maréchal,

---

any individual dared to work a mine in the region 'les fermiers se déchaînent comme des furieux'. B. de N., Alles to Richard, 13 Mar. 1780.

[47] It was agreed that dividends would be paid every three months and that Sugier's fee should be one-quarter of the price of the annual lease of the mines. A loan of 5,400 *livres* from the shareholders would be repaid according to the proportion of shares each one held. *AN* 306AP 482, *mémoire pour M. le maréchal de Castries contre J. Sugier, avocat.* See also Castries, *Papiers de famille*, 304.

but his fellow associates.[48] Dividends were never forthcoming; share-holders took money out, leaving IOUs in the desk drawer; 'bookkeeping' was reduced to farcical proportions, with the overall result that by the beginning of 1783 half of the shareholders sold out to Castries, who now owned five-eighths of all the shares, 'ce qui le rendit maître de la situation'.[49] Faure wisely decided to resign: Sugier was dismissed.

It was at this time that Castries decided to place Pierre Crozade, a *notaire* in Alès, in overall charge of his financial affairs so far as the *comté d'Alais* and the *terre de Trouilhas* were concerned. The region's financial wizard, Louis Dhombres, was called in to sort out the immediate chaos, ultimately discovering that instead of the 6,329 *livres* which Sugier claimed Castries was owed, the sum was in fact 19,381 *livres*![50] Sugier was taken to court for the recovery of the money and Castries had made a mortal enemy in the Alès region, someone who would exact his revenge in 1788. The Sugier affair was not so much bound up with a conscious desire to swindle great nobles, it was more a reflection of the *ad hoc* manner in which the coal-mines in the region had been managed. When he was asked for his books, for example, François Faure replied that 'we are not in habit of keeping records; we have always used single sheets of paper'![51]

Sugier's close friend and fellow conspirator in 1788 was Jean-François Soustelle, son of Jean-Jacques Soustelle, *lieutenant de juge du vicomté de Portes* and seigneur of Saint-Cécile-d'Andorge, which was situated at the head of the Grand-Combe valley. The mines in the *vicomté de Portes*, like all the mines in the Alès coalfield, had traditionally been farmed out every nine years to property-owners and silk manufacturers like the Soustelles.[52] Ever since the 1740s and the take-off in the raw-silk industry, the Soustelles had been eager to benefit from subleasing mines. In 1782, at the height of the coal-fever in Alès, Soustelle *père* wrote to Joly de Fleury to request permission to open a second mine on their property, authority to work the first having

---

[48] The duc de Castries writes that 'Cette affaire était très révélatrice d'une mentalité fort commune en Languedoc, qui est de penser que les gens de la société sont inaptes aux affaires'. *Papiers de famille*, 305.

[49] When Faure was originally asked for his books he produced a *Journal de la recette* in which only one and a half pages had been filled in since 1780! *AN* 306AP 482, *mémoire pour M. le maréchal*.

[50] Castries, *Papiers de famille*, 304.

[51] *AN* 306AP 482, *mémoire pour le maréchal de Castries*.

[52] Galy, 'L'Exploitation des houillères en Languedoc', 180.

been obtained as early as 1745.[53] The request was challenged by Tubeuf on the grounds that the mines on the Soustelle estates fell within the boundary of his concession.[54] Three years later, Jean-François Soustelle, who had followed his father as an *officier* of the prince de Conty, was dismissed from his office by Monsieur the king's brother, who had recently purchased the mines of the Portes region from the Contys. Like his friend Sugier, Jean-François Soustelle regarded himself as the victim of outside entrepreneurs and great nobles alike, all intent upon undermining the power of local coalowners and manufacturers. At the meeting of the Third Estate in Alès at the beginning of March 1789, two men marched into the hall, each with his own version of the local *cahier*; one was Cabane de Camont, intent upon preserving what he could of the rights and privileges of his patron Castries as well as those of the Estates of Languedoc; the other was Jean-François Soustelle, his version a broadside against the Estates, the composition of the diocese of Alès, and the rights of certain seigneurs to name the town's *consuls* and seigneurial judges.[55]

Both de Camont and Soustelle were 'lawyers', a fact of little importance. What really mattered is the experience of the two men and their relatives and friends during the turbulent years of the 1780s. The former had benefited from the incursion of great seigneurs in the lives of the Alèsians, the latter had not. At the beginning of 1785—by which time he had seized almost all the shares in the *société des fermiers de la Grand-Combe*—Castries sent a mining expert named Prévost to report on the potential of the Grand-Combe. At roughly the same time, Monsieur was being briefed on the *mines de Portes* by his own expert, Faujas de Saint-Fonds. Prévost's report was severely critical of the destruction wrought by Faure and his men,[56] but he

---

[53] *AN* F14 7682, Jean-François Soustelle to Joly de Fleury, 15 June 1782. A second mine had been opened in 1767 but not worked for long according to Soustelle. Jean-Jacques Soustelle had sought permission to work coal-mines on his *seigneurie* as early as 1745, having rented them out to the *fermiers de son Altesse royale, M. le prince de Conty*. The Soustelles were also involved in a *société* for the exploitation of coal in the Alès region in 1767. Bardon, *L'Exploitation du bassin houiller d'Alais*, 53–61.

[54] *AG* 58J 4, Tubeuf to Joly de Fleury, 29 June 1782. Tubeuf visited Sainte-Cécile and failed to find any trace of a mine. Clearly the Soustelles were anxious to pre-empt any move by Tubeuf—or Castries—to seize coal-mines worked only sporadically by *fermiers* since the 1740s.

[55] *AN* 306AP 490, Crozade to Castries, 9 Mar. 1789.

[56] This is confirmed by another report compiled the following year which describes how Faure had made several openings half-way up the Grand-Combe mountain, pushed a few score feet inside, then, when the mine filled up with water, withdrew, pulling

went on to explain that, mined efficiently, the Grand-Combe could make the maréchal even richer than he already was, concluding with the statement that he 'had never seen such rich reserves of coal which would not be exhausted for several centuries'.[57] Prévost was right, and the maréchal was convinced. He told Prévost to stay in overall charge, recruited Tubeuf's German ex-*maître-mineur*, Gantzler, to undertake the skilled mining, and appointed Crozade as financial director.[58] By the middle of the following year, two new levels had been reopened in the Grand-Combe mine and the first real *galerie d'écoulement* blasted out of the rock to drain the water from the old workings. Production quadrupled, and with Gantzler employing all the skills he had learned with Tubeuf, a few hesistant steps in the modernization of the medieval Grand-Combe mine had begun.

Although, during the late 1780s, the maréchal de Castries and Monsieur were being drawn more deeply into 'industrial capitalism', the differences between their involvement and that of a bourgeois entrepreneur like Pierre-François Tubeuf were striking and significant. For one thing, the former were obliged to operate at several removes from the pit-head. What went on in the Grand-Combe or Portes was filtered through stewards and secretaries in Alès and Versailles, which made it extremely difficult for Castries to know exactly what was going on, and even if he did the technical or management side of it would have made very little sense to him. Given this understandable ignorance, the role of his agents and stewards in the Cévennes was obviously crucial. The tragedy was that they were often no better equipped to oversee the transition from medieval to modern mining than their masters;[59] their primary concern was with balancing the books as well as serving the interests of the local élites. The outcome was, unlike that which occurred at Rochebelle where the excellent partnership of Tubeuf and Renaux was laying the foundations of the nineteenth-century coal industry in the Cévennes, that most of the maréchal's

down the blocks of coal supporting the roof (*piliers*) as he went, 'thus destroying the mine'. *AN* 306AP 487, 14 May 1786.

[57] *AN* 306AP 486, 4 July 1785.

[58] Gantzler was given 840 *livres* a year and, since the *château de Trouilhas* was too far away for his lodgings, a new house was to be built nearer the mine. *AN* 306AP 485, 8 Feb. 1785.

[59] When Castries introduced his 'New Deal' for the Grand-Combe in 1785, Crozade accepted that Faure had not done too good a job but then admitted that 'Je suis peu au fait de ces sortes d'exploitations.' *AN* 306AP, 2 Jan. 1785.

half-hearted initiatives in the direction of modernization foundered on the rock of local ignorance and popular resistance, reflected, more often than not, in the opinions of his steward Crozade.

From the beginning of Castries's 'New Deal' in 1785, Crozade had made it abundantly clear that he was not in favour of any radical change in the way the coal-mines were being operated. Indeed, in November he was pressing Castries to lease out the mines for a fixed annual sum (*bailler l'extraction à forfait*), a much better way of making a profit in his humble opinion. Prévost, in the meantime, had been pushing for direct control (*une régie*), which prompted Crozade to press for his dismissal. In a way, Prévost, like Tubeuf, was also an outsider. The quarrel between the two men was temporarily resolved by a curt admonishment to Crozade from Castries's secretary at Court: 'When a seigneur has made a firm decision, one must know when to give in.'[60] Wisely, on this occasion at least, Crozade took the hint.

The rearguard action went on, however. The following year, another of Castries's advisers suggested that the maréchal should launch a real industrial venture by setting up a blast furnace near the Grand-Combe. Crozade's reply to this radical suggestion, which would really have drawn Castries in the direction of a modern industrial plant, was extremely revealing, founded as it was upon the traditional *négociant* mentality which Tubeuf had challenged. Crozade began his letter by suggesting that the maréchal was being given very bad advice:

Large undertakings like this are only suitable for individuals who can manage them directly, and who can devote their energies to finding the appropriate outlets for the goods produced. We are talking about real manufacturing concerns (*entreprises de manufacture*), which rarely succeed in the hands of a *grand seigneur* like yourself. These kinds of venture must always, and necessarily, be infinitely more costly and less lucrative than they would be for ordinary individuals (*simples particuliers*).

Can any statement be more revealing of the structural and mental gap which divided 'real' nobles from 'capitalist' bourgeois in the eighteenth century? Crozade, continuing to reflect his thoughts through the prism of a protoindustrial society founded upon textiles and viticulture, asked why Castries should bother with such risky undertakings anyway. Coal consumption and, therefore, profits were rising. Surely the maréchal would not want to be involved in something which might degenerate into 'une véritable entreprise de commerce'? Far better to

---

[60] *AN* 306AP 486, 17 Nov. 1785.

risk 50 or 100 *livres* to transport coal a few kilometres than to 'run the risk of failure, having disbursed fifty or sixty thousand *livres* on the construction of a blast furnace (*haut fourneau*) and its workshops'.[61] Again, could we find a greater contrast to the massive injection of capital by Tubeuf? The fear of 'venture capital', the even greater fear of *dérogeance*, everything was exploited by Castries's steward to keep the maréchal within the context of an *ancien régime* society and an *ancien régime* system of production. And this was by no means the only example of resistance to change on Crozade's part. When a mining engineer named Dietrich was sent to the Grand-Combe to check on Crozade's conclusion that the opening of a new level and the intro- duction of new machinery was unacceptable on grounds of cost, he reported that, like Rochebelle, which he had visited, the Grand-Combe should be 'modernized' (*exploiter en grand*), and that Castries should not worry too much about the costs at this stage 'because you will soon see a return on your investment'.[62]

It was obvious, given Tubeuf's example, that change was necessary, but, as a result of the lack of a skilled work-force, the rearguard resistance of his steward, creatures as they were of the community they both served and exploited, as well as the maréchal's reluctance to part with the huge sums involved in modern coal-mining, only partial and temporary improvements could be made. The French nobility in the eighteenth century were indeed involved in the growth of industrial capitalism, but they were even more deeply involved in the traditional fiscal and social relationship with their vassals, their *censitaires et fermiers*. *Gens d'affaires* like Crozade were the professionals who had vested interest in the perpetuation of this social system. The consequence for the mines of the Grand-Combe valley was disastrous. In July 1786, the richest and most easily worked seam in the Grand- Combe, that which Faure and his men had pillaged in the early 1780s, collapsed when miners pulled down some of the pillars of coal which were used to prop up the roof. According to Crozade, this 'error' had only occurred because the *maître-mineur* had not been present, but this was the traditional method of mining in the Cévennes, ripping out the pillars as you retreated from a particular 'stall'.[63]

---

[61] *AN* 306AP 487, 25 June 1786.
[62] *AN* 306AP 487, 27 Dec. 1786.
[63] Later on in the year Crozade was told by Soleiret, Faure's old *maître-mineur*, that he had plans to open another mine further along the mountain! *AN* 306AP 487, 22 Nov. 1786.

The last real attempt to introduce a 'managerial revolution' failed when negotiations to attract Tubeuf's brilliant, and loyal, mine director, Renaux, to the Grand-Combe fell through. Again, Crozade's role was crucial. Recommended to Castries as a 'genius' by the marquis de La Fare, Crozade told the maréchal that in his opinion Renaux was far too young and inexperienced for the job![64] Renaux's replacement, Adam Forster—another German miner who had worked for Tubeuf—did make some improvements, reopening a new seam and draining some of the workings, but the dreadful weather of the late 1780s, together with the political and economic crisis, meant that Forster was struggling against the odds.

It was almost inevitable, however, that, even if Forster had been more successful in expanding production in the Grand-Combe, Castries would increasingly have been confronted with the same kind of local resistance which had helped to ruin Tubeuf's plans. Clear evidence of this may be found in the history of the mines of the *vicomté de Portes*, where Monsieur, through his steward, Roussel, also *sub-délégué du diocèse d'Uzès*, was in fact pushing a little harder for meaningful change. Roussel was anxious to ingratiate himself with the king's brother by closing down 'uneconomic pits', just as Tubeuf had done, and therefore provoking a reaction which threatened to become another *masques armés* revolt. In one of his more purple passages, the historian Achille Bardon could scarcely contain his anger:

Roussel was truly unbelievable. He was blind to the trouble which was spreading throughout the country; he failed to hear the winds of revolt which were blowing so strongly throughout France; he sought to increase the number of disgruntled people, the poor workers, the small property-owners in the hills. His only aim was to please *les Grands*, Monsieur, the Court. The idiot![65]

It seems that this linkage between early industrialization, economic recession, political upheaval, and social rebellion was indeed very much in the minds of officials in the Cévennes. For Louis Dhombres and Pierre Crozade it was a factor in the complicated equation between profit and social stability. On the eve of the Revolution, following Castries's unjust victory over Tubeuf at Court, the maréchal was considering the possibility of taking the fight into Tubeuf's

[64] *AN* 306AP 487, 24 Sept. 1786. In December, Crozade expressed his preference for Forster and Soleiret as joint *maître-mineurs*, a disastrous decision, given Forster's inability to speak good French (let alone the local *patois!*) and the contempt with which he was treated by Soleiret and his Alèsian friends.

[65] Bardon, *L'Exploitation du bassin houiller d'Alais*, 322.

backyard by trying to gain control over some of the mines in the Rochebelle area. On this occasion again, Crozade advised caution; if the maréchal did move into this region then

It would be necessary to lease the mines out *en société*. Those who take up the leases would assume the responsibility for all production costs and you would receive so much a *quintal* for the coal which is sold. If you adopt this approach, you will be certain of making a profit. If, on the other hand, you assume direct control over the mines then you will lose this possibility, because production costs will eat up all the profit.[66]

It was still the same old story—No direct control *à la Tubeuf*, no major, costly investment; lease out the mines in the traditional way to the small property-owners and mine-owners of the region, many of whom, after all, were Crozade's friends and clients. For Castries and the property-owners and lawyers of the lower Cévennes, it had to be a traditional partnership, with profits shared between the maréchal and the local *propriétaires*.

Further proof that agents like Crozade were worried about the social and political consequences of pushing too far in the direction of real change comes in a long letter which Crozade wrote to Castries's secretary, Dufraisse, at Versailles, who had asked Crozade if the maréchal's coal-mines could possibly produce around 500,000–600,000 *quintaux* a year to satisfy important new customers from Arles. Shades of Tubeuf's contract with Richard, Carrouge et Cie began to fall over Crozade's desk. He explained that such a level of production was way beyond the capacity of Castries's mines; that the method of transport by carts prevented coal being mined throughout the year; and—the crucial issue for Crozade—even if the figure could be achieved it would undoubtedly provoke 'un murmure général' amongst the local population.[67] It seems that Castries, having invested reasonable, if insufficient, sums in his mines since 1785, was now expecting greater profits, profits which he now began to realize were not forthcoming, given the resistance of local agents, property-owners, and workers.[68]

---

[66] *AN* 306AP 490, 6 Mar. 1789. Crozade added that he had talked to the maréchal's son during a recent visit to Montpellier and that he was in full agreement.

[67] *AN* 306AP 488, to Dufraisse, 6 Mar. 1787.

[68] See Crozade's reply in July 1790 explaining why expenses had been higher than income for the last quarter of 1789 and for every month, so far, in 1790. The blame was placed on the cost of recent improvements and the fact that the deeper the miners dug into the mountain, the fewer the loads (*faix*) they were able to bring to the surface. *AN* 306AP 488, 25 July 1790.

The pressure which Castries's secretaries in Versailles and in Montpellier were exerting upon Crozade forms part of the 'seigneurial reaction' whose existence revisionist historians still contest despite the strong evidence provided by historians like Peter Jones.[69] What is not always clear is the precise nature of this reaction, particularly the relationship between its constituent parts. Before endeavouring to illuminate this matter, it is important to recall that we are dealing with a protoindustrial not a purely agricultural region of France. As Castries's lawyers reminded the maréchal in 1781: 'If one travels through this vast stretch of land granted as a concession to sieur Tubeuf, one sees an open countryside peopled with an immense number of workers. All one sees are workshops, warehouses, and buildings of every conceivable kind.' They were most impressed with the coalmines 'which are beginning to produce *en grand* and which impress one with the regularity of their operations, the solidity of the workings themselves, and the great number of miners who are employed in them'.[70]

In the Alès region, as in many other regions of France, the seigneurial reaction involved not only the increased exaction of 'feudal' dues but the exploitation of the seigneur's political and judicial powers to increase revenues from other sources. Mougel's study of the management of the Conty estates will highlight the main issues. The estates of François-Louis de Conty in the south-east were second in importance to the prince's land in the Vexin français; more significantly for us, they originally included the lion's share of Tubeuf's coal concession covering the *vicomté de Portes* and the *comté d'Alais*. As we have seen, the latter estate was sold to Castries in 1777 whilst the former went to the king's brother in 1783. The management of the Conty estates had established the pattern for seigneurial estates in Alès region. It involved (1) an increasing emphasis on the farming out of land and the collection of tolls and dues on short (six- to nine-year) leases, an obvious disincentive to long-term industrial development;[71]

---

[69] P. Jones, *Politics and Rural Society*, 160.

[70] *AG* C194, *observations pour M. le syndic-général des États du Languedoc*, 1781.

[71] F. C. Mougel, 'La Fortune des princes de Bourbon-Conty: revenus et gestion, 1655–1791', *Revue d'histoire moderne et contemporaine*, 18 (1971). Mougel states that 'Il y a donc bien un renversement de politique au XVIIIᵉ siècle en ce sens, qu'il y a une orientation générale vers la constitution d'un important domaine foncier au détriment des sources nouvelles de richesses alors en plein essor.' p. 38. Such examples throw further doubt on Chaussinand-Nogaret's thesis concerning the dynamic, capitalist leanings of the nobility.

(2) proper concern for the maintenance of 'feudal' rights—*cens, banalités, lods et ventes,* etc., the Contys being 'très exigeante en ce qui concerne l'affirmation de leurs droits'.[72] However, as we have seen, the coal boom of the 1780s would nudge both Monsieur and Castries in the direction of industrial ventures.[73]

If we now examine in some detail the management of the *comté d'Alais* and the *terre de Trouilhas,* we shall discover how the pattern outlined above was repeated by Castries's agents, the overall approach being to press ahead with increased revenues from coal-mining but always within the framework of the old seigneurial system. Guy Lemarchand reminds us that the system was always undergoing change, but that if, by 1789, 'we are no longer talking of a direct link between man and man, the landed and fiscal relationship, founded on the fief remained'.[74]

By 1789, the maréchal de Castries's annual revenues stood at one-third of a million *livres,* beside the income from his wife's fortune, estimated to be three-quarters of a million *livres.* Half of the maréchal's annual income came from the rewards of his successful military and political career; of the remaining half, the income from the *comté d'Alais* represented the single most important source of revenue collected from the family estates scattered throughout France.[75] An examination of his accounts for the family seat at Castres as well as for those from the *comté d'Alais* immediately reveal the very significant increase in revenues during the two decades prior to the Revolution. Under stewardship of his agent Pégat in Montpellier, income from the Castries estate rose annually during the 1770s, with a significant increase after 1778. In the words of the duc de Castries, 'In under ten years, the honest Pégat had managed to double the revenues of the marquisat, despite the cost of expensive repairs to buildings and improving the vineyards. . . . the following years secured the prosperity of the marquisat.' Most of the annual increase stemmed from a

---

[72] Ibid. 48.

[73] Ibid. 44.

[74] Lemarchand, 'La Féodalité et la Révolution', 538. The author also stresses the increased pressures being exerted upon the poor as a result of demographic and cultural (ability to read French etc.) factors as well as by the seizure of land by seigneurs and their *gens d'affaires.* p. 549.

[75] His lands at Bruyères grossed 32,164 *livres,* those in the Auvergne, 29,196 *livres,* at Castries, 20,063, Lézignan, 25,000, and Ollainville, 14,500 *livres.* The *comté d'Alais* brought in 50,070 *livres.* Income from his military functions came to 145,591 *livres* annually, in addition to which he received a pension of 20,000 *livres* as a former Minister. Castries, *Papiers de famille,* 315.

re-evaluation of the *droits féodaux—cens, banalités,* and *lods et ventes,* 'as well as by the successful renewal of leases'.[76]

The accounts of the *comté d'Alais* reveal a very similar pattern, with one notable exception, the income from the mines of the Grand-Combe and Abilon. In 1787, Pierre Crozade wrote a personal letter to the maréchal requesting a substantial increase in his salary, in fact, no less than three times his 600 *livres* per annum! His case was a good one, based as it was upon the dramatic increase in revenues from the *comté d'Alais,* which, in the early 1780s, had averaged around 12,000 *livres* a year but which, by 1787, had reached over 50,000 *livres.*[77] In support of his claim, Crozade underlined the vital importance of a good steward: 'Experience has proven that revenues are low when things have been neglected and that they will not rise substantially unless one makes a really extraordinary effort.' This effort had been directed in Crozade's case towards the objective of raising the income from annual leases. On 12 September 1785, after an inauspicious beginning, he reported that the leasing-out process had exceeded his wilder dreams. The *ferme* of the *moulin neuf* had been raised from 3,000 to 4,425 *livres,* the *pré de pradelle* from 416 to 1,350, the lease covering the collection of tolls etc. from 2,300 to 3,100 *livres.* It is interesting, given the increasing opposition to feudal dues on the part of the peasantry, that Crozade believed that the lease relating to the collection of this form of income (*cens, albergues,* etc.) would have fallen in value; in fact, it rose by just 5 *livres.*[78] It is also interesting to learn that Crozade had not managed to raise the price of leases on one of the six *métairies* belonging to the *terre de Trouilhas.* It seems that the Protestant *seigneur–négociant* Pierre Deleuze, who had owned the land until Castries's purchase in 1782, had already pushed his *fermiers* to the limit.[79]

---

[76] Castries, *Papiers de famille,* 317–18.

[77] Crozade went on to explain that, apart from looking after the coal-mines, 'les fermes demandent aussi des visites pour empêcher les dégradations et maintenir la bonne culture des terres, la recette des lods assujetie à des recherches particuliers pour parvenir à les découvrir et en assurer la rentrée à laquelle nombre de redevables s'étudient à échapper par les fraudes; à tout cela se joint une correspondance suivie et fort étendue'. *AN* 306 AP488, 17 Mar. 1787. Crozade added that in Languedoc it was the custom for a *régisseur* to be paid one *sol* for each *livre* collected, so that on the estate's annual income of around 50,000 *livres* he should be paid 2,500 *livres.* He was happy, however, to settle for 1,800.

[78] *AN* 306AP 486.

[79] Ibid. Crozade did in fact express his opinion that 'M. de Trouilhas avait porté ses fermes à un trop haut prix.'

What of 'feudal' dues? How important were they in the total annual income of Castries's land in the south-east? Stressing that *rentes foncières* constituted the most important item, Guy Lemarchand states that 26.5 per cent of the total income of 37,688 *livres* for a *seigneurie* in Normandy in 1777 related to feudal dues, and 34 per cent of 90,000 *livres* for a *seigneurie* in Burgundy in 1780.[80] On the Castries estate, as late as 1790, Pégat was still collecting what he termed *droits féodaux* worth 4,210 *livres*, compared with 17,108 *livres* from *les fermages*.[81] Given the considerable difficulty of collecting feudal dues at this time it would surely not be an exaggeration to conclude that, in an average year, they certainly represented around a quarter of the total income of the Castries estate in the Hérault.

The accounts for the *comté d'Alais et la terre de Trouilhas* reveal an even higher percentage of overall income from feudal dues. The balance-sheet for 1789 for the *comté d'Alais* provides us with figures of 9,405 *livres* for *les fermages*, and 3,263 *livres* from *cens, albergues,* and the *lods et ventes* alone. The figures for the *terre de Trouilhas* were 2,501 and 1,130 *livres* respectively. It is abundantly clear that the *lods et ventes*—fixed in the Alès region at one-sixth of the price of land bought or sold—was by far the most lucrative of the *droits féodaux*.[82] Taking the average income from the *lods et ventes* for the last four years of the *ancien régime*, we arrive at a figure of 4,958 *livres* for the *comté d'Alais*.[83] So far as the *terre de Trouilhas* is concerned, feudal dues would not have been terribly important 'without the *directe* which M. de Trouilhas exercised in the town and immediate vicinity of Alais'.[84] The importance of the *lods et ventes* is highlighted in the correspondence between Castries and Crozade at the beginning of the Revolution

---

[80] Lemarchand, 'La Féodalité et la Révolution', 541.

[81] Castries, *Papiers de famille*, 319.

[82] *AN* 306AP 496, *relevé des revenus et charges du comté d'Alais et terre de Trouilhas.*

[83] *AN* 306AP 496, *relevé des droits des lods et ventes.*

[84] *AN* 306AP 485, 3 Mar. 1785. Legal battles over the *lods et ventes* were commonplace and Crozade fought tenaciously to exact his last feudal *livre* of flesh. The sale of the *domaine de Gardies* provoked a year-long battle between the maréchal de Castries, the baron de Vibrac, and the abbé de Sauve over the 39,000 *livres* which was at issue. Although Castries eventually won the lion's share, Crozade complained that the maréchal should have been awarded the entire amount since he exercised complete sovereignty over 'la mouvance féodale du domaine'. *AN* 306AP 488, 16 Oct. 1786; 489, 22 June 1787. The average income from 'cens, albergues et autres droits féodaux', however, covering the same period, 1785–9, was 1,526 *livres*, a not inconsiderable sum. What is noticeable is the declining trajectory concerning the payment of *droits féodaux*—1,707 *livres* in 1786, 1,401 in 1789. *AN* 306AP 496, 16 Dec. 1791, *recettes des censives, albergues . . . de M. le maréchal de Castries.*

when considerable confusion reigned concerning those dues which were to be abolished without compensation and those which were to be made redeemable. In a letter dated 13 September 1789, Crozade explained that 'If dues are to be redeemed, the crucial issue for M. le Maréchal will be the *droits seigneuriaux*, whose value is considerable, always supposing that the *lods et ventes* are to be included.' The steward went on to explain that if the *cens* and similar feudal dues were alone to be made redeemable, then the maréchal stood to lose a great deal 'because there are very few *censives* in the town of Alais, whereas the *lods* represent a sizeable sum because of the frequent sales and purchases of property which occur'.[85]

Castries, through the tireless work of his steward, fought hard to protect his rights during the 1780s, winning one legal battle against the *communauté* of Saint-Paul-Lacoste, 'au sujet des droits de leude', in 1786[86], and yet another against the town of Alès itself, represented by the vicomte d'Alais, over the payment of feudal dues such as 'le droit du quintalage, du courtage et autres droits'. In this latter case, Crozade again successfully defended the rights of his lord by proving, at least to the satisfaction of the court, that the right to levy such dues had been granted by the 'consuls et la communauté d'Alais à Madame Charlotte de Montmorency, comtesse d'Alais, le 5 septembre 1634' and that, therefore, as the comte d'Alais, Castries enjoyed full legal entitlement.[87] At times, Crozade and Roussel, *sub-délégué* of the diocese of Uzès and steward of the *vicomté de Portes*, pooled their expertise in obtaining money from increasingly recalcitrant tenants. On one occasion, Roussel had sent his bailiffs from Bagnols to force the *sous-fermiers* of M. le baron de Fontenède to produce the 2,000 *livres* they allegedly owed on the spot. Learning of this rather heavy-handed tactic (we have already noted Achille Bardon's denunciation

---

[85] *AN* 306AP 491, 13 Sept. 1789. Many Alèsians were anxious to redeem the *droits casuels*, particularly the *lods et ventes* following the publication of the Assembly's decree of 3 May 1790. They sought, however, to invoke the application of Article 25, which effectively would have redeemed a *lods et ventes* of, say, 7,200 *livres* for 500 *livres*, whereas Crozade fought hard to apply Article 35, which set the redemption price at five-sixths of the *lods*. Given that the *lods et ventes* on 7,200 *livres* was established in the Alès region at one-sixth, or 1,200 *livres*, a redemption price of five-sixths would have netted 1,000 *livres*. Crozade actually wrote to Merlin de Douai—who had played a leading role in the committee dealing with the abolition, or redemption, of feudal dues—seeking his adjudication. Merlin wrote to say that Crozade's interpretation was the correct one. *AN* 306AP 493, to Castries, 10 Sept. 1790; Merlin de Douai to Crozade, 11 Oct. 1790.

[86] *AN* 306AP 488, Crozade to Castries, 19 Oct. 1786.

[87] Ibid.

of Roussel 'the idiot'!), Crozade advised a more cautious approach: 'I wrote to M. Roussel to inform him that the best way of getting paid was to follow up the *banisements* [*sic*] (notices to quit) which may have been served on *fermiers* who have fallen into arrears, several of whom offer to pay up as soon as they are presented with the official notices to leave.'[88]

As well as defending feudal rights from individuals and communities who may have read their Boncerf,[89] agents like Crozade and Roussel were also obliged to protect the rights and perquisites associated with the seigneurial courts of justice from Bourbon centralization. When, following the resistance of the Paris *parlement* in May 1788, Lamoignon introduced his 'legal revolution' with the creation of the *grands bailliages*, Crozade expressed the opinion that, despite the protestations of the government, 'this move represents a heavy blow aimed at the seigneurial courts of justice'.[90] Although the government stated that it was not its intention to undermine the judicial power of seigneurs, this was unquestionably the consequence of Lamoignon's action. In August, Crozade reported that already several cases had been taken from Castries's *siège des appeaux* to the *grand bailliage de Nîmes*. It is not so much the financial benefits of seigneurial courts of justice which explain the fight for their retention—the *greffe* of Castries's *cour des appeaux* was sold for just 500 *livres* a year—it was the justified fear of a reduction in the general authority of the seigneur over his vassals.[91] Again, we must bear in mind not just the financial, but the social and political, reality of seigneurial power.

The most striking fact concerning the accounts of the *comté d'Alais et la terre de Trouilhas* after 1783, however, one which distinguishes them from those of the previous decade as well as from the stewardship of the Hérault estates, is the increasing importance of profits from the sale of coal. The possibility of profit from the mines of the *comté d'Alais* had been one of the factors predisposing Castries in favour of purchasing the fief in 1777; it had been the overriding factor so far as the *terre de Trouilhas*, with its rich Grand-Combe mine, was

---

[88] *AN* 306AP 486, 8 Nov. 1785.

[89] See J. Q. Mackrell, *The Attack on 'Feudalism' in Eighteenth-Century France* (London, 1973).

[90] *AN* 306AP 490, to Castries, 18 May 1788.

[91] *AN* 306AP 490, 6 Aug. 1788. The costs of running the court, estimated at 200 *livres*, had to be deducted from the 500 *livres* received, thus reducing even further the financial significance of suppressing seigneurial courts of justice. *AN* 306AP 491, 13, Sept. 1789.

concerned. On 3 March 1785, Crozade explained to the maréchal that 'Trouilhas is only beneficial to M. le maréchal because of the mines which are farmed out at present for 1,500 *livres* but which could bring in 12,000 *livres* after the leases have been renewed.'[92] As we have seen, Castries decided to ignore his steward's advice concerning a *ferme*, choosing instead to acquire overall control (a *régie*) with Crozade in financial control. The decision was the right one from a financial standpoint. Following Castries's 'New Deal' of 1785, income from the mines rose every year until the Revolution. In 1780, the mines had been farmed out for 1,500 *livres*. In 1785, as we have just noted, Crozade thought that he could raise this sum to 12,000 *livres*. However, the balance-sheets for the *comté d'Alais et la terre de Trouilhas* for 1789 reveal that the profit from coal-mining, all administrative costs deducted, stood at 35,740 *livres*, representing no less than 68.7 per cent of the total revenue from both the *comté* and Trouilhas. No wonder that Castries repulsed every advance which Tubeuf made to him over the Grand-Combe! And no wonder that, just like Monsieur in the *vicomté de Portes*, Castries pushed further in the direction of a *monopole*, thus risking his position as seigneur–protector of the community in the Alès region.

We are now in a better position to understand the crucial importance of defeating the industrial pretensions of a Pierre-François Tubeuf, even though a victory might imperil the social relationship between Castries and his vassals. Danger cones had been hoisted by Crozade as early as 1785 when he warned the maréchal that: 'If sieur Tubeuf manages to seize control of the mines of the Grand-Combe, not only would M. le maréchal see himself deprived of the very significant rise in income which the coal-mines will bring, but, in addition, he would see the income from his mine at the *forêt d'Abilon* fall, since the competition from the Grand-Combe would be absolutely ruinous.'[93] This analysis of the situation rests upon Crozade's vision of producing for a local economy; essentially it was the same vision as that of François Faure and his supporters, for whom it was preferable to close down either the Grand-Combe or Abilon (given that they only had a handful of traditional miners to play with and that Abilon was simply an extension of the seams running through the Grand-Combe, it really did not matter which) to protect their very slim profit margins. When Tubeuf agreed to hand the Abilon and

[92] *AN* 306AP 485.   [93] Ibid.

Mas-Dieu mines to Castries without a fight in the early 1780s, he did so because he knew that the real source of the coal wealth of the valley lay in the Grand-Combe and that, armed with a plan, sizeable investment, and his manager Renaux, he could soon kill off the competition from Abilon, indeed he could have reached it simply by working the seams of the Grand-Combe along their natural length. It was simply a matter of modern mining techniques rather than digging foxholes.

The 'pre-Revolution' in Alès, then, must be viewed against the backcloth of a narrowly based municipal élite whose legitimacy was being threatened, the economic recession of the 1780s, which affected the silk industry in particular, and, finally, the bitter struggle for control of the potentially rich coal reserves of the region. All this was linked to the wider problems of international economic crises associated with changing markets and fashion, the challenge of increased competition from countries such as Spain, intent upon building up their own manufacturing base, as well as the incursion of modern industrial capitalist ideas synonymous with the work of Pierre-François Tubeuf. It was Tubeuf, with his grand vision of production for international markets, who became the focus of opposition from a traditional, protoindustrial community, composed of smallholders, *fermiers*, *sous-fermiers*, colliers, carters, and lime-burners, and it was the local *officiers*, stewards, and *gens d'affaires* who articulated the ideas of this traditional socio-economy. The social rebellions which erupted during the 1780s and early 1790s must be analysed within the context of the 'Dual Revolution', socio-economic and political, capitalist and revolutionary. It is surely not coincidental that the *masques armés* revolt, the *Grande Peur*, the Catholic royalist *camps de Jalès* from 1790 to 1792 all occurred within the region of the northern Gard–southern Ardèche; nor that the *bagarre de Nîmes*—the most violent manifestation of counter-revolution in France before the Vendéen rebellion—involved Protestant merchants and their protoindustrialized workers from the Cévennes and small Catholic masters and textile workers in Nîmes.

The significance of the rebellions known as the *masques armés* and the *camps de Jalès*, as well as the relationship between them, has been analysed in some depth by Michael Sonenscher and, more recently, by Gerard Sabatier.[94] Both scholars have emphasized the central

[94] Sabatier, 'De la révolte de Roure', 123, which stresses the involvement of the local *gens d'affaires* in the 1670 revolt.

importance of peasant indebtedness and the role played by the local *gens d'affaires*. For Michael Sonenscher, 'This local élite, composed of *hommes de loi*, could . . . extend their role as the servants of a seigneurial system into that shadowy region where credit, trade, and all the individual arrangements arising from the sale, leasing, and inheritance of land came together!'[95] At the highest level of provincial life, this was the function of the Dhombres and the Roussels, although their political and administrative responsibilities demanded a very sophisticated and tactful approach to the potentially explosive relationship between central government and the Estates of Languedoc, and the wishes of great princes and nobles like Monsieur and Castries and those of the local population. Both men were implicated in the *masques armés* revolt. Louis Dhombres is surely the 'M. Dhombres, *procureur* of the *parlement* of Toulouse' who received a warning for the legal harassment of Jacques and Jean Chamboredon, whilst it was Roussel who thought that 'le germe de tous les troubles' was a quarrel over the appointment of a judicial official whose installation was opposed by the local seigneur, Louis-Joseph Bastide.[96]

Of particular relevance to this present study, however, are the similarities which Gerard Sabatier finds between the revolt of the comte du Roure in 1670 and that of the *masques armés* a century later. In 1670, the local *gens d'affaires* were already being denounced for squeezing the poor by means of 'the farming-out of seigneurial rights and dues'. Of even greater interest is the attack on the 'monopoleurs et des enchérisseurs du charbon de terre'.[97] As early as the seventeenth century, the price and control of the region's coal reserves could help to initiate popular rebellion. *Ancien régime* riots do not all occur around grain carts and barges. In 1783, as in 1670, rebellion was 'legitimized' by invoking the support of the aristocracy. One of the leaders of the *masques armés* revolt, subsequently hanged for his rebellion, allegedly stated that 'they had the support of M. le Prince de Conti and that of the Comte du Roure'. We have noted how the former encouraged the maréchal de Castries to purchase the *comté d'Alais*, whilst the comte du Roure, a vassal of the 'Prince de Conti', had opposed Tubeuf's operations in the region from the beginning.[98]

---

[95] 'La Révolte des masques armés', 248.
[96] Ibid. 250–5.
[97] 'De la révolte de Roure', 140.
[98] Sonenscher, 'Royalists and Patriots', 261.

It is necessary, therefore, to insist upon the 'protoindustrial' nature of Alèsian society, upon the fact that the region affected by the *masques armés* revolt and the 'Catholic royalist' *camps de Jalès* from 1790 to 1792 corresponded, in the main, to the area covered by the concession granted to Tubeuf in 1773. The epicentre of the two rebellions, the commune of Banne, was the original base for his mining operations as early as September of that year. By 1780, Tubeuf was extracting over 7,000 *quintaux* of coal a month from his Pigère mine near Banne on land which belonged to the comte du Roure. It should also be noted that Jacques and Jean Chamboredon, the victims of Dhombres's machinations, were coal-miners.

As for 'le germe de tous les troubles', it was on 19 November 1782 that the commission appointed by the government to investigate the problems associated with Tubeuf's concession gave Tubeuf the green light to move against the small coal-owners or *fermiers* in the region.[99] Armed with what he understandably regarded as the final legitimization of his *privilège*, Tubeuf harried the Intendant into providing armed force to close down the many small mines in Robiac, Castilhon, Courry, and Banne, communes directly involved in the *masques armés* revolt.[100] It was on 19 January 1783, on the very eve of the revolt, that the inhabitants of Meyrannes decided to hold a public meeting in the square, denouncing Tubeuf for unleashing 'the most terrible misery; for placing a number of people in the situation of having to leave the village; for ruining the production of silk and closing down the workshops which it supplies, thus affecting the collection of royal taxes'. Tubeuf was also accused of 'farming out these mines to the very people he has just robbed and of selling at exorbitant prices the coal which nature has freely given them'.[101] Significantly, it was in the immediate aftermath of the *masques armés* affair, by which time Tubeuf had become one of the most hated men in Languedoc, that Tubeuf decided to sell off his concession to the abbé Bréard. The revolt coincided exactly with the implementation of Tubeuf's 'final solution'. The scale of the repression—three men hanged and five

---

[99] At the end of the month, Tubeuf and his family returned from a stay in the capital determined to act upon the government's decree and to stay in Alès until Pierre-François had recouped all his losses. *AG* 58J 2, 30 Nov. 1782.

[100] On 11 Nov. 1782, Tubeuf wrote in his Journal that the letters he had sent to du Boullaye in the Conseil des mines had finally elicited a positive response: the Intendant had told him that he would receive the armed force he had requested. *AG* 58J 4.

[101] Rouff, *Tubeuf*, 61–2.

more sent to the galleys—finally induced him to concentrate his attention on his native Normandy and on the mines he had discovered on the outskirts of Paris.[102]

Once Tubeuf had effectively lost his struggle to exploit his concession *en grand*, due in no small measure to the resistance of the *masques armés* and the miners who stoned him at the Grand-Combe a year later, the Roussels, the Dhombres, and the Crozades could pursue their difficult task of working for *les Grands* whilst protecting the interests of local *négociants* and *propriétaires*. The lessons to be learned from the *masques armés* revolt were not taken to heart. Whenever bad harvests, whether of grain, silk, or wine, pushed the subsistence levels of the protoindustrial workers of the Cévennes too low, the threat to the local élite became more overt. We have already noted that some of the worst outbursts of violence during the early years of the Revolution were to occur in the department of the Gard. However, as we have done with the *masques armés* revolt, we need to reassess the factors which contributed to the *Grande Peur*, the *bagarre de Nîmes*, and the *camps de Jalès*, not only in the light of the *longue durée* of religious antagonism between Catholics and Protestants, but within the context of the economic forces affecting the region since, at least, the 1770s.

For example, although the *Grande Peur* in the south-east of France does, indeed, appear to follow the classic lines drawn over half a century ago by Georges Lefebvre, it seems from Pierre Crozade's own account that the movement affected the protoindustrial workers of the Cévennes just as much as the peasantry, and that their concern for their raw silk and finished goods was just as profound as the fear of the grain harvests being ruined in the fields. As Lefebvre indicates, there were two *peurs* in the Alès region, the first occurring at the end of March—not unassociated, surely, with the political excitement generated by the meetings held to draw up the *cahiers de doléances*—the second at the end of July.[103] As a further gloss upon political issues, it is noticeable that the fear which spread from Montélimar southwards down the Rhône valley, and westwards to Saint-Jean-du-Gard appears to have found its origins in the Dauphiné, whose newly created Estates provided the model for the political demands of the *patriotes* in Alès

---

[102] It is significant that he should have confided at this time in Louis Dhombres, undoubtedly the most influential public figure in the region. See *AG* 58J 4, 27 July 1783.

[103] Lefebvre, *La Grande Peur*, 29.

and Nîmes. On 29 July, Crozade reported to Castries that six men from the commune of Rivière had delivered a letter to the municipality in which 'they begged to be given rifles and shot to defend themselves against a troop of brigands, 3–4,000 strong, who were at present in the neighbourhood of Montélimar but making their way towards Pont-Saint-Esprit'. By the evening of the same day, emissaries from les Vans in the Bas-Vivarais increased the sense of panic in Alès by announcing that 'they had been informed that an army of 10,000 piedmontais had entered the Dauphiné, marching in good order'. For two days, every shop and house in the town remained shuttered and barred.[104]

The religious aspect of the affair is illustrated by the way in which, as Lefebvre, notes, 'the *Grande Peur* recalled la pâou des Higounaous', the fear of the Huguenots which swept through Catholic communities in the seventeenth century.[105] But the sacks which 'peasants' from the cévenol countryside carried behind the safety of the city walls of Alès as *les brigands* approached were filled not with grain, but with raw and reeled silk. It is also evident that the municipality of Alès, led by its *politique* mayor, Firmas-Périès, was more concerned about the *foire de Saint-Barthélemy*, which was due to be held in the town, than any re-enaction of the Massacre of St Bartholomew! At the peak of the *Grande Peur*, he dispatched letters to Nîmes and to the editor of the *Courrier d'Avignon* announcing that all merchants and visitors to the fair would be safe, since the town had 1,500 men under arms, as well as a detachment of regular soldiers. Some of the venom associated with religious hatred had already been drawn by adopting the traditional practice of calling a 'general assembly' of citizens, and by organizing 'a great procession of local dignitaries, Catholic and Protestant', which ended with an impressive firework display.[106]

However, the snake had been scotched not killed. The most horrific consequences of the *conjoncture* between historic religious antagonisms and economic recession, aggravated by the revolutionary crisis, came with the *bagarre de Nîmes*, the first manifestation in France of counter-

---

[104] *AN* 306AP 491, 3 Aug. 1789. It is interesting that a general panic over the rumoured arrival of Catholic royalist troops swept through Protestant towns and villages in this same region as late as the 1820s. See G. Lewis, 'A Cévenol Community in Crisis: The Mystery of "L'Homme à Moustache"', *Past and Present*, 109 (1985).

[105] Lefevre, *La Grande Peur*, 62.

[106] *AN* 306AP 491, 3 Aug. 1789. Crozade stated that during 'la frayeur ou une terreur panique', 100 *quintaux* of silk were brought into Alès in just two days.

revolutionary activity on any sizeable scale. The facts, including the prominent part played in the months leading up to the massacre by François Froment, have already been established in my *Second Vendée*.[107] What that study, concerned as it was to emphasize the *continuity* of counter-revolution in the Gard during the Revolution and Empire, did not adequately stress was the fact that the link between the protoindustrial workers in the Cévennes and the merchant élite of Nîmes provides a central explanation for the *bagarre*. Again, there can be no doubt that the merchants, anxious to seize administrative control of the department, exploited the age-old religious antagonism which divided the two communities. No doubt also that Froment's leading role can be explained by the dismissive treatment meted out to his father, an official on the city municipality, by the Protestant élite in the 1780s.[108] However, in a most revealing pamphlet entitled *Charles Sincère à Pierre Romain*, written by Froment some months before the *bagarre de Nîmes*, it was the 'capitalist' crimes of the Protestants, not their religious or political errors, which assumed pride of place.

The pamphlet concentrates on issues which have underpinned the argument so far in this present work: the extension of industrial work throughout the Cévennes, the elimination of the independent master, the importance of the *propriétaire foncier*, the problems confronting a protoindustrial society, already divided along religious lines, of economic recession and political upheaval. For this reason it is worth examining in some detail. The brunt of the attack is levelled against 'ces riches négociants' who could not, as they had allegedly done in Geneva, exploit the law to gain exclusive control of the commercial and manufacturing life of the region. Having failed in their attempt, Froment accused the Protestant merchants of forming 'a secret league for the purpose of weakening or ruining Catholic commercial houses, to such good effect that, until the present day, they are not able to extend their activities beyond a certain point'. Capitalizing upon religious hatred and the mass recession which had affected urban workers in particular, Froment insisted that the Protestants had decided upon the ruin of the independent master-craftsman. It was also the intention of the 'comité secret des fabriquans [*sic*] à Nîmes' to reduce the poorer 'cultivateurs et les ouvriers' to a state of abject misery. How? By controlling the prices paid for raw silk and finished

---

[107] G. Lewis, *The Second Vendée* (Oxford, 1978), 1–40.
[108] Sonenscher, '*Royalists and Patriots*', 54–71.

products. Every year, silk merchants gave spinners money to buy the necessary cocoons, the latter promising to produce raw silk at an agreed price. Froment alleged that, when demand was low, the wages paid to the spinners could be 20, 30, or even 50 *sols le livre* below the normal payment. In addition, the same merchants controlled the supply of bread by purchasing grain and then selling some of their stocks at low prices early in the season in order to force down the price paid to small producers, then dramatically raising the price later in the season having stockpiled their own grain to benefit according- ly.[109] There can be no doubt that hoarding and speculation in grain, and other basic commodities, was widespread: Castries's agent fre- quently indulged in such 'immoral'—so far as the eighteenth-century consumer was concerned—practices.[110]

In addition to the above crimes, 'Charles Sincère', as Froment modestly, but revealingly, described himself, also accused the Protes- tant *négociant* of putting out work only to their co-religionaries in the Cévennes, 'who can live more cheaply than those in the town and who are willing to accept lower wages for their work. As a result of these activities, dictated by *fanatisme* and greed, agriculture is deprived of a great number of workers and the Protestants, having disseminated a general desire for luxury amongst all classes of citizens through the introduction of the silk industry, perpetuate the misery and moral corruption which is the inevitable consequence.' Here we have the voice of the 'traditional' Catholic community, looking more to the plough than the loom, denouncing the consequences of the protoin- dustrialization of their region, arrogating to itself the moral high ground. Turning to another bone of contention during this period to which we have already referred, that of taxation, Froment explained, ironically, that 'these wealthy *négociants*, these men of integrity, these citizens who are so useful and keen to dominate everything, do not exhibit any qualms about avoiding the payment of taxes . . . of swearing in public that their fortunes have been reduced to zero, with the result that it is those who own land, *les vrais citoyens*, who support almost the entire burden of taxation'.

---

[109] *AG* ADXVI 37, *Charles Sincère à Pierre Romain*, 3–4.

[110] In one letter to Castries, Crozade explained that almost all his *métairies* were leased out in return for certain amounts of mulberry leaves. Crozade stockpiled the leaves until the silk-cocoon harvest was well advanced in order to obtain the highest price. In 1786, at the peak of the harvest, Crozade was able to charge twice the price which had been asked earlier in the spring. *AN* 306AP 487, 3 July 1786.

Froment's unique contribution was to *politicize* the problems associated with the commercialization and industrialization of a society caught in a prolonged recession as well as in the time-warp of religious hatred. More than any other single figure in the south-east, he managed to translate the social, cultural, and economic values of a traditional Catholic community into the more politicized world of counter-revolution. Associating the Protestants in the Midi with the alleged long-term plot to overthrow the monarchy, with the aid of 'perfidious Albion', a theme which would be adumbrated by the abbé de Barruel, Joseph de Maistre, and his successors on the Right, Froment stated that 'It is a well-known fact that the *cabinet de Londres*, for over a century, has embraced the project of creating a Protestant republic in Bas-Languedoc, based in the Cévennes and the Vivarais.' This theme of a *République protestante du Midi* would affect relationships between the two religious communities in the region well into the nineteenth century.[111]

The Revolution, by granting the Protestants complete religious freedom, and by enabling them to seize administrative and political power through the bullet and the ballot-box in the Gard, was to complete the alienation of the majority of Catholics, particularly those who had been content to trade off economic for municipal power under the *ancien régime*. The Protestant merchant élite was certainly not loath to exploit its economic stranglehold over the region. In the old woollen town of Sommières, for example, the *négociants* scarcely bothered to mask the fact that those who paid the Catholic pipers were now in a position to call the tune. Describing themselves, like their colleagues in Alès and Nîmes, as *patriotes* dedicated to the annihilation of *les aristocrates*, they sent a petition to the Constituent Assembly in 1790 explaining that, despite their defeat at the polls, *les aristocrates* were attempting to regain control of the municipality and had disbanded the largely Protestant *milice bourgeoise*. The merchant élite explained that, regrettable as it might be, they might now 'have to abandon fifteen to twenty thousand individuals whom we employ in the town and immediate vicinity of Sommières to the horrors of destitution'.[112]

---

[111] See Lewis, 'A Cévenol Community in Crisis', 151–2.

[112] *AG* ADXVI 37, Nov. 1789. The merchants explained that the majority of people 'était pour cette compagnie [the *milice bourgeoise*] composée d'honnêtes citoyens, la plupart chefs de famille et fort contribuables'.

The history of Federalism and of the Terror in the south-east of France, which involved the execution of 133 individuals in Nîmes alone, a sizeable percentage of whom were merchants and lawyers implicated in the Federalist revolt, can only truly be comprehended if one appreciates the reality of the emerging class war between those who owned if not always the means of production then certainly the means of reproduction, and those who saw themselves being stripped of their skills and craft status, reduced to 'the humiliating and perpetual condition of an ordinary worker (*ouvrier*)'.[113] When the master-craftsmen and textile workers of Nîmes combined politically to form the Société populaire de Nîmes in 1792, attracting significant support from *both* religious communities, they rejected all overtures for a merger with the wealthy Société républicaine, denouncing 'the seductive appeal of a society in which every kind of wealth . . . is concentrated'.[114] For their part, 'ces riches négociants', who had seized control of the department as a consequence of the *bagarre de Nîmes* in 1790, lost no opportunity of denouncing the members of the popular society as the remnants of Froment's followers, dispatching emissaries to societies throughout the Cévennes, as they had done in 1790, 'to stir up the inhabitants against the *club populaire de Nîmes*, telling them that it was only composed of the *houpettes de 1790* (the name for Froment's supporters).[115] As Christopher Johnson has shown with reference to the textile workers of the neighbouring Hérault department, master-craftsmen were to be very disillusioned by the dawn of independence which they thought they glimpsed in the early years of the Revolution; hence their widespread involvement in the Terror, in Paris and in the provinces.[116]

Some time before the Jacobin Terror had left its historic mark on the department of the Gard, however, the two great protagonists for control of the coal reserves of the Alès basin had left French shores, never to return. As a confidant of Marie Antoinette, it is hardly surprising to learn that the maréchal's attitude to the events of 1789 was hostile. An avowed enemy of Loménie de Brienne and Calonne, Castries was especially concerned about the latter's land tax and his

---

[113] Lewis, *The Second Vendée*, 56.
[114] *AG* ADXVI 37, *pétition de la société populaire de Nîmes*, 2 Nov. 1792.
[115] *AG* ADXVI 37, 8 Apr. 1793.
[116] Johnson, 'Artisans versus Fabricants', 21.

partial attack on honorific privilege.[117] He fought a rearguard action at Versailles against the convocation of the Estates General and, having failed in this, the doubling of the Third Estate and the vote by head. In recognition of his counter-revolutionary leanings, Castries was invited to join the government the day before the fall of the Bastille. Not surprisingly he refused. On 20 October 1789, he emigrated with his friend Necker to Switzerland, to the *château de Coppet* on the shores of Lake Leman.[118] Two years later, Castries received the title of *représentant du Roi auprès des princes émigrés*, using his influence to secure close links with the Spanish court.[119] By 1794, Castries had triumphed over his arch-enemy Calonne, replacing him as the unofficial prime minister of the counter-revolution. A year earlier, the comte de Vaudreuil had penned an extremely unflattering comparison of the two courtiers: 'Certainly there is a very great contrast between the pigmy Castries, who is in control today, and the person we are speaking about [Calonne]. I saw the former at work at close quarters. He has limited intelligence; he is a pen-pusher, obsessed with his paperwork written illegibly and in poor style, still seduced by the redundant maxims and bombastic phrases of the Genevan charlatan [Necker].'[120] As a friend of Calonne's, Vaudreuil's opinion can hardly be described as objective; the duc de Castries suggests that his forebear tried hard to limit the more foolish excesses of the *émigrés* at Coblentz.[121] None the less, it is difficult to avoid the conclusion that Castries's influence at Court, whether from a political or an economic standpoint, had been anything but pernicious.

Whatever the maréchal's faults, however, there can be no doubt that he and his family were forced to pay a heavy price during the Revolution. The *château de Castries* was pillaged in 1793, his estate being auctioned off in 144 lots. When the maréchal eventually died at the *château de Wolfenbütel* in 1800, his liquid capital had been reduced to just 50,000 *livres*, 'misérable débris d'une immense fortune'.[122] It

---

[117] J. Hardman (ed.), *French Revolution Documents* (Oxford, 1973), ii. 37–8.

[118] Duc de Castries, *Notice historique et descriptive* (Paris, n.d.), 10.

[119] M. Hutt, *Chouannerie and Counter-Revolution: Puisaye, the Princes and the British Government in the 1790s* (Cambridge, 1983), 109–14.

[120] Hardman, *French Revolution Documents*, ii. 419. Vaudreuil went on to say that, since Calonne's departure, the result of Castries's plotting, 'ressources, énergie, moyens, activité, tout a été anéanti et la nullité a été complète'.

[121] Castries, *Notice historique*, 10.

[122] Castries, *Papiers de famille*, 196. The Château and part of the landed fortune was reconstituted in the 1820s by the second duc de Castries, Edmond-Eugène-Hercule (1787–1866), a former aide-de-camp to marshal Davout. Castries, *Notice historique*, 11.

was to be left to his son to salvage something from the wreck of the maréchal's mining interests in the Alès region.

Pierre-François Tubeuf was destined to die much further afield, in Virginia, America in fact. His energies had never been exclusively confined to Bas-Languedoc. He was, after all, a Norman by birth and had extended his mining activities in that province by acquiring concessions at Saint-Sauveur-le-Vicomte, Saussey, and du Plessis.[123] In 1788, he was pressing Joly de Fleury to provide more support for his mining interests in the region 'since they stretch from Glanville to Cherbourg' and would be significant in defeating the competition of English coal landed at Cherbourg.[124] In addition to his base in Normandy, he had been granted a concession on the outskirts of Paris at Villeneuve and Luzarches, not far from Saint-Germain-en-Laye, on 10 April 1779.[125] A report by the Inspecteur-général des mines notes that Tubeuf had constructed a kiln near his Parisian mines to produce bricks and plaster for the *plâtriers de Paris* who had been forbidden to use wood by order of the city council. Tubeuf's Journal for this period reveals his interest in the 'new technology', recording several visits to the famous Chaillot works run by the Périer brothers culminating in the purchase of new pumping equipment to solve the age-old problem of flooding underground. It was the Périers who had popularized Watt's invention in France leading to the production of forty steam-engines between 1778 and 1791.[126] It was typical of Tubeuf that he should have been one of the first to benefit from the pioneering work of the Périers in France.[127]

Not only was Tubeuf learning to adapt to the new technology associated with the age of iron and steam, he had also learned to involve the government more closely in his plans, a necessity given his sad experience in Alès and the scale of his debts to the Chaulieus.

---

[123] *AG* 58J 4, letter of 10 Feb. 1781 asking for confirmation of a concession in the Cotentin region.

[124] *AG* 58J 5, 4 Mar. 1788. Anxious not to miss a trick, Tubeuf thought that Joly de Fleury might like to let his wife in on all this so that she might benefit [*sic*] from future share issues! This is 'Court capitalism' in the making.

[125] *AG* 58J 4, 27 Dec. 1786. Tubeuf finally discovers coal and states his intention of publicizing the news in order to attract investors.

[126] Chaussinand-Nogaret, *The French Nobility in the Eighteenth Century*, 104–5.

[127] e.g. *AG* 58J 5, 18 June 1788, which confirms an order for 'deux coupes de pompes de 8 pieds de longueur et 8 pouces de circonférence'. It seems, however, that this machinery, intended for his works at Luzarches, was to be run by horse- not steam-power. On 4 Aug. 1788, he explained to Renaux that he now had 12 horses at Luzarches, which would be enough 'pour faire aller notre machine'.

On 12 September 1784, Tubeuf and two of his *directeurs* met de La Boullaye, head of the Conseil des mines, to confirm that the government would provide advance funds to cover the mounting costs of discovering coal on the outskirts of Paris.[128] Despite assurances of assistance, however, the persistent problems of local resistance and debt continued to undermine his work. On 31 October 1781, Tubeuf had been obliged to write to a *propriétaire* at Saint-Martin, near Luzarches, informing him that if he did not seal up the entrance to his mine he would have no alternative but to call in the law. The letter has a depressingly familiar preamble: 'Today, I am warning you for the last time . . .'!'[129] Just as the government was making preparations for the meeting of the Estates General in Paris, Tubeuf was writing to the Conseil des Mines over the threatened loss of his concession in Normandy. Recalling his traumatic experience in Bas-Languedoc, he asked 'Do I have to fear a repetition of these misfortunes in Normandy? No, Monsieur, you cannot possibly allow it,' a conclusion, one suspects, written more in despair than in hope.[130]

However, the Revolution appears to have rejuvenated him. Perhaps now he would receive the recognition and support which had been sadly lacking under the old dispensation, at least among some Court circles. As always, he busied himself with the preparation of *mémoires* and petitions, besieging ministers and deputies, pestering anyone with even half a foot in the corridors of power. As one of the most experienced specialists in coal-mining in France, he was, in fact, listened to with some attention: his influence on the legislation eventually passed in 1791, sadly deficient as it proved to Tubeuf, was obvious and important. It became clear after discussions he held with Mirabeau quite early on, however, that the Revolution, despite the latter's unequivocal support for his ideas, would not return to him the untrammelled exercise of his concession in Bas-Languedoc, or indeed in Normandy.

Ultimately disappointed in his expectations of legal redress—the Revolution was to be a revolution of *propriétaires* after all—and crushed by the continuing burden of his debts, Tubeuf made what would surely have been for any ordinary mortal, given his age and injuries,

---

[128] For Tubeuf's experiments on *les fours perpétuels*, see *AG* 58J 5, 14–27 Mar. 1789, and entry for 16 Nov. 1789 for details of his 'four perpétuel d'une construction particulière'.

[129] *AG* 58J 4, 31 Oct. 1781.

[130] *AG* 58J 5, to Milliner, 8 Apr. 1789.

the extraordinary decision to emigrate to the New World.[131] In May 1791, accompanied by his elder son, François Tubeuf, he set sail from le Havre on the *Pétite Néande*, bound for Virginia under the command of captain Pitalugi. The equally remarkable Marie-Margueritte Tubeuf had agreed to live with their younger son and the widow of their principal creditor, the marquise de Chaulieu, in their Paris apartment in order to protect the family's mining interests in France.[132] Pierre and Marie were never to see each other again.

Tubeuf had been making plans to emigrate as soon as it became clear that the Revolution would not solve all his problems, at least not immediately. At the beginning of August 1790, he had taken 'un ancien négociant anglais' named Smith to visit his works at Luzarches, eventually persuading him to purchase his 300 shares in the company in return for 55,000 acres of land in Virginia.[133] Never slow to exploit a good bargain, Tubeuf managed to offload some of his shares in his American investment before he left France.[134] On 13 November, he met a deputy from the French colony of Saint-Domingue, who had lived in Virginia and who managed to dispel any lingering doubts which Tubeuf may still have been harbouring. His investment, Tubeuf was told, 'was the source of an immense fortune'.[135] At last, he would be able to pay off all his debts and, with more luck than he had enjoyed in France, create a coal empire in America.

During the winter of 1790–1, Tubeuf finalized his plans. They were, in brief, to set up a French *colonie* in Russell County, Virginia, which would include 'a number of people with the appropriate talents and skills'. On 4 November, he wrote to John Harvey, secretary to the

---

[131] On 1 May 1791, he wrote to the marquis de Lafayette asking for a letter of recommendation to take with him to America. In this letter, Tubeuf refers to 'la renversement de ma fortune occasionnée par la nouvelle constitution'. *AG* 58J 5. Many entries in his Journal for Feb. 1791 refer to his many debts, however.

[132] *AG* 58J 5, 3 Mar. 1791: 'Madame de Chaulieu nous ayant demandé un logement chez nous, elle y est descendue en venant de Beauvais, avant-hier mardi, 4 de ce mois. Je lui ai proposé d'habiter desormais après mon départ pour la Virginie toute la maison avec ma femme et d'en partager la dépense en commun ainsi que celle de la nourriture.'

[133] *AG* 58J 5, 1 and 2 Aug. 1791. On 2 Sept., he took all the correspondence relating to his purchase of land in Virginia to Joly de Fleury, who told him that 'j'avais fait une excellente affaire'.

[134] On 26 Apr. 1791, he sold a further 250 acres of his land to a M. Warnier, *administrateur du département de l'Aisne*, for 12 *livres* an acre, thus making a profit of 750 *livres*. On 12 May, another 170 acres went to M. Julien, *aide-de-camp du marquis de Lafayette*, and 300 acres to his clerk. M. Hardy. These lucky purchasers would accompany Tubeuf on his voyage of discovery to America. *AG* 58J 5.

[135] *AG* 58J 5, 13 Nov. 1790.

Land Commission in Richmond, Virginia, seeking replies to a host of questions. What is the nature of the soil? What markets are there in the county? What is the climate like? And, with what was to prove commendable foresight, 'Should we not fear raids by savages (*Sauvages*)?'[136] The replies were most reassuring, the surveyor of Russell County describing his land as 'generally hilly, but of a very fertile soil, equal, I believe, to any in the State. It is well watered with a great variety of placid streams and cool fountains and plentifully stored with a great variety of excellent timber.' Even more interesting to Tubeuf was the comment: 'I have been told that there is a great appearance of Iron Ore on the lands you have purchased.'[137] Armed with letters of recommendation from two figures known to all students of the French Revolution—the marquis de Lafayette and Governor Morris—Tubeuf eventually left in May 1791 accompanied by his 18-year-old son, 'eighteen *maîtres* and twenty-five servants, skilled and unskilled workers'.[138] The future *colonie* also included Tubeuf's niece, a priest, the abbé Dubois, and his son's former mathematics professor. The *Traité de société* was finally signed at le Havre on 21 May, the eve of their departure.[139]

Tubeuf might have sailed out of France and history were it not for one of the most exciting and human documents to be unearthed during the research for this work—Pierre-François's handwritten diary which he kept during his awful voyage across the Atlantic. Fate was never kind to Tubeuf! The diary etches a few last lines into the portrait of a quite remarkable eighteenth-century entrepreneur, someone who was, despite some appearances to the contrary, extremely fond of his wife—the diary has many references to 'ma tendre amie'—a man who, in late middle age, was looking forward to the challenge of opening up a new frontier for the age of coal and iron in a region known to be full of hostile Indian tribes.

If the passengers on the *Petite Néande* had known what awaited them they would probably have never mounted the gangplank, for the voyage to Chesapeake Bay, and hence to Richmond, capital of Virginia, proved a nightmare. Due to calm seas and contrary winds, it

---

[136] *AG* 58J 5, 4 Nov. 1790.

[137] For John Harvey's reply to Tubeuf's queries, see Rouff, *Tubeuf*, 106.

[138] Bardon, *L'Exploitation du bassin houiller d'Alais*, 342.

[139] The *traité* was very detailed, Article 4, for example, stipulating that each *sociétaire* would have to clear his land and sow crops immediately on arrival. Article 6 stated that the first harvest would be shared in common. *AG* 58J 8, *traité de société*.

would take no fewer than seventy-four days to reach port![140] The ship's larder of biscuits, vegetables, beef, live sheep, pigs, and chickens had been reduced to a few mouldy biscuits, one small pig, and a few *haricots verts* by 25 July. As the intense tropical heat persisted, the little water they had left became almost undrinkable. On 28 July Tubeuf wrote: 'We have spent a terrible night surrounded by all the horrors of the sea.' Heat and hunger tested character to the limit. On 14 July, the captain had decided to celebrate the anniversary of the Revolution by firing several shots of cannon, much to the annoyance of the good abbé Dubois, who refused to associate himself with the godless events of 1789. It is significant that the pragmatic Tubeuf should have asked the *abbé* to co-operate by saying Mass: to no avail.[141] The 'class struggle' on board appears to have become more pronounced as tempers became more strained, with the servants taking a particularly dim view of Dubois' counter-revolutionary tendencies.[142] By the end of July, personal morals had also begun to deteriorate: 'The conduct of Mlle Laporte with the captain', Tubeuf informed his wife, 'has become extremely scandalous: il la tutoyait!'[143] Clearly, the captain regarded himself as *un vrai sansculotte*! Fortunately, the winds and events took a turn for the better at the beginning of August. On the eighth, the ship was restocked with water from a 300-ton packet-boat destined for Amsterdam, and, over the next few days, they ran into a shoal of tuna fish, some of them 80 pounds in weight.

The immense relief of sighting land is captured in Tubeuf's entry for 15 August: 'Land, *ma tendre amie*, land, after a seventy-four day crossing and all the problems which have made things so difficult! In order to imprint this day for ever in my mind, I propose to call the first home which I shall build on my lands *Sainte-Marie*.' His wife's

---

[140] The following references are taken from Tubeuf's diary of his passage to America, which was kindly loaned to me by M. Pierre Firmas-Périès. The diary covers the period from 7 June to his arrival in Jamestown, Virginia on 16 Aug. 1791. The duration of the journey was not all that unusual: the American ship taking Léger Sonthonax, *commissaire* of the French Republic, to Saint-Domingue in the summer of 1792 took two months to reach port. See R. C. Stein, *Léger-Félicité Sonthonax* (Cranbury, NJ, 1985), 45.

[141] The strain imposed on all the passengers as a result of the unforeseen length of the voyage completed the alienation of Tubeuf and his immediate entourage from the *abbé* and his friends, the Warniers and the Grandidiers. There was to be no 'communal' sentiments left by the time they reached Jamestown!

[142] Tubeuf revealed that, after the *abbé's* refusal to celebrate the 14 July, the servants 'en murmuraient tout haut'.

[143] Apparently Mlle Laporte was besotted with the captain, who treated her with 'beaucoup d'indécence et comme il la pourrait faire avec une fille publique'.

name was, of course, Marie.[144] The strain of the voyage had proved too much for the cohesion of the *colonie*, however, and a few days after their arrival, Tubeuf, together with his son, a few friends, and some workers, split off from the abbé Dubois and his group. The Revolution had accompanied them to America, dividing the *colonie* into New World *patriotes* and Old World *aristocrates*. It is typical of Tubeuf that he should have embraced his new life unreservedly, swearing an oath to the American constitution in the presence of the Governor of Virginia shortly after his arrival. In the eighteenth century, legal requirements and diplomatic niceties did not stand in the way of making good Americans.[145] On 8 September 1791, Tubeuf dispatched his ship's diary to his wife with an accompanying letter telling her not to worry, that he was about to leave for his new lands in Russell County beyond the Appalachian mountains, and that he would send news of his activities every month. With this, Tubeuf passes from the sight of this observer, until, that is, May 1795, when a death certificate to be found in the Tubeuf family papers records that Pierre-François Tubeuf was massacred by Red Indians 'on his property in Russell County in Virginia'.[146] It was a sad but perhaps not an entirely surprising end to a colourful career.

We have followed Tubeuf across the Atlantic and to his untimely death in order to emphasize the fact that it was not so much that entrepreneurs were lacking in *ancien régime* France as that *ancien régime* France did not always welcome his kind of entrepreneurial skills, as one member of the government actually told him. In his reply Tubeuf wrote:

You reproach me with the accusation that I am too enterprising. I have nothing to fear on this score, since I have only undertaken projects which have proved successful, those which have proved useful to the public good, and since I actually heard a minister say out loud that the State would be happy indeed to find ten individuals who devoted themselves to such work as successfully and with the same zeal as I have done.[147]

[144] It may have been the contrast with the horrors they had all endured on board ship which induced Tubeuf to describe the bay, Jamestown, and Richmond, the capital of Virginia, in glowing colours—substantial, pretty houses, rich farming land, an abundance of food and clean water, sturdily built men, including the 'nègres', who comprised two-thirds of the local population according to Tubeuf.

[145] According to the law, Tubeuf should have lived in the colony for two years before qualifying for American citizenship.

[146] According to Marcel Rouff, his fellow *sociétaires* finally abandoned Tubeuf in May 1793. *Tubeuf*, 109. The official report on Tubeuf's death stated that he had been killed whilst prospecting the furthermost point of Russell County, which boasted very few, if any, Frenchmen or women, indeed, very few visitors of any nationality.

[147] *AG* 58J 5, letter to Milliner, 8 Apr. 1789.

The 'minister' in question would almost certainly have been Bertin, a man with some vision, forced out of office, like the Turgots and the Calonnes, by a combination of weakness, intrigue, and Court favouritism. So far as Tubeuf's work in Languedoc is concerned, Achille Bardon provides the best assessment: 'What is absolutely certain is that one can ask anyone in this region who was the founder of the modern coal industry in the Alais basin and they will reply without hesitation—Tubeuf. So far as the local people are concerned, his name is synonymous with progress.'[148]

However, what Bardon failed to stress, since it was not part of his brief, is the fact that Pierre-François Tubeuf had a wife and two children who were to make their own contribution to the saga of the Tubeuf family as well as to the history of trade and industry in Bas-Languedoc. From his departure in May 1791 to the early years of the Empire, Marie-Margueritte Tubeuf, aided by her two sons François and Alexandre (the former having escaped the fate of his father), fought, and fought successfully, to reconstitute the Tubeuf empire. Indeed, for a few brief and productive years in the 1800s, they were to enjoy the full fruits of the original concession granted by Louis XV, something the father had never really been able to do. In the course of preparing scores of petitions to the government during the 1790s, Marie-Margueritte produced the best epitaph for her husband, 'who, for forty years, devoted his life to the discovery of new ventures which were useful to the State, his ceaseless labour leading him to his death without having received the rewards he deserved'.[149] History has done him a similar disservice.

[148] Bardon, *L'Exploitation du bassin houiller d'Alais*, 347.

[149] This proud and personal epitaph is by no means exaggerated in its assessment of Pierre-François Tubeuf's ability. Roger Dugrand, referring to the potential riches of the Alès coal-basin in the late 18th century, writes: 'Le seul qui à l'époque l'ait compris fut Tubeuf, grand chef d'industrie moderne qui entreprit la concentration et la modernisation des puits d'extraction de la zone d'Alès.' *Villes et campagnes en Bas-Languedoc*, 382.

4

REVOLUTION, RECESSION, AND THE RIGHTS OF PROPERTY-OWNERS

IN the departments of the Gard and the Ardèche, as in most other textile regions of France, the recession of the 1780s continued well into the Revolution. Recoveries were to be of brief duration, halted by the impact of war, federalism, *coups d'état*, and the 'red' and 'white' terrors which punctuate the dramatic history of the south of France during the 1790s. Little wonder that Protestant *négociants, fabricants,* and *gens d'affaires* alike welcomed with open arms the arrival of Napoleon, promising, as he did, protection against the threat of a return to the *ancien régime* and an economic 'New Deal', one which appeared to have materialized—at least in part—by 1807. This date marks not only a return to the coal production levels of 1789, but the beginning of a rise in production which, despite a temporary set-back during the last turbulent years of the Empire, was never again to dip below the 1807 figure. Throughout the Revolution and Empire, however, the small *propriétaire* and coal-owner would fight a successful rearguard action against the encroachment of the State and 'monopoly' capitalism. They would be assisted in their task by the political and administrative revolution which handed effective power into the hands of town and village élites, as well as by the persistence of the protoindustrial forms of production outlined earlier.

The severe climatic conditions of 1788 and 1789, allied to the political upheavals of the period, could only aggravate an already ailing economy.[1] The textile industry was, of course, peculiarly susceptible to revolutions and wars. Producers of raw silk in the Cévennes and Bas-Vivarais found it almost impossible to sell their produce at the

---

[1] As the delegates to the Estates General in Paris prepared to confront the King, heavy rain and giant hailstorms seriously damaged vineyards and olive trees, as well as the silk-cocoon harvest: 'Le mauvais temps est survenu dans l'état qui est le plus critique pour ses insectes,' Crozade explained to Castries, although later reports suggested that the damage was not irreparable. In Aug., however, Crozade reported that a severe hailstorm had ruined many vineyards and olive trees. *AN* 306AP 491, letters of 5 June and 21 Aug. 1789.

first August fair to be held in Alès since the fall of the Bastille, a serious matter, as Pierre Crozade explained, 'since this will not offer much encouragement to next year's spinners . . . it is vital for this region that the silk trade takes off soon'.[2] The failure to sell their silk meant that the protoindustrial workers of the region fell deeper into debt and therefore into the hands of Protestant *négociants* and *commissaires-fabricants*. As we have seen, it was to be the 'Catholic royalist' craftsmen and textile workers of Nîmes who were to pay the price for the serious economic situation during the bloody *bagarre de Nîmes* one year later. The guild records for the *cardeurs de filoselle* reveal the scope of the misery being inflicted upon them and their families; they also underline the link between the harvest failure and the manufacturing recession. In October 1789, the *syndic* of the guild reported that 'every branch of commerce is inactive; agriculture offers little alternative employment for our workers, a sad consequence of last year's rigorous winter . . . these calamities have plunged the majority of workers, not just in our *corps* but in all other branches of the industry, into the most desperate condition'. The guild decided to contribute 60 *livres* a month to the *bureau de bienfaisance* which had been organized by the municipality and the wealthier merchants.[3] One year later the position had deteriorated: 'our plight at the moment is such', the *cardeurs* reported, 'that our business seems to have collapsed . . . as a result, our workers, deprived of employment, are in a most miserable state, and, to add insult to injury, the price of food has risen to exorbitant levels'. The guild agreed to donate another 600 *livres* 'pour le soulagement des ouvriers'.[4]

Understandably, the successive blows dealt to the agricultural and manufacturing sectors were also felt by coal producers. Crozade's reports to Castries stress the link between climatic, economic, and political factors during the first years of the Revolution. Heavy rainfall was undoubtedly responsible for the collapse of the number 3 seam in the Grand-Combe in May 1790.[5] Two months later, Crozade highlighted the *bagarre de Nîmes* in his explanation for the continuing decline in coal sales: 'The present circumstances have led to the

---

[2] *AN* 306AP 491, 9 Sept. 1789. Crozade noted that those who had chosen not to sell their silk on the first day of the fair, relying on the prospect of higher prices as the days went by, were to be bitterly disappointed.

[3] *AG* IVE 139, 31 Oct. 1789.

[4] *AG* IVE 139, 16 Dec. 1790.

[5] *AN* 306AP 493, 7 May 1790.

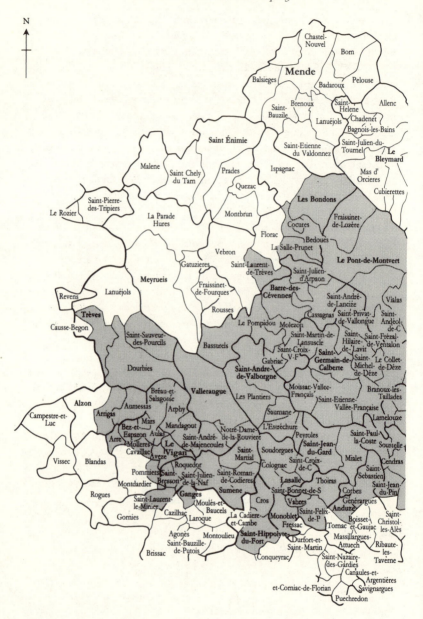

MAP 4.1. Administrative boundaries of the Cévennes region.
Taken from Philippe Joutard, *Les Cévennes de la montagne à l'homme* (Toulouse, 1979)

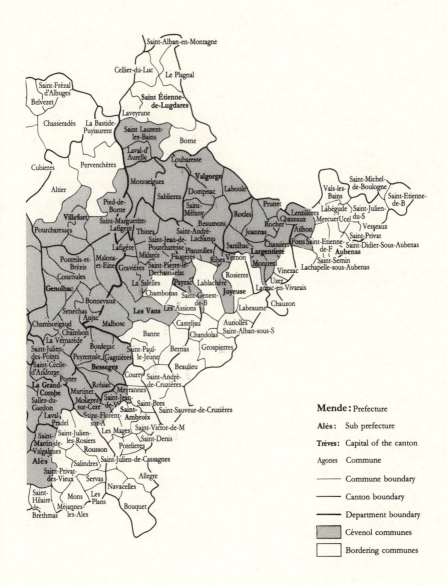

Saint-Alban-en-Montagne

Cellier-du-Luc   Le Plagnal

Saint-Frézal
d'Albuges
Belvezet

Saint Étienne-
de-Lugdares

Laveyrune

Chasseradès   La Bastide-
Puylaurent

Saint Laurent-
les-Bains

Borne

Cubières   Pervenchères

Laval-d'
Aurelle

Loubaresse

Altier

Montselgues

Valgorge

Dompnac   Laboule

Pied-de-
Borne

Sablières

Saint-Michel-
de-Boulogne

Vals-les-
Bains

Saint-Étienne-
de-B

Villefort

Saint-Marguerite-
Lafigère

Saint-
Mélany

Roclès

Prunet

Lentillères
Chazeaux

Labégude   Saint-Julien-
du-S

Mercuer Ucel

Pourcharesses

Thines

Beaumont

Rocher
Ailhon

Joannas

Vesseaux

Lafigère

Saint-Jean-de-
Pourcharesse

Saint-André-
Lachamp

Sanilhac

Chassiers

Fons Saint-Étienne-
de-F   Aubenas

Saint-Privat

Saint-Didier-Sous-Aubenas

Ponteils-et-
Brézis

Malons-
et-Eize

Malarce

Planzolles
Faugères

Vernon

Ribes

Largentière

Montréal

Saint-Sernin

Lachapelle-sous-Aubenas

Concoules

Gravières

Saint-Pierre-le-
Dechausselat

La Salelle

Rosières

Vinezac

Uzer

Genolhac

Bonnevaux

Chambonas

Payzac   Lablachère

Joyeuse

Laurac-en-Vivarais

Senechas

Les Vans

Saint-Genest-
de-B

Labeaume

Chauzon

Chamborigaud   Chambon
Aujac   Malbosc

Les Assions

Casteljau

Auriolles
Saint-Alban-sous-S

La Vernarède

Banne

Chandolas

La Vernarède

Bordezac

Saint-Paul-
le-Jeune

Berrias

Grospierres

Saint-Julien-
des-Points

Peyremale

Gagnières

Saint-Cécile-
d'Andorge

Bessèges

Courry

Beaulieu

Portes

Robiac

Saint-André-
de-Cruziéres

La Grand-
Combe

Martinet

Meyrannes

Salles-du-
Gardon

Molières-
sur-Ceze

Saint-Jean-
de-V

Saint-Bres

Saint-Sauveur-de-Cruziéres

Laval-
Pradel

Saint-Florent-
sur-A

Saint-
Ambroix

Saint-
Martin-de-
Valgalgues

Saint-Julien-
les-Rosiers

Les Mages

Saint-Victor-de-M

Saint-Denis

Alès

Rousson

Potelières

Saint-Julien-de-Cassagnes

Salindres

Allegre

Saint-Privat-
dès-Vieux

Servas

Navacelles

Saint-
Hilaire-
de-
Brethmas

Mons

Les
Plans

Méjannes-
les-Ales

Bouquet

Mende: Prefecture

Alès: Sub prefecture

Trèves: Capital of the canton

Agones   Commune

—— Commune boundary

—— Canton boundary

—— Department boundary

▒ Cévenol communes

▢ Bordering communes

closure of all the workshops as well as to the failure of the cocoon harvest, a failure aggravated by the sad happenings in Nîmes. There has been a terrible carnage; we have witnessed some horrific sights.'[6] As a direct consequence of the *bagarre*, some Protestant manufacturers sought to ruin Catholic coal producers, refusing, for example, to order any more coal from Castries's mines. The bitter prologue to the Revolution had led to the imposition of an economic 'Test Act'.[7] And it was not only Castries but Tubeuf who was beginning to feel the pinch of recent economic and political events. On 12 July 1790, he expressed the hope that when things had returned to normal after the shock of the *bagarre*, 'the commerce and sale of our coal will take off again'.[8] Two months later, coal sales had in fact dropped to a new low.[9] Despite the overwhelming problems he was facing, however, Renaux managed to keep fifteen men gainfully employed in Roche-belle, with another six producing small coal for the local lime-burners at an old mine on the Brouzon mountain.[10]

The introduction of the *assignats* as convertible currency posed yet another headache for communities which depended upon a sophisticated and complicated system of barter and exchange. As early as September 1790, Crozade had warned Castries that

the *assignats* have provoked a great deal of discontent in this *pays*. Those inhabitants of the Vivarais who attended the *foire de Saint-Barthélemy* to sell their silk chose to take it back home with them rather than accept *assignats* in payment. The fear of another issue of two million new *assignats* has reinforced the attraction for hard cash, which is becoming increasingly scarce.[11]

The antagonisms which were building up at local level against the stewards of the bigger estates arose not only from the confusion which

---

[6] *AN* 306AP 493, 7 July 1790. See also letter of 12 Dec., in which Crozade *fils* blames the collapse in coal prices on the recession in the textile industry.

[7] Plantier, one of the wealthiest Protestant *négociants* in Alès and the owner of the biggest silk-spinning mill in the town, refused to purchase Castries's coal for several weeks after the *bagarre*. It was only the very poor quality of his alternative supplies which forced him back to the Grand-Combe. *AN* 306AP 493, 25 July 1790. Crozade to Castries.

[8] *AG* 58J 5, 12 July 1790, to Renaux.

[9] *AG* 58J 5, 13 Sept.

[10] *AG* L4108, *état où sont situées les mines de charbon qui fait exploiter le sieur pierre-françois Tubeuf*, 6 July 1792. The *mine de Cendras* was employing, regularly, 1 *maître-mineur*, 1 *receveur*, 1 *maréchal*, 4 *boiseurs*, and 8 *piqueurs*. Brouzon had 2 *toiseurs* and 4 *piqueurs*.

[11] *AN* 306AP 493, 27 Sept. 1790.

surrounded the so-called 'abolition of feudalism' but also from their refusal to accept *assignats* in settlement of *rentes* and seigneurial dues. Consumers, whether urban workers or protoindustrialized peasants, were being asked to pay for their daily bread in hard currency at the same time as the former were being forced to accept *assignats* in their pay-packets and the latter were finding it impossible to pay off their debts in the rapidly depreciating paper money. Always keen to exploit a situation which promised pecuniary advantage, Tubeuf offered Renaux some good advice on how to force *assignats* on his workers:

As for the shortage of hard currency which is creating difficulties for you when it comes to paying the workers at the end of the month, you should do what I do. Keep a record of the payments due to each of your workers on the same sheet of paper and when the amount has risen to a few hundred *livres*, give them *assignats* to the value of two or three hundred *livres* which they will divide amongst themselves on the basis of what is due to each of them.

Tubeuf warned his *directeur* never to give them cash, so that eventually 'the workers will get used to the idea of being paid in *assignats*, not being in a position to do anything else'.[12] No wonder disillusionment amongst wage-earners spread during the early years of the Revolution. The 'democratization of local government'[13] and the subsequent rise of the sansculotte movement is inexplicable without reference to the economic and social upheavals of the 1780s and early 1790s.

It is also inexplicable without an appreciation of the lengths to which the bourgeoisie in France were prepared to go to protect property. The Constitution of 1791 was to make it abundantly clear that if all men were indeed equal, property-owners were more equal than most. The *honnêtes gens* who framed the early legislation of the Revolution, lawyers and landowners almost to a man, many of them steeped in the physiocratic notion that land was the source of all real wealth, sought to square their egotistical concern for property with their fear of rural and urban rebellion. According to Patrice Higonnet, the uneasy alliance between the bourgeoisie and the peasantry must

[12] *AG* 58J 5, 18 Oct. 1790. Tubeuf added that the government was about to print 50-, 60-, 70-, 80-, and 100-*livre* notes so that regular payments to workers could be simplified.

[13] Lynn Hunt's description of the social composition of the 'democratic' movement of the Year II fits the situation in the Gard admirably: 'In the next wave were the artisans and shopkeepers, cutlers and carpenters, clothiers with a few employees, merchants for a limited regional market.' *Politics, Culture and Class*, 168–9.

also be explained by the cultural inheritance of the former, genuine believers in universal, if not egalitarian, rights: 'Caught as they often were between their particularist leanings and their craving for virtuous community, the French *classes moyennes* rummaged for ersatz solutions which would not endanger their social supremacy but might placate *le peuple*.'[14] Whatever proportion of altruism or *vertu* we wish to attribute to the bourgeoisie, the problem of placating the smallholding and share cropping peasantry was very much in the forefront of their minds, hence the complicated and contradictory legislation of 1791, including the Constitution itself. As Albert Soboul pointed out a generation ago, the Assembly refused to draw the logical conclusions from Heurtault de Lamerville's demand that the countryside should be set free,

which would have involved the ending of *vaine pâture* which was contrary to the 'natural and constitutional rights of property'. The Constituent Assembly refused to countenance this radical measure . . . the Rural Code, finally passed on 28 September 1791, did not follow logically from the general principles which had been adopted: enclosure was permitted but *vaine pâture* and the *droit de parcours* were to be retained if they were founded upon custom or title. The poorer peasant, unprovided or insufficiently provided with land, was to defend his collective rights for a very long time; even Napoleon did not dare to use his authority to deprive him of them.[15]

What has all this to do with coal-mines? A great deal, since the legislation which was to decide the future of the coal industry in France until the end of the Napoleonic Empire was passed, like the Rural Code, in 1791, and, like the Rural Code, it suffered from the same ambiguities and compromises, the same obsession with the rights of private property, with disastrous consequences for coal-mining *at a crucial stage in its evolution*. For it was precisely during the 1790s and 1800s that the British coal industry was laying the foundations of its subsequent world supremacy—8,850,000 tons in 1775, 15,045,000 tons in 1800, 22,265,000 tons in 1815.[16] What a contrast with output in the Alès region where, as we shall see, production levels in 1815 were

[14] P. Higonnet, *Class, Ideology, and the Rights of Nobles during the French Revolution* (Oxford, 1981), 264.
[15] A. Soboul, *Précis d'histoire de la Révolution française* (Paris, 1962), 156. Following the publication of Anatoli Ado's work on the peasantry in the French Revolution, Soboul was to revise his thesis (borrowed largely from Georges Lefebvre) concerning the relationship between the poorer peasant and the retardation of capitalism in the countryside. See P. Jones, *The Peasantry in the French Revolution* (Cambridge, 1988), 124–8.
[16] Flinn and Stoker, *History of the British Coal Industry*, 26.

hardly to rise above those of 1789. Tubeuf had shown himself eager to grasp the opportunity of legislating for a modern mining industry; few entrepreneurs, after all, were better equipped to understand the relationship between economics and politics. In a letter to Renaux just after the *bagarre de Nîmes*, he stressed the need for patience: 'We must hope that Nîmes will soon be back to normal, and that the commerce and sale of our coal takes off again. In the meantime, I would suggest that you keep on those workers you think are useful, telling them that you will be giving them work again as soon as the *affaire des mines* has been resolved [in the Assembly].'[17] The workers would have to wait for another year, during which time Tubeuf tried his level best to shape the legislation which was being discussed in accordance with his own ideas and experience. His eventual disillusionment helps to explain his decision to leave for Virginia.

As early as 25 January 1790, Tubeuf could have been discovered scurrying along the corridors of power surrounding the Constituent Assembly armed with multiple copies of a *mémoire* he had prepared on the future of coal-mining in France. On 6 February, he had passed the entire morning making final corrections to 1,500 copies 'since the printer has made a terrible glaring error which I have had to correct by hand'.[18] In addition to his many other duties, Tubeuf was his own secretary. For the rest of the year, his Journal is peppered with references to his exertions on behalf of himself and his fellow entrepreneurs like Desandrouin, manager of the rich Anzin mines,[19] as well as to visits made to the Bureau des mines and to his old patron Joly de Fleury.[20] When the Assembly finally got round at the beginning of 1791 to debating some of the major principles relating to mining, Tubeuf launched himself into another hectic burst of activity, corresponding frequently with the *rapporteur* appointed to oversee the new legislation, and distributing 900 copies of his redrafted *mémoire*, now entitled *Idées générales sur les mines du charbon de terre, sur leurs concessions, avec un projet de substituer les mineurs des mines de Royaume aux mineurs de l'armée*, to members of the Assembly and any other interested parties.[21] When one recalls that Tubeuf was still overseeing

[17] *AG* 58J 5, 12 July 1790.

[18] *AG* 58J 5. On 9–10 Mar., Tubeuf was particularly busy pressing copies of his *mémoire* into the hands of any deputy who was passing.

[19] *AG* 58J 5, meetings of 18 Feb. and 13 and 27 Mar., etc.

[20] *AG* 58J 5, 31 Aug. 1790.

[21] Bardon, *L'Exploitation du bassin houiller d'Alais*, 336–9.

the production of coal near Paris as well as in Languedoc, and that he was in the final stages of organizing his *colonie* to settle in Virginia, one can only wonder at the energy he generated.

What were the main elements of Tubeuf's programme, and how many of his ideas were incorporated into the eventual law of 28 July 1791? His main preoccupation was obviously to curtail the power of *les Grands* like Monsieur and Castries who had engineered his own defeat in the Alès region—and what a good time to do so. Tubeuf's spirits rose as the antifeudal feeling in France gathered momentum. As early as 20 April 1789, he had informed Renaux that the Estates General were bound to discuss the future of mining and that, at last, *concessionnaires* like himself would obtain justice.[22] However, as the months, indeed the seasons, elapsed, his natural buoyancy became somewhat deflated. He would return from meeting after meeting armed only with the knowledge that the serious debate on mining would not take place 'for at least another month'.[23] Throughout this period, Tubeuf consistently endeavoured to defend the interests of those *concessionnaires* who possessed real technical and managerial skills as opposed to landowners anxious to protect their property and medieval mining practices. In his *mémoire*, first drafted in January 1790, he had pointed out that serious coal-mining demanded long experience, technical know-how, and immense capital reserves, adding that 'one does not often find a landowner prepared to invest this kind of money; it is even more rare to discover that he is prepared to take the risks involved'. It was his concern for the wider national interest which attracted Tubeuf to the comte de Mirabeau, then the outstanding orator in the Assembly, who was to play a very important part in the early debates on mining in France. On 24 March 1791, Tubeuf sent him a personal letter, enclosing a copy of his *mémoire*.[24] Armed with Tubeuf's detailed information, Mirabeau, in one of his last speeches before his early death, spoke out against the untrammelled rights of individual *propriétaires*. 'Our experience shows . . . that the individual freedom to work coal-mines only destroys their potential or ruins them completely.' This had always been the main burden of Tubeuf's critique of the current situation.[25] Mirabeau attracted the

[22] *AG* 58J 5.
[23] *AG* 58J 5, letter to Renaux, 27 Mar. 1790.
[24] *AG* 58J 5, letter to Mirabeau.
[25] Rouff, *Les Mines de charbon*, 48. Tubeuf, reflecting his own bitter experience, was also eager to ensure that once a concession had been awarded, the *concessionnaire* should

support of deputies like Regnauld d'Épercy, who suggested that if the State allowed every individual to own and exploit the coal on his land then French industry would soon be completely mortgaged to Britain.[26]

Unfortunately for Tubeuf and his supporters, Mirabeau was to die in April and the most powerful advocate for their cause disappeared from the scene. The legislation which was finally passed on 28 July 1791 proved to be an extremely untidy and unworkable compromise between the interests of the nation and those of the individual.[27] Mirabeau had stood in the same line as *hommes d'état* like Bertin and Joly de Fleury, and there can be little doubt that the majority of the members of the Constituent Assembly appreciated the force of his (and Tubeuf's) arguments. However, for *propriétaires*, concerned, above all, about 'despotic' ministers and the encroachment of the 'corporate' and 'feudal' State upon their lives, the 'rights of property' had to take precedence.

According to one exasperated *concessionnaire* writing during the Bourbon Restoration, the legislation passed in 1791 represented nothing more than 'un assemblage ridicule de dispositions incohérentes',[28] an exaggerated conclusion containing, however, more than one grain of truth. For example, the opening words referring to the 'nationalization' of all coal-mines was about as meaningful as the opening words of the famous decree of 4 August promising to abolish feudalism 'in its entirety', since, as we shall see, all that was meant by 'nationalization', in practice, was that the individual landowner was supposed to take the legislation pertaining to the extraction of coal and the safety of miners seriously. It is true that certain articles were designed to strengthen the *étatiste* themes of the law passed in 1744 stipulating, for example, that anyone sinking a pit had to have the necessary technical skill and financial backing.[29] However, such provisions were to be respected more in the breach than in the observance. Article 4 was also designed to defend the rights of *concessionnaires* who already

---

be 'inattaquable par qui que ce fût d'autant que les contestations qu'attirent leurs succès sont trop souvent la ruine des concessionnaires et des entrepreneurs'. Bardon, *L'Exploitation du bassin houiller d'Alais*, 335–6.

[26] Rouff, *Les Mines de charbon*, 433.

[27] See Bardon, *L'Exploitation du bassin houiller d'Alais*, 336–8.

[28] *AN* 306AP 481, *mémoire concernant la proposition faite à ce sujet par M. Dugas des Varennes*, 11 Apr. 1816.

[29] See Article 9.

possessed legal entitlement to their mines, granting them, in some instances, a lease of fifty years, but very few *concessionaires*, as we have seen in Tubeuf's case, enjoyed unchallenged rights to their concessions. In addition, Articles 1 and 3 effectively established the *propriétaire* as the real arbitrer of the coal-mines on his land until the end of the Napoleonic Empire. Article 1 stated that 'Owners of the surface of the land will also enjoy the rights to their mines . . . to a depth of 100 feet only', a weak attempt to protect serious coal entrepreneurs like Tubeuf who were beginning to dig deeper and deeper coal-mines. It does not take much imagination to foresee the legal battles which would take place between *propriétaires* digging down to 100 feet and *concessionnaires* taking over below this depth.[30] It simply did not make technical sense. But Article 3 was the real prize offered to the landowner. It stated that 'Owners of the surface must always be given preference and the freedom to work the mines which might exist on their property, and permission for them to do so cannot be refused once a request has been made.'

It is abundantly clear that the real issue at stake in 1791 was *property*, as it had been since the legislation of 1744. The law of 28 July, however, must be seen as the victory of the bourgeois landowner over the 'feudal' authority of *les Grands* like Monsieur and Castries as well as over *les grands concessionnaires* like Tubeuf. Given the importance of the attack on 'feudalism', huge concessions were viewed in much the same light as huge *capitaineries*. It was none the less a severe blow to those who saw the State as the handmaiden of industrial progress. For this reason it is difficult to accept Achille Bardon's conclusion that 'In the final analysis, Tubeuf's ideas had triumphed.'[31] Marcel Rouff is much nearer the mark: 'Caught between reality and theory, the Constituent Assembly tried to evade the issue. Pressed hard to resolve it, it failed to take positive action. Never was a debate so troubled, so lacking in passion; never was a law so ambiguous and devoid of courage.'[32] This approach has much in common with that of Patrice Higonnet referred to above. One thing is clear: Tubeuf, crippled with debts and increasingly conscious of the fact that he was

---

[30] Indeed, the law was to multiply the number of disputed cases between landowners and mining entrepreneurs: 'La loi jetait donc le trouble dans toutes les anciennes concessions; elle ouvrait carrière à une infinité de procès.' Bardon, *L'Exploitation du bassin houiller d'Alais*, 343.

[31] Ibid. 344.

[32] *Les Mines de charbon*, 585.

never going to recoup his huge losses in Languedoc, was finally convinced that his salvation lay not in the Assembly, but in the New World. He had known, for example, as early as February 1791 that all concessions were going to be reduced to 12 square miles, one-third of his original concession in the Alès coal-basin.[33] The legislation of 1791, shaped as it was by the circumstances of the period, not only provided the epilogue to Tubeuf's career in France, it was to be the prologue to a period of stagnation or partial collapse for the French coal-mining industry which was to last throughout the Revolution and Empire.

The victory of the local *propriétaire* over the *concessionnaire* was sealed by the seizure of *biens nationaux* from the Church and the *émigrés*: from the spring of 1792 these *biens nationaux* would include the mines formerly owned by Monsieur, Castries, and Tubeuf, all three having been placed on the *émigré* list. Merchants, lawyers, and landowners all joined in the scramble for land, emphasizing the shift away from industry to agriculture. Much of the land purchased would go to increase the acreage claimed by the vine and the mulberry tree. No one would be immune from the virus of land-grabbing. In 1790, François Renaux, one of the leading mining engineers in the Midi, ploughed what little capital he had saved into what proved to be a successful enterprise for the production of silk-cocoons, although he continued to protect and administer the Tubeuf family's mining interests in the Alès region.[34] In the same year, Gantzler, Tubeuf's *maître-mineur* at Rochebelle, left his employment after purchasing a few acres of land planted with vines.[35] Given the prolonged recession in the silk industry, and the temporary collapse of raw-silk prices, vines and the distilling industry seemed a safer bet. One of the most vocal minorities to be heard in the Constituent Assembly from 1789 to 1791

[33] On 14 Feb. Tubeuf had sent Renaux the *projet de décret* which he had obtained from his friends in the *bureaux des mines*. On 15 Mar. 1791 Renaux replied that it was really not feasible to divide the original concession into three parts and hope to acquire three new concessions. *AG* 58J 5. His wife subsequently wrote: 'Ne pouvant supporter alors la spoliation qui venait d'être commise sur ces biens [Castries's legal victory and the reduction of his concession during the Revolution], he decided to emigrate to America'. *AN* F14 7683, *mémoire par la veuve Tubeuf, Brumaire An X*.

[34] *AG* 58J 5, letter of 7 June 1790.

[35] Tubeuf wrote of Gantzler's 'treachery': 'Ce qui vous me dites de Gantzler me surprend beaucoup. Je l'ai cru honnête homme', adding that he did not believe that his new acquisition would bring him prosperity. *AG* 58J 5, 24 Aug. 1790.

were the wine-growers of the Gard and the Hérault, pressing hard for the abolition of duties on wines and spirits. The *vignerons* of these departments may not have been renowned for their *grands crus*; they did, however, produce increasing quantities of cheap wine which could be distilled into the Languedoc brandies.

As Achille Bardon pointed out, landowners, busily buying up national lands and 'seizing control of common lands', were well represented amongst the active citizens of the region—taxation still being based primarily upon landed wealth—and they could always organize a powerful opposition group to any *étatiste* ideas on mining.[36] In September 1791, a *propriétaire* from Pont-Saint-Esprit, Jean Barbut, petitioned for possession of the coal-mines to be found on land 'formerly owned by the Chartreuse de Valbonne'. Barbut based his claim on the law of 28 July 1791, which, according to his reading of it, as well as that of all other *propriétaires* in the region, opened the way for the return of the mines 'to landowners who were working them before the granting of concessions'. It is interesting, and significant, that the Directory of the Department turned down his request not because he had misinterpreted the law of July 1791 but because coal-mining might have devalued the *biens nationaux* seized from the Chartreuse de Valbonne. For the wealthy land-owning Directors of the Gard, agriculture, including in this case forest land, was far more important than coal.[37] Apart from a few voices crying in the wilderness, most of the landowning inhabitants of the region continued to regard coal as a local commodity, not as a national, or even a regional, resource.

During the early years of the Revolution, partly as a result of the economic recession which had afflicted the Alès region for over a decade and partly as a consequence of the law of 28 July 1791, the pioneering work of Pierre-François Tubeuf was seriously undermined, as indeed were the less impressive achievements of his former *maîtres-mineurs* in the Grand-Combe. Many traditional coal-mining communities were determined to return to the happy days before Tubeuf's name had ever been mentioned, and before the maréchal de Castries had tried to imitate the action of the great entrepreneur. In June 1790, for example, the inhabitants of the commune of Laval had forced Castries's clerk at the Grand-Combe to sell them coal at the 'just

---

[36] Bardon, *L'Exploitation du bassin houiller d'Alais*, 336–8.
[37] *AG* L770, *Notice aux administrateurs du directoire du département du Gard*, Sept. 1791.

price' of 4 *sols le quintal*, or about half the current market price. Crozade instructed the clerk, Puechlong, to put a stop to this prodigality, with the result that the villagers marched *en masse* to the Grand-Combe demanding their 'droits anciens' to be provided with coal at 5 *sols* for 3 *quintaux*! Crozade informed Castries that he could try and hold up the inevitable by pretending to search through his archives for the relevant *titre*, a good example of the 'feudal' approach to mining, but given that, in his opinion, no documentary evidence existed this might prove to be a complete waste of time. The steward concluded gloomily 'There would never have been any such demand if it had not been for the Revolution.'[38] At the end of 1790, the maréchal's old gamekeeper, Pignol, opened up a small mine near the Grand-Combe which was more convenient for the carters to reach and which posed serious problems for sales from the Grand-Combe.[39] A few months later, Renaux explained that production from Rochebelle was being seriously affected by the reopening of those 'petites entreprises' which Tubeuf had fought so hard to shut down.[40]

The law of 28 July 1791 appeared to legitimize the seizure and reopening of the scores of small coal-mines in the Alès basin: it soon became the charter of the *petit propriétaire*. A brief examination of the individuals and families involved will reveal that they had all been in the vanguard of the struggle against Tubeuf since his arrival in Languedoc. The Larguier family, which owned a small plot of land— the *mas de la Tronche*—near the mine of the same name which they commandeered at the beginning of the Revolution, had fought alongside Pierre Rozier, the first landowner to take Tubeuf to court, in 1776.[41] The Larguiers had been involved in mining for generations and enjoyed the full support of the local landowning and manufacturing bourgeoisie, like Desparcieux, who was to act as their protector and patron throughout the Revolution and Empire. In one of his many petitions to the government, Desparcieux explained that he based his defence of the Larguiers on the law of 28 July 1791.[42] The Gillys, a minor noble family involved in glass-making, had been the

[38] *AN* 306AP 493, 3 June 1790.

[39] *AN* 306AP 493, Crozade to Castries, 12 Dec. 1790.

[40] *AG* 58J 5, 21 Mar. 1791.

[41] *AG* 8S 104, *procès-verbal* of the mayor of Sainte-Cécile, 5 Mess. Year IX.

[42] *AG* 8S 104, petition to Conseil des mines, 24 Vend. Year XII, in which Desparcieux described himself as 'l'un des plus forts contribuables de cette commune', and *AG* 8S 104, letter to prefect, 20 Apr. 1806, in which he refers to the law of 1791.

co-ordinator of the campaign involving the forty-nine individuals who had petitioned the government to cancel Tubeuf's concession in 1780.[43] The eventual compromise included the provision that, although Gilly could retain control of his own coal-mine, all others in the Saint-Jean-de-Valériscle area would have to close. By the end of the 1790s, six of these mines had been reopened, most of them leased out by Jean-Louis Gardies, another wealthy landowner with an interest in the production of raw silk.[44] Finally, in the Meyrannes valley, the Gazaix family had been the sharpest thorn in Tubeuf's side since 1775 when he had been forced to pay Jacques Gazaix 60 *livres* a year to compensate the family for the closure of their coal-mine.[45] In 1784, Tubeuf had unsuccessfully requested the use of troops to oblige 'Gazaix et ses complices de Meyrannes' to observe the law.[46] By 1795, Jean-Louis Gazaix was in charge of a coal-mine in the *forêt de Portes*. In the same year, five mines were operating in the Meyrannes and Robiac valleys.[47]

Crucial to the success of the landowners and their coal-miners was the decentralization of power to the municipality and the district. Under the *ancien régime*, Tubeuf could, and did, appeal to the Intendant against the interests of the municipality of Alès. The last Intendant, Ballainvilliers, had been one of Tubeuf's strongest supporters. The introduction of an electoral system to choose mayors and local councils gave the provincial bourgeoisie the kind of power which had previously been refracted through great nobles and archbishops. Members of the Gazaix family are listed as mayors or members of the municipality of Portes at various times during the Revolution alongside *propriétaires* who had been associated with coal-mining for several generations, like Jean-Louis Dautun.[48] Louis Gabourdes, who worked the Abilon mine 'illegally' throughout most of the 1790s, was to

---

[43] *AN* 306AP 481, *arrêt* of 15 May 1781.

[44] *AG* 8S 21, mayor of Saint-Jean-de-Valériscle to subprefect of Alès, 4 Prair. Year IX, and 8 S 105, Simon Martin to prefect, 11 Therm. Year XIII. Jean-Louis Gardies was one of the 500 highest taxpayers in the department. Simon Martin claimed that his family had opened his Deslieures mine and that, therefore, the law of 1791 gave him precedence over Tubeuf.

[45] *AG* 58 J2, 27 Mar. 1775, which records the payment to Gazaix, 'propriétaire du terrain'.

[46] *AHC, papiers de Tubeuf*, Cambis to Tubeuf, 9 July 1784.

[47] *AG* 8S 21, mayor of Portes to subprefect of Alès, Year IX.

[48] *AG* 8S 104, *procès-verbal* of mayor of Portes, 6 June 1806.

become mayor of Saint-Andéol-de-Trouilhas (renamed Laval during the Revolution) in 1803.[49] Another long-standing opponent of the Tubeufs, Jean Larguier, had replaced him by 1807.[50] These families could no longer appeal to the maréchal de Castries or the Archbishop of Narbonne; they turned instead to the kind of *notable* thrown up by the Revolution, leader of the *patriote* party in Alès in 1786 and deputy to the Constituent Assembly, Jean Soustelle. Member of a family which had a very real interest in coal-mines and the silk industry,[51] Soustelle had helped to orchestrate the campaign waged by the inhabitants of Laval to be supplied with coal at 5 *sous* for 3 *quintals*, doubtless to win the support of the mining communities, for by 1794 we find his younger brother managing a small coal-mine in the *forêt de Portes*.[52] The Soustelles had always been the sworn enemies of great nobles and great entrepreneurs like Monsieur and Tubeuf. The Revolution, for very different reasons, had turned both into *émigrés*.

The way in which the 'nationalized' mines of the Alès coal-basin were to be administered by the new municipalities and districts, far closer to the needs of local industry than previous administrations, was to aggravate the problem of their proliferation and exhaustion. During the course of 1792, both Castries's and Tubeuf's mines were placed 'at the disposal of the nation'.[53] The coal-owners of the region had not, however, bothered to wait for this official decision; they had simply reoccupied the mines they had always regarded as their own. In January 1792, the Directory of the Gard had written to the mayor of Laval expressing the hope that the villagers were showing the greatest possible respect for the new Constitution, which meant, in its opinion, respect for the mines belonging to the *ci-devant* maréchal de Castries.[54] The unwritten reply must surely have been that whereas the maréchal was in Switzerland, they were *in situ* and that, in any case, they had always regarded the mines as their birthright. It was a

---

[49] *AG* 8S 95, letter of prefect, 8 June 1806.

[50] *AG* 8S 95, Larguier to subprefect of Alès, 30 Aug. 1807.

[51] Jean Soustelle, *avocat*, was one of those who had signed a petition organized by bishop Béthizy and sent to the government in 1780 stressing that families like the Soustelles had owned their mines 'de tems immémorial'.

[52] *AN* F14 4240, *rapport sur les mines de Portes*, 18 Frim. Year II.

[53] F. Rouvière, *L'Exploitation des mines nationales du Gard*, 1792–1810 (Nîmes, 1901), 3–4. Castries's lands in the Gard during the Revolution were valued at 94,522 *livres*. *Rentes* from the Castries's estate were placed at the disposal of the *hôpital d'Alais*.

[54] *AN* 306AP 496, 26 Jan. 1792.

very important issue for the wealthy landowners of the region. If villagers seized mines legally belonging to *émigrés*, what was to stop them seizing the vast tracts of land taken from the Church under the pretext that they, or their forefathers, had always regarded the fields or forests they had toiled in as their own?

Many municipalities represented the less well-heeled members of society, and were inclined to favour sansculotte economic theories— no person should own more than one farm or one workshop or one coal-mine. This was evident in the legal battle between Georges Vairauch, who had worked a small mine in the le Vigan district for many years, and a forge-master named Combet, who was challenging his legal rights. In their letter to the Directory of the Department of the Gard, the municipality of le Vigan stressed that 'The injustice of M. Combet's demand is all the more despicable, given that he is rich and Vairauch is poor, that the law affords special protection for the latter against the former, and that Vairauch depends for his livelihood upon the mine into which he has sunk all his money.'[55] There is no record of who won the battle, but Vairauch's odds must have been poor given the naivety of his defenders, added to the fact that Combet was *procureur-syndic* of the district of le Vigan!

Officially, all the mines belonging to Monsieur (Levade, la Tronche, Champcloson in the *forêt de Portes*), the maréchal de Castries (the Grand-Combe, Abilon, the Mas-Dieu), and Tubeuf (Rochebelle–Cend-ras) were placed under the control of the Régie de l'enregistrement de la domaine nationale, an impressive title which meant, in practice, that in the Alès region the fate of its coal-mines was handed over, lock, stock, and winding-gear, to the municipalities of Alès and Uzès. It is significant that the local official responsible for leading the struggle against Tubeuf in the diocese of Uzès before the Revolution, Alexis Trinquelaque, had been chosen as mayor of the town in 1789 as a result of his Catholic faith and his determination to continue his struggle to defend *les petits contre les gros*. Eventually, he would be drawn, somewhat reluctantly, into the Counter-Revolution and the *camps de Jalès*, being forced to 'emigrate' in 1792.[56] His choice of political option may well have been facilitated by the fact that his brother, a wealthy planter in Saint-Domingue, had been ruined by the slave revolt in that colony. The Trinquelaques had no reason to love

[55] *AG* L770, 27 Apr. 1791.
[56] Lewis, *The Second Vendée*, 11–12.

the Revolution. In overall charge of the Régie was another old enemy of Tubeuf, Stanislas Serres, who, as *receveur des domaines nationales*, encouraged the disastrous policy of farming out the mines to his old landowning and manufacturing friends. As a Protestant and more inclined to the *patriote* party by virtue of his education and manufacturing interests, Serres had no problem in accepting the Revolution, at least in the early and late 1790s: few of the wealthier Alèsian bourgeoisie were to enjoy the Terror.

One of the first to benefit from the leasing-out policy adopted by the Régie was Pierre Soleiret, owner of a plot of land in the *forêt de Portes*, *maître-mineur* for Castries before the Revolution. He acquired the Portes and Champcloson mines. Jean Larguier was given control of la Tronche, whilst Stanislas Serres himself took over at Levade, his *maître-mineur* being none other than the son of François Faure, who had organized the attack against Tubeuf at the entrance to the Grand-Combe as a result of which Tubeuf had been blinded in one eye.[57] As for the many mines on the Cendras and Montaud mountains near Alès which Tubeuf had fought so hard and so long to close in order to concentrate production in Rochebelle, most were reopened and returned to his old adversaries the Devèzes and the Aubrespins, whilst Stansilas Serres seized control of Rochebelle itself for a brief spell during the 1790s.[58] Finally, the Grand-Combe and Abilon mines were placed in the hands of Adam Forster, ostensibly as an agent of the Régie, in reality as *maître-mineur* for local landowners and silk producers Gabourdès and Sauvezon.[59]

Every official report compiled during the Revolution—and it should be remembered that, after 1794, we can rely upon the inspectors of the newly created Agence des mines—stresses the serious damage inflicted on the coal-mines of the Alès region during the administration of the Régie. 'Nationalization', in effect, meant power to the *propriétaire*, not to the people. The mines were handed back to the landowners, raw-silk producers, and coal-miners who had wreaked such havoc in the coal-basin before the arrival of Pierre-François

[57] Information on the ownership and running of coal-mines during the 1790s is contained in the reports by mayors of Laval to the subprefect of Uzès and Alès. e.g., *AG* 8S 21, 29 Prair. and 8 Flor. Year IX. See also reports of Mahieu to the Directeur de l'enregistrement des domaines nationales du Gard, 27 Mar. 1807, *AG* 8S 95–6.

[58] *AG* 58J 5, *pétition du madame Tubeuf*, 4 Mess. Year X.

[59] *AN* F14 7683, report of the municipality of Alès, 25 Germ. and 2 Frim. Year III. Also *AN* 306 AP 496, report of 27 May 1806.

Tubeuf. It is hardly surprising that an organization created to deal with the transfer of Church lands should have made such a mess of running the coal industry. No fewer than nine small landowners or coal-mining families, amongst whom we find the familiar names of the Soleirets, Dautuns, and Laupiès, were working mines in the Portes region by 1801.[60] A report prepared by the Inspecteur des mines, Figuières, in the spring of 1796 warned the district of Alès that there would be 'an incalculable loss if you continue to place the mines at the mercy of *les fermiers*, who only work the rich and easily mined seams, who spend only what is strictly necessary, and who have no concern for the general upkeep of their mines . . . even pulling down the coal supports (*piliers*) in order to get out all the good coal with the least possible expense'. The Levade mine, the report added, was well on the way to total ruin.[61] A history of the Grand-Combe during the Revolution found in the Castries family papers states that, due to the damage inflicted by the agents of the Régie during the Revolution, only the injection of considerable sums of money could return the mine to working order.[62] The first prefect of the Gard reported that having ripped out the coal near the surface of the Grand-Combe, the miners had moved to the nearby Abilon mine to inflict the same damage there. He concluded that the administration of the Régie had been an unmitigated disaster, placing the ultimate responsibility, however, on 'landowners who do everything possible to retain control of the mines which are then worked without technical know-how or plans, something which cannot, in the public interest, be allowed to continue'.[63]

Even before the disruption caused by war and the Jacobin Terror, the more optimistic national and international vision of Pierre-François Tubeuf had faded in favour of the old, localized 'village economy'. The scale and rhythms of production were again being determined by the demands of the lime-burners and silk producers of the Cévennes and Bas-Vivarais, although a few coal-owners continued to provide fuel for the distillers of Nîmes and the Lunel region. At the lowest level of production came the tiny 'open-cast' mines of Barjac, the centre of Tubeuf's original concession, which were only worked for

---

[60] *AG* 8S 21, mayor of Portes to subprefect of Uzès, n.d. Year IX.

[61] Rouvière, *L'Exploitation des mines nationales du Gard*, 13–15.

[62] *AN* 306AP 495, *mines de la concession de monsieur le duc de Castries*, 1816.

[63] *AG* 8S 96, *avis du préfet du Gard*, Year XI.

most of the Revolution by 'a handful of individuals when they have
no other work to do. They dig a few holes in their fields from which
they extract a few baskets of poor quality coal . . . in order to produce
a couple of sacks of lime for their fields.' This was the old medieval
link between coal-mining and agriculture. The mayor of Sainte-Cécile,
referring to the three mines under his jurisdiction, explained that 'It
has always been the custom for the owners of these mines to work
them at certain times of the year only, just for their own needs, and
no one has bothered them.'[64] Higher up the scale came men like Jean
Larguier, *fermier* of la Tronche: he sold his coal in the Hautes Cévennes
to silk-spinners and chestnut-dryers.[65]

The odd exception to the dismal catalogue of disasters which befell
the great majority of the mines of the Alès coal-basin during the
Revolution—even the Grand-Combe had ceased production by
1794[66]—concerns former employees of Pierre-François Tubeuf, particularly Jean-Baptiste Mahieu and, of course, François Renaux. Both
men were trained mining engineers, but they lacked the necessary
capital and the support from the local authorities to do much more
than hold the line at Abilon and Rochebelle. In Vendémiaire Year IV
we learn that a *chaufournier* named Blancher and a certain François
Renaux had taken out a five-year lease on a couple of mines on the
Montaud mountain for 1,100 *livres* a year.[67] Renaux was clearly continuing to serve the interests of the Tubeufs despite the trying circumstances. He was aided and abetted in his schemes by Mahieu. The
two men were to remain very close friends throughout the Revolution
and Empire.[68] It is not surprising that Stanislas Serres should have
launched his bitterest invective against Mahieu and Renaux, the first
being denounced as someone who spread 'fear and terror' throughout
the region,[69] the second criticized as 'the paid and confidential agent
of Tubeuf, who brought him to these parts in the beginning, putting
him in charge of the mine called Chaulieu [Rochebelle]'. The continued animus against the Tubeuf family may be judged by the reference

[64] *AG* 8S 21, to subprefect of Alès, 29 Prair. Year IX.

[65] *AG* 8S 96, Chabrol to prefect, 24 Mess. Year XIII.

[66] *AN* 306AP 482, *mémoire sur les mines de charbon de terre de l'arrondisssement d'Alais,
An II.*

[67] Rouvière, *L'Exploitation des mines nationales du Gard*, 62.

[68] By 1806, according to the subprefect of Alès, 'il est notoire que le sieur Mahieu
mange presque toujours chez madame Tubeuf à Rochebelle et loge chez le sieur Renaux'.
AG 8S 104, to prefect, 27 Oct. 1806.

[69] Rouvière, *L'Exploitation des mines nationales du Gard*, 206–7.

to Mme Tubeuf as 'la citoyenne Brochet, self-styled widow of Tubeuf'.[70]

The tragic consequences of the *bagarre de Nîmes*, added to the destructive consequences of the 'nationalization' of the mines in France, did not prevent coal production from rising briefly in 1791 and 1792. However, the advent of war was to pose particular problems. It might be thought that, with its increased demand for armaments, war would have acted as a spur to increased production. The Littry mines in Tubeuf's native province of Normandy, after all, were doing quite well in 1792 delivering coal to armament manufacturers in Caen and Coutances. By the end of 1794, however, the Littry mines were already experiencing major problems leading to a dramatic fall in production. Increased demand for coal would benefit the Belgian rather than the French coalfields in the 1790s. Does the experience of the coal industry in the Gard provide corroboration for Jean-Charles Asselain's conclusion, confirmed by other economic historians like Bonin and Crouzet, that 'The revolutionary period, after 1792–1793, experienced a real economic collapse, easily explicable in terms of the conjuncture of civil war in certain provinces, external war, and inflation.'[71] The answer, on the whole, is yes; although the explanation Asselain offers, so far as the coal industry is concerned, is too limited in scope, omitting the crucial issue of the legislation of 1791 and its link with property-owners.

It would also be wrong to think that the Jacobins were ignorant of the major problems coal-owners were experiencing in France: indeed, it was to be during the Terror, just a few weeks before Robespierre fell, that a major reorganization from above occurred. On 18 Messidor Year II (1 July 1794), it was decided to create the Agence des mines. It is quite clear that war was the decisive factor behind this extremely important reorganization of the mining industry in France, given that the new agency was to be a subsidiary of the Commission des armes et poudres. The Agence des mines was to be composed of a three-

---

[70] Rouvière, *L'Exploitation des mines nationales du Gard*, 65.

[71] J.-C. Asselain, *Histoire économique de la France du XVIIIe siècle à nos jours* (Paris, 1984), i. 120. See also H. Bonin, 'La Révolution française, a-t-elle brisée l'esprit d'entreprise?', *Information historique*, 47 (1985); F. Crouzet, *De la supériorité de l'Angleterre sur la France* (Paris, 1985). On p. 293 Crouzet points out that although there was some increased demand, the Napoleonic wars, 'dans la mesure où elle garantissait aux maîtres de forges un marché stable pour leur production, elle était plutôt un frein à l'innovation'.

member executive, 8 inspectors, 12 *ingénieurs des mines*, and 40 *élèves*. Its first task would be to establish 'an inventory of the number of mines, foundries, and workshops in the control of the Republic'. In the pursuit of collecting and collating information, and in the hope of improving the techniques associated with mining, certain members of the newly created Agence would spend eight months of their year travelling in the eight administrative *arrondissements* created by the decree. In Vendémiaire of each year, a conference of inspectors and engineers would be held in Paris to compare notes and plan future activity.[72] An indication of the importance attached to this development was the fact that the decree of 18 Messidor was signed by almost every member of the Committee of Public Safety.[73] A year later, the first issue of the *Journal des mines*, the most important publication on mining yet to appear, would be published. In his first editorial, Charles Coquebert underlined the significance of the recent developments in the field of mining: 'The Committee of Public Safety has seen that the interests of Liberty require that the mining industry should be revived. An Agence has been organized . . . This Agence will preside over a *Maison d'Instruction*, which will include a *cabinet de Minérologie*, a *Bibiliothèque*, a *Laboratoire*, and a Département de Desseins et de Modèles.' It was the Revolution which introduced France to the scientific age of mining.[74]

By the time the first issue of the *Journal des mines* appeared on the desks of mine directors throughout France, the Agence was pressing them and 'les *propriétaires* des mines de houille' to send them reports on production figures every decade.[75] As so often during the Revolution, enthusiasm for the creation of a 'modern' state was oustripping common sense. Far more sensible was the growing recognition that the Régies de l'enregistrement were proving a major obstacle to their plans for a revolution in production. Letters had been received from entrepreneurs stating their willingness to increase production for the armament industry on the understanding that private enterprise was the real key to success. One entrepreneur stated that the existing

---

[72] *Journal des mines publié par l'Agence des mines de la République* 1(1) (1794), 103. On 18 Mess. Year II, it settled the salaries of its personnel. An *inspecteur* was to be paid 6,000 *livres* a year, *ingénieurs*, 3,000, and *élèves*, 1,500 *livres*.

[73] *AG* L1048, *extrait du registre des arrêtés du Comité du Salut Public, 13–18 messidor An II*. The *arrêt* was signed by Robespierre, Carnot, Prieur, Collot, Lindet, Billaud, Couthon, Barère, Jeanbon Saint-André, and Saint-Just.

[74] *Journal des mines* 1(1) (1794), 4.

[75] *AG* L1048, *extrait du registre des arrêtés du Comité du Salut Public, 22 frimaire An II*.

system would have to be ended since he 'regards the *régies* as ruinous for the industry'.[76]

Once again, as a result of war and the consequent centralization of government, the municipality of Alès saw itself confronted with the return of 'monopoly production' and the arrival of new 'Tubeufs' seeking to concentrate the industry and shut down small pits. As early as the spring of 1793, Henri Isnard had written to the administrators of the Gard seeking their permission and support 'to set up forges in the Midi for the purpose of making canons for the navy'. Isnard also wanted to 'open a second workshop in the district of Alais for making iron with desulphurated coal; and also a second glassworks [Pierre Gilly's had been the first] based upon English methods of production'. Isnard concluded that the Alès coal-basin 'contained all the basic materials for launching an industry whose products are eagerly sought by the foreigner. The coals of Alais are of particular importance, notably those of the Grand-Combe.' The offer, on account of its scale and objectives, obviously evoked the memory of Tubeuf's doomed arrangement with Richard, Carrouge et Cie fifteen years earlier. It also looked forward, however, to the plans which Tubeuf's younger son, Alexandre (with his brother in America at this time), would implement in the Alès coal-basin a decade later. Isnard was the *directeur* of the government glassworks at nearby Montcenis and, consequently, well informed about the coal industry and local conditions. In his petition he noted that tests on the iron-ore deposits near Alès had proved very promising, and that 'the same industry which had been started at Montcenis could also be started in the Alais region, but with this essential difference; that the workshops and the machinery one could set up there would not demand either the same costs or the same sacrifices which had characterized the opening of the Montcenis works'.[77]

It is evident that the brains behind Isnard was Tubeuf's loyal *directeur*, François Renaux, referred to by Isnard as 'Renau, ingénieur et directeur des mines nationales du district d'Alais'. In his notes on the project, Isnard, obviously basing his statement on Renaux's advice, thought that it would be necessary to close down the mines which

---

[76] *AG* L1048, letter from steel manufacturer to district of Alès, 4 Fruct. Year II.

[77] *AG* L1048, *pétition et mémoire aux citoiens administrateurs du département du Gard*, 13 Mar. 1793. One of Isnard's advisers was Faujas de Saint-Fonds, an expert on mining who had been promoted to an important position in the Jardin national des Plantes, and who had once been an adviser to Monsieur, Louis XVI's brother.

had belonged to 'Castries and Monsieur, brother of the last king of the French, in order to ensure that there would be no untoward competition'. However, deeply conscious of the lengthy battle between his old *patron* Tubeuf and the *propriétaires* represented by the municipality, Renaux had clearly warned Isnard that some form of leasing out of the smaller mines would be necessary, or, as Isnard phrased it, 'citizens who intended to associate with *l'artiste* Isnard would be encouraged to buy or lease the necessary mines at competitive prices'. Isnard also promised that he would 'bear in mind the duty of supplying the department, also setting up workshops which entrepreneurs might think appropriate'. The *patriotes* would obviously have been particularly pleased with the plan to seize Castries's *château de Trouilhas* and transform it into a workshop, a good example of industry availing itself of opportunities provided by the sale of *biens nationaux*.[78] There was, therefore, something for everyone in Isnard's plan, *propriétaires*, entrepreneurs, as well as the municipality, which would have the coal it needed to exchange for grain. Not surprising, therefore, that in April 1793, in the course of a public meeting, the departmental administrators suggested that the offer should be taken seriously. By the end of the month the *administrateurs du district d'Alais* had also given the scheme their blessing.[79] In a final letter to the Directory of the Gard, Isnard underlined what Tubeuf had grasped twenty years earlier—that there was at least as good a chance of creating a successful mining and metallurgical enterprise in the Alès region as at Montcenis or Givors, given Alès's close proximity to the Rhône and to Marseille.[80]

Unfortunately for the landed, mercantile, and professional élite which was in control of the department at this time, the *patriotes de 1793* were about to replace the *patriotes de 1789*. The former had created the Société des amis de la Constitution three years earlier

---

[78] It is interesting that Isnard was worried about the projected division and sale of all *émigré* property and was anxious to secure (for himself and his fellow 'artistes') a base for his coal and iron-ore mining activities before the Castries's estate was split up into small lots. *AG* L1048, Isnard to Agence des mines, 26 Mar. 1793. It is probable that Renaux, who argued against seizing the *château de Trouilhas*, was extremely concerned about any move to take over *émigré* property, given his loyal service to Tubeuf who had also, of course, been placed on the *émigré* list. See *AG* L1048, comments of the Conseil d'administration du district d'Alais, 26 Apr. 1793.

[79] Ibid. A public meeting was held on 8 Apr.; Isnard's proposals were officially sanctioned on 27 Apr. 1793.

[80] *AG* L1048, 10 Aug. 1793.

'supported essentially by *négociants*, merchants, *fabricants*, but also by landowners and lawyers'. Schemes such as those proposed by Isnard were obviously in tune with the interests of this élite. It certainly did not have the same attraction for the members of the Société populaire des amis de la Constitution, which was almost exclusively composed of master-craftsmen and textile workers, victims of the prolonged economic recession and the exploitation of the *négociants*. The latter threw themselves into the ill-fated Federalist revolt in the south-east, issuing a declaration on 22 June 1793 which exhorted its followers: 'Vous qui avez des propriétés, armez-vous.' As Anne-Marie Duport notes, 'This text clearly reveals that the fear of unrest and disorder which was so harmful to trade, to business in general, was linked, in the minds of the property-owners, to the fear of losing their land.'[81] Following the miserable failure of the Federalist revolt, the sansculottes of the Société populaire were to seize the main administrative positions on the municipal and district councils throughout the department, as indeed was to be the case in many other towns in France.[82] Attempts to re-create the atmosphere of 1790, when religious differences were exploited for political ends, failed in the face of the severe economic problems which the textile industry, and other industries in the Gard, were experiencing, producing a class alliance of Catholic and Protestant small masters and workers against the *négociant* and *propriétaire*.[83]

This failure was to have important repercussions in the Alès region. On 12 September 1793, the members of the Directory of the department were all dismissed and a month later the représentants Rovère and Poultier arrived in Alès, flanked by emissaries from the Société populaire de Nîmes, to arrest leading members of the merchant and legal élite which had held power since 1789. Jacques-André Sugier, who had played a major role in the pre-Revolutionary period in Alès,

---

[81] Duport, A.-M., 'Le Fédéralisme gardois: de la théorie à la pratique', in *110ᵉ Congrès national des sciences sociales* (Montpellier, 1985), ii: *Histoire moderne*, 173–89.

[82] Of the 12 members of the Comité de surveillance de Nîmes, 5 were *faiseurs de bas*, 2 were small merchants, 1 was a *fabricant d'étoffes*, and there was 1 *relieur*, 1 *mécanicien*, 1 *blanchisseur*, and 1 *apprêteur d'étoffes*. Lewis, *The Second Vendée*, 73.

[83] During the spring of 1793, the leaders of the Société républicaine sent *commissaires* into the Gardonnenque to enlist support for their cause, denouncing the members of the Société populaire de Nîmes as Catholic royalist followers of François Froment, the *émigré* agent held responsible for unleashing the bloody *bagarre de Nîmes* in 1790. Undoubtedly some had supported Froment against the Protestant *négociants* in 1790, just as they supported the new mayor, Courbis, in 1793 and his campaign against the *négociants* and lawyers who were leading the Federalist revolt. Ibid. 65.

Louis Rocheblave, one of the most influential silk merchants in the town, and Stanislas Serres, member of the Régie de l'enregistrement, who had benefited so much from the 'nationalization' of the coal-mines, were all imprisoned in the *fort d'Alais* for alleged complicity with the Federalists of Nîmes. Sugier was subsequently guillotined in Nîmes. The purged municipality was to be drawn from much the same stratum of the population as at Nîmes, with Pignol as mayor flanked by a silversmith, a druggist, a baker, and wigmaker. The indispensable Louis Dhombres, who had been appointed *procureur-syndic* at the beginning of the Revolution, tactfully left his post announcing that, in his *politique* opinion, the new municipality would do a wonderful job and that it enjoyed his full support![84] The smaller coal-owners and colliers were doubtless impressed by a remarkable missive from the Administration générale des armes portatives de la République to the district authorities in the spring of 1794 which underlined the need for weapons and hence greater supplies of coal in semi-mystical terms. The district was told to scour the countryside for 'those who are capable of opening coal-mines. Amongst the poorer class (*la classe la moins aisée*) it is possible to find devoted men who only need encouragement for them to develop their considerable talents.' The district was told that they should ask for the assistance of the popular societies in order to facilitate its task.[85] Jacobin ideas were percolating through to the work-place as well as to the town hall, and the smaller land-owners and mining families were not unresponsive.

However, those who shouldered the responsibility for expanding production, the trained mining engineers like Renaux, Mahieu, and Forster, saw things in a very different light.[86] On 13 Messidor Year II (1 July 1794), Renaux explained to the administrators of the district of Alès that he could no longer continue production given the financial constraints imposed by the maximum of prices. Large coal from his Cendras mine, which had sold for 10 *sous le quintal* in 1790, had been fixed at 12 *sous* by the municipality (if only the municipality had enjoyed these powers in Tubeuf's day!), and, given escalating costs

---

[84] Bruyère, *Alès, capitale des Cévennes*, 434–6.

[85] *AG* L1048, 3 Flor. Year II.

[86] See *AN* F14 7688, Mahieu to Agence des mines, 24 Pluv. Year III, which states that, apart from himself, only Renaux and Forster had any real engineering ability. Many others were working mines, but 'aucun n'a de principes et presque tous sont illitérés et toute leur science consiste à extraire du charbon où ils en trouvent le plus à portée'.

of production, particularly wages, he was selling at a considerable loss. Renaux explained, as all mine directors and manufacturers were obliged to explain, that he was, of course, a *bon patriote* and therefore did not wish to break the law 'by selling at a higher price than that fixed by the municipality or by giving short weight, as many do'. So, he had decided to lay off some of his workers.[87] A few months later Jean-Baptiste-Mahieu, who was now managing the Abilon mine for its original owners, Gabourdès and Sauvezon, sent a detailed report to the Agence des mines explaining that, despite formidable obstacles, he had succeeded in doubling production from 31,000 *quintaux* for the year ending December 1790 to 63,000 *quintaux* in 1793. However, his report continued, he was now facing a considerable drop in production 'since the maximum fixed on the price of coal sold in Nîmes and Montpellier is far too low when compared with the price allowed in Alais'.

One of the main problems for Mahieu and his fellow producers in the Alès basin was the cost of transport. Coal suitable for the larger spinning-mills and distilleries had been fixed at 16s 9d a *quintal* in Alès, but could only be sold in Nîmes at 19s. As a result, the carter received just over 2 *sous le quintal* for carrying the coal over 25 miles. In 1790, the same carters would have charged around 10 *sous le quintal* for this distance.[88] The position was much the same a year later when Mahieu explained to the Agence des mines that a severe shortage of carts was preventing him from supplying 'coal-powered workshops and forges since all the carts have been requisitioned for the army'. Things were so bad, Mahieu went on, that he had to use green wood in his own house because he could not get coal delivered![89] Production at the rich Grand-Combe mine had ceased, again primarily on account of transport difficulties.[90] The evidence is conclusive: coal production in the Alès basin was severely interrupted by the cost of transport as well as by the shortage of horses and mules requisitioned by the army.

Equally serious as a brake on production was the requisitioning of men for the army. In his report of 27 Brumaire Year II (17 November 1793), Mahieu had stressed the difficulty he was facing as a result of 'the law of the maximum and the loss of fifteen young miners who

[87] *AG* L1048, 13 Mess. Year II.

[88] *AG* L1048, Mahieu to *les citoyens administrateurs du département du Gard*, 27 Brum. Year II.

[89] *AN* F14 7688, 24 Pluv. Year II.

[90] Rouvière, *L'Exploitation des mines nationales du Gard*, 8.

have been called up'. He begged the Agence des mines to ensure that the municipality of Laval did not requisition skilled workers like Jean-Louis Gabourdès (son of the mine's owner), who was his *conducteur des travaux*, nor Jean-Antoine Quensac, a shot-firer and haulier.[91] During periods of full production, Mahieu explained, the Abilon mine employed about 30 men; since the *levée en masse* he had only 13 full-time workers on his books.[92] The complaint was repeated a year later when Mahieu replied to charges that he, and other coal suppliers, were not providing enough coal for the gunpowder factory in Montpellier. He stressed that the fault was not his since 'the small number of miners I have left since the *levée en masse des volontaires* have been working around the clock'.[93] This loss of manpower was also felt by the smaller producers: in the Robiac valley, for example, where only one mine, belonging to Charles Polge of Castilhon, was working by the early spring of 1795;[94] and at the Levade mine, whose manager had filed a request for 'a greater number of workers' in the winter of the previous year.[95] The importance of maintaining levels of output for the war effort was underlined by the municipality of Laval when it reported that if the Grand-Combe and Abilon mines (usually worked alternately) did not produce coal 'for the forges of Nîmes, Montpellier, and other towns, for the distillers in the Vaunage, as well as for the saltpetre works which is so vital for the production of gunpowder . . . all these *fabriques et forges* would have been forced to shut down, it being common knowledge that the other mines in the region cannot produce enough'.[96]

The terrible winter of the Year III obviously exacerbated the problems faced by coal producers, now confronting the increasing demands of the army. As the first issue of the house journal of the Agence des mines suggests, war continued to be the spur to action: 'We are entering a more scientific era of coal-mining,' the editor explained to his readers. 'If we are beginning to make better use of nature's gifts, if we are beginning to rely more on our soil and our industry, it is to the war that we must pay hommage.'[97] In the winter

---

[91] *AN* F14 7688, 27 Brum. Year II.
[92] *AG* L1048, *état concernant les mines de charbon de terre de la forêt d'Abilon*, 14 Brum. Year II.
[93] *AN* F14 7688, 24 Pluv. Year II.
[94] *AG* L1048 *rapport sur les mines du Gard*, n.d.
[95] Rouvière, *L'Exploitation des mines nationales du Gard*, 14.
[96] *AG* L1048, *extrait des registres de la commune de Laval*, 27 Oct. 1793.
[97] *Journal des mines*, 1(1) (1794), 3.

of 1795, the Commission des armes et poudres again expressed its concern to the authorities in Alès over the temporary closure of the gunpowder factory in Montpellier, 'a consequence of the lack of fuel which it gets from the coal-mines of your district'. The Commission instructed the *agent national près le district d'Alais* to ensure that 'the exploitation of these mines are actively pursued and that they fulfil all the demands made upon them, particularly those from this important *raffinerie de salpêtre*'.[98] The *agent national*, like any good bureaucrat, passed the buck on to the man who was—theoretically at least—in charge of overall production in the Alès basin, the *receveur des domaines nationales*, who replied that, as far as he could ascertain, 'there was plenty of coal available, but no carts to transport it'.[99] The following month, the Commission fired another broadside over the bows of the beleaguered *agent national* instructing him to make absolutely sure that mine directors like Renaux were supplied with sufficient powder for blasting rock. On 24 Pluviôse Year III (12 February 1795), Mahieu summed up the technical and economic problems he was facing: 'The most pressing requirement for the exploitation of the mines is *la poudre à mine* which would enable us to undertake the necessary drilling in the rock, iron for tools, and, throughout the region, more food, the price of which rises daily.'[100] Iron was indeed in short supply: in September 1794, the only three workshops in the district of Alès which were turning out bayonets for the army were closed due to a severe shortage of this raw material.[101] The crisis of production in the coal industry was not confined to the Alès region: a letter written by Mahieu the following spring informed the Agence des mines that a forge-master from Bordeaux had told him that the price of coal in the port was now so high, as a result of the war, that he was considering ordering it from Alès. Mahieu explained to the Agence that 'when he arrives, I shall do my level best to convince him that he should forget all about the greedy English'.[102]

As Georges Lefebvre has pointed out, the same problems had been bedevilling coal production in the Littry mines of Normandy. Noel,

---

[98] *AG* L1048, 3 Niv. Year III.

[99] *AG* L1048, *receveur* to *agent-national*, 15 Niv. Year III. The former's uncompromising reply was that the Commission des armes had to ensure that transport to deliver coal was available.

[100] *ANF*14 7688, to Commission des armes. Mahieu asked for at least one *livre* of gunpowder a day.

[101] *AG* L1048, *état indicatif des mines de charbon de terre dans le district d'Alais*.

[102] *AN* F14 7683, 22 Vent. Year III.

Directeur des mines de Littry, informed the government that 'The *maximum*, requisitioning in the markets, the increasing shortage of basic commodities, mean that we can hardly continue production without the assistance of the local authorities; in addition, the *levée en masse* threatens to deprive us of our work-force.'[103] The privations caused by the winter of 1795 led to strikes and the periodic suspension of all production. It is clear that in the Gard, the *paysans-mineurs* were less dependent upon the mines for their survival. It had been traditional for the unskilled coal-miner to move from the pits to work associated with the textile industry or the harvesting of chestnuts and grapes. Coal-mining was inserted into the local labourer's diary in accordance with the seasons not with the thought that he would be spending fifty weeks a year underground.

It was, however, the old problem of the multiplicity of small-owners which aggravated the situation in the Gard. At Littry, there would be a pronounced turn for the better by the end of the Directory: in March 1800, the first steam-engine from the Périer brothers would be installed.[104] In the Alès coal-basin on the other hand, although, as we shall see, the position was not as bad as we have been led to believe, the rule of the *petit propriétaire* continued to exercise a baleful influence on coal production. In the spring of 1796, Faujas de Saint-Fonds (who had prepared a report for the king's brother on the *mines de Portes* before the Revolution) reported to the government that most of the coal-mines in the Gard were being ruined by a combination of ignorance and greed: 'These abuses, if tolerated for much longer, will inevitably lead to the loss of our coal-mines, a fall in manufacturing output, and consequently the ruin of much of the activity and industry associated with this *pays*.'[105] An official report drawn up in the summer of 1797, which noted the importance of the coal industry for the 400 silk-spinning mills in what used to be the Bas-Vivarais, now the southern Ardèche, concluded: 'Unfortunately . . . work in the mines in this part of France is left to isolated individuals who have neither the means, the know-how, nor the

---

[103] G. Lefebvre, 'Les Mines de Littry, 1744–an VIII', in *Études sur la Révolution française* (Paris, 1963), 177.

[104] Ibid. 192.

[105] *AN* F14 7688, *observations sur les mines de houille du département du Gard*' Flor. Year IV. The report stressed that particular attention needed to be paid to the Grand-Combe and Levade mines, which had either been underworked, as was the case with the former, or become waterlogged, as in the case of the latter.

necessary farsightedness and spirit of improvement.' Banne, which, according to the same report, had been well managed in Tubeuf's day, 'is now abandoned to the arbitrary efforts of the *gens du pays*: everything has been turned upside-down and ruined. No precautions have been taken to ensure the circulation of air and water or the safety of the mine; the *piliers* have all been attacked and serious roof-falls have been the result of this blind greed.'[106] According to an earlier report, the inhabitants of the Gard had neither the interest nor the financial means to involve themselves in modern mining techniques.[107] There was, however, one glimmer of hope. In the winter of 1794, the Committee of Public Safety had informed all *agents nationales* that 'according to the principles adopted by the Committee, no more *régies nationales* would be accepted since they are always costly to the Republic and because they involve unnecessary expenses. Besides the Régisseur, occupied more with his own affairs than the interests of the public good, is rarely concerned with improving things.'[108] This was an excellent comment on the attitude of legal officials and stewards, who had constantly, both before and during the Revolution, interposed themselves between the local population and those entrepreneurs and officials who favoured 'modernization'.

If mining experts and central government knew what had to be done, local officials and property-owners continued to raise almost insuperable obstacles. Here again, we must stress one of the major themes of the present study—the link between politics and economics, between property-owners and the perpetuation of outmoded forms of mining. The overthrow of the *patriotes de 1793* by the men who had run the department during the early years of the Revolution (those who had not been guillotined that is!) involved a strident reaffirmation of the rights of property. Their attitude was succinctly, if dramatically, summed up by Olivier Gérente, one of the *représentants-en-mission* to the Gard in 1795, who informed the Convention that, 'having learned from the misfortunes which resulted from the *journée* of 31 May [1793]', he and his friends were ready 'to rush to the defence of the Convention and to make a rampart of their corpses . . . ready to perish a thousand times over rather than fall once again beneath the yoke of bloodthirsty and rapacious men. Speak', he concluded, 'and at your voice you will see a phalanx of *républicains propriétaires* marching

---

[106] *Journal des mines*, 46 (Mess. Year V), 631.
[107] *Journal des mines*, 13 (Vend. Year IV), 54.
[108] *AG* L1048, 6 Frim. Year III.

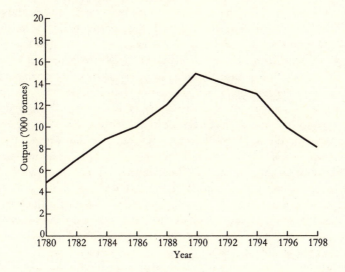

FIG 4.1. Production in the Alès coal-basin, 1780–1798

from the departments of the Gard and the Hérault'.[109] Following the White Terror of 1795, which accounted for the lives of hundreds of 'terrorists' in the south-east, including Courbis, the mayor of Nîmes during the Terror, the wealthy Protestant *négociants*, *propriétaires*, and *avocats* again seized the main departmental and municipal offices in Nîmes and the larger towns. In Alès itself, the new municipal council was chosen by the *représentant*, Girot-Pouzols, who appointed Jacques-Louis Dhombres as mayor. Throughout the Directory and Empire, the families which had traditionally dominated the civic life of Alès—the Dhombres, the Périès, the Rocheblaves—would tighten their grip on political and economic power, although on the smaller municipalities like Laval, the *petits propriétaires* would continue to protect their own interests. On 27 July 1795, the 'return to normality' would be symbolized by the rededication of the cathedral in Alès and the return to their nursing duties of the *Sœurs de la charité*.[110]

Fig. 4.1 underlines the impact of war, the Terror, and successive political upheavals upon coal output in the Gard during the Revol-

[109] Lewis, *The Second Vendée*, 81.
[110] Bruyère, *Alès, capitale des Cévennes*, 45.

ution.[111] In the spring of 1794, the district of Alès estimated that
annual production for the most important mines only was as shown
in Table 4.1. If we take the higher figures given in the table, this
makes a total annual production of 350,000 *quintaux*, or 14,000 tonnes
for 1793, which compares quite favourably with the figure of approximately 15,000 tonnes for 1789.[112] It must also be noted that the
production figures for mines like Saint-Jean-de-Valériscle are not
included. The impact of war, the Terror, the winter of 1794–5, and
the political upheavals of the Directory are evident from the decline
in production during the following years. They are, however, not quite
as dismal as previous estimates have suggested.[113] Production figures
for the Year III (September 1794–September 1795) are shown in Table
4.2. These figures give us a total of 162,190 *quintaux*, or almost 7,000
tonnes. However, Table 4.2 does not include the figures for the Portes
or the Robiac mines, nor those of the small mines on the Montaud
mountain. The reports from which these figures have been taken make
it very clear that coal was still being produced in all these mines but
that it was impossible to obtain reliable estimates of production.[114]
Renaux was convinced that one should add at least one-third to the
total official production figures to cover the output of 'les mines
illicites'.[115] Total production for the Alès basin for 1794–5, therefore,
must have been nearer to 10,000 tonnes than the 7,000 referred to
in the table. Basing our conclusions from figures for individual mines,

[111] The statistics for this graph have been taken from *AG* L912, *tableau des mines qui
se trouvent dans le district d'Alais*, 29 Brum. Year II (confirmed by figures for individual
mines like Abilon, *AG* L1048, 14 Brum. Year II); *AG* 8S 21, *aperçu de ce que fournissent
annuellement les mines de houille des environs d'Alais et des communes voisines*, Year XI; as well
as from the official figures published in the *Journal des mines*, e.g. the excellent report
published in no. 71 (Therm. Year X), *aperçu général des mines de houille exploitées en France,
de leurs produits, et des moyens de circulation de ces produits*, which was based on reports
received by the Agence des mines over a seven-year period. pp. 357–8 cover the Alès
coal-basin.

[112] *AG* L1048, *rapport sur les mines du district d'Alais*, 28 Vent. Year II. Because
production was moved to Abilon (easier to mine, or rather to despoil), figures for the
Grand-Combe drop from 58,728 *quintaux* for the Year IV to 47,200 for the Year VII
and 37,320 for the Year VIII.

[113] See e.g. D. Woronoff, *The Thermidorean Regime and the Directory* (Cambridge,
1984), 64.

[114] *AN* F14 4240, *observations générales sur les mines de houille du département du Gard*, Flor.
Year IV.

[115] *AG* 8S 21, letter to subprefect, 19 Vent. Year XI. The previous report, *observations
générales* (which François Renaux helped to compile), makes it perfectly clear that small
mines on the Montaud mountain as well as many in the Meyrannes, Robiac, and *forêt
de Portes* districts were producing coal throughout this period.

TABLE 4.1. *Estimated annual production for major mines, Alès district, April 1793–April 1794*

Mine	Mine director	Production (*ancien régime quintaux*)
Cendras	Renaux	70,000–80,000
Montaud	Devèze (and others)	40,000
Abilon	Mahieu	80,000–90,000
Grand-Combe	Forster	70,000–80,000
Portes	Soleiret	40,000–50,000
Robiac	—	10,000

TABLE 4.2. *Estimated annual production for major mines, Alès district, September 1794–September 1795*

Mine	Production (*ancien régime quintaux*)
Cendras	43,693
Saint-Jean-de-Valériscle	21,312
Abilon	56,647
Grand-Combe	31,818
Pomeirol	3,720

it would be fairly safe to assume that production continued to decline until the Consulate.[116] By the Year XI (September 1802–September 1803), *before*, as we shall see, very positive steps were taken to improve the situation, production had returned to just above the 1794–5 figures.[117] Renaux estimated that the mines in the immediate vicinity of Alès itself were producing 2,400 tonnes: 1,800 tonnes being sold in the department, 400 in the Hérault, and 200 in the Lozère, Aveyron, and the Bouches-du-Rhône.[118] It is hardly surprising, however, that the government during the Consulate should have been extremely worried about the situation in the Gard, particularly when one notes that production at the Anzin mines, which had fallen to 65,000 tonnes in 1794, had risen to 138,000 in 1796, and 213,000 tonnes by 1798.[119]

[116] See Rouvière, *L'Exploitation des mines nationales du Gard*, 80.

[117] It is possible that a new agreement with entrepreneurs like Puech and Goirand helped to improve the situation. See ibid. 28.

[118] *AG* 8S 21, Renaux to subprefect of Alès, 19 Vent. Year XI.

[119] Woronoff, *The Thermidorean Regime*, 115.

What galled government officials most was the fact that the Gard was 'one of the departments in the Midi where this fuel [coal] is the most abundant'.[120]

1795 was an important year in the public calendar of the French Revolution—the *journées* of Germinal and Prairial in Paris, the White Terror in the south-east, the Vendémiaire uprising and the birth of the Directory. The same year had been no less momentous in the private history of the Tubeuf family—the violent and untimely death of Pierre-François and, as a kind of epitaph to his pioneering work, the first signs of the re-creation of his concession in the Alès coal-basin. Marie-Margueritte Tubeuf had always intended to continue where her husband had left off and, given the disgrace and exile of their arch-enemies Monsieur and the maréchal de Castries, there was always that glimmer of hope to beckon her on. It was one such ray of hope which prompted her to reopen her husband's Journal. On 16 Ventôse Year III (6 March 1795), she wrote, in her usual poor French: 'aujourdhui que la justice et a loudre du jour et que mes affaires dont se moment semble prometre un avenir plus heureuse, je reprent mon compte' (today, now that justice is the order of the day and my affairs seem at the moment to promise a happier future, I am reopening my accounts).[121] It would be easy to make an unfavourable comparison between Marie-Margueritte's poor French and equally poor bookkeeping and those of her husband. Although she had obviously started out with the intention of carrying on his work in his customary efficient manner, her entries in Pierre-François's last Journal following his departure for America in 1791 are perfunctory to say the least. They consist, in the main, of scattered references to receipts and repayments to her creditor and companion the marquise de Chaulieu.[122]

However, if her husband had been a truly remarkable man, Marie-Margueritte was no less a remarkable wife, mother, and advocate for her family's interests. Described in her *certificat de résidence*, dated 1797,

---

[120] *Journal des mines*, 71 (Therm. Year X), 357, *Aperçu général*.

[121] *AG* 58J 3.

[122] Ibid. On 15 May 1791 Mme Tubeuf made her first entry: *Compte de recette et de despense à commencer depui le dépar de mon mari pour lamérique avec mon fils, le 15 de la moy de mai*. However, apart from the few scattered references to payments made to Mme Chaulieu and deposits from the ever-faithful Renaux, no serious attempt was made to record credit and debit accounts. There is nothing at all in the Journal from 8 Nov. 1793 to 16 Vent. Year III. This was the period of Marie-Margueritte's 'personal Terror'.

as being 'five feet in height, with auburn-coloured hair and eyelids, grey eyes, a high forehead, long nose and average-sized mouth',[123] Marie-Margueritte had never been trained to assume the reponsibilities of running a sprawling industrial business, still less to cope with a revolution, the violent death of her husband, and the departure of her only two sons for America—Alexandre, the younger boy, having joined his brother François some time during the mid- or late 1790s. Living in very straitened circumstances at the Boulevard du Pont aux choux in Paris, saddled with massive debts, she devoted her entire energy to the reconstitution of her husband's 'empire' in Languedoc. Her greatest asset in this regard was undoubtedly François Renaux: without his loyalty and expertise, and knowledge of the treacherous local situation in Alès, it is doubtful whether or not she would have been as successful as she eventually proved to be. Marie-Margueritte was big enough to acknowledge this fact. In a letter to her son, Alexandre, referring to 'monbon Renaux', she wrote: 'This man is precious to us. We must look upon him as the best of our friends, frank and straight . . . in a word, *un parfait, honnait homme.*'[124] Chaucer could not have phrased it better, nor with greater justification.

In a forty-page *mémoire* intended for the eyes of Napoleon Bonaparte himself, Madame Tubeuf, through her lawyers, provided the government with a résumé of her husband's epic battle with the maréchal de Castries and her own valiant efforts to be recognized as the legitimate heir to her husband's estate.[125] Her ultimate objective, doubtless on Renaux's advice, was the control of all the productive mines in the Alès coal-basin, including the Grand-Combe. The document stressed, quite rightly, that the legal victory won by Castries in December 1788 had been 'a mockery of justice', and that, until the prefect of the Seine had crossed her husband's name off the *émigré* list on 2 Messidor Year IX (21 June 1801), her life during the Revolution had been a catalogue of disappointments.[126] It was the action of the prefect of the Seine which had prompted her to organize

---

[123] *AG* 58J 8, 22 Aug. 1797.

[124] *AG* 58J 7, 8 June 1801.

[125] See *AN* F14 7683, *mémoire par la veuve Tubeuf*, Brum. Year X. This document refers to her husband as 'l'artiste qui, depuis quarante ans, se livrait à des découvertes utiles à l'Etat et que ses travaux de toute espèce ont conduit au tombeau sans avoir reçu la recompense qu'il méritait'.

[126] On one occasion Marie-Margueritte had threatened to break into Bonaparte's private office and fling herself at his feet unless she received some reply to her letters! *AN* F14 7684, 27 Flor. Year IX.

a final assault upon the government, one that was at last to prove successful. By a consular decree dated 7 Thermidor Year X (15 July 1802), Marie-Margueritte Tubeuf, *née* Brochet, was *provisionally* granted control, not only of the mines of Cendras and Rochebelle, but also of the prize which had always eluded her husband, the Grand-Combe itself. The decision officially annulled the infamous decree of December 1788.

The task of bringing the more productive mines of the Alès coal-basin back to full production, which involved repairing the damage inflicted upon them during the mid- and late 1790s, may be judged by a remark made by Marie-Margueritte to a close friend: 'Would you believe, madame, that I have had to employ sixty workers to reopen the mines. The Grand-Combe, which was run by the Régie, is in a terrible state, everything smashed, ruined.' There can be little doubt that the owners of small 'illicit mines' had done everything they could to end the ruinous competition from rich mines like the Grand-Combe and Rochebelle, neither of which were working when the Tubeufs took over again in 1802. For a time, Madame Tubeuf was to be caught in the old vicious circle that had surrounded her husband: she could not afford to invest considerable sums of money in 'modernizing' productive mines like the Grand-Combe and Rochebelle, whilst the Soleirets, the Larguiers, and the Gabourdès continued to sell coal from the easily worked 'illicit' mines in Portes, the *forêt d'Abilon*, and the Montaud mountain. And these mines could not be closed without provoking howls of protest from the local landowners, silk-spinners, lime-burners, and distillers who depended upon the traditional small, seasonal deliveries of coal; some of them were also *fermiers* who benefited from renting out the small mines, thus securing coal for the manufacturing side of their business interests at cheap prices.[127] In addition, her efforts were to be further impeded by a more enterprising breed of coal-owner who had exploited the opportunities afforded by the sale of land and the 'nationalization' of the mines during the Revolution to carve out a promising future. As we shall see, Jacques Puech and Pierre Goirand were to prove the most successful 'Goriots' of the Alès region.[128]

---

[127] *AG* 58J 7, to Mme de Montschanque, 1801.

[128] Puech and Goirand had obviously done extremely well out of the many land transfers which took place in the Gard during the 1790s. They were also far-sighted enough to secure long leases on some of their deals. For example, on 22 July 1793 they had acquired Champcloson from Pierre Soleiret on a 40-year lease for 800 *livres* a

The most immediate and threatening problem confronting Marie-Margueritte and her trusted expert François Renaux in 1802, however, was the spectre of the maréchal de Castries's ghost haunting the battlements of the Grand-Combe. The maréchal himself had died two years earlier, but not before he had helped to file a claim to his coal interests in the name of his daughter Adélaide-Hortense-Gabrielle de Mailly, who, in turn, was acting on behalf of her nephew, the marquis de Castries.[129] All the bitter memories of the long and costly struggle which Mme Tubeuf and her husband had suffered before the Revolution returned to trouble her last years. As she explained in a personal letter: 'I am continually unwell. These coal-mines are killing me! How I wish for peace and the end of the pain which one has to suffer in this life. I trust that the next life will be infinitely more tranquil. What misfortune to live only this kind of life, and to know that one is always its victim.'[130] However, the times were still out of joint for the maréchal's heirs and, for a few years at least, Marie-Margueritte, Renaux, and her younger son Alexandre (who had left his brother François in America in 1801 in order to assist his mother) could concentrate on the unenviable task of getting the mines back into full production, which would ultimately involve a sustained attack on the owners of the 'illicit mines' in the region. Alexandre appears to have been the favourite son (hardly surprising given that he had originally stayed with his mother when her husband left in 1791), and was rewarded with many instances of Marie-Margueritte's maternal affection. He undoubtedly deserved such favour: on one occasion, having

year. On 6 Vend. Year VII they obtained the same lease to the Plusor mines from Agniel for 2,800 *livres* a year; on 6 Vend. and 7 Pluv. Year IX, the important lease to the Trescol mine from Antoine Baldy (500 *livres* a year) and Jean Coste (2,400 *livres*). However, most of their deals were concentrated in the old *vicomté de Portes*, mines formerly owned by Monsieur and therefore still 'nationalized' property. The Soleirets, Agniels, Baldys, and Costes were simply acting as they and their fathers had done for decades, leasing out property with scant regard for the legal niceties of the Revolution! See *AG* 8S 96, prefect of the Gard to Minister of the Interior, n.d. (Year XI). This was to cause considerable difficulty when the government eventually decided to regularize the confused situation in the Alès coal-basin at the end of the Empire.

[129] The maréchal de Castries's rights to his coal-mines in the Gard had been divided between his daughter, the vicomtesse de Mailly, and his grandson, Eugène-Edmond-Hercule, marquis de Castries. Mme de Mailly eventually conceded her share to the marquis de Castries in return for an annual *rente* to be paid to her daughter, Elizabeth de Mailly, duchesse de Caylus. When the latter died prematurely in 1814, Mme de Mailly agreed to forgo her rights. Castries, *Papiers de famille*, 309–10.

[130] *AG* 58J 7, to Mme de Montschanque, n.d. (but almost certainly 1801).

sent his mother the sizeable sum of 10,000 *francs*, she thanked him not just for the money, but because 'tu et [*sic*] mon fils et de plus mon ami'.[131]

Slowly, but surely, despite many misgivings associated undoubtedly with her sad memories of the 1780s and the uncertain state of her health,[132] Marie-Margueritte was won over to the 'expansionist' ideas of her son and Renaux. It was no easy task. On one occasion Mahieu (now working for the Tubeufs, not Gabourdès and Sauvezon) explained to Alexandre that he had suggested taking on more workers, 'but your mother, fearful as always, thought it better to dismiss some of the workers and to cancel our contract with several carters'.[133] None the less, Alexandre and Renaux pushed forward as best they could with the work of drying out the flooded seams and propping up the collapsed roofs of the Grand-Combe, and, on Renaux's advice, some workers were kept on the books during the winter months to undertake the same work in Rochebelle, where the seams were deeper, requiring far more preparation and investment than at nearby Cendras.[134]

Eventually, good management, the concentration of production at the Grand-Combe and Rochebelle, and the closure of a few small mines produced results. By the autumn of 1803, monthly sales figures had doubled (compared with the previous year's) and looked to be set on an upward curve.[135] There can be no doubt whatsoever that much of the credit went to François Renaux who was not only

---

[131] *AG* 58J 7, 8 June 1801. Madame Tubeuf ended her letter with the touching farewell: 'A dieux monbon a lexandre, a dieux mon fils.' François, the elder brother, who was 27 in 1801, was still in America at this time looking after the family's commercial business, which had been launched some time after the death of his father.

[132] Given the great potential of the Grand-Combe mine it is sadly ironic that Marie-Margueritte Tubeuf should have bemoaned the fact that the family had been given possession not of the Abilon and Mas-Dieu mines in the Grand-Combe valley, but the Grand-Combe itself. Her well-grounded fears about the enormous cost of restoring the mine to full production is evident in one of her letters to Alexandre: 'la grende Combe ne peuvent fournir du charbon car gros frais, puise qu'il sont [*sic*] épuisée'. *AG* 58J 7, 25 Prair. Year XI.

[133] *AG* 58J 7, 8 Vend. Year XI.

[134] *AG* 58J 7, 16 Brum. Year XII. Renaux suggested that 'la saison morte' (for coal sales) had begun and that this might provide an opportunity to move men from Cendras to Rochebelle in order to prepare production for the following spring. According to the ever-worried Mme Tubeuf, they had already spent 10,000 francs pumping water out of Rochebelle. *AG* 58J 7, to Mme de Montschanque, n.d.

[135] *AG* 58J 7, Renaux to Alexandre Tubeuf, Vend. Year XI. In Mess. and Therm., 23,000 francs-worth of coal had been sold at their Alès warehouse. Renaux estimated that they would sell coal to the value of 24,000 francs in Vend.

overseeing the engineering side of the business but also busily promoting sales. On 10 August, he had reported upon a tour of the
Vaunage during which he had contacted old clients and discovered a
few new ones: 'I was well received everywhere,' he wrote to Alexandre.
'I am returning with many orders which have to be met in two months
. . . our coal-depot is well stocked,' adding that he was just off to
Beaucaire to buy new tools for their workers.[136] Transport difficulties
were also faced, 60,000 francs having already been earmarked for the
completion of a new road from the Grand-Combe to the main
highway.[137] By the spring of 1805 despite, as we shall see, constant
battles with the *propriétaires* of the small mines in the region, the
Tubeuf company had, to all intents and purposes, monopolized
production in the Alès region.[138] A year later, Alexandre and his
brother François—who had now also returned from America to assist
in promoting the family fortune[139]—could write to their creditors:
'Our production of coal is now so great that we have outstripped
consumption in our own department.'[140] Fig. 4.2 illustrates how the
production of coal in the Alès basin had risen by this time well above
pre-Revolutionary levels.[141]

The years 1806–8, however, would record the high point of achieve-
ment for the Tubeuf *fils*. The twin forces of economic and political
change were henceforward to move against them. It was perhaps
fortunate that Marie-Margueritte, who had fought so valiantly to
re-create her husband's empire, had died a year earlier. She may, at
least, have recaptured something of 'le bon vieux temps' of her youth.
Scarred, however, by half a century of personal drama and revolutionary conflict, a 'foreigner' in the hostile Cévennes, she had always
appreciated that industrial success during the Revolutionary and Napoleonic period was bound to rest upon rather shaky foundations. It

---

[136] *AG* 58J 7, 22 Therm. Year XI.

[137] *AG* 58J 7, Mme Tubeuf to Mme de Montschanque.

[138] Rouvière, *L'Exploitation des mines nationales du Gard*, 233.

[139] See the first entry in *AG* 58J 10, 14 Jan. 1804, which records that his brother
had decided to join him in Alès.

[140] *AG* 58J 7, to Devienne *frères*, 12 Nov. 1806.

[141] The figures are based upon those provided in the Tubeuf Journal, *AG* 58J 7,
tableaux des dépenses et des produits des mines de Tubeuf) for 1807–8, corroborated by the
very reliable estimates contained in the Beaunier report (see below), which suggests that
2,000 tonnes of coal was being produced in 'illegal' mines not part of the Tubeuf
empire.

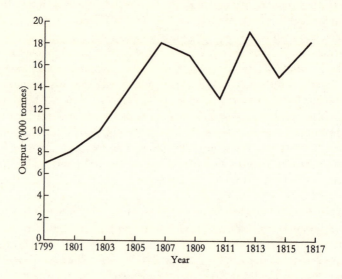

FIG 4.2. Production in the Alès coal-basin, 1799–1817

should also be recalled that the consular decree of Thermidor Year X had been *provisional*: there was always the threat from the descendants of the maréchal de Castries hovering in the background. More immediately, there was the battle with the local opposition, land-owners, old mining families, and municipalities which represents the most consistent theme in the history of the coal-mines in the Alès region since Pierre-François Tubeuf had first carried his young bride over the threshold of their home in the Cévennes some forty years earlier.

As we have seen, the Revolution had strengthened the resistance of the *propriétaire*, who had been well pleased with the provisions of the 1791 legislation on mining. François Renaux, who knew the situation better than anyone, put it in a nutshell when he wrote that 'most of the mines which fell within the boundaries of Tubeuf's concession would have produced a great deal of coal by now but for the fact that they have been worked for years by certain individuals, *propriétaires du terrain*, who have seized control of them, resisting every attempt to dispossess them, above all since the Revolution'.[142] Jean

[142] *AG* Q150, *régie nationale des biens de François-Pierre Tubeuf*, Renaux to the Tribunal correctionnel d'Alais, 11 Germ. Year VII.

Larguier had seized the mines of la Tronche, near Portes, which had been worked by the *fermiers* of Monsieur before the Revolution, at the beginning of 1797: in one of his many petitions against his old enemies the Tubeufs he argued that 'the owner of the land must be preferred to *un étranger*'.[143] The 'owner of the land' was a relatively wealthy landowner from the commune of Laval, who supported Larguier's claim by direct reference to the law of 28 July 1791.[144] In August 1806, Larguier was to spend a short spell in prison as a 'dévastateur des propriétés nationales', having refused to accept the prefect's ruling that he must stop his 'illicit mining'.[145] Another old adversary of Pierre-François Tubeuf, Jean Rouquette, *propriétaire* of a few acres in the commune of Sainte-Cécile, had actually taken the prince de Conty to court in 1782 to defend his rights to the Levade coal-mine, which his family had worked for decades. Not surprisingly, he had lost the case, which did not prevent him from reasserting his claim during the Revolution, basing it upon the law of 28 July 1791.[146] Jean-Pierre Devèze, *propriétaire* of a plot of land in the *quartier de Brouzen*, 'profiting from the upheavals from which France is still suffering', had seized a coal-mine during the Revolution which was just a few hundred yards from Tubeuf's Rochebelle mine. The medieval techniques employed by Devèze's miners were primarily responsible for the flooding of the Rochebelle mine. As late as 1808, Devèze was still protesting that the mine he and his family had 'owned' for generations had been illegally seized by 'la dame Tubeuf'.[147]

Destined to become the most important of the local coal-owners during the Bourbon Restoration, Jean-Jacques Puech, a *propriétaire d'Alais*, and Pierre Goirand, *traiteur d'Alais*, were to lead the local fight to defeat the re-creation of the Tubeuf 'monopoly' during the Napoleonic Empire, having laid the foundations of their success by buying out the rights of the inhabitants in the former *vicomté de Portes* during the Revolution and Consulate. According to the Ingénieur en chef du département du Gard, Puech and Goirand had organized the collective petitions which poured into the prefect's office in the summer of 1806 and again in 1807, representing, in the opinion of

---

[143] *AN* F14 7670, *pétition de Jean Larguier*, 30 Fruct. Year XII.

[144] *AG* 8S 104, letter of Desparcieux to the prefect, 20 Apr. 1806.

[145] *AG* 8S 104, prefect to Minister of the Interior, 7 Apr. 1807.

[146] *AG* 8S 104, *réponse des habitants de la commune des Portes*, 1 Brum. Year XIII, which stressed that Jean Rouquette was the *vrai propriétaire* of the Levade mine.

[147] *AG* 8S 95, letter to the prefect, 13 Aug. 1808.

the Ingénieur, 'the opinions of a few individuals who are jealous of seeing order reign at last over this important industry'. As for the *propriétaires*, they were mainly 'inhabitants of these parts who managed to get their hands on this source of public wealth during the Revolution and who have fought ever since to legitimize their usurpations'.[148] Just as Pierre Gilly had organized petitions against Pierre-François Tubeuf in the 1780s, so Puech and Goirand rounded up support for the attack on his wife and sons during the Empire. The script had hardly changed in thirty years! Accusing 'la dame Tubeuf' of doing her best to dispossess them of 'une propriété sacrée', the signatories to the petitions, including all the old familiar names— Larguier, Aubrespin, Dautun, Devèze, etc.—stated that 'A foreigner, with no rights other than those acquired by intrigue, cannot enjoy the right to dispossess us.' The decree of 7 Thermidor Year X was attacked in words almost identical to those used to denounce the decrees won by Pierre-François Tubeuf in the early 1780s: 'subversive of the right of property and ruinous for every class of citizen, since it would establish a scandalous monopoly in the distribution of a commodity which has become essential for everyone'.[149]

As had been the case in the 1780s, it was the municipality of Alès, supported now by the little mining communes of Laval, Saint-Cécile, Portes, and Robiac, which gave political shape to the opposition. As a result of the decentralization of power and the electoral influence of the landowner, Larguier, Gabourdès, and Jean-Louis Dautun all became mayors of their respective communes during the Consulate and Empire. They could now claim, with some justification, to be protecting the interests of the local inhabitants they represented. Jean Larguier told the prefect that, so far as the mines in his village were concerned, 'I only look upon them from the standpoint of the advantages which the inhabitants of this commune derive from their exploitation and the livelihood which they provide for a great many of them.'[150] Jean Rouquette told the mayor of Saint-Cécile that he 'only opened up the [Levade] mine when they asked him to do so'.[151] The inhabitants of the commune of Pradel explained in their petition

---

[148] *AG* 8S 95, July 1807. For the involvement of Puech and Goirand see the *arrêté préfectoral*, 8 June 1806.

[149] *AG* 8S 95, *aux citoyens composant le conseil municipal de la commune d'Alais*, n.d. (probably 1807).

[150] *AG* 8S 46, mayor of Saint-Andéol-de-Trouilhas, 17 Pluv. Year XIII.

[151] *AG* 8S 104, Chabrol to subprefect of Alais, 5 Mess. Year IX.

that they were 'miners from generation to generation; that they knew their mines and the ways of preserving the coal in them'. This was the key issue for many villagers—*preserving* the coal in their mines for their children. They underlined this point in a telling remark, having accused 'monopolists' like Tubeuf and—stressing the rising threat of their increasingly powerful partnership—Puech and Goirand, of ripping out all the coal in their mines with no thought for the future: 'these mines are for the time being the coffers of Croesus; in a short while, abandoned . . . we shall be reminded more of Job!'[152] The mayor of Robiac told the subprefect of Alès that he was defending the rights of his villagers only on account of '*les pauvres misérables*, whose plaintive cries over the fear of being deprived of their daily bread inspire pity in me'.[153]

Again, as in the 1780s, the increasing opposition to the remarkable degree of success which had crowned the efforts of the Tubeufs and François Renaux was to be channelled through the agency of the municipality of Alès. As early as 1799, Jacques-Louis Serres, acting on behalf of the municipality as Receveur des domaines nationales, had sought permission from the *tribunal correctionnel d'Alais* to seize Roche-belle, its mines, equipment, house, and land, using the pretext that the Tubeuf's were *émigrés*.[154] Was this a 'holding operation' on behalf of the Castries family? Probably. Whether it was or not, over the next decade, faithful to the spirit of resistance mounted by the local community over thirty years, Serres was to launch a sustained bure-aucratic guerrilla war against the Tubeuf family.[155] On 26 Germinal Year XI (16 April 1803), echoing the sansculotte economic theory championed by Alexis Trinquelaque before the *masques armés* revolt of 1783, the Conseil d'arrondissement d'Alais denounced the growing threat of another Tubeuf 'monopole' in the following terms: 'First, there can be no doubt that in placing the exploitation of the numerous mines which are to be found in the first *arrondissement* in the hands

---

[152] *AG* 8S 95, petition to prefect, Brum. Year XII.

[153] *AG* 8S 21, 30 Mess. Year IX.

[154] *AG* Q520, *régie nationale des biens de François-Pierre Tubeuf.* The Tubeufs had fallen foul of the post-Fructidorean legislation against *émigrés* passed in Brum. Year V. Patrice Higonnet explains the increasing ferocity of the attack on *émigrés* as a 'quest for ideological surrogates'. *Class, Ideology, and the Rights of Nobles*, 259.

[155] On 1 Germ. Year XI, 'une scène scandaleuse' took place in Serres's office in Alès when Alexander Tubeuf, accompanied by his two faithful industrial retainers Renaux and Mahieu, tackled Serres about their legal rights. Rouvière, *L'Exploitation des mines nationales du Gard*, 180–1.

of a single individual, the quantity of coal extracted will drop appreciably.' All that *concessionnaires* achieved, the council believed, was to push up wages and the price of coal. Finally, asserting the long tradition of provincial independence, once associated with the Estates of Languedoc, the council noted: 'Natural law, Roman law, a series of royal *ordonnances* from the time of Charles VI to the Revolution, all confer the ownership of coal-mines upon the *propriétaire des fonds*.'[156] The words of this song hardly varied throughout the Napoleonic Empire. In 1807, the Conseil-général du département told the government that 'An exclusive *privilège* is therefore a curse;' three years later, that it was about time the government put an end to the Tubeuf's 'vaste ressort'.[157]

As under the *ancien régime*, the Napoleonic administration began by taking a firm line but then, as adversity struck, pusillanimity became the order of the day. Despite, as we shall discuss, the passing of one of the most important laws in the history of French coal-mining to the present day, the lessons to be learned from Pierre-François's success in the 1780s and his sons' achievements in the 1800s (with the personal contribution of François Renaux acting as the essential bridge between the two) were ultimately sacrificed in return for local and aristocratic support during the dying years of the Empire. During the early years of the Empire, the prefect of the Gard did everything he could to support the Tubeufs, following the arguments of *ancien régime* ministers like Bertin that coal was vital for industrial growth and that France should not be totally reliant on British imports. In addition, coal had now became very important as a source of domestic heating.[158] However, prefects were also sensitive to the importance of property-rights and the ideological significance of competition. The *avis du préfet* sent to the Minister of the Interior by prefect Dubois in 1804 reflects most of these points: 'The consular decree of 7 Thermidor Year X,' Dubois explained, 'which restored to Mme Tubeuf the rights granted to her husband, has unleashed all the passions to be found amongst the majority of landowners, who will fight to the death to protect their mines, which are run without technical know-how or plans, something which, in the public interest, can no longer be tolerated.' The prefect went on to explain how these landowners had worked through the municipalities of Alès, Portes, and Laval, to

[156] Rouvière, *L'Exploitation des mines nationales du Gard*, 222–6, meeting of the Conseil-général, 26 Germ. Year XI.
[157] Ibid. 297–304.
[158] Ibid. 286.

spread the 'false' notion that the Tubeuf concession was 'une calamité publique pour toute la contrée'. 'Unfortunately,' the prefect concluded, 'most people, above all the landowners, cannot be persuaded that limits might be placed upon property-rights.'[159]

Initially, prefects did the best they could in the circumstances. In the spring of 1803, the first order relating to the closure of all 'illegal' mines had been issued, asking all mayors to provide the prefecture with details of all coal-mines operating within their jurisdiction.[160] In the summer of the following year, the prefect ordered Jacques Serres, the Receveur des domaines nationales and an avowed enemy of the Tubeufs, to hand over the rights of mines like Levade to the Tubeufs.[161] It is obvious that these moves were only partially success-ful since they had to be repeated on several occasions, notably on 8 June 1806, following yet another official report referring to 'la dévas-tation la plus effrayante' in some of the smaller coal-mines.[162] On this occasion, an exasperated prefect named the offenders—the Soleirets, the Larguiers, the Laupiès, Gabourdès, and Desparcieux—and de-manded that the gendarmerie visit their coal-mines to block up the entrances with walls at least two metres thick.[163] Two months later, Larguier, who had done his best to ignore even this order, was incarcerated in Alès prison 'pour encourager les autres'.[164] Such dra-conian measures were only partially successful: after all, the Larguiers had been fighting authority for generations. When the gendarmerie made their visit to Larguier's mine they were told, in the strongest possible cévenol language, to leave, which they apparently did.[165] Having forged close links with the local élites on municipal councils and tribunals, the 'independent colliers' of the Cévennes felt that they had little to fear—and they were right. As the Ingénieur des mines explained to the Conseil des mines, local officials were loath to implement the law since they did not wish to make enemies of their friends and relatives in their respective communes.[166]

---

[159] *AG* 8S 96, *avis du préfect*, n.d. (1804).
[160] *AG* 8S 95, *arrêté préfectoral*, 26 Germ. Year XI.
[161] *AN* F14 7670, Renaux to Conseil des mines.
[162] *AG* 8S 95, *arrêté préfectoral*.
[163] *AN* F14 7683, Ingénieur-en-chef des mines to the Conseil des mines, 21 Vent. Year XIII.
[164] *AG* 8S 104, *arrêté préfectoral*, 7 Apr. 1807.
[165] *AG* 8S 22, *rapport sur la rebellion des exploitants des mines de l'arrondissement d'Alais*, 8 May 1806.
[166] *AN* F14 7683, Ingénieur-en-chef des mines to the Conseil des mines, 25 Vent. Year XIII.

Local officials were indeed in a most difficult position, frequently obliged to resort to defensive tactics in order to placate the higher authorities. The mayor of Portes told the Ingénieur des mines that, in his experience, there was absolutely no point in walling up the entrance to the mines worked by Soleiret and Gazaix since the masons who had previously been dispatched to undertake the work 'had allowed themselves to be intimidated by certain threats made against them'. The mayor failed to explain that he was himself a *propriétaire* who leased out the rights to work the mines on his land![167] The excuses offered by the mayor of Saint-Andéol-de-Trouilhas, another *propriétaire*, sounded more credible: they included the observation that blocking the entrances to mines was really quite pointless because of the 'considerable number of openings which have been dug in the hillsides of Pradel and the immediate vicinity. Since the coal-seams break through the surface of the ground, it takes people less than a day to dig another entrance.'[168] There was a final consideration in the minds of the local authorities—the fear of popular rebellion, not to be underestimated in a region which, since the *masques armés* revolt of 1783, had seen more bloodshed than most regions of France. At the peak of the popular agitation over the recreation of Tubeuf's 'monopole', the Ingénieur-en-chef des mines drew up a report in which he stated 'that certain people were fanning the flames of rebellion amongst the workers of this region' and that he was convinced that the entrepreneurs in Alais who controlled the coal warehouses were involved, adding that the coal-mines were being worked 'by strangers to the region who would have to be watched very closely'.[169]

From the beginning of the 1800s, ministers, prefects, and mining engineers had all been convinced that positive measures would have to be taken by the State to shake the inhabitants of the Cévennes, and indeed other regions of France, out of their traditional 'routine vicieuse'. Experts in the Agence des mines were unanimous in favouring an *étatiste* solution to the problem, particularly since 'the last law on this matter, that of 28 July 1791, is somewhat incoherent so far as its general principles are concerned and has already given rise to a great number of legal battles which have proved extremely

---

[167] The mayor was Louis Dautun, an old enemy of the Tubeufs. *AG* 8S 95, 20 Flor. Year XI.

[168] *AG* 8S 95, letter to the prefect, 26 Flor. Year XI.

[169] *AG* 8S 22, *rapport sur la rébellion*, 8 May 1806.

damaging'.[170] However, the Conseil-général du département, like the *assiettes des diocèses* of the *ancien régime*, was equally determined to protect its citizens from the Tubeufs and all the horrors of a 'monopoly'. As soon as her success became evident, it had stepped up its campaign against 'la dame Tubeuf', suggesting to the government that, in place of her monopoly, separate concessions should be granted to cover the mines of the Grand-Combe, Abilon and Pradel, Trescol, Portes, and Rochebelle–Cendras.[171] Meanwhile, by 1807, the Tubeufs, reaping the benefits of their hard work over the past few years, were looking to the future with the launch of an ambitious scheme involving setting up a glassworks and iron-works. In the same year, the government decided to act, charging one of its leading mining experts with the task of preparing a comprehensive report on every aspect of coal-mining in the Gard, particularly the issue of who should control which mines. In 1810, the government would introduce legislation—destined to govern coal-mining throughout the nineteenth century—to rectify the anomalies contained in the 1791 law. Was this, at last, to be the beginning of a 'revolution' in coal-mining in France, and in the Cévennes in particular? The Tubeuf *fils* undoubtedly believed that they were on the threshold of a new and exciting chapter in the history of their family. However, the dying years of the Empire were to bring deception and disappointment rather than fulfilment, as our next chapter will reveal.

---

[170] *AN* F14 7684, *Beaunier, rapport général sur les mines des environs d'Alais, Portes et Saint-Ambroix pour satisfaire aux dispositions du décret impérial rendu sur le fait de ces mines, 18 Sept. 1807.* This report, by far the most important and professional to be written on the mines of the Alès coal-basin during the Revolution and Empire, was 166 pages long and was compiled by the Ingénieur-en-chef des mines, Beaunier. He had been sent to the Gard to draw up a definitive study of the coal-mines in the department which would provide the basis (although, for important reasons which we discuss below, some of Beaunier's main suggestions were not accepted) for a final decision on the granting of coal concessions.

[171] Rouvière, *L'Exploitation des mines nationales du Gard*, 233.

5

THE RETURN OF THE TUBEUFS:
AN ABORTIVE 'TAKE-OFF'

ONE of the pre-conditions for the success of Tubeuf's reconstituted concession was social and political stability, a *desideratum* shared by merchants and landowners alike, particularly those who had benefited from the Revolution. The departments of the Gard and the Ardèche had suffered more than most from the enervating blows of civil and foreign wars. The bitterness and hatred engendered by the *bagarre de Nîmes* and the consequent seizure of the main political and administrative offices by the Protestants would pass from one generation of Catholics to the next. Throughout the period of the Directory and Napoleonic Consulate, the south-east of France had been adversely affected by the organized activities of the Catholic royalist *égorgeurs du Midi*, responsible for individual crimes as horrible as any committed by the Jacobins and their sympathizers during the Terror. Returning priests and seigneurs had joined forces, after 1794, to re-create the social alliance between traditional élites and the poorer sectors of the community. In this region, Catholic royalism was to be the preferred ideology of the more protoindustrialized and traditional producers: François Froment's attack had always been directed against 'les gros', the mainly Protestant bankers and *négociants* of the region. The late 1790s and the early 1800s had marked the degeneration of the economic and political life of the south-east, as of many other troubled areas of France. No wonder brigandage had flourished, exploiting as it did the 'general sense of demoralization, the contempt for human life learned during the upheavals of the Revolution, a serious economic crisis, extreme misery . . . deep social divisions, a timid and ineffective policy of repression'.[1]

What evidence is there to support the association of political instability with economic distress? A great deal, particularly after the *coup d'état* of Fructidor Year V, when the activities of the Catholic

---

[1] M. Marion, *Le Brigandage pendant la Révolution* (Paris, 1934), 77.

royalist *égorgeurs* were directed against the economic and administrative infrastructure of the south-east. In the winter of 1800, the authorities in Marseille had informed the government that it had been 'three years since anyone has been able to travel safely in the countryside around the city', whilst, a year later, the first prefect of the Basses-Alpes reported: 'We are sitting on a volcano here.'[2] We have first-hand knowledge of the impact of brigandage upon the Alès region from someone who was destined to emerge from the Revolution as a leading coal-owner, Pierre Goirand. Having been reprimanded by the prefect of the Gard in the winter of 1800 for not doing his bureaucratic homework, Goirand blamed 'the brigandage which has been afflicting these parts for some time now, organized by the self-styled *chouants* [*sic*] who have already done so much harm to our *honnêtes citoyens*, forcibly entering their homes in order to extort money from them'.[3] Even more distressing, but equally revealing of the anti-industrialist *mentalité* of the Catholic royalist movement, was the murder of an 80-year-old Protestant landowner at his home in the southern Lozère. His name was Barrot; his son had been a member of the Legislative Assembly; his grandson Odilon Barrot would become a member of the Chambre des députés during the Bourbon Restoration and, more directly relevant to our argument, another of the new breed of coal-owners destined to displace the Castries and the Tubeufs as nineteenth-century industrial capitalism at last effectively challenged the protoindustrial structures of Bas-Languedoc.[4] One should not underestimate, therefore, the impact of Catholic royalist guerrilla warfare upon the economic life of those departments which had traditionally provided markets for cévenol coal—the Lozère, the Ardèche, the Hérault, and, to a lesser extent, the departments on the right bank of the Rhône. It reinforced the 'village economy' of the region: locals would continue to fill the odd sack of coal for drying chestnuts, making lime, boiling cocoons, or distilling wine, but carters were not going to risk life and limb distributing coal to far distant parts.

The advent of Napoleon Bonaparte did not transform the picture overnight, although the hiatus in the lengthy series of European wars after 1801 did enable the First Consul to turn the might of his army

[2] G. Lewis, 'Political Brigandage and Popular Disaffection in the South-East of France, 1795–1804', in G. Lewis and C. Lucas (eds.), *Beyond the Terror: Essays in French Regional and Social History, 1794–1815* (Cambridge, 1983), 196.

[3] *AN* F14 7671, Goirand to prefect, 10 Niv. Year IX.

[4] Lewis, 'Political Brigandage', 204–5.

against his internal as opposed to his external enemies. Military courts began to mete out summary justice in the south-east, often against young men who had only joined the *égorgeurs* to escape military service. On a more ideological front, it was the Concordat with the Papacy, ratified in 1802, which took the sting out of the Catholic royalist tail, particularly in a region which had witnessed recurrent bouts of religious warfare since Calvin's message first echoed through the hamlets of the cévenol hills. So far as the Catholics were concerned, the Revolution had not only involved a substantial shift of power towards the Protestant community, it had also involved the loss of a bishopric in Nîmes and the relegation of the cathedral of Alès to the status of a parish church.[5] By 1802, the twin traditional protectors of the Catholic *propriétaires*, coal-owners and colliers—the maréchal de Castries and the Bishop of Alès—had both disappeared from the scene, the former having died in Switzerland in 1800, the latter by his acceptance in 1802 of a government pension, supplemented by the unofficial payment of the *dîme* from die-hard Catholic royalists like the marquis de Calvières of Vézénobres. After 11 Ventôse Year VIII (2 March 1800), the sceptre of power passed to the first prefect of the Gard, Jean-Baptiste Dubois.

Dubois, together with his immediate successors, baron d'Alphonse and baron Rolland (1804–10), were to earn for themselves the undying hatred of the majority of Catholics by their unstinting support for the Tubeuf family. This support was resented not only by contemporaries but by eminent local historians like François Rouvière, who could conclude as late as 1901 that Dubois, 'neglecting his duties', had exhibited 'an almost servile indulgence' towards the Tubeuf family.[6] It is certainly very doubtful that the Tubeufs could have re-created their 'empire' without the support of these prefects, just as a generation earlier Pierre-François Tubeuf had been obliged to lean upon the Intendant of Languedoc and his friends at Court. Unlike their father, however, who had no option but to suffer the exhausting journeys from Paris to Alès, his sons Alexandre and François simply had to travel the few dozen kilometres to Nîmes to petition the prefect. The decentralization of power in the 1790s had enabled municipalities and the property-owners who elected them to control their own local economies. Napoleonic centralization involved a swing

---

[5] Bruyère, *Alès, capitale des Cévennes*, 476.
[6] Rouvière, *L'Exploitation des mines nationales*, 317.

of the pendulum back towards the State and the *grand concessionnaire*, at least until the troubled final years of the regime.

The beneficial effects of peace, military and religious, allied to the introduction of administrative order and authority, were clearly making an impact upon the inhabitants of the Basses-Cévennes by the winter of 1802. On 3 December, one of Pierre-François Tubeuf's former *directeurs des mines*, Mahieu, was writing to Chaptal on behalf of the Tubeuf family seeking the minister's permission to reopen the Abilon mine near the Grand-Combe.[7] To embellish his claim, Mahieu reminded Chaptal that modern economic growth depended upon a strong coal industry. Explaining that he actually delivered coal to Chaptal's workshops at Martines in the Lozère, Mahieu concluded with the comment that 'steam-powered workshops in the Gard and the Hérault, which are just resuming production as a result of the benefits which peace has conferred upon us, are giving their support to large-scale producers of coal (*exploitants en grand*)'.[8] This was the point to make—one that Pierre-François Tubeuf had reiterated—that if a modern French economy were to develop, it was essential that the government support large-scale, modern concerns. At the dawn of the nineteenth century, encouraged by 'scientific' ministers like Chaptal, it was clear that coal was increasingly being accepted as the basis of a rejuvenated economy. A lengthy report by the Ingénieur des mines for the Gard at this time included a reference to coal as 'le régénérateur et le soutien de l'industrie française'.[9] Much had not changed, particularly from a technological standpoint: what had changed, however, was a more general acceptance by government, by manufacturers and industrialists, that if political theory had been England's most important export in the seventeenth century, coal had replaced it by the end of the eighteenth.

The advent of peace, then, provided an excellent opportunity for tackling the economic problems bequeathed by a decade of internal and external conflict.[10] What official statistics reveal, however, confirming

---

[7] It seems that Rouvière was unaware of Mahieu's long service in the Tubeuf camp. He writes: 'Un ingénieur du nom de Mahieu . . . se fait le plat valet des Tubeufs.' Ibid. 316–17.

[8] *AN* F14 7682, 12 Frim. Year X.

[9] *AN* F14 7863, 18 Pluv. Year XIII.

[10] Christopher Johnson has suggested that the 1800s witnessed a significant economic recovery: 'It seems probable that during the 1800s the Empire saw a decade (1800–10) of revival, and therefore, Lévy-Leboyer's massive "deceleration" thesis for the whole of

one of the main arguments of this study, is that the origins of the recession of the early 1800s must be sought in the serious collapse of the textile industry in the Bas-Languedoc region during the reign of Louis XVI. Some reports, for obvious reasons, give 1789 as their starting date, like the *État des fabriques et manufactures dans la commune d'Anduze*, which provides the figures given in Table 5.1. It is noticeable that the majority of these workers were female—silk-throwers, spinners, embroiderers, seamstresses. It was the loss of the woman's earnings which provoked hardship for families in the main urban areas like Nîmes. It seems clear, however, highlighting a trend which was to characterize the silk industry in Lyon and Nîmes, and elsewhere, in the early decades of the nineteenth century, that the smaller *bourgs* and hamlets of the Cévennes did not suffer as much of a decline, at least in certain branches of the textile industry, as Nîmes itself. Terror in the city—the *bagarre de Nîmes* of 1790, the Jacobin Terror, and the White Terror after 1795—must have pushed many small-scale manufacturers and workers back to their family roots in the cévenol hills. For the mayor of Anduze, writing in 1798, the 1790s had none the less been a pretty miserable decade: 'You will appreciate how manufacturing industry has declined since the Revolution, and how the prospects for the future look even worse.'[11] The mayor was determined to look on the bright side, explaining that, in his opinion, if everyone worked hard then things could get back to normal. His optimism was ill-founded. Detailed official reports for 1806, which adopt a longer-term perspective, constantly refer to the damage sustained by all sectors of the textile industry, although they again suggest that the Alès region had suffered less than Nîmes. What they also emphasize is the importance of the major recession of the late 1770s and 1780s.

In 1806, the number of workers involved in producing *étoffes de soie* (various articles which often contained a mixture of poor silk and cotton) was 2,000–2,500. At the peak of its activity in the early 1770s, at least twice that number of workers would have been involved in the industry. The number of workers making printed fabrics (*toiles peintes*) had dropped from 300 in September 1804 to 120 by 1 January

the Revolutionary and Napoleonic era needs some modification.' 'The Revolution of 1830 in French Economic History', in J. Merriman (ed.), *1830 in France* (New York, 1975), 143.

[11] *AG* 9M 6, *état des fabriques et manufactures dans la commune d'Anduze*, Vend. Year VI.

TABLE 5.1. *Report on the state of manufacturing in the Commune of Anduze 1789 and Year VI*

Product	Year	
	1789	Year VI
Woollen goods		
(*molletons, pessots,* etc.)		
Number of workers	1,000	200
Number of items produced	3,000	750
Hats		
Number of workers	100	25

Note: The number of workers in the manufacture of silk stockings, however, remained static at 420.

Source: AG 9M 6.

1806. In his revealing report, the mayor of Nîmes laid particular emphasis on the importance of changing fashions. In the good old pre-Revolutionary days, the merchants of Nîmes had produced material for over a hundred articles, stockings, dresses, handkerchiefs, blouses, waistcoats, gloves, ribbons, etc. By 1806, it was the large and colourful shawls which were dominating production: 'Demand for this kind of product has increased substantially over the past five or six years.' But shawls, along with an increasing demand for home furnishings, curtains, rugs, carpets, would never fully compensate for the collapse of the silk-stocking industry as well as for that of the *fabrique des étoffes de soie*.[12]

It was a similar tale for the woollen industry in and around Sommières, which had sustained serious damage since the 1770s when 6,000 workers, scattered throughout the Vaunage and the Gardonnenque, had been busy with the production of the famous woollen blankets, the *molletons de Sommières* and the *molletons d'Anduze*.[13] In the 1780s, the merchants of Sommières had produced 16,000 pieces of finished cloth (each of 38 metres in length). By 1811, this figure would drop to 6,000.[14] Again, some of the smaller cévenol towns and villages, centred around le Vigan and Alès, appear to have suffered less harshly than Nîmes, however. The explanation for this does not lie entirely

---

[12] *AG* 9M 6, mayor to prefect, 10 Mar. 1806.
[13] See p. 67–8.
[14] *AG* 9M 7, *nombre des ouvriers employés autrefois et à présent dans les manufactures de Nîmes,* 19 June 1811. See also Rivoire, *Statistique du département du Gard,* 56.

in the political *bouleversements* which had shaken the fabric of life and industry in Nîmes, but also in the severe shortage of water which was so vital for the bleaching and dyeing industries, as well as for many other manufacturing processes.[15] Water was also needed to turn the water-wheels of industry. It was partly for this reason that the le Vigan region became the centre of the cotton industry in the Napoleonic period, employing around 6,000 workers and producing approximately 120,000 kilograms of spun cotton, mainly from Sauve, Saint-Hippolyte, and le Vigan. Saint-Hippolyte and its immediate hinterland alone were producing 7,000 dozen pairs of stockings annually by 1811.[16] No wonder the old silk-stocking industry of Nîmes was declining. In addition, Alès, Anduze, Saint-Jean-du-Gard, Bagnols, as well as towns and villages in the southern Ardèche and the Drôme better served with water, were rapidly becoming some of the most important centres in France for the production, drawing, and spinning of raw silk and silk thread. Before the Revolution, Nîmes had boasted over a hundred *moulins à ovale* for the drawing of silk thread, representing around two-thirds of the departmental figure. By the end of the Napoleonic period, only a few dozen would still be working.[17]

In 1811, the authorities in Nîmes produced the most detailed and revealing figures concerning the fate of its textile industry. They chart the seriousness of the recession of 1810–11 as well as the general decline of an industry which had once commanded markets world-wide. We shall return to the significance of the economic crisis of 1811 later. What we need to emphasize at this point is the sharp decline, in some cases the virtual collapse, of the older branches of the silk industry in Nîmes, particularly the manufacture of silk stock-ings and gloves. In the *bon vieux temps* of the 1760s and 1770s, 6,000 looms had been engaged in the silk-stocking industry in what became the department of the Gard, with more than half this number working in Nîmes itself. By 1810—a more representative year given the deep recession of the following year—one could almost count the number of looms working in three, rather than four, figures. In the *étoffes de soie* branch of the industry, 2,600 workers had produced around 120 different articles in the 1770s; by 1810, this figure had fallen to just over a thousand, well over a third of whom were producing cheap

---

[15] The above report states that whereas Nîmes could boast of 150 dyers before 1789, only a handful were still working 20 years later.

[16] *AG* 9M 6, *état des filatures de coton établies dans le département du Gard*, 26 Mar. 1806.

[17] *AG* 9M 16, *état de l'industrie textile, 1808–1812*.

TABLE 5.2. *The decline of the textile industry in Nîmes, 1790–1811*

Workers	Year			
	1790	1803	1810	1811
Tireurs de soie	900	500	600	200
Taffetassiers	2,500	1,500	3,000	900
Fabricants de bas	4,000	1,800	1,000	600
Couturières et brodeuses	2,300	1,500	900	300
Cardeurs	700	500	500	300
Ourdisseurs	45	30	50	20
Ovaleuses	100	60	40	25
Mouliniers de soie	150	20	20	20
Rubaniers	120	140	150	100
Dévideuses	900	450	600	150
Teinturiers	166	120	150	60
Tondeurs et pareurs	56	45	60	30
Tanneurs	40	30	30	30
TOTAL	11,977	6,695	7,100	2,735

handkerchiefs. All this, as Table 5.2 illustrates, spelled disaster for thousands of dressmakers and embroiderers, silk-throwers and spinners. Many must have returned to relatives in the Cévennes to participate in the partial revival of the silk-rearing and spinning industry in the towns of Alès, Anduze, Saint-Jean-du-Gard, and le Vigan.[18]

One of the main points to note is that the reports of the Chamber of Commerce in Nîmes lay greater emphasis on the pre-Revolutionary origins of manufacturing decline, referring, in particular, to 'le coup mortel' delivered by the Spanish government as a consequence of the prohibitive duties placed on the import of certain textile goods in 1778.[19] Apart from the raising of duties, what were the long-term structural reasons for the decline of manufacturing industry in Bas-Languedoc, and how did this decline affect the fortune of the Tubeuf family?

A la longue durée, trade continued to shift from the Mediterranean to the Atlantic ports, from the Levant to the Americas, from Venice and Marseille to Amsterdam, Liverpool, and Bristol. Roger Dugrand having suggested various reasons for the decline of manufacturing

[18] *AG* 9M 7, *notice sur les produits de l'industrie du département du Gard*. This detailed report was drawn up by the Chambre de commerce de Nîmes and sent, marked confidential, to the Minister of Police on 22 July 1811.
[19] Ibid.

industry in the region—lack of investment, an unfavourable climate for certain processes in the textile industry, imports of Japanese silk into Europe—focuses particular attention on the shift in 'les grandes centres de gravité économiques nationaux'.[20] The most striking evidence of this shift in world trade is the drop in the volume of goods traded at the international Beaucaire fair, held each summer and situated on the river Rhône just 24 kilometres from Nîmes. Fig. 5.1 illustrates not just the overall decline from 1802 to 1815 but also the brief recovery of the mid-1800s, followed by the consequences of the British government's Orders in Council in November 1807 and the war with Spain the following year.[21] Of the 217 ships which had berthed in Beaucaire during the summer of 1802, 63 had been Spanish; in 1809 not one Spanish vessel was to be spotted.

The value of goods sold at the fair fell from 46 million francs in 1802 to 16 million in 1815.[22] Denis Woronoff notes that France was evidently losing the battle for the Central and Latin American trade, a vital blow to the manufacturers of Bas-Languedoc. Further west, Bordeaux's trading links with the United States had broken down by 1797: 'Gradually a new map of French trade emerged, in which pride of place was held by northern Europe—the markets of Brussels, Amsterdam, Hamburg, Copenhagen—and central Europe, thanks to the restoration of relations with Berlin.'[23]

This attraction of northern and central European markets, as opposed to those in the Americas, which were being drawn increasingly into the English commercial orbit, is reflected in official reports on the economy of the department of the Gard during the Napoleonic Empire. An *état des fabriques de tissus de coton pur ou mélangé* for 1806 explains that whereas the products of the region had been sold mainly in the Levant before 1789, new markets had been found in England

---

[20] Dugrand, *Villes et campagnes en Bas-Languedoc*, 395. See also J. Thomson, 'Variations in Industrial Structures in Proto-industrial Languedoc', in Berg *et al.* (eds.), *Manufacture in Town and Country*, 88–9. Roger Dugrand also comments on the 'selfishness' of the port of Marseille, which, even after the Revolution, continued to enjoy favourable treatment in terms of duties charged on foreign ships when compared with Sète, which would have been the most appropriate port for the coal producers of the Cévennes.

[21] J. Tulard, *Napoleon: The Myth of the Saviour* (London, 1984), 156. The author notes that between July and Nov. 1807, almost all continental ports were closed to British trade.

[22] 'Le Mouvement économique du Gard sous le Consulat et le premier Empire', in *Mémoire de l'académie de Nîmes* (Nîmes, 1892), 77–98. See also Fitzpatrick, *Catholic Royalism in the Department of the Gard*, 5–7.

[23] Woronoff, *The Thermidorean Regime*, 110–11.

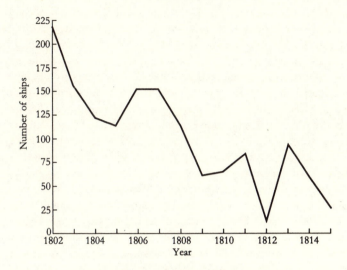

FIG 5.1. Ships entering Beaucaire, 1802–1815

during the peaceful years 1801–2. Since the recommencement of hostilities, however, the only outlets were local markets in Languedoc, Provence, Dauphiné, and Burgundy.[24] Five years later, the mayor of Nîmes pointed out that in the 1770s most of the silk stockings made in the region had been shipped to the Indies, to Mexico, and to Peru, but that since the Spanish embargo of 1778 no comparable markets had been discovered.[25] The adverse effects of a decade of revolution and war upon the economic map of France, and indeed Europe as a whole, can also be traced in the reports emanating from other textile centres like Lyon and northern Italy. In 1806, the authorities in Lyon informed the government that 'the continental war had paralysed our manufactures',[26] whilst Alain Dewerpe concludes that 'the transfer of the mediterranean axis towards the Atlantic axis profoundly reshaped the bases of economic power in Italy'.[27]

Embargoes and blockades, Napoleon's Continental System, the war with Spain in particular, obviously aggravated the problems confronting

[24] *AG* 9M 6, report of 26 Mar. 1806.
[25] *AG* 9M 7, 22 July 1811.
[26] *AN* F12 611a, *état de la situation du commerce*, 7 Mar. 1806.
[27] Dewerpe, *L'Industrie aux champs*, 122.

most French businessmen. Although the Spanish embargo of 1778 had struck a serious blow at manufacturers in Languedoc, a thriving smuggling trade had softened the impact. In 1790, the district of Uzès had explained that stockings, hats, and gloves (mainly cotton) from Sauve and Saint-Hippolyte were still entering Spain despite the heavy import duties since Catalonian and Spanish merchants were happy to meet their Languedocian counterparts at 'unofficial border crossings' to purchase goods which were then sold under Spanish 'brand names'.[28] Trading relationships, some dating back for several generations, could not be severed overnight. There is further evidence of the importance of contraband trade with Spain and Portugal, and, therefore, of the adverse effects of the 1808 war with Spain, in the Chamber of Commerce report from Nîmes in 1811. Stressing, yet again, the importance of the Spanish connection, the report explains how the associated loss of Latin American business had helped to create the recession. During the early 1800s, and despite high import duties, trade to the Iberian peninsula itself had continued, with American shipping moving to Bordeaux to find silk goods for the colonies. But when, in November 1807, the British government passed its legislation attacking neutral shipping (one of the major causes of the brief war with America), the silk industry in Bas-Languedoc was struck another severe blow. What exacerbated the problem was the increasing difficulty of building up alternative networks of trade to the north: 'For a long time now, the war has seriously restricted, if not entirely closed, the number of outlets for our manufactured goods, already excluded from Cadiz and Lisbon, which we had managed to secure in Germany and Russia.'[29] If, as a result of prohibitive import duties and the recurrent difficulties associated with Napoleon's interminable wars, merchants could not sell their wares, then the future looked bleak, particularly at a time when increasing investment in modern machinery like the Jacquard loom and steam-powered engines was becoming vital if France were to compete with Britain. And if things looked bleak for textile manufacturers, they were equally depressing for coal producers like the Tubeufs.

The importance of 'modernization' was not lost on the more perceptive members of the Chamber of Commerce in Nîmes. Commenting upon the availability of modern spinning machines, its report for 1811

[28] *AG* 9M 6, *réponses aux diverses questions sur les manufactures*, 1790.
[29] *AG* 9M 7, *notice sur les produits de l'industrie du département du Gard*, 22 July 1811.

noted that 'It is astonishing that no comparable machines (*filatures à grandes mécaniques*) exist in this region which produces such a large quantity of cotton goods.' Silk-spinning was, of course, more difficult to mechanize, but at least one leading manufacturer, M. Gensoul of Bagnols, had introduced 'un appareil à vapeur' to accelerate the process of silk-throwing and spinning. It appears, however, that Gensoul was the only devotee of the steam-engine in the Gard, so far as the silk industry was concerned. The firm of Aigoin and Delord were making fine cotton white stockings *à l'anglaise*, but sadly, in the opinion of the Chamber of Commerce, even 'This industry is still in its infancy.' Some concentration of production—again noticeable above all in the cotton industry—was taking place in Nîmes where Foussard and Astier had achieved success by manufacturing printed cotton fabrics. The design, printing, and dyeing of their goods was all carried out under one roof with around 200 employees working as 'une industrieuse colonie'. The Chamber of Commerce thought that this was worthy of particular praise, given the shortage of water supplies to the city.[30]

So far as heavy industry is concerned, one firm in particular, Jean Méjean et Cie, was at least trying to push forward into the nineteenth century. The Méjean example is an extremely interesting one since it illustrates the pitfalls awaiting families which had made their fortunes in the textile industry only to lose the greater part by shifting resources to the heavy industrial sector, in Méjean's case iron foundries. During the second half of the eighteenth century, Méjean had built up one of the most successful silk- and cotton-spinning concerns in the le Vigan area. Such families had been instrumental in establishing the reputation of the *bas de Ganges*. Jean Méjean had left the textile side of the family business to concentrate on iron-smelting, using the well-known 'forge à la catalane'.[31] The late 1800s seemed to be an auspicious time for iron-masters, given the demand created by Napoleon's wars. Méjean would doubtless have heard of the achievements of the iron-masters in the Ariège, assisted, as in the Gard, by sympathetic prefects and legislation restricting the rights of workers. Production from the iron-ore mines of Rancié had doubled between 1789 and 1811, the period 1805 to 1811 being decisive with the modernization and expansion of production.[32] During this very same

[30] Ibid., 22 July 1811.
[31] *AN* F14 7677, *supplément du rapport général*, by Beaunier, 26 Aug. 1808.
[32] See R. Garny, *La Mine aux mineurs de Rancié, 1789–1848* (Paris, 1970).

period, Jean Méjean, assisted by one of his sons, Frédéric, made four attempts to produce good-quality iron for the production of tools and nails.[33] Despite significant improvements in the quality of the iron produced, the poor quality of the iron-ore and coal which he was using, allied to the lack of skilled workers, meant that by 1811 Méjean felt obliged to give up his entrepreneurial venture. According to his son, Méjean had spent 300,000 francs in five years and had no capital left to mount another 'campaign'. Doubtless the economic crisis of 1811 helps to explain why, in July of that year, 24,000 of the 74,285 kilograms of iron produced during Méjean's fourth 'campaign' remained unsold.[34]

The main conclusion drawn by the Chamber of Commerce in Nîmes from its broad survey of the economic situation in the Gard obviously applies to Méjean's failure to produce good-quality iron: 'These imperfect instruments have nothing in common with English machinery, and if one had used the latter instead of having been forced to abandon them . . . the beneficial results we would have obtained, as is the case everywhere they are used, would have encouraged others to adopt them.'[35] The fact was, as François Crouzet has pointed out, that the lack of competition and English technical expertise did exercise a deleterious effect upon French industry.[36] It was even more serious in the Gard where the successive blows of shrinking markets, revolution, and war only served to reinforce the protoindustrial mentality of the vast majority of its inhabitants.

In 1772, a *mémoire* prepared for the government of the day had described how the inhabitants of the Cévennes 'manufacture woollen and linen goods, but they only do so for part of the year when the lack of agricultural work leaves them some spare time'. Industry was only 'a supplementary resource. It is the same for the numerous woollen and cotton spinning-mills which are springing up everywhere in the countryside.'[37] It is quite remarkable that, forty years later, no

[33] *AN* F14 7671, *pétition de Jean Méjean*, 27 July 1808.

[34] *AN* F12 1605, prefect to Minister of Interior, 12 Nov. 1811. The prefect's letter was based upon a report drawn up by Frédérick Méjean, who explained how in 1809, when things were going very well, 'la pierre sur laquelle frappe le gros marteau ayant été endommagée, on fut obligé de cesser les travaux de la forge et de renvoyer les ouvriers'. In 1810, floods destroyed the culvert which had been built to bring water to the forge.

[35] *AG* 9M 7, *notice sur les produits de l'industrie du Gard*, 22 July 1811.

[36] F. Crouzet, 'Guerres, blocus et changement économique, 1792–1815', in *De la supériorité de l'Angleterre sur la France*, 280–98.

[37] Dutil, *L'État économique de Languedoc*, 289.

really significant structural change had occurred in manufacturing except that *négociants*, *marchands-fabricants*, and *commissionnaires* had tightened their control over their workers. By the time of the Revolution, the majority of inhabitants in the hills of the Cévennes had become completely dependent upon industry for the purchase of their daily bread. The municipality of Saint-André-de-Valborgne, commenting upon the problems of growing silk, stated that 'There is no business that demands so many hands. One has to cut levels into the hills like those in an amphitheatre to plant our mulberry trees which require continual care. The production of silkworms is even more demanding; then comes the spinning of the raw silk, which engages the hands of carders and spinners during the long winter evenings.'[38] The sale of every kind of silk thread was now vital to the existence of these predominantly Protestant hillsmen and women. No wonder that thousands had been prepared to march on Nîmes during the *bagarre* of 1790 to slaughter Froment and his 'anti-capitalist' Catholic royalist followers. It was as much a question of bread as of the Bible.

In 1806, in the *arrondissement* of le Vigan, centre of the department's cotton industry, forty merchants (including the Méjean *frères*) were still employing workers scattered throughout and around the towns and villages of Saint-Hippolyte, Sauve, Aulas, Bréau, and Valleraque. Each house had its 'domestic industry': 'We find poor people spinning cotton thread on their spinning-wheels for *entrepreneurs*, that is to say merchants engaged in the putting-out industry.' There was not a single mule-jenny to be found in the department: 'the vast majority of poor workers use the hand-wheel, each one works at home for a few *entrepreneurs* . . . the inhabitants of the countryside spin at home when the fancy takes them'.[39] In 1811, the Nîmes Chamber of Commerce informed the government, in tones of some regret, that

manufacturing industry in this department is not concentrated in a few workshops in which all the relevant workers, now scattered throughout the countryside, might be housed under one roof. It is rare, even in the countryside, to find a home without a loom in it, almost all of them the property of the workers, irrespective of whether they are working for themselves or for piece-rates. The word *fabricant* here is used for someone who employs a certain number of isolated workers, providing them with the prepared material, paying them only for their labour. These manufacturing entrepreneurs

---

[38] *AC Anduze*, 2F 3, *pétition à l'Assemblée nationale de la municipalité de Saint-André-de-Valborgne*, 1790.
[39] *AG 9M 6, état des filatures de coton établies dans le département du Gard*, 26 Mar. 1806.

are very numerous, above all in the silk fabric and hosiery branches of industry.[40]

For the cévenol population the main objective was to retain some association with the land of their fathers. The few daily *sous* which women might earn was a supplement to the family income, especially during the trying winter months when food was short and expensive. The craft of spinning had been handed down from mother to daughter since medieval times and still, as the Napoleonic Empire neared its end, many communes between Nîmes, Anduze, and Alès were still producing hemp to satisfy the ordinary needs of their inhabitants— sheets, shirts, sacks, etc. The 'sack-dress' may have been a twentieth-century fashion fad, but it was a basic item of clothing to many a cévenol. Just as in many parts of late eighteenth-century Ireland where domestic linen production 'took place within the context of a land-holding society . . . the model household was the farmer-weaver growing flax, wife and children spinning it into linen'.[41] According to an inquiry of 1812, the commune of Saint-Christol produced 180 kilograms of hemp a year: 'In the main, women occupy themselves with this work either during the season or when they have some leisure time.' In Ribaute, a few women spun 'the red cloth which property-owners wear'. The Protestant commune of Ners produced 340 kilograms a year: 'most of those who harvest the hemp also get their wives and daughters to spin it during the winter'.[42] This village boasted six weavers, who not only wove material produced in Ners itself, but also spun the yarn brought to them by women from the surrounding hamlets. Clearly, far less hemp was being grown than, say, a century before. Alès produced just 430 kilograms a year, although its five weavers also did work for the population of the immediate neighbourhood. In his reply, the mayor noted that not much hemp was being grown in the territory under his jurisdiction, particularly since the locals had adopted 'the custom of growing potatoes and maize . . . in the kind of soil appropriate to the cultivation of hemp'.[43] The authorities in Anduze, where six weavers

---

[40] *AG* 9M 7, *notice sur les produits de l'industrie du Gard*, 22 July 1811.

[41] B. Collins, 'Proto-industrialisation and Pre-famine Emigration', *Social History*, 7 (1982), 130.

[42] *AG* 6M 799, *enquête sur la filature et tissage de chanvre et lin*, July 1812.

[43] Ibid. The peasantry of Cardet, for example, took their hemp to Anduze for it to be made into blankets and sacks for mulberry leaves. Boucoiran produced 960 metres a year, most of it for the manufacture of rope and cord.

and twenty spinners (earning 1.80 francs and 50 centimes a day respectively) were employed intermittently throughout the year finishing 11,200 metres of hemp into sheets, sacks, and rope, also noted that production was declining, although, just one year earlier, they had informed the prefect that 'in recent years, more hemp has been planted in this region despite the fact that the soil is poor and there is little fertilizer to be had'.[44] A few other communes had also decided to grow hemp again, almost certainly a reflex response to the severity of the 1810–11 economic crisis.[45]

All this, however, reflected little more than a post-medieval subsistence economy. Money was still scarce for the purchase of grain, land, and farm and textile machinery and tools, and that money could only be earned by working the land or the loom. Increasingly during the Empire, work on the land took precedence. The shift, which had been observable long before the Revolution, away from manufacture to the cultivation of the *mûrier et la vigne*, became more pronounced as the uncertainties of urban, commercial, and industrial life confirmed the advantages of one's *lopin de terre*. This is evident from the official reports on hemp-growing for 1811. The mayor of Anduze explained that whilst slightly more hemp had been grown in recent years, it was the mulberry tree which was now dominating the countryside.[46] One year later, the mayor of Sénéchas reported the same phenomenon in his locality.[47] Philippe Joutard suggests that the planting of mulberry trees fell into temporary disfavour during the 1790s, only to recover during the first years of the Napoleonic Empire.[48] Maurice Agulhon is probably nearer the truth when he concludes that the cultivation of raw silk began to be affected some time before the Revolution, associated with the recession in the textile industry after 1778.[49] The planting of the mulberry tree was directly related to the fortunes of

[44] *AC Anduze* 3F 2, *réponses aux questions contenues dans la lettre de monsieur le préfet,* 12 Aug. 1811.

[45] *AG* 6M 799, *enquête sur la filature.* The reply from the commune of Vézénobres noted that less hemp was being grown in the commune than in the old days, but that 'les pauvres gens . . . après la levée du chanvre, ils y mettent de navets, des aricots [*sic*] et des pommes de terre, objets qui viennent à merveille dans le terrain propre au chanvre'.

[46] *AC Anduze,* 3F 2, *réponses aux questions.*

[47] *AG* 6M 799, *enquête sur la filature.*

[48] Joutard, *Les Cévennes de la montagne à l'homme,* 154.

[49] Agulhon, *La Vie sociale en Provence intérieure,* 22. The author notes that the production of silk cocoons began to drop before the Revolution, to fall increasingly into disfavour during the 1790s.

the silk industry, which had obviously been seriously affected before
the Revolution broke out, as a report for 1800 confirms: 'People dug
up their [mulberry] trees, and none were planted for ten or fifteen
years. Now people are beginning to speculate on the future and have
borrowed money to do so.'[50] Maybe this optimism was not unrelated
to the beginning of a new century?

Whatever the truth of this speculative remark, there was a pronounced
shift to the cultivation of raw silk during the first decade of the
nineteenth century, although the production of silk-cocoons did not
surpass the 1789 figure until the early years of the Bourbon Restoration,[51] the economic crisis of the late Empire putting a firm brake on
earlier growth. In 1813, an official report confirms both the growing
popularity of the *mûrier* during the Empire as well as its recovery after
the crisis of 1811–12. Although precise figures were not available, the
report stressed that the number of people involved in the production
of raw silk 'is very considerable, given that the mulberry tree is
cultivated in almost 350 communes, and the fact that few families, in
the countryside primarily, are not engaged in this type of industry,
which is invariably a lucrative one. The high price of silk over the
past couple of years has encouraged the planting of mulberry trees,
something which had been neglected for a long time.'[52]

The same process was observable across the Rhône in the department of the Vaucluse. Before the Revolution, Avignon had 2,000–
2,200 looms making silk goods, the *doubles* and *mi-Florences*. In 1806,
only half this number were still operating, whereas the number of
moulins à ouvrir la soie had increased from 90 to 140.[53] Alain Dewerpe,
referring to the later years of the Empire, notes that 'Henceforward,
Italy will become an exporter of the raw material or half-finished
products.' Production of raw silk increased in value from 1,860,000
livres in 1800 to 3,840,000 in 1820.[54] What was happening was a
structural shift, in the south-east of France as well as in northern

---

[50] M. Riou, 'La Terreur blanche dans le département du Gard: aspects économiques
et sociaux', in *Économie et société en Languedoc-Roussillon de 1789 à nos jours* (Montpellier,
1978), 387.

[51] *AG* 6M 202, *situation morale et politique d'Alais*, 1818. The subprefect's report included
the comment: 'on s'efforce de réparer les pertes eprouvées pendant le régime révolutionnaire où cette culture fut méprisée. Malgré tous les efforts on n'a pas encore
atteint les produits antérieurs à 1793.'

[52] *AG* 9M 16, *statistique industrielle et manufacturière: tableau des produits en soie*, 1813.

[53] *AN* F12 611a, *état de la situation du commerce dans six départements*, 1806.

[54] Dewerpe, *L'Industrie aux champs*, 127 and 18.

TABLE 5.3. *Production of silk-cocoons in the département of the Gard (kilos)*

Year	Silk-cocoons
1808	1,260,000
1809	1,200,000
1810	1,280,000
1811	1,160,000
1812	770,000
1813	800,000
1814	930,000

Note: Figures for the Vaucluse, 1808, were 1,689,000 kilos; Ardèche, 998,400; Drôme, 622,246; Hérault, 517,000.

Source: *AN* F12 2291, *état comparatif des mûriers en France*.

Italy, from a manufacturing to a semi-agricultural socio-economy, a very significant stage in the 'de-industrialization' of Bas-Languedoc and Provence. These Mediterranean provinces were being transformed into 'colonies' producing the raw material for manufacturing centres like Lyon, Tours, Paris, and Saint-Chamond. By 1815, three-fifths of the raw-silk output of the Gard was being 'exported' to these places.[55] And the pace of this change would accelerate during the first half of the nineteenth century. Little wonder that: 'Since the end of the last century . . . until 1816, no significant change has occurred in the type of loom used to manufacture the various materials employed by *l'industrie nîmoise*'. The Jacquard loom was only introduced by the Roux-Carbonnel firm in 1816.[56]

But if in the hills of the Cévennes the mulberry tree was spreading, its domination was being challenged by the vine, particularly in the plain around Nîmes and along the left bank of the Rhône valley.[57] The Revolution, by releasing and subdividing land, provided a considerable boost for the small *vigneron*. If, as Roger Dugrand states, the period 1670 to 1789 marks 'la première explosion du vignoble',[58] then, in contrast to the uneven development of the *mûrier*, the period of

[55] *AG* 9M 16, *tableau des soies*.
[56] Rivoire, *Statistique du département du Gard*, 24.
[57] Before the Revolution, vines were commonplace around Saint-Gilles, Beaucaire, Bagnols, Pont-Saint-Esprit, Saint-Ambroix, and Alès.
[58] Dugrand, *Villes et campagnes en Bas-Languedoc*, 356.

the Revolution and Empire is one of 'take-off'.[59] In 1788, 51,000 hectares of vine had been tended in the Gard; by 1808, this figure had risen to 71,000 hectares and to 74,000 hectares by 1818.[60] This figure was not to be surpassed until the 1850s as, in the intervening years, the mulberry tree continued to compete for the hearts and pockets of the peasantry.[61]

The massive Napoleonic armies did not wear silk culottes, but they did drink considerable quantities of wine and spirits. The Napoleonic army marched on its liver rather than its stomach! Distillers had always provided a good market for coal-owners: one of Pierre-François Tubeuf's important customers had been the seigneur de Chusclan, who had made his money out of the sale of wine and brandy.[62] The Chamber of Commerce report from Nîmes in 1811 pays particular attention to the distilling industry, charting its successful course, excluding the severe crisis of the 1780s, from the reign of Louis XV to that of Napoleon. It recorded the fact that every village with a sizeable vineyard had its own distillery, and that about forty communes in the Gard were occupied for the greater part of the year in the cultivation of the vine and the production of *eaux-de-vie*. The region around Nîmes and Montpellier, with Lunel as its distribution point, housed some of the better-known distilleries in France: Aiguesvives alone, a commune to the south of Nîmes with a population of around 1,500, dispatched 3,000 barrels of spirits annually to Paris during the 1800s.[63] All this was of vital importance to the coal industry, which relied heavily on the silkworm and the grape. As one report in 1805 explained: 'The conversion of our excess wine into brandies, the drawing and spinning of silk thread, the preparation of silk, and the many different manual activities associated with its manufacture constitute the main branches of the commerce and industry of this department, allowing us to trade with the interior of France as well as with foreign countries.' The same report estimated that around 5,000 tonnes of coal was used by the distilling industry annually; just 2,000 on the production of silk.[64] The increasing shortage of wood

[59] Tulard, *Napoleon*, 199.

[60] *Nîmes et le Gard*, 41ᵉ Congrès de L'Association Française pour L'Avancement des Sciences, 1–8 Aug. 1912, 2 vols. (Nîmes, 1912), ii. 27.

[61] See Huard, *Le Mouvement républicain en Bas-Languedoc*, 34.

[62] Bardon, *L'Exploitation du bassin houiller d'Alais*, 98.

[63] *AG* 9M 7, *notice sur les produits de l'industrie du Gard*, 1811.

[64] *AN* F14 7683, report of *ingénieur-des-mines* for the Gard, 1805. Other industries listed as using coal were those engaged in the manufacture of cooking-oil, soap, beer, skins, as well as iron foundries outside the department.

had 'forced every distiller, for a long time now, to use coal, which they have to transport, at great cost, from the mountains fifty or sixty kilometres away'.[65]

When the Tubeuf family sat down in 1806 to undertake a major review of their situation, they were confronted with certain constraints within which they were obliged to operate—a rapidly declining textile-manufacturing industry, little technological innovation or concentration of production, considerable uncertainty concerning the export trade given the continuation of war, but signs of growth in the cultivation of raw silk and even rosier prospects in the sale of wines and spirits, even though production of these products remained 'protoindustrial'. Before reaching any firm decisions as to future plans, Marie Tubeuf and her two sons Alexandre and François, admirably counselled by the ever-faithful Renaux, would have recalled the tragic failure of their father—hundreds of thousands of *livres* poured into the development of a 'modern' coal industry only for him to be defeated by a combination of aristocratic power linked to a small property-owning, protoindustrial society. Certainly the power of the aristocracy had been scotched, if not killed off, but the socio-economic foundations upon which Castries had constructed his successful opposition to the Tubeufs had, if anything, been strengthened, whilst wars and rumours of wars made long-term planning a nightmare. No wonder Mme Tubeuf went into fits of the vapours when anyone mentioned the possible investment of substantial sums in her mines. She had lived through extraordinary and tragic times, including the financial ruin and physical loss of her husband: she was clearly not going to allow Renaux and her two sons to throw away everything she had won as a result of her tenacious struggle to regain control of her former husband's 'empire'.

And what of Marie's two sons? Their experience during the 1790s and early 1800s not only provides us with a new chapter in the extraordinary history of the Tubeufs; it also serves as an illustration of the pitfalls awaiting anyone unfortunate enough to have been involved in commercial ventures during a period of revolution and war on an international scale. Retracing the steps of the Tubeufs, *mère et fils*, allows us a glimpse at least of the international commercial network which bound France to the Americas as well as emphasizing

---

[65] *AG* 9M 7, *notice sur les produits de l'industrie du Gard*, 1811.

the increasing domination of English financial and commercial know-how by the 1800s. We move from Alès to Paris, from le Havre and Liverpool to Richmond, Virginia, and thence to Port-au-Prince and le Cap in Saint-Domingue where Toussaint L'Ouverture was writing his own chapter in the history of black emancipation. The commercial experience of the Tubeuf *frères* in the Americas was to determine, in part, their attitude to the coal-mines which had come into their possession. Given the example of their father, and the reality of what was happening in the Gard, would it not be wiser to link coal to the commerce of wines and spirits (something they knew about), as well as to the manufacture of raw silk, rather than to costly forays into forges and iron foundries, for which there was no massive local demand and, given the Continental Blockade, even less technical know-how?

'Francis Peter Tubeuf'—for this was the 'American' son whom Pierre-François Tubeuf had taken with him to America in 1791—had been 21 when he had been confronted with the savage murder of his father in the 'Back Country' of Virginia.[66] He was put into the care of a certain Claybourne Watkins, who found him a job as a secretary in the office of a 'Mister Skipworth'. Sometime in 1797, François's brother Alexandre joined him in America and, one year later, the Tubeuf *frères* had set up an export–import business dealing, mainly, in wines and spirits from Saint Petersburg, Virginia.[67] They had already settled some of their father's American debts by disposing of certain 'assets', like the 'negro woman and her children [who] had better be sold to pay Mister English'.[68] They retained possession, however, of the estate which their father had purchased, and extended, in Russell County.[69]

For a time, their business prospered, and in September 1801, François left his brother to look after things in Saint Petersburg whilst he established a new commercial house in Saint-Domingue, first at le Cap, then at Port Républicain, which, as François explained, was more

---

[66] *AG* 58J 8, letter of recommendation by William Alexander, 1801. 'Peter Francis' had clearly inherited some of his mother's more obvious characteristics. He was described as being 5 ft. 4 in. in height with chestnut-coloured hair, blond eye-lashes, and greyish-blue eyes.

[67] *AG* 58J 8, letter of introduction from Skipworth, which describes 'Peter Francis' as 'a fine young man, worthy of every confidence', n.d., 1798.

[68] *AG* 58J 8, letter of William Alexander, 10 Aug. 1797.

[69] When the brothers left America in 1803, the land still in their possession amounted to 45,000 acres. *AG* 58J 9, letter to Mr Omealy in Norfolk, 11 Mar. 1803.

peaceful and less subject to the cut-throat competition of American traders.[70] The brothers also decided to diversify their interests, importing textiles and salt, as well as wines and spirits, from France, Portugal, and Spain, to which they added flour and tobacco from Virginia. The early 1800s, however, was not the most propitious time for international trade, with Britain and France hovering between war and peace and Saint-Domingue itself about to lapse into another spasm of bloody anarchy as Napoleon considered the reimposition of slavery upon what had been France's richest colony.[71] As François explained, events in Europe 'keep the people here in a tremor; the market is consequently extremely dull and colonial produce is falling sensibly'.[72] At the end of 1801, Napoleon dispatched General Leclerc, at the head of 12,000 men, with orders to capture the now legendary black leader Toussaint L'Ouverture. In February of the following year, just after Leclerc had landed at le Cap, one of Toussaint's lieutenants, Christophe, burned the port to the ground.[73] The savage brutality and byzantine complexity of the struggle eventually forced François to rejoin his brother in the comparative calm of Virginia.[74] The French were ultimately to be successful in capturing Toussaint L'Ouverture, transporting him to a miserable death in a French provincial prison. Toussaint's cowardly capture and subsequent death may be thought to represent not the least of the crimes attributable to the great Napoleon.[75]

The general situation in Virginia on François's return was not, however, totally reassuring, even if life and limb were better protected. In a letter to a friend who had stayed on in Port Républicain he explained that 'The European war has had the dreaded effect;

[70] *AG* 58J 9, letter of François, 10 Oct. 1801, in which he explains that there were only six houses still trading with the European continent and that white table wine could sell in Saint-Domingue for 7 or 8 francs more.

[71] In one of his letters to Alexandre, François underlined the fragility of business in the Caribbean at this time: 'It is to be observed that having very few capitalists, if any, this place for its commerce depends entirely upon foreigners.' He added that everyone trusted to luck with '10 vessels entering on one day followed by a fortnight with no soul in sight'. *AG* 58J 9, 29 Sept. 1801.

[72] *AG* 58J 9, 25 Nov. 1801.

[73] See C. L. James, *The Black Jacobins: Toussaint L'Ouverture and the San Domingo Revolution* (London, 1982), 296. When he entered le Cap, Leclerc found that only 59 out of 2,000 houses were still intact. James remarks that the burning of the port 'was the beginning of a devastation which threw San Domingo back half a century'.

[74] *AG* 58J 9, François to Alexandre, 14 Mar. 1802: 'Les troubles de Saint-Domingue m'est ramené à Norfolk [County].'

[75] James, *The Black Jacobins*, 333–4.

businesses are most annihilated, nothing but a few shipments of tobacco to France has been done since my arrival. The West Indies produce finds no purchasers and everybody stands on the qui vive, waiting for a clear day to scatter the heavy fog obstructing our sight.'[76] The Tubeuf brothers, strong in maritime metaphors but weak in hard cash, were hardly encouraged by a string of bankruptcies 'up country in New York and Baltimore'.[77] A few months later, François underlined the dangers inherent in their position, caught as they were between a European continent about to embark upon yet another suicidal round of warfare, and a colony, Saint-Domingue, involved in bloody rebellion: 'Toussaint's refusal to recognize the officers sent by the French government created much fear in this colony [Saint-Domingue], as well as in Guadeloupe, both colonies being, for a long time now, a prey to disorder and dissension.'[78]

The situation was bedevilled by the stranglehold exerted over traders like the Tubeuf brothers by English merchants and finance houses. From the beginning, they had realized the importance of establishing links with commercial and financial centres in London.[79] In May 1802, François had written to a business contact in Cadiz saying that things were very quiet and that they would probably 'continue in the same state of languor till Europe is restored to perfect tranquillity', adding that Norfolk County in America was now 'filled up with agents of English houses pouring out constantly the produce of their manufactories'.[80] Increasingly, England ruled not only the waves but the colonial warehouses. Business from Europe to America was becoming impossible without going via the City of London, 'since the purchase of convoys and advances are generally made in drafts on England'.[81] Reflecting a trend that would be continued until Europe embarked upon yet another suicidal round of war in 1914, French traders like

---

[76] *AG* 58J 9, to Mr Smith, 26 Jan. 1802.

[77] On 27 Jan. 1802, François told his brother that there had been 'plusieurs faillites au nord', including one that involved a close friend in New York. Despite this fact, François was still inclined to indulge in a little self-deception, explaining that 'J'ai toujours eu de la répugnance pour les affaires de New York.' Perhaps he was trying to cheer up his younger brother, who, we must recall, was still only 22 years of age in 1802. François was 27.

[78] *AG* 58J 9, 14 Mar. 1802.

[79] *AG* 58J 8, letter of recommendation from William Alexander, written in 1801, which stressed that the Tubeuf brothers were seeking to establish links with commercial houses in London.

[80] *AG* 58J 9, to the Ferry brothers, Cadiz, 25 May 1802.

[81] *AG* 58J 9, to Mr Thelluson, London, 20 Jan. 1803.

the Tubeufs tried to offset English superiority in manufactured goods by importing high-quality brandies and sherries from Spain,[82] as well as the 'vins de Champagne, vins de Bourgogne, prunes, articles de Paris, porcelaine', all of which were on board the last shipment which the Tubeuf *frères* organized from France to America in 1803.[83] One cannot over-emphasize the fact that the expertise which the Tubeuf brothers had gained in their commercial endeavours from 1797 to 1803 was to be crucial in explaining the options which they chose back in the comparative calm of Bas-Languedoc a few years later.

François's brother Alexandre had left Saint Petersburg for France as early as November 1801, having just learned that he and François had been struck off the *émigré* list, thanks to the tenacious lobbying of their mother. The main reason for his visit was the prospect of reopening their mines in the Alès coal-basin. Alexandre had always been less pessimistic than his brother about recovering their property rights in Languedoc, possibly because François had spent the formative years of his life in America. How often must his father have told him the dismal story of his epic struggle with the maréchal de Castries during the long Virginian *veillées*? As François explained, he had himself 'spent three years in the pursuit of our property [in Languedoc]'.[84] None the less, the bitter accidents of fate which had separated the family throughout the Revolution also served, paradoxically, to bind them closer together. In a very touching letter to his brother, François wrote in March 1802:

If we should fail to regain full possession of our property, the next time you happen to be with mother reassure her about the future, and although it is not possible for us to be together at present . . . kiss her a thousand times for me. Do everything that you can to make her forget her worries. She deserves everything that we can possibly do for her.[85]

François's filial affection had masked, perhaps, his mother's grim determination and Renaux's technical domination of the mining scene in the region: there was also his brother's financial and commercial experience. Once it became clear that Marie Tubeuf had successfully

---

[82] See the letter to the Ferry brothers in Cadiz, asking for good-quality 'Brandy, Oporto, Sherry, Malaga, etc.' *AG* 58J 9, 25 May 1802.

[83] *AG* 58J 8, list of merchandise aboard the Neptune, 10 July 1802.

[84] *AG* 58J 9, 25 Nov. 1801. He wished his brother all the best, but expressed the belief that his mission was doomed to failure.

[85] *AG* 58J 7, 14 Mar. 1802.

regained the Grand-Combe as well as the Rochebelle complex, and given the deteriorating situation in the Caribbean,[86] the brothers decided to shut up shop in America and return, like many other *émigrés* caught up in the ideologies of revolution, to their homeland for good. The final blow for François had been the loss of the *Neptune*, the ship he had chartered to bring that valuable cargo of wines, porcelain, and 'articles de Paris' to Virginia. The debts associated with this loss would follow him to France.[87]

On New Year's Day 1803, François wrote to Messrs Willings and Frances in Philadelphia asking them if his firm might continue to count on their custom since the Tubeuf *frères* were about to move their commercial house from Virginia to le Havre. From the outset then, commercial, rather than industrial, interests were to dominate the thinking of the Tubeuf family. If their father had failed to create international links for the sale of coal, they had established international links for the sale of wines and spirits. Like the smallest *vigneron* in the Cévennes, the Tubeufs placed their ultimate trust in land: their father's mining interests were to represent little more than collateral for their wider commercial interests, as one of François's letters makes abundantly clear. Commenting on the good news that the French government had given the family back 'our estate in Languedoc', François explained, in one of his last letters from America, that 'we have determined to extend our interests by the foundation of a commercial house in le Havre, and to realize it by organizing the sale of our landed property in Virginia. We want to sell here because we do not wish to touch our property in France, for on it rests our independence as men and our respectability and credit as merchants in this country.'[88] Unlike their father, the second generation of Tubeufs, despite being drawn increasingly, as the nineteenth century progressed, into industrial ventures, would think of themselves, first and foremost, as merchants.

---

[86] On 8 July 1802, François wrote, in his rather clumsy English, to John Galloway, explaining that 'business here is in a languishing state.' *AG* 58J 9.

[87] The value of the cargo lost with the sinking of the *Neptune* may be judged by the fact that the commission payable to the Tubeufs at 2% was estimated at £291. 19s. 6d. The *Neptune* went down in October, just 30 leagues from the American coast. A few days after the receipt of this news, François wrote to several customers asking for their bills to be paid since he was 'in want of all the money we can raise'. See e.g. *AG* 58J 9, letter to Prosser, 31 Oct. 1802.

[88] *AG* 58J 9, 1 Jan. 1803.

None the less, by the time that François had joined his brother in Alès in 1804,[89] Alexandre and their *directeur des mines*, Renaux, had already discussed plans for rescuing the mines now under their control from the years of neglect and plunder. Two years later, they would launch a three-year project at the Grand-Combe to dry out the workings and construct a regular drainage canal for the Airolle workings which would allow them to regain entry to the rich number 7 seam.[90] Once again, Renaux, armed, it must be stressed, with the provisional decree of Thermidor Year X which gave the Tubeufs only *temporary* ownership of the Grand-Combe, but backed now by the international commercial expertise and contacts of the Tubeufs, was planning to mine *en grand*.

It was still, however, more a task of returning to the original plans of Pierre-François Tubeuf than of embarking upon a really major strategy of digging deeper pits and exploiting the benefits of the steam-engine, one of Périer's engines from his famous Chaillot works having been placed in the Littry mines at the end of the previous decade. If Renaux and Alexandre, spurred on by the economic boomlet of the mid-1800s, had a rush of blood to the head, François and his mother were always on hand with a word or two of caution. In any case, the legislation of 1791 had confirmed the Gilly family in possession of the Saint-Jean-de-Valériscle mines whilst the Tubeuf *frères* never expressed any real interest in the Robiac–Meyrannes mines in the neighbouring Cèze valley, nor in the old fiefdom of Monsieur, the *mines de Portes*, including the Champcloson mine. Henceforth, it would be the mines along the river Gardon, from Rochebelle to the Grand-Combe, which would consume the interests of the Tubeufs. A lot of money would be spent on improving roads, particularly the link between the Grand-Combe, the Gardon valley, and the Villefort–Alès road, thus opening up markets in the Lozère department. Nearly 50,000 francs would be poured into this undertaking, eliciting considerable praise from the government's Inspecteur des mines, who described it as 'véritablement digne d'éloge'.[91]

Even more revealing of their 'commercial', as opposed to their 'industrial', vision was the determination to build a glassworks near

---

[89] *AG* 58J 10, entry by Alexandre for 14 Jan. 1804, stating that his brother was about to join him in Alès.

[90] For a detailed account of the work conducted by the Tubeufs see *AN* F14 7684, Beaunier, *rapport général sur les mines d'Alais*.

[91] Ibid. 36.

the Rochebelle mine, using its fairly poor-quality coal. This plan dovetailed neatly into the increasing production of wine in Bas-Languedoc and the commercial interests of the Tubeuf brothers. As we have established, the Tubeuf *frères* were international figures in the wine business,[92] and, upon their return to France, had established commercial houses not only in le Havre, but also in the Mediterranean port of Sète. The brothers were now speaking confidently about 'entering upon the European trade'.[93] The Tubeufs exemplify that general shift in French history, from an 'Imperial' to a 'Continental' strategy, one which was forced upon France and Napoleon as much by the eighteenth-century victory of Britain over France at sea as by the economic consequences of the Revolution. Indeed, the 'economics' of the Revolution cannot be separated from this wider defeat, already evident in the reign of Louis XVI.

The marked increase in coal production consequent upon the hard work of Renaux during the early 1800s meant that, by the end of 1806, production was outstripping demand: the mini-recession of the previous year must obviously have been a factor. Not surprising, therefore, that it was in 1806 that the Tubeufs finalized their plans for a major glassworks at Rochebelle, producing green and black glass. As Alexandre explained to their creditors in November: 'The stagnation in industry and the desire we have already shown to make good use of your funds prompt us to inform you of the current plans which we are about to launch.'[94] Paradoxically, technical changes in the distillation of wine following Adam's new process which involved the burning of less fuel seem to have been yet another factor in their decision to go in for glass-making.[95] The final approval from the Conseil des mines had to wait until 1808, by which time production from the Tubeufs' mines alone (that is, excluding Robiac, Saint-Jean-

---

[92] See the letter written by the *agent commercial des États-Unis à Paris* certifying that François and Alexandre Tubeuf, *négociants*, had lived for several years in Norfolk, Virginia, where they had enjoyed 'un commerce considérable, particulièrement avec la France; que la solvabilité de ces négociants est connue et leur crédit solidement établi'. *AG* 8S 95, 4 Sept. 1802.

[93] *AG* 58J 9, letter of François Tubeuf, 1 Jan. 1803.

[94] *AG* 58J 10, 12 Nov. 1806, to Devienne *frères*, for example. For reassurance, Alexandre added: 'Nos charbons sont si abondantes que la consommation de notre département ne pas les employer.'

[95] See *AG* 58J 8, Alexandre to prefect, 16 Feb. 1809: 'La consommation de ce combustible [coal] n'est plus aussi considérable à cause de la nouvelle manière employée dans les fabriques, dans les distillations'.

TABLE 5.4. *Output, profit, and costs at the Tubeuf mines, 1807–1808*

Mine, year	Total production (*ancien régime quintaux*)	Sales (francs)	Production costs (francs)	Profit (francs)
Rochebelle				
1807	84,906	23,747	20,880	2,867
1808	81,717	24,751	19,690	5,061
Grand-Combe				
1807	114,529	39,403	26,512	12,885
1808	143,988	45,980	36,265	9,715
Trescol				
1807	107,726	30,435	24,029	6,406
1808	115,350	28,802	25,090	3,712
TOTAL				
1807	307,161[a]	—	—	22,148
1808	341,055[b]	—	—	18,488

[a] = 12,286 tonnes
[b] = 13,642 tonnes.

Source: AG 58J 7, tableau des dépenses et des produits des mines de Tubeuf, 1807–1808.

de-Valériscle, and the *mines de Portes*) were approaching the figures reached in 1789 for the entire Alès coal-basin. In 1809, the Tubeufs would purchase a third furnace for the production of white glass.[96] The figures shown in Table 5.4 offer an indication of the increase in production—particularly for the Grand-Combe—during the late 1800s, as well as of the costs involved.

Not only were the 1800s the most successful years for the Tubeufs, their own 'Second Empire' in the Alès coal-basin, but it seemed as if the State would give them the official and legislative backing they needed, firstly, by regularizing the provisional arrangement of 7 Thermidor Year X, and, secondly, by introducing the law of 12 April 1810 which was to govern mining procedures in France until the twentieth century. This very important piece of legislation represents the victory of the State and the *concessionnaire* over local interests spearheaded by the *propriétaire*.

On 18 September 1807, the government dispatched 'un ingénieur extraordinaire' to the department of the Gard to make an exhaustive inquiry into the state of every mine in the Alès coal-basin. Just under

[96] *AG* 58J 8, letter to prefect, 16 Feb. 1809.

a year later, Beaunier produced his 166-page report, the first comprehensive and detailed analysis of the geological, technical, and economic
problems affecting the mining industry in The Basses-Cévennes.[97]
Such reports mark a very significant stage in the relationship between
industry and the State in France, and the capacity of the government
to modernize mining procedures. In his preface, Beaunier noted that,
whilst, in their present state, the mines of the Cévennes were nothing
like as productive as those of Anzin and the Rive-de-Gier, they were
none the less worthy of serious consideration and that 'nothing must
be neglected in the task of ensuring that those responsible for
operating the mines do so in a way which guarantees their future'.[98]
Throughout his report, Beaunier made it clear that the only mines
being worked in a modern and professional way were those belonging
to the Tubeuf family. The report includes a series of general observations as well as a detailed technical plan for each mine. For the
Tubeufs, however, the vital issue was Beaunier's recommendations to
the government concerning the number and ownership of the mining
concessions for the region.

His general conclusions were that, at present, the mines did not
require huge capital investment on new machinery given that so much
of the coal lay near the surface; that transport from the Alès mines
to commercial centres like Saint-Ambroix was far too costly; and that
the main demand for coal came, as we have noted above, from
distillers and textile manufacturers, 'les deux branches principales de
commerce de ce département'.[99] The report also included a major
criticism of the considerable number of working mines which had not
even received a provisional sanction from the government: these
'mines illicites' in Beaunier's estimation produced around 1,000 tonnes
of coal a year.

But it was the boundary of the Tubeufs' 'empire' in the coal-basin
which mattered most. What should the family receive, and who should
be granted the remaining concessions? In his recapitulation of the
long and chequered history of the coalfield, Beaunier remarked that
the root of the conflict lay in the fact that Pierre-François Tubeuf's
original concession in 1773 had been far too extensive. However,
given that the latter had agreed, in the 1780s, to concede the Abilon

[97] *AN* F14 7684, Beaunier, *rapport général sur les mines d'Alais.*
[98] Ibid. 8.
[99] Ibid. 5–6. Beaunier explained that most of the distilleries in the region were to be
found in and around Nîmes, Montpellier, and, in particular, Lunel.

and Mas-Dieu mines to the Castries family and Saint-Jean-de-Valériscle to the Gilly family, and that the sons did not now wish to claim entitlement to the Robiac and Meyrannes mines, nor those in the *forêt de Portes*, the government should agree to the following concessions:

1. *Concession d'Alais*, for the Tubeufs: Rochebelle, Cendras, Trescol, Pradel, Grand-Combe.
2. *Concession d'Abilon*, for the Castries: Abilon, Mas-Dieu.
3. *Concession de Portes*, for the Puech–Goirand company: Tronche, Levade, Champcloson, Fenadou (the old *mines de Portes* which had belonged to Louis XVI's brother before the Revolution).
4. *Concession de Saint-Jean-de-Valériscle*, for the Gillys: mines of Saint-Jean-de-Valériscle.
5. *Concession de Meyrannes et Robiac*, for the Suffrens: Meyrannes, Robiac.

There can be no question but that the Tubeufs would have been delighted with this division of the spoils: included within their proposed concession was the jewel in the cévenol crown, the Grand-Combe, the mine that Pierre-François had fought so hard for, losing the sight of an eye in the process during the vicious attack upon him in 1784 by the traditional *fermiers de la Grand-Combe*. In justifying his decision, Beaunier pointed out that not only had Pierre-François Tubeuf laid the foundations of modern mining in the region,[100] but also the work already completed for his sons by his *directeur*, François Renaux, after 1802 'must, in the future, provide untold advantages, amply rewarding the owners for the expenses which they are incurring today. Once finished, this work will ensure the easy exploitation of the seams for many years to come.' Beaunier concluded that it would only be after the realization of Renaux's plans 'that we may date, properly speaking, the regular working of the mines of the Grand-Combe'.[101] Thus, justice appears to have been done. The family which, more than any other, and *on two separate occasions*, before and after the Revolution, had raised the coal-mining industry in Bas-Languedoc from its medieval origins were about to receive what was plainly due to them. Or were they?

---

[100] Ibid. 24. 'C'est ainsi que M. Tubeuf jetta dans le pays d'Alais les premiers fondements d'une exploitation régulière.'

[101] Ibid. 34. The Inspecteur stressed that it was the Grand-Combe which had made Alès famous for its coal, and that it was this mine which had proved to be 'la source d'un grand profit pour le maréchal [de Castries]'. During the Revolution, however, the Grand-Combe had been 'ruined', denying a similar 'profit pour l'État'.

Beaunier, one of the more experienced graduates of the École des mines, was obviously representative of that school of State officials, beginning with Pierre-François Tubeuf's friend in the Conseil des mines during the reign of Louis XVI, La Barbérie, and continuing with one of the founder-members of the reformed Agence des mines in the 1790s, Lefebvre d'Hellancourt,[102] who embraced a national vision of industry, as opposed to the regional and local vision held by those officials who had staffed the offices of the Estates of Languedoc in Montpellier before the Revolution and the departmental directories and municipalities after 1790. The latter, representatives of a seigneurial and protoindustrial socio-economy, appealed to the tradition, epitomized in the legislation of 1791, which elevated the rights of the *propriétaire* above those of the *concessionnaire*. The La Barbéries and the d'Hellancourts preferred the claims of the latter, possessing, as most of them did, a more *étatiste* angle of vision, as exemplified in the new legislation of 21 April 1810.

As early as the summer of 1801, Lefebvre d'Hellancourt had posed the crucial question in an article which was published in the *Journal des mines*: 'Should mineral deposits, whose extraction depends upon the skills of the miner and the mineralogist, be considered public property or as property inherently attached to the land? The answer to this question is fundamental in determining the principles upon which any legislation should be based.'[103] D'Hellancourt himself had no doubts about the matter: individual landowners with mines on their property were ruining France. The legislation of 28 July 1791 had been 'incoherent, provoking many disputes'. What the government should do now is to appreciate that there existed a *scientific* solution to the old problem of who owned what: mineral deposits, of whatever kind, 'are to be found in positions which bear no relationship either to the surface land or to the way in which they have been divided up'.[104] Contemporary articles in the *Journal des mines*, written by other experts, also stress the distinctions which had to be drawn—on scientific, geological lines—between ownership of land and ownership of any mineral deposits which might lie beneath it.[105] We are entering

---

[102] See the *liste des officiers des mines* chosen by the Committee of Public Safety. *Journal des mines*, 1 (Vend. Year III).

[103] *Journal des mines*, 60 (Fruct. Year IX), 887, 'Considérations relatives à la legislation et à l'administration des mines, par M. Lefebvre, membre du Conseil des mines'.

[104] Ibid. 908.

[105] See e.g. an article in the *Journal des mines*, 86 (Brum. Year XII), 137, 'Sur l'administration des mines en Allemagne', by M. Duhamel, Inspecteur des mines, which

a new age, one in which science is employed in the legitimization of the State, *une et indivisible.*

The final outcome of this development was the law of 21 April 1810, which—like the decrees of 1744 and 1791—represents a very significant landmark in the history of mining in France. It finally grasped the nettle of the relationship between the State and individual property-rights, and, in terms of the ownership of coal and iron-ore deposits, it was the individual property-owner who was stung. Compared with the legislation of 1791, that of 1810 made it abundantly clear that ownership of *la surface* did not entail ownership of *le sous-sol.* Article 19 stated that, from the moment a concession was granted, it became a 'different kind of property' from that enjoyed by the former landowner.[106] Other sections of the bill made it equally clear that no landowner would be allowed to own a mine unless he or she possessed the necessary financial and technical resources, and that these would be checked by the prefect and the relevant government bodies. What the legislation of 1810 did was to undo the work of the French Revolution in regards to individual property-rights. It expressed, in more scientific jargon, what had seemed pretty obvious to eighteenth-century Bourbon bureaucrats, as embodied, for example, in the legislation of 19 March 1783, that 'mines form a kind of property distinct from that enjoyed by the landowner: they belong to the sovereign'.[107] In this domain also, Napoleon Bonaparte was imitating the action of his royal predecessors.

J. M. Gaillard has interpreted the allocation of new concessions in 1809, allied to the new legislation governing the mining industry, as 'l'élan décisif à l'exploitation du charbon dans le bassin houiller du Gard'.[108] From a juridical standpoint there is little doubt that he is right; but then much of the complexity of the Revolution is explicable in terms of the gap which existed between new juridical and old social and economic realities. From the standpoint of a 'take-off' in the

reminded the government that 'Dans toute l'Empire d'Allemagne, ainsi qu'en Bohême et en Hongrie, des mines et minières ont de tout tems été regardées comme propriétés nationales' (underlined in the original text). Also *Journal des mines,* (Apr. 1806), 277–305, 'Articles fondamentaux de la jurisprudence des mines dans les pays d'Europe', which hammers home the same point.

[106] Tulard, *Napoleon,* 202.

[107] Bardon, *L'Exploitation du bassin houiller d'Alais,* 266.

[108] Gaillard, J.-M., 'La Naissance d'une entreprise industrielle au XIXe siècle: la compagnie des mines de la Grand-Combe', in *Mines et mineurs en Languedoc-Roussillon et régions voisines de l'Antiquité à nos jours* (Montpellier, 1977), 191.

production and distribution of coal in the south-east of France, Gaillard's comment has little, if any, validity. The 'élan décisif' did not occur until the end of the Bourbon Restoration; for the end—or the beginning of the end—of the *political* economy of a traditional, protoindustrial society. The private correspondence of the Tubeuf brothers records the fact that the latter years of the Napoleonic Empire represent as disastrous a period in their history as the latter years of the reign of Louis XVI was for their father. How can we explain the difference between this potential for growth in the coal industry and the relative stagnation in production which characterizes the period 1810 to 1830? As in the days of Pierre-François Tubeuf, the lack of a heavy industrial base, the periodic absence of demand associated with economic recession, as well as the cost of transporting coal obviously have to be brought into the equation. However, we have seen that, even in the 1770s, Pierre-François Tubeuf did not regard these obstacles as insuperable. The major obstacle he, and his sons, were forced to confront was the strength of local opposition to any 'monopolistic' plans, opposition spearheaded by aristocratic families like the Castries.

Although, as we have seen, the maréchal de Castries had died in exile in 1800, the government's decree of 7 Thermidor Year X had not, in fact, disinherited his heirs. It is true that the Grand-Combe mine itself had been given, provisionally, to the Tubeufs,[109] whilst most of Castries's *rentes* in the Alès region had gone to the *hospice d'Alais*.[110] However, the mines of Abilon and the Mas-Dieu, which Pierre-François Tubeuf had—under pressure—transferred to the maréchal de Castries in the early 1780s, were still, technically, nationalized as *émigré* property. In fact, like the Grand-Combe, they had been ravaged during the Revolution and early Empire by local landowners and their colliers.[111] Following the eradication of the Castries name

---

[109] According to the government's decree of 7 Therm. Year X, the mines of Abilon and Mas-Dieu had been excluded from the new provisional Tubeuf concession. *Journal des mines*, 77 (Pluv. Year XI), 390, Articles 1 and 4.

[110] Rouvière, *L'Exploitation des mines nationales du Gard*, 3–4. The value of the land and goods belonging to the maréchal which were sold during the Revolution was estimated at 94,522 *livres*. In addition there were the *rentes* given to the *hospice d'Alais*.

[111] In 1804, when the government's Ingénieur-en-chef des mines visited the Abilon mine, which was being worked illegally by Gabourdès, Mahieu, and Sauvezon, he found 'partout . . . l'inexpérience de les extracteurs par l'irrégularité de leurs travaux et l'insuffisance de leurs moyens pour les perfectionner'. Gabourdès had already ruined 'la

from the *émigré* lists on 15 Brumaire Year X, Abilon and the Mas-Dieu had passed into the hands of the maréchal's daughter Adélaide-Hortense-Gabrielle, the widow of Alexandre-Louis Mailly, and his grandson, the marquis de Castries.[112] On 19 April 1808, unquestionably prompted, in the first place, by the financial rewards now beginning to flow into the Tubeuf coffers after all Renaux's hard work, and, in the second, by the news that the government was about to make a definitive decision on coal concessions, the Marquis de Castries wrote to the prefect of the Gard asking him how much he thought the 75 hectares of land in the *forêt d'Abilon* and the 30 hectares in the *forêt de Trouilhas* were worth. It is instructive that Mme de Mailly and her nephew should have been more interested in the value of the land than in the coal-mines to be found beneath it. The prefect replied that it was up to the family to send its own valuers down; he did add, however, that the suffering which the Castries had endured during the Revolution suggested that they deserved the government's sympathetic attention.[113] Prefectoral *politesse* or more evidence of that mid-Empire concern for the *ralliement* of the aristocracy? I prefer the latter interpretation.

Whichever is correct, the return of the Castries must have given the Tubeufs many a sleepless night. Was all the work which they had accomplished since the early 1800s, work which had so impressed Beaunier, to be put at risk? And were the Castries, yet again, to be the beneficiaries?

The answer, incredible as it might seem, was—yes! When, on 12 November 1809, the government announced its decision concerning the concessions to be granted in the cévenol coalfield, it became clear that the advice of its expert, Beaunier, was to be disregarded: the Tubeuf 'empire' was to be reduced, more or less, to the limits established by the infamous decree of 24 December 1788. In all, eight concessions were announced, the geographic limits of the majority to be decided after further expert inquiry. The eight concessions were:

---

petite veine', and was currently ruining seams linked to the nearby Grand-Combe mine, officially, if provisionally, belonging to the Tubeufs. *AN* F14 7683, report to Conseil des mines, 21 Vent. Year XIII. The entire report is a lengthy indictment of the coal-owners in the Alès region and the destruction which they were wreaking upon 'their' mines.

[112] *AN* 306AP 494, prefect of the Seine to M. Brot, 6 Therm. Year X.

[113] *AN* 306AP 494, letter of prefect, 19 Aug. 1808.

1. *Concession de Tubeuf*: Rochebelle, Cendras.
2. *Concession de Castries*: Grand-Combe (Abilon and Mas-Dieu to be decided after more advice).
3. *Concession de Puech–Goirand*: Trescol, Pradel.
4. *Concession de Champcloson*: mines of the *forêt de Portes*, (provisionally given to its traditional mining families).
5. *Concession de Méjean*: Tronche, Levade.
6. *Concession de Gilly*: Saint-Jean-de-Valériscle.
7. *Concession de Serres*: Fenadou.
8. *Concession de Suffren*: Robiac, Meyrannes.[114]

Apart from the increased number of concessions—from five to eight—the most obvious departure from Beaunier's proposals concerns the transfer, from the Tubeufs, of the Grand-Combe to the Castries family, and of Trescol to the Puech–Goirand company. The renewed threat, as local opinion had always perceived it, of another Tubeuf *monopole* had been averted. In addition, we must note the emergence of a new coal company, under the direction of the Berard de Suffren family, in the Cèze valley: the mines of Robiac and Meyrannes would form the foundation of the later nineteenth-century Bessèges coal company.

To understand the reasoning behind the government's decision to ignore some of the major suggestions made by Beaunier in his detailed report we need to remind ourselves of the general political and social situation in France during this period. By 1809, the strains inherent in Napoleon's grandiose economic and military policies were taking their toll. War in Spain was draining the Empire of money and men, whilst, internally, the *ancien régime* nobility continued to refuse communion with revolutionary parvenus like Napoleon. This is very clear from some of the comments made in a letter sent by the minister of police to the prefect of the Gard at this time: 'The majority of older families are opposed to our forms of government and seek only to ally with each other, because they have convinced themselves that in so doing they will revive, and add greater lustre to, the titles which the Emperor does not recognize.' In the face of this opposition, the minister advised tact, caution, and the reconciliation of all classes.[115] In the Gard, the older aristocratic families were the Castries, the Berard de Suffrens, and, on a far humbler level, the Gillys. The

---

[114] *AN* F14 7673, *rapport sur les concessions des mines de houille des environs d'Alais.*
[115] *AG* 6M 671, 4 Oct. 1810.

Castries could boast a rare maréchal de France; the Suffrens, a not so rare but still very prestigious amiral de France. The representative of the Castries family in 1810, the marquis de Castries, was serving in the Napoleonic army, as an aide-de-camp to the prince d'Eckmuhl. He had, therefore, hardly had time or occasion to visit his industrial fief in the Grand-Combe. Indeed, his absence prompted the Tubeufs to enquire whether or not they could be given authority to run the mines belonging to the Castries until a representative of the family did appear.[116] But war was war, and it would not be until 1814, when the duc de Castries bought the mines from his sister, that the family did make an appearance, and then only by proxy! In the meantime, Napoleon needed the support of these old families, both for the army and in the pursuit of his policy of *ralliement*.

So far as the Tubeuf brothers were concerned, the main consequence of all these alarums and excursions, representing, as they unquestionably did, a major blow to their more optimistic plans, was surely to confirm them in their judgement that glass-making and continued involvement in the commerce of wines and spirits was now the only possible course of action. Producing only relatively poor-quality coal at Rochebelle, this decision brought the Tubeufs into competition with the Gillys at Saint-Jean-de-Valériscle, whose family had been engaged in the glass-making business for many decades, but which was now branching out into distilling and silk-spinning.[117] Likewise, the Serres family secured continued use of Fenadou on the understanding that it would establish the only tool-making workshop in the region;[118] whilst Jean Méjean, who had acquired Tronche and Levade, had his iron foundries to consider. All of this brings us to the second major factor explaining the government's creation of eight concessions in 1809—the need for competition. This was, at least, what the government said it wanted, but one wonders whether this was not simply a rationalization of the pressures exerted upon it by the various powerful interests and families involved, just as the government of Louis XVI had capitulated in the trying times of the late 1780s.

---

[116] *AN* F14 7683, Tubeuf to Conseil des mines, 3 Apr. 1810.

[117] *AN* F14 7670, *observations faites par le sieur Gilly*, 28 Sept. 1806.

[118] *AN* F14 7684, Stanislas Serres to prefect, 1809. This letter shows that Serre's real occupation was the growing of mulberry trees and the traditional drying of chestnuts for sale.

However, cynicism where Napóleon Bonaparte is concerned has to be tempered by the evidence, and there is at least some to suggest that the need for competition was a factor which the government felt obliged to consider seriously. Anti-monopolist sentiment was not absent from the corridors of power, even if most of Napoleon's bureaucrats and engineers were convinced that it would be more advantageous to make an exception in the case of the coal industry. In any case, given the protoindustrial structures of the economy in Bas-Languedoc, competition might stimulate the economy. This appears to be the thinking behind a report by the Ingénieur des mines in 1809 which confirmed that the granting of the Champcloson and Suffren concessions was motivated by the need to restimulate trade and industry around the old trading town of Saint-Ambroix, particularly with Pont-Saint-Esprit on the river Rhône, as well as to supply coal to the southern Ardèche (the old Bas-Vivarais).[119] Does this suggest that the somewhat artificial departmental boundaries introduced in 1790 had disrupted the old economic relationships between the northern parts of the Gard and the southern parts of the Lozère and Ardèche? Quite possibly. A year later, the Gilly family were instructed to shake up their ideas and start thinking in wider terms than simply producing coal for the drying of chestnuts and silk-spinning.[120] Finally, in 1811, when the Berard de Suffrens complained that 11 kilometres of land in the commune of Robiac had not been included in their concession despite the fact that one of their major seams of coal lay beneath this land, the prefect replied that he wanted to see mining concentrated on the right bank of the river Cèze in order to encourage trade with manufacturers in the Ardèche and the Lozère.[121]

Finally, there can be no question that the new concessions granted in 1809 did go, in the main, to those who had the necessary financial and technical resources. The exceptions were the owners of the two small concessions of Champcloson and Fenadou, and these would be swallowed up by their bigger competitors within a very few years. An examination of the amounts paid in land taxes by the victors and losers of the 1809 share-out of the old Alès coal-basin confirms the conclusion that mines and money were at last becoming synonymous.

[119] *AN* F14 7671, *rapport de l'ingénieur des mines*, 1809.
[120] *AN* F14 7670, *rapport au Conseil des mines*, 2 Feb. 1810.
[121] *AG* 8 S 105, *pétition de madame Berard-Montalet de Suffren*, 5 July 1811.

The two aristocratic families who received what were potentially the richest mines, the Castries (Grand-Combe) and the Suffrens (Robiac–Meyrannes), paid, respectively, 1,464 and 1,672 francs. In itself, this reveals an interesting personal revolution in family fortunes, given the massive wealth of the maréchal de Castries compared with that enjoyed by the Suffrens on the eve of 1789.[122] Jacques Méjean (Tronche–Levade) paid 416 francs, but his family owned one of the the biggest silk-spinning works in the region. Puech (Trescol) paid only 76 francs and thus would seem to belong to *les petits* rather than *les gros*. However, in his letter of application for a concession sent to the prefect he explained that his partner and financial backer Pierre Goirand had chosen not to join with him in this venture and so had not included his tax-return! Goirand had, in fact, become a wealthy man during the Revolution as a result of his transport business and his mining links with Puech.[123] The two partners would emerge as the richest coal-owners in the Gard by 1830, the triumph of the local bourgeoisie over the national nobility represented by the Castries family.

The losers in 1809, almost all small landowners, their sons, or 'independent colliers' who belonged more to the eighteenth than the nineteenth century, were not in the same financial, or social, league. Louis Gabourdès, who had worked the Abilon mine illegally during the Revolution and Empire, paid 50 francs; Jacques Larguier of la Tronche, 20. Maurice Nouvel, who had been digging pot-holes in the Meyrannes hills for years, was excluded for quoting his father's *contribution foncière* of 94 francs. Nouvel had the (rudimentary) technical know-how, but not the necessary financial reserves. Pierre Sauvezon, representative of an old mining family in the region, also had to admit that he was too poor to qualify and referred the authorities to the landowner from whom he farmed his mines, David Verdelhon, who paid 104 francs. Another small landowner, Jean-Pierre Devèze, informed the prefect that he paid only 24 francs, but, in a very revealing comment regarding the dangers of taking land taxes as representative of an individual's *real* wealth, he regretted the fact 'that the hard cash

---

[122] *AN* F14 7684, tax-returns sent to the prefect of the Gard in 1808. 'La dame veuve Mailly' paid 677 francs for property in the 10th *arrondissement* of Paris; her nephew, 'Lacroix de Castries', paid 786 francs (26 July 1808). In 1789, the maréchal de Castries had paid 500 *livres capitation* tax, the vicomte de Suffren, 140, the vicomte Alais-Montalet, 110. *AG* C1846, *rôle de repartition de la capitation des vigueries d'Alais et d'Anduze, année 1789.*

[123] *AN* F14 7684, letter of Puech to prefect, 6 Aug. 1808.

(*numéraire*) which someone might have at his disposal is not taken into account'.[124] Pierre Goirand had been very aware of this fact, wishing rather to hide his not inconsiderable liquid assets! But then he was a representative of that commercial and industrial bourgeoisie who would only really come into their own after 1830.

As is usually the case in history, the real losers in 1809 were the poorest sections of the community, those families who were totally dependent for their daily bread upon the few sacks of coal they had traditionally scraped out of the hillsides. A petition from the inhabitants of the *forêt de Portes*, written in 1815, adopts a retrospective approach, underlining the meaning for them of '1809'. Explaining that 'from time immemorial', everyone who had a plot of land 'would work the mines to be found in the entrails of his property. He would put the coal to good personal use, for silk-spinning, the end-product of his [raw-silk] harvest, which is so precious in this *pays des Cévennes*. The decree of 9 November 1809 changed this order of things.' The petitioners went on to stress that, for them, the legislation of April 1810 represented the *coup de grâce*. Giving full rights of the *sous-sol* to mining entrepreneurs would transform them into owners of the land itself: 'Such munificence was beyond the wildest dreams of the *concessionnaire*'.[125] The same small-landowning, protoindustrial approach was taken by André Argenson, a *propriétaire* and silk-spinning manufacturer from the Meyrannes region, in his attack upon the powerful Suffren family, which—like Tubeuf a generation earlier—had been closing down many of the smaller mines in the Cèze valley.

I simply want to make the point that political necessity alone demands that these mines stay open, above all during the period when the silkworm is being reared and the silk being spun. It would be both difficult and costly for the inhabitants living in this concession, as well as in the neighbouring communes of Courry and Saint-Brès where consumption of coal is high, to organize the transport of coal from mines a half-day's journey away, when they have it, so to speak, on their doorsteps.[126]

Politically dangerous! Was Argenson recalling the peasant-miner revolts of the *masques armés* in 1783, or the various *jacqueries* which had

---

[124] This is the point which the mayor of Nîmes stressed in a letter to the Minister of Police on 31 Oct. 1812. *AG* 6M 671.

[125] *AN* F14 7671, 15 Aug. 1815. The petitioners added that since the 1809 decree 'les propriétaires des Cévennes gémissent sous une mesure qui les prive d'user de la houille dont ils ont besoin'.

[126] *AG* 8S 105, mayor of Meyrannes to subprefect, 20 May 1813.

punctuated the revolutionary 1790s? Poverty had been a prominent recruiting-sergeant for these upheavals: it threatened to be so again as the Empire drew to its bloody end. Jean Tulard has pointed to the scale of economic distress associated with the disruptive and destructive policies of Napoleon Bonaparte.[127] By the spring of 1812, the prefect of the Gard was reporting that, out of a total population of 312,144 inhabitants, no fewer than 89,407 were surviving on 'soupes populaires'![128] Although the position was to improve over the following year, any conceivable economic take-off was to be sabotaged—yet again—by a combination of foreign and civil war in 1814 and 1815.

[127] Tulard, *Napoleon*, 287–9.   [128] Lewis, *The Second Vendée*, 158.

6

THE BOURBON RESTORATION: 'PLUS ÇA CHANGE . . .'

THE second, more ignominious, return of the Bourbons in the summer of 1815 heralded the last, bloody chapter in the history of religious conflict between Catholics and Protestants in Bas-Languedoc. During the First Restoration—1814–15—the Protestants had retained the contested hegemony achieved as a result of the *bagarre de Nîmes* in 1790 when several hundred Catholics had been brutally slaughtered, many by Protestants from the protoindustrial *bourgs* of the Basses-Cévennes. The return to France in 1814 of the royalist leader who had done more than anyone else to provoke the violent collision of the *bagarre*, François Froment, had been an ominous portent of things to come for the Protestant community. As during the early years of the Revolution, economic recession and unemployment in 1814 and 1815 would provide Froment and his friends with fertile ground for the recrudescence of popular religious hatred. Froment's handwritten memoirs provide ample evidence of the pressure which the *émigrés*—who had learned a great deal but who had certainly forgotten little—exerted upon the corpulent frame of Louis XVIII and his courtiers. Refused an audience with the king in 1814, Froment wrote to the duc de Blacas, asking him if he believed that he could 'ever abandon my relatives, my friends and the thousands of royalists who, under my orders, were the first to oppose the white flag to the *tricolore*'.[1] The excesses of Protestant and Bonapartist sympathizers during the Hundred Days provided Froment with what he undoubtedly regarded as a heaven-sent opportunity of putting his plans for a *coup* against the Protestant élite into action.

During the summer of 1815, using unofficial Catholic detachments of the National Guard, Froment and his friends in high places unleashed a reign of terror in Nîmes and the Basses-Cévennes which culminated in the killing of around 200 Protestants. In Alès and the

---

[1] G. Lewis, *The Second Vendée*, 168.

smaller cévenol towns and villages of the Gardonnenque, Protestants armed themselves, as they had done in 1790, to repulse a rumoured invasion from Nîmes: 'Agitators spread the rumour yesterday that they [*les brigands*] would arrive on the day of the *foire d'Alais* . . . at Saint-Jean-du-Gard, Anduze, and other communes of the Gardonnenque in order to massacre the Protestants.'[2] That day—24 August—was the most emotionally charged date in the Protestant calendar, commemorating as it did the Massacre of Saint Bartholomew. In the event, a detachment of Austrian soldiers—part of the Allied occupying force—was sent with the blessing of the Catholic royalist authorities in Nîmes leading to the slaughter of possibly 100 Protestant peasant-artisans who had gathered to defend the region from their historic enemies. The 'White Terror of 1815' in Nîmes formed part of a wider plan aimed, nationally, at the installation of an 'ultraroyalist' administration in Paris and, locally, at the overthrow of the Protestant political hegemony in the department of the Gard. It was successful on both counts, with the election of the ultraroyalist Chambre introuvable in Paris, and the appointment, during the most violent period of the White Terror of 1815, of the marquis de Calvières from Vézénobres as temporary prefect of the Gard, to be replaced after a few months by the ultraroyalist marquis d'Arbaud-Jouques.[3]

The return of the Bourbons to France in 1814, Napoleon's romantic but utterly destructive return from Elba the following year, culminating in Bas-Languedoc with yet another bout of 'white' terror and the installation of a Catholic royalist administration, guaranteed that the political economy of the Calvières and the Froments would triumph over that of Protestant bankers and merchant-manufacturers. This is not to argue that for 'ultraroyalism' one should read 'late-feudalism', for 'Protestant republicanism', 'early-industrialization'. For one thing, not all Catholics were royalists and not all Protestants—certainly not the élite—were republicans. The restored Bourbon regime would also reveal brief glimpses of 'liberalism', as under the presidency of the duc de Decazes between 1817 and 1820. It is also true that, given the hammer-blows of political crises and economic recession which had characterized the previous two decades, venturing into the realm of industrial capitalism was not for the faint-hearted, and the hearts

---

[2] Ibid. 212–13.

[3] Ibid. 191. Toulouse became the headquarters of the ultraroyalist movement in the south of France, its 'occult government' determining the appointment of 'prefects, sub-prefects, military commanders, mayors, municipal councillors and judges'.

of most Protestant manufacturers were pretty faint. One of the immediate consequences of the White Terror of 1815 was the emigration—to Lyon and Paris, as well as to Switzerland—of many of the richest Protestant *négociants* and *fabricants*, as well as of hundreds of skilled textile workers. An English agent, Colonel Ross, estimated that around 1,500,000 francs in capital was drained from the economic infrastructure of the Gard. Possessing long historical memories, the Protestants of the Basses-Cévennes would make the comparison with the Revocation of the Edict of Nantes.[4]

It is legitimate to argue, however, that the development of modern capitalism, *particularly* after the successive crises of the Revolution and Empire, required positive encouragement from the State and that this was not forthcoming; indeed, as the Restoration progressed, the reverse would prove to be true. In 1822, the political fortunes of France would be placed in the hands of Jean-Baptiste de Villèle: 'His approach provides us with the most famous example of his class: passionately attached to the land, hostile to industrial capitalism, he considered his principal task the maintenance of social immobility.'[5] His cévenol counterpart was the marquis de Calvières, one of the leaders of the White Terror of 1815.

For the Villèles and the Calvières it was very much a question of salvaging something from the wreckage, political, economic, *and* moral, of the Revolution and Empire. An analysis of the social structure of our region after twenty or so years of revolutionary upheaval will indicate that there had been a significant shift of power away from the nobility towards the various elements of the bourgeoisie, but that provincial nobles like the Calvières continued to exercise considerable political and social influence, at least until the Revolution of 1830.

'Les Grands' had never exercised great influence in Bas-Languedoc. In 1812, the prefect of the Gard had prefaced his *renseignements sur les principales fortunes du département* with the remark that there were a few representatives of the *ancienne noblesse* in his jurisdiction, but that they included no great names: 'there are very few fortunes in the department which we can describe as considerable; there were very few illustrious families living here before the Revolution, and those have been dispersed since 1789'.[6] Apart from the *émigrés*, like the maréchal de Castries, it was those nobles whose income had depended, primarily,

[4] Lewis, *The Second Verdée*, 196.
[5] R. Lafont, *La Revendication occitane* (Paris, 1974), 64.
[6] *AG* 6M 671, 4 Oct. 1812.

upon feudal dues, who had obviously lost most. 'Noble Jacques Domergue' of Saint-Jean-de-Valériscle was eking out a miserable existence in Montpellier in 1815. On 22 February, he appealed to the comte d'Artois for help, explaining that he had owned 'the seigneurial estate of Saint-Jean-de-Valériscle as his only means of income . . . its revenues being made up solely of feudal and seigneurial dues'. Since the Revolution had abolished the latter, 'your supplicant, like the other members of his family, have been plunged into a state of misery . . . almost an octogenarian, I do not have enough bread to eat'.[7] Chabrol hailed from a wealthy professional bourgeois family which had bought into the landed nobility before the Revolution. In his petition, he explained that 'my fortune has been greatly reduced as a result of the Revolution'. His father had been an *avocat au ci-devant parlement de Toulouse*, and he had 'inherited' the position, as well as that of *juge-général des terres des ci-devant prince de Conti*. Not only had he lost the income from these two posts but 'I have also lost all the fiefs which I possessed in the Cévennes, which were quite extensive and of which no trace remains'.[8] In his detailed study of *les notables* in Bas-Languedoc towards the end of the Napoleonic Empire, André Ducel writes that certain nobles 'who did not, however, emigrate, found themselves in difficulty as a consequence of the suppression of feudal dues which constituted the major part of their income, above all in the mountainous regions'. The author mentions, as an example, 'Debroche, ancien seigneur de Saint-André-de-Valborgne', who married his own servant.[9]

However, the region could still boast a clutch of provincial nobles of some economic and social standing, like the marquis de Calvières, the 'prefect of the White Terror of 1815'. Ducel lists twenty-five nobles amongst the highest taxpayers for the Gard in 1810.[10] A successor in Calvières's prefectoral chair, appointed by the liberal administration of the duc de Decazes, emphasized 'la grande influence' which these provincial nobles exercised over the poorer elements of the Catholic population: 'A common religion which, throughout the

---

[7] *AN* F14 7671, to the comte d'Artois, 22 Feb. 1815. Domergue added that he had spent two years in prison during the Terror and that his family could boast of 'dix commissions de capitaine, cinq crois de Saint-Louis', etc.

[8] *AC* 8S 96, Chabrol to the prefect of the Gard, 24 Mess. Year XIII.

[9] A. Ducel, 'Les Notables dans le Bas-Languedoc à l'époque napoléonienne', in *Economie et société en Languedoc-Roussillon de 1789 à nos jours* (Montpellier, 1978), 363.

[10] Ibid. 362.

different epochs of our history, weighed equally upon the people and its nobility, has cemented a confraternity between them which nothing can destroy. It is to this that we must attribute its power and this difference between the people of the Cévennes and those of other French provinces'.[11] This sociological observation helps to explain the longevity and influence of a distinct, *ancien régime*, Catholic culture in Bas-Languedoc, with its preference for landed, 'protoindustrial' as opposed to urban, industrial values.[12] Roger Dugrand has estimated that, by 1820, 44.8 per cent of small country estates (*mas*) owned by town-dwellers belonged in fact to the nobility, including a few members of the *noblesse de l'épée* like the Montlaurs and the Vogüés, the latter being substantial landowners in the Uzès region.[13]

This link between the provincial nobility of Bas-Languedoc and the land had been forged long before the Revolution.[14] The *capitation* rolls of the mid-eighteenth century had produced the following average annual payments (in *livres*):[15]

196	*gentilshommes ou gens vivant noblement*	38. 8. 2
381	*bourgeois*	18. 5. 4
73	*avocats et médecins*	27. 0. 7
83	*procureurs et notaires*	13. 15. 11
155	*marchands et négociants*	29. 10. 1.

The list of 61 *figures les plus imposants* drawn up in 1811 confirms the continued wealth and influence of the landowner, many of them nobles. Of the 55 names whose profession we can establish fairly confidently there were (with their average annual income, in francs):

31	*propriétaires*	11,000
9	*marchands et négociants*	8,000
11	*avocats et notaires*	6,100
4	*médecins et docteurs*	3,400.

However, of the five families receiving an annual income of over 20,000 francs we find the Calvières of Vézénobres with 40,000; Jacques Destrem *aîné* and Bosanquet-Cardet strengthened the

---

[11] *AG* M6 202, *situation morale et politique d'Alais*, 1818.

[12] Brian Fitzpatrick has argued that this power and influence was to remain evident throughout the 19th century. *Catholic Royalism in the Department of the Gard*, 116.

[13] Dugrand, *Villes et campagnes en Bas-Languedoc*, 348.

[14] Dugrand notes that by the mid-18th century, 'nobles' had become 'masters of the land'. Ibid. 129.

[15] *AG* C512, *état des capitales du diocèze d'Alais, distingués par leurs classes et qualités*, 1736. This list excludes the three *receveurs de taille* whose average payment was 48. 8. 4.

representation of the provincial nobility with annual incomes of 25,000 francs each. Possessing an estimated annual income of 30,000 francs, we find our old friend Louis Dhombres, who had served as *receveur des tailles* and *sub-délégué de l'Intendant* before the Revolution. The Dhombres would integrate into the Napoleonic nobility and emerge as one of the most powerful families in Bas-Languedoc during the nineteenth century. Also amongst the 'top five', with an annual income assessed at 20,000 francs, we find Alexandre Tubeuf. Opposite his name, however, we read the description *'négociant'*, not 'entrepreneur' or even 'manufacturier'.[16]

This analysis of the *statistique personelle de l'arrondissement d'Alais* would confirm Jean Tulard's opinion that the *notable* who emerged from the crucible of the Revolution tended to be 'a landowner (very often a former nobleman), a rentier, an important tradesman, a lawyer, unusually a notary or a solicitor whose income from real estate was generally above 5,000 francs'.[17] However, it is a measure of the very modest levels of wealth in the Alès region that 21 of the 61 individuals chosen to represent the leading families received less than 5,000 francs' income a year.[18] It seems that, from official lists like the above, few considerable fortunes were made in the Gard during the Revolution and Empire. In addition, the 'back to the land' movement which the period had favoured with the sale of vast tracts of 'national lands' meant that *la vigne et le mûrier* was preferred over the coal-mine and the iron foundry, attracting many former Protestant manufacturers and bankers. The Restoration would do little to reverse these trends; indeed, as Roger Dugrand has noted, Protestants who had put their money into the purchase of *biens nationaux* and their energies into public affairs, wide open to them for the first time as a result of the Revolution, were reluctant to plough their profits back into heavy industry.[19]

Given that many provincial nobles—certainly not all—emerged from the Revolution bloody but financially unbowed, one should not conclude that, in social terms, very little had changed since the 1780s.

---

[16] *AG* 6M 671, *registres de la statistique personnelle des principaux familles de l'arrondissement d'Alais, 1810–1812.*

[17] Tulard, *Napoleon*, 184.

[18] See, however, Ducel, 'Les Notables dans le Bas-Languedoc', 350: 'Le notable, dans le Bas-Languedoc, apparaît comme un citadin, âgé, entouré d'une famille déjà peu nombreuse, et disposant d'un revenu souvent inférieur à 5000 francs.'

[19] Dugrand, *Villes et campagnes en Bas-Languedoc*, 348–52.

Reliance upon tax-rolls and 'estimated incomes' can produce a very misleading picture indeed, one which is almost entirely framed by *landed* wealth. The above list does not include the truly international banking, manufacturing, and commercial families whose wealth was of the more liquid kind and therefore far more difficult to contain within outmoded taxation brackets. This point was forcibly driven home by the subprefect of Nîmes in 1812 when, rather wearily, he complained about the problem of drawing up more meaningful estimates of the income of those under his jurisdiction. As he explained, in his *arrondissement* there were 'very few old noble families and very few big landowners'. It was 'commerce . . . which would have given most substance to the *statistique personelle*, but you know, monsieur le baron, how difficult it is to discover the real financial situation of the *négociant*'. The subprefect ended by pointing out a fact which would remain a constant in the history of French taxation well into the twentieth century, namely, that poor old officials like him would simply have to guess a *négociant*'s income 'from the scale of his business affairs'.[20] If we take the leading *négociants* and *marchands-fabricants* in Nîmes, Alès, and Anduze at the end of the Empire, we shall reveal something at least of the considerable wealth of the banking, commercial, and manufacturing élite, whilst emphasizing the continued, but declining, dominance which the city of Nîmes exercised over the region.

The *liste des notables du département du Gard* for 1810 underlines the economic supremacy of the Protestant community in particular; it includes some of the wealthiest families in Bas-Languedoc.[21] 'La première maison de commerce' was that of Vincens, Devillas et Cie, whose activities were now concentrated on continental markets. A banker and *commissionnaire*, as well as a shareholder in a large textile business in Nîmes, Jean-Alexandre Vincens-Mourgues, 50 years of age, was reckoned to enjoy a capital value of 900,000 francs, and an estimated annual revenue of 70,000 francs, almost twice that of the biggest landowner in the Gard, Calvières-Vézénobres. Daniel Murjas, a wholesale textile merchant, enjoyed 'un crédit immense', with a capital value of 800,000 francs and an annual income of 60,000. The average capital value of the fifteen leading 'manufacturiers et fabricants de Nîmes' in 1810 was 337,000 francs; their estimated annual revenue,

---

[20] *AG* 6M 671, letter to the Minister of Police, 31 Oct. 1812.
[21] *AN* F12 936B, *liste des négociants et commerçants les plus distingués du Gard*, 6 Sept. 1810.

9,000. In contrast, the average capital value of the thirteen 'négociants et commerçants les plus distingués d'Alais'[22] was 64,000 francs and their annual revenue just 3,600. This tends to disguise the fact that industrialists like Louis Rocheblave and Jean-Louis Guiraudet, representatives of Protestant families whose business origins could be traced back at least to the beginning of the eighteenth century, enjoyed far greater economic security, although they were not in the Vincens-Mourgues class. The average capital valuation placed on the leading six *négociants* of Anduze was precisely the same as that of their Alèsian counterparts, 64,000 francs, but their estimated annual revenue was slightly higher at 5,500.[23] André Ducel notes that of the 17 leading industrialists mentioned in the *statistique* of 1810, 6 lived in Alès, 6 in Nîmes, and 5 in Saint-Hippolyte and le Vigan.[24] This underlines the growth of the cévenol *bourgs* as manufacturing and industrial centres, as opposed to the banking and commercial strength of Nîmes. To underscore this point, we should note the success of David Dhombres-Roux, heading a recently formed business based in Nîmes—Frat, Dhombres et Laurens—who was related to the influential Dhombres family of Alès.[25]

There can be no doubt that, in most regions of Languedoc, the Revolution had confirmed the social and economic power of the wealthy provincial bourgeoisie, particularly, like the Dhombres, those with one foot firmly embedded in the soil. 'Multiplying the number of manufacturing concerns, providing the impetus behind the large-scale maritime trade, grouping together for their own profit the scattered plots of the peasantry, the big urban families, whether or not they lived in small towns or in the local capitals, have become the masters of the economic and administrative life of the province.'[26] In the Basses-Cévennes, although still dependent to a considerable extent upon *les gros* in Nîmes and Montpellier, it was the merchant and manufacturer of modest means who oiled the wheels of trade and industry. Of the 1,222 *marchands-fabricants* in the Gard in 1809, no fewer than 654 lived and worked in the Basses-Cévennes region.[27]

---

[22] *AG* 9M 24, *liste des négociants et commerçants les plus distingués par la fortune et le succès*, 11 Aug. 1810.

[23] *AG* 9M 24, *liste des négociants d'Anduze*, 27 July 1810.

[24] Ducel, 'Les Notables dans le Bas-Languedoc', 359.

[25] Dhombres-Roux's business had a capital value of 200,000 francs and an annual revenue of 25,000. *AN* F12 936B, *liste des négociants*.

[26] Dugrand, *Villes et campagnes en Bas-Languedoc*, 423.

[27] Ibid. 386.

Bourgs like Valleraugue were typical, dominating the upper valleys of the Hérault department, acting as a transport and trading post. Of its 1,462 inhabitants, 360 heads of families were engaged in trade or industry, including 19 *marchands-fabricants*, 12 silk-stocking manufacturers, 39 small workshop masters, and 9 innkeepers.[28] At the centre of the cluster of greater and lesser *bourgs* stretching from le Vigan in the west to Pont-Saint-Esprit on the Rhône stood the 'capital of the Cévennes, the town of Alès, now beginning to emerge as "une petite ville" '.[29] One should recall, however, that, with its 10,000 inhabitants, it was only one-quarter the size of Nîmes. In 1815, Alès was still in the process of making that painful and slow transition from a protoindustrial to an industrial town.

Whilst tax-rolls exaggerate the continued importance of the nobility, other contemporary documents confirm that the Revolution and Empire had wrought a social revolution in the expectations and tastes of the middle and lower classes. 'Jacques' may still not have been as good as his noble or merchant master, but he, and a far greater number of his friends, thought that they were. Whatever 'revisionist' historians claim about a noble and bourgeois élite dominating French society and politics from the mid-eighteenth to the mid-nineteenth century, many officials thought that the real victors to emerge from the Revolution were 'the middling sort of people'. In a detailed and most illuminating official report which was written towards the end of the Napoleonic Empire and entitled *Changements survenus dans la manière à vivre et dans le prix des choses nécessaires à la vie*, the anonymous author concluded:

It seems that, in general, the Revolution has produced an amelioration in the situation of the most numerous class of society. The subdivision of the large estates, the suppression of several onerous *ancien régime* dues, the clearing of the common lands, the acquisitions made in *assignats*, the rise in the cost of labour, all of these factors have increased the standard of living of *le peuple*.[30]

This levelling process was most evident to our social analyst in 'life-styles'. Whereas, before the Revolution, the ordinary *cultivateur des Cévennes* was content with his *aigo-boulido*,[31] rye-bread, dried chestnuts,

---

[28] Dugrand, *Villes et campagnes en Bas-Languedoc*, 432.
[29] Ibid. 354.
[30] *AG* 6M 651. This interesting document was probably the work of the subprefect of Alès.
[31] A kind of thin soup, laced with garlic.

TABLE 6.1. *A comparison of annual average incomes, Basses-Cévennes, 1789 and 1805*

Social category	Annual average income	
	1789	1805
Wealthy landowner (*propriétaire le plus riche*)	14,600	10,950[a]
Bourgeois	3,000	3,852
Small farmer (*plus petit propriétaire*)	1,022	1,040
Carpenter (*menuisier*)	896	1,095

[a] This is practically the same figure as that produced on p. 256 as the average annual income of *propriétaires* in the Alès region.

Source: *AG* M 651.

potatoes, and a *picquette* of wine, by 1807, he was frequently to be found eating white bread, 'pork or mutton once a week and drinking wine with his meals'. His coarse woollen or hemp smock had been replaced by cotton-mixed coats, whilst his daughter 'thought her vanity wounded if she had to dress up on fête-days in her grandmother's old outfit'. The report concluded: 'It is, above all, amongst the middling sort of people (*la classe intermédiaire de la société*) that the unfortunate consequences of this ridiculous change in life-styles has been felt most profoundly. The lowest *bourgeois*, seeking to appear something he is not, sacrifices any savings he might have to satisfy this mania.' Presumably, our official was from the higher ranks of the bourgeoisie!

As for basic food supplies in the Alès region, the price of salt had been halved, but bread and wine cost about the same. Meat prices, however, had risen very sharply due to increased demand and the continuing secularization of society, 'non-observation est devenue presque générale des jours d'abstinence'.[32] The economics of the 'bourgeois revolution' are contained in a table comparing average incomes (in francs in 1789 with those in 1805 (see Table 6.1). Taking a family of five as the norm, the report concludes, the outlay on food and lodgings which the wealthy landowner had to find had increased from 6.30 francs a day in 1789 to 8.25 in 1805; for the *bourgeois*, 4.65

[32] *AG* 6M 651, *sommes nécessaires à chaque individu pour son entretien par jour.*

to 6.50; for the small farmer, an increase from 1.40 to 1.80; and for the carpenter, from 1.30 to 1.65, suggesting a further levelling between the wealthier and the poorer members of society.

As we have seen, the Revolution had provided an excellent opportunity for consolidating the power of those smaller landowners, silk manufacturers, and mine-owners who had done so much to undermine the pioneering work of Pierre-François Tubeuf before the Revolution. Let us take the example of two of Tubeuf's bitterest opponents—Jacques Aubrespin and Jean-Baptiste Deveze. The former was a typical Alèsian manufacturer owning a silk-spinning works and land on the Montaud mountain near the Rozier family, which had organized the first resistance to Tubeuf in the 1770s.[33] By the 1800s, Aubrespin had extended his activities to include lime-kilns and the lease of the Abilon mine, which was worked for him by Louis Gabourdès. The Aubrespins, heavily dependent upon coal for their small and various manufacturing ventures, maintained their opposition to the Tubeufs throughout the Revolution and Empire, particularly when Mme Tubeuf regained provisional control of her dead husband's concession in 1802.[34] Jean-Pierre Deveze had even worked, briefly, for Tubeuf as a 'un simple ouvrier' in his Rochebelle mine before the Revolution. On 5 Messidor Year III (13 August 1795), he had purchased a small plot of land on the Montaud mountain for 7,000 *livres*, paid in pretty worthless *assignats*.[35] Deveze then reopened many of the small levels which had been dug into the mountainside over many years with the intention of supplying the many locksmiths, cutlers, and coppersmiths of Alès and the immediate vicinity. In 1804, it was Jean-Pierre Deveze who had organized a petition supported by local artisans against the Tubeuf family's 'monopole' of production.[36] By 1808, he had joined with other small landowners, manufacturers, and mine-owners to launch yet another assault upon the Tubeufs. In the words of the Inspecteur des mines, Deveze was typical of 'the so-called *propriétaires* who got their hands on the nation's riches during the Revolution and who have sought ever since to consolidate their usurpations'.[37]

[33] See p. 85.

[34] *AG* 8S 104, *pétition de Jacques Aubrespin*, 4 Germ. Year X.

[35] *AN* F14 7684, Beaunier, *rapport général sur les mines d'Alais*, 52.

[36] *AG* 8S 95. This petition claimed that the Tubeufs had raised the price of small coal from 3 to 5 *sols le quintal*. Pre-Revolutionary petitions against their father had made similar (justified) accusations.

[37] *AG* 8S 95, *rapport de l'ingénieur-en-chef des mines au préfet*, 13 Aug. 1808.

However, by the time that Louis XVIII was trying to fit his corpulent frame to the throne of France for the second time in 1815, a new breed of coal entrepreneur, more exclusively concerned with mining and the transportation of coal—always a vital factor in the success or failure of early coal-mining—had emerged in the persons of men like Jean-Jacques Puech and Pierre Goirand. These two men were destined to triumph over the Castries and the Tubeufs, neither of whom were prepared (after the hammer-blow of the 1809 concessions in the case of the Tubeufs) to devote themselves exclusively to the coal-mining industry. Puech and Goirand were to play a major part in the creation of the modernized Grand-Combe mining company after 1830. Jean-Jacques Puech came from a reasonably wealthy landowning and manufacturing Alèsian family; Pierre Goirand, as we have noted, was a *traiteur* in Alès, whose store became the base for the early coal warehouses established by the partners.

During the Revolution, Puech and Goirand had secured the leases of as many mines as they could lay their money on, Goirand being the 'front man' on account of Puech's social standing in the region and the royalism which his branch of the family had espoused. On 27 July 1793, for example, Pierre Goirand, flanked by a couple of associates, had leased some of the mines in the *forêt de Portes*, formerly the property of the king's brother.[38] The terms of these leases—800 *livres* a year for forty years—were yet another example of the compliant administration of the Régie de l'enregistrement in Alès. In 1801, prompted by the news that the Tubeufs were about to regain their old concession, Puech and Goirand began to search feverishly for new seams of coal, digging up vineyards and gardens, becoming, in the words of the local population, 'the plague of our commune'.[39] A couple of years later, the Tubeufs were obliged to recognize officially the influence of Puech and Goirand in the Portes region. However, as the Tubeufs increased their own power and influence during the early years of the Empire, resistance to their 'monopole' increased,

[38] See *AN* F14 7677, letter of six inhabitants of Champcloson to the prefect, 4 Apr. 1808. These six inhabitants—Pierre Soleiret, Jean-Louis Dautun, Louis Dautun, Jean Ginestoux, Louis Gazaix, and Jean Polge—had all participated in the resistance to Pierre-François Tubeuf before the Revolution. The agents of Monsieur, who had secured the Portes concession in 1784, had concentrated their attention upon the mines of Levade, Fenadou, and la Tronche, leaving Champcloson to the six individuals listed above. On 21 Oct. 1786, these men had received 3,000 *livres* compensation for their agreement to withdraw from the three other mines.

[39] *AN* F14 7675, Louis Dautun to subprefect of Alès, 28 Vent. Year XI.

leading to the 'insurrection' of 1806. According to the prefect of the Gard, the principal instigator of this concerted resistance was Pierre Goirand, who had 'sown discord amongst the workers of this region'.[40] A year later, Goirand and his associates set up a *société* to protect their investments. It is clear, however, that the *éminence grise* behind this move was the relatively wealthy Jean-Jacques Puech.

As a result of the pressure which Puech was able to exert in Paris, he and his partner had succeeded in wresting the Trescol mine from the Tubeufs in the great shake-up of 1809: it was to mark a very important milestone in their journey to power as the region's most influential mine-owners. Puech had very useful family connections. His brother-in-law was the ex-member of the National Convention Barrot, whose family owned land and a textile manufacturing business near Villefort in the neighbouring Lozère department. Puech's daughter had married a wealthy Paris manufacturer named Fabre, who was also to become involved, as an investor, in the cévenol coal-mines.[41] Puech and Goirand formed the conduit through which Parisian money would trickle into the coffers of the local coal-owners. This trickle would only become a torrent with the arrival of the Rothschilds and the Talabots after the Revolution of 1830.

The rise of entrepreneurial companies like the Puech–Goirands necessarily involved the fall of the traditional 'independent collier' families. Men like Jean-Pierre Soleiret, whose family had mined for coal in the forest of Portes for generations. Jean-Pierre himself had filled the post of *maître-mineur* under Adam Forster in the Grand-Combe during the 1780s. The Revolution provided him with the opportunity of running his own small mine in the region.[42] By 1815, he was described as 'un salarié' of the duc de Castries, who was, on no account, to be given a position of any real trust or authority.[43] Soleiret was by now a member of 'les vieux', the last exponents of the art of medieval mining. (During a recent underground tour of the Blaenant pit in South Wales, the guide, pointing to an early shaft

---

[40] The Inspecteur des mines noted that 'les entrepreneurs d'Alais qui font magasin de houille [the Goirands] ne sont pas étrangers à cette rébellion'. *AG* 8S 22, *rapport sur la rébellion des exploitants des mines de l'arrondissement d'Alais.*

[41] Barrot, who had lived with the Puechs in Alais during part of the Empire, had traditionally been supplied by coal-mining families like the Soleirets whose mines in the *forêt de Portes* provided coal for parts of the Bas-Vivarais. *AN* F14 7683, Ingénieur des mines to the Conseil des mines, 18 Pluv. Year XIII.

[42] *AG* 8S 95, *pétition du citoyen Adam Forster*, 20 June 1793.

[43] *AN* 306AP 488, *demandes pour être placées aux mines de M. le duc de Castries.*

which had been dug into the hillside, spoke to me in very respectful terms of 'the old ones', whose ghostly footsteps he could still hear if he listened very carefully!) On 28 Pluviôse Year V, Jean Larguier, again the representative of a very old mining family, had secured, with the connivance of the Régie de l'enregistrement, a three-year lease on the la Tronche mine in the commune of Saint-Andéol, which he continued to work, off and on, until 1808. Larguier, like Soleiret, derived his political clout from his friends and neighbours, who had elected him mayor of Saint-Andéol at the beginning of the Revolution. And he returned the favour. As he explained to the prefect, he had defended the local coal-mines from 'les étrangers', not for reasons of personal gain, but on behalf of his fellow citizens.[44]

This was the very understandable, protoindustrial perspective through which old families like the Soleirets and the Larguiers viewed economic issues. The latter, like so many other *charbonniers* in the region, was supported to the end by small property-owners like Desparcieux, who described himself in one petition as 'one of the highest taxpayers in this commune'. Desparcieux leased out the coal-mines on his property, receiving, in return, cheap supplies of coal for his small silk-spinning mill and glassworks. In a letter to the Conseil des mines, he explained that 'From time immemorial, these mines have been worked for local consumption, bringing in money for us to pay our taxes.'[45] Jean-Baptiste Larguier said that he had mined coal on his own property as well as leasing coal-mines from men like Desparcieux 'depuis son enfance'.[46] An inveterate enemy of the Tubeufs since the 1770s, the Larguier family was being forced to adjust its line of fire to cover the Puech–Goirand company by the 1800s— 'cette société des spéculateurs d'Alais'—providing, in his own defence, the manifesto of the traditional independent collier families: 'These families cannot pursue any other profession than that of coal-mining. The ancient right which they possess to work these mines represents a form of ownership (*titre*) which commands all the more respect when one considers that they cannot be deprived of their rights without endangering the livelihood of the many families who depend

---

[44] *AG* 8S 95, *Ingénieur-en-chef des mines* to prefect, 27 Mar. 1807.

[45] *AG* 8S 95, *pétition de Desparcieux de Pradel au Conseil des mines*, 24 Vend. Year XII. In 1806, Alexandre Tubeuf had described Desparcieux as 'un brigand', probably on account of the fact that the latter was thinking of setting up a glassworks on his property! *AG* 8S 104, Ingénieur-en-chef to prefect, 11 Sept. 1806.

[46] *AN* F14 7683, *pétition de J.-B. Larguier*, Year IX.

upon them for their daily bread.'[47] This was the classic statement of the eighteenth-century 'moral economy', of the customary rights which were being eroded, on and beneath the land, in favour of a modern contractual system. All to no avail. By 1826, we find that Jean-Pierre Larguier was working for Puech and Goirand in the very Trescol mine that he had 'owned' for a time during the Revolution and Empire.[48] There are many similar cases, like that of Louis Gabourdès, who had worked the Abilon mine for Jacques Aubrespin and who had led the revolt against the Tubeufs in 1806. In 1816, we find him petitioning the duc de Castries for a job in the Abilon mine.[49] 'Independent colliers' were in the process of being transformed into the nineteenth-century mining proletariat.

It had been the legislation of 1810, of course, which had delivered the legal *coup de grâce* to 'les vieux'. When asked to justify his right to a concession, Desparcieux could only fall back upon the 'property-owners' charter' of 1791, but families like the Gabourdès and the Laupiès possessed neither the legal expertise nor the required degree of literacy to play the new game of concession-bidding properly. Laupiès did write to the prefect to explain that if he did not legally own the mine which he was working, it was only 'through my ignorance of the law'. He did, however, decide to take his case against Puech and Goirand to the *tribunal de première instance d'Alais*, arguing that the mine he rented should be treated like any other 'bien rural'. He lost.[50] The inhabitants of Champcloson in the *forêt de Portes*, led by the Soleiret family, complained that the coal-mines in their region had been wrongfully seized and divided between Jean Méjean and Puech and Goirand simply because 'the person charged with the defence of our interests did not draw up our petition in the correct manner'. They suggested to the prefect that an industrialist like Jean Méjean was the really guilty party given his 'insatiable avidity and his determination to reduce six families and fifty local inhabitants to a state of complete despair'.[51] Puech and Goirand had exploited the

---

[47] *AG* 8S 104, Larguier to prefect, 15 Vent. Year IX.

[48] *AG* 8S 36, *mémoire sur les mines d'Alais*, 1826.

[49] *AN* 306AP 495, *mémoire sur les mines de la forêt d'Abilon*, 1816. It was suggested that he should be employed 'comme corporal, au moins'.

[50] *AG* 8S 105, Laupiès to prefect, 25 Vent. Year IX.

[51] *AN* F14 7677, *mémoire sur les concessions de 1809*. Thirty years earlier the same families, Soleirets and Dautuns, had bitterly criticized Pierre-François Tubeuf for his 'insatiable avidity'. *AN* F14 7677, *délibération du 5 Oct. 1780* (signed by 42 other families).

economic crises of 1811 to buy out some mining families for a few hundred francs.[52]

All these complaints fell upon prefectoral ears which were tuned to receive only the message of the new 1810 legislation, which insisted upon the importance of the technical and financial resources of prospective *concessionnaires*. A comparison of the taxes paid by the future coal-owners of the region with those paid by the old mining families will not just reveal a difference of class but will tell us something about the real 'winners' and 'losers' of the French Revolution.

Let us start with the men whose names would figure amongst the shareholders of the future Grand-Combe mining company, which would be formed in 1828. We have already discussed the financial position of Puech and Pierre Goirand. As for their financial backers, Barrot and Fabre, the former owned property in Paris and the Lozère, on which he paid 387 francs; the latter paid 575 francs for his Parisian properties.[53] Gardies, a wealthy property-owner in the Gard, had bought the Destieures mine from the representative of another traditional mining family, Simon Martin of Saint-Jean-de-Valériscle. Gardies, typical of those Protestant urban bourgeois who had benefited from the purchase of national lands and who had extended their financial control over the countryside, boasted, in addition to his property in Alès, a fine country house and farm near Ribaute, stocked with merino sheep.[54] Guiraudet-Laliquière, the Protestant silk-manufacturing family from Alès which had helped to spearhead the resistance to the maréchal de Castries on the eve of the Revolution, owned property in Alès, Salindres, and Saint-Christol, paying a total in taxation of 1,051 francs. Deleuze, descended from another Protestant family, who had sold the *terre de Trouilhas* to the maréchal de Castries in the 1780s, had property in Alès, Portes, and Robiac, upon which he paid 415 francs. These families were hardly in the Rothschild class, but compare their financial standing with that of 'les vieux'. Polge, Joseph and Louis Dautun, and Pierre Gazaix, all of whom had once managed mines in the Portes region and who had been hopeful of securing something from the 1809–10 'revolution', paid just 6, 8, 10,

---

[52] *AN* F14 7677, Ingénieur-en-chef des mines to prefect, 26 Mar. 1816.

[53] The figures for this case, and those that follow, are taken from *extrait des rôles de contributions*, 1816. *AN* F14 7677.

[54] *AG* 8S 105, Ingénieur des mines to prefect, 7 Feb. 1807.

and 6 francs respectively. Not surprisingly, their hopes were quickly dashed by the prefect.

It is evident, therefore, that there was meaningful social change in the Alès and Nîmes region during the Revolution and Empire. 'Les Grands', as well as those nobles who had been dependent for a significant part of their income upon feudal dues, certainly lost in economic as well as in social terms. When he died in 1800, the maréchal de Castries had left only 50,000 *livres*.[55] If certain Catholic royalist nobles in Bas-Languedoc continued to wield significant political power, it was due, not so much to their economic strength, but to the persistence of that unique form of snobbery which (still) places an impoverished duke above a wealthy mine-owner, as well as to the immediate consequences of the White Terror of 1815, which blocked the political pretensions of the Protestant community for almost a generation. It would be an exercise in counterfactual history to speculate on the possible accelerating pace of industrial change had not so many Protestant bankers and manufacturers fled the region— some temporarily it must be noted—in 1815, and we have already established that land and the production of wine and raw silk, not investment in heavy industry, attracted both Protestants and Catholics during the Revolution and Empire. But there can be no doubt that crises like the White Terror further inhibited the move towards investment in new machinery and new methods of production. Michel Riou has analysed the events of 1815 against long-term socio-economic trends, correlating the periodic bouts of violence with high levels of unemployment and changing patterns of production, and insisting that political crises sharpened the old antagonisms between Protestant masters and Catholic workers. It would be several years before confidence returned.[56]

No wonder so many small manufacturers, merchants, and artisans persisted in defending protoindustrial structures of production which promised, at least, some defence against the massive risks of monopoly capitalism and costly fixed capital investment on the one hand and the miserable rigours of proletarianization on the other. Government officials were also well aware of the revolutionary dangers of economic and political upheavals. The prefect of the Gard during the relatively

---

[55] Castries, *Papiers de famille*, 196.
[56] Riou, 'La Terreur blanche dans le département du Gard', 387–98.

good years of the mid-1800s and again during Napoleon's ill-fated Hundred Days, baron d'Alphonse, insisted upon the uneasy peace which only held in prosperous times, concluding that 'The last thing that we want to see here is a political upheaval.'[57]

However, despite the widespread attraction of landed wealth which the Revolution bequeathed to the restored Bourbons and the economic buffeting which shook the whole of France periodically during the Napoleonic Empire, it would be just as misleading to suggest that no meaningful technical change occurred in the manufacturing sphere during the Restoration as to argue that the Revolution had no social consequences. There was indeed change, although not enough, before 1830, to revolutionize the structures of the textile industry and, in consequence, those of the coal industry, nor to entice enough investors away from the lure of *la vigne et le mûrier*. The degree of change which did occur, however, the transformation—in part a technical one—of the silk industry in Nîmes, further redefined its relationship with the towns and villages of the Basses-Cévennes. It confirmed the role of the latter as 'colonies' for the production of raw and spun silk, gradually reducing the numbers and political clout of the small, independent textile manufacturer and craftsman, eventually eroding the base of political opposition to the introduction of massive 'monopoly' investment in the coal industry. However, this was only to become evident after the Revolution of 1830 which severely curtailed the political and economic influence of Catholic royalism in Bas-Languedoc and facilitated the rise of modern industrial capitalism.

By far the most important technical change concerned the introduction of the Jacquard loom, itself 'une belle conquête industrielle' according to one historian. It revolutionized production by increasing the quality and design of fabrics, whilst reducing the number of workers necessary for the production of the new range of products— scarves, cravats, printed dresses, and, in particular, shawls and house furnishings like curtains and carpets.[58] André Cosson argues that it was the installation of the Jacquard loom in Roux-Carbonnel's workshops which pulled Nîmes out of its post-Napoleonic economic recession, enabling it to emerge with a number of new products and

---

[57] A. Cosson, 'Industrie de la soie et population ouvrière à Nîmes de 1815 à 1848', in *Économie et Société en Languedoc-Roussillon*, 191.

[58] E. Parisot, *Les Industries de la soie* (Lyon, 1890), 353; *Nîmes et le Gard*, 324–5, which notes that the 'take-off' in the manufacture of printed scarves, cravats, etc. began around 1820 and prospered until the 1850s.

a somewhat shaky confidence in the future.[59] The subsequent technical refinements to the loom introduced by Grégoire and Tirian in 1827 and 1834 respectively would further modernize the processes of production, particularly so far as the hosiery branch of industry was concerned. It is very relevant to note that it was Guiraudet, the Protestant Alèsian manufacturer directly involved in the development of the coal industry in the Alès region, who was to install the first steam-engine in his factory specializing in the production of silk thread from the original cocoons.[60] Contemporary reports reveal how very important these years were for what might reasonably be termed a minor renaissance in the fortunes of industry in Bas-Languedoc as a whole, but certainly in the Basses-Cévennes. The subprefect of Alès commented in 1820 upon 'the astonishing progress which has occurred in the spinning of silk'. In 1818, Alès had 107 small spinning concerns, but just one *filature à vapeur*, the one which Guiraudet had installed in his workshop: two years later, there were no fewer than fourteen mills worked by steam-power. Similar developments were taking place in Saint-Jean-du-Gard and Anduze.[61] The populations of these two *bourgs* would reach their peaks in the 1830s—5,500 and 4,300 respectively, almost twice today's figures.[62] It was not just the manufacturing revival in Nîmes which provided the impetus for this growth: the rebirth of the silk industry in Lyon would create a major demand for raw and spun silk during the first half of the nineteenth century. As for the old hub of the industry's wheel, Nîmes, it was specifically the demand for shawls, which surfaced again around 1820, that would boost the industrial recovery of the period with 5,000 looms providing work for 12,000 workers by 1825.[63]

These developments, along with the rapidly changing world of fashion, itself part of the transition from an aristocratic to a bourgeois society, with trousers and cotton and woollen socks or stockings replacing the breeches and silken hose of the eighteenth century, introduced a period of wildly fluctuating fortunes for manufacturers and workers alike. Employment figures rose and fell alarmingly during the Restoration as capitalist cycles of trade impacted upon the lives

---

[59] Cosson, 'Industrie de la soie et population ouvrière à Nîmes', 192.

[60] *AG* 6M 202, *situation morale et politique d'Alais*, 1818.

[61] *AG* 6M 202, report for 1820.

[62] *AG* 6M 2, *tableau des mouvements de la population du département du Gard de 1800 à 1834*. See also *AG* 6M 100, 102, 104, and 651.

[63] Dugrand, *Villes et campagnes en Bas-Languedoc*, 390.

of the tens of thousands of protoindustrial workers in town and countryside. Cosson states that the number of workers employed in the silk industry in Nîmes rose from just 4,500 in 1819 to 14,500 two years later. In 1823, this figure dropped to only 6,000; two years later, it rose again, this time to 26,630![64] It was to be during the mid-1820s, fuelled in part by the social consequences of these dramatic alternations of boom and recession as well as by the political impact of the accession in 1825 of the last of the Bourbons—the ultraroyalist Charles X—that yet another, albeit it a relatively non-violent, collision occurred between the Catholic royalist authorities in Nîmes and the predominantly Protestant inhabitants of the Basses-Cévennes.[65] After 1827, trade and industry was to experience a prolonged recession culminating in the Revolution of 1830.

As the acreage devoted to the planting of mulberry trees increased, and the drawing and spinning of silk thread became the main concern of the inhabitants of the Basses-Cévennes, so the vine began to move southwards to the sandy plains around Nîmes, where today's Listel wines are produced, and east to the department of the Hérault, still one of the chief sources of cheap table wines. Before the Revolution, Bellegarde, Vauvert, and Aiguesvives were already producing cheap wine for local consumption or for the production of *eaux-de-vie*, but, at the beginning of the nineteenth century, grapes had still been a popular crop in the old Bas-Vivarais (southern Ardèche), around les Vans and Joyeuse.[66] However, the acreage covered by the vine in the department of the Gard did not increase significantly during the first half of the nineteenth century—71,000 hectares in 1808, 74,000 in 1818, rising to just 78,000 by 1852.[67] During the Bourbon Restoration, the mulberry tree triumphed over the vine as *the* 'spoilt child' of the inhabitants of the Basses-Cévennes. A prefectoral report of 1828 included the following comment: 'It is certainly true that this increase [in the production of raw silk] is very noticeable and that, in different localities, this form of production has replaced viticulture. The fall in the price of wine and, above all, the difficulty of finding markets, has

[64] Ibid. 192–212.

[65] Lewis, 'A Cévenol Community in Crisis', 156–7.

[66] Laurent, R., 'Les Quatre Âges du vignoble du bas-Languedoc et du Roussillon', in *Economie et société en Languedoc-Roussillon*, 11–12. Laurent notes that, due to transport difficulties, the vine spread its branches mainly around towns and along the canal du Midi and the port of Sète, where the Tubeufs established a *maison de commerce*.

[67] *Nîmes et le Gard*, 17–28.

produced this result.'[68] The transition phase appears to have fallen, as one might expect, towards the end of the Napoleonic period, with the loss of a protected market and the disbanding of Napoleon's huge armies. The same report states that it was during 'the period 1814 to 1820' that local inhabitants moved decisively from cultivating grapes to the rearing of silkworms, 'above all during the early years of the Restoration when the advent of peace saw the price of silk-cocoons rise to three francs *la livre ancienne*. As a result, landowners began to plant mulberry trees . . . they had already sacrificed their olive trees in the Cévennes around le Vigan; they now began to sacrifice their chestnut trees'.[69]

The sacrifice seems to have been worth it. The number of *mûriers* in France rose from nearly 10 million in 1820 to nearly 15 million in 1834. In 1828, the department of the Gard alone sheltered 3,430,000 mulberry trees, a figure which, according to the prefect, had increased threefold since 1809. Again, we note that the 'take-off' comes around 1820. In 1818, the subprefect of Alès explained that whilst the planting of mulberry trees in his jurisdiction was on the increase generally, their numbers had still not exceeded those recorded in 1793: 'people are working hard to repair the losses experienced during the revolutionary regime when this form of production fell into some disfavour'.[70] By 1834, the Gard would produce a figure of 5,709,466 mulberry trees, twice that of the Drôme and around two and a half times that of the Vaucluse and the Ardèche. At this time, the inhabitants of the Gard were tending a quarter of all the mulberry trees in France.[71] Strong demand explains why the price of a kilogram of silk-cocoons rose from 1.80 francs in 1811 to 3.75 in 1820, and 4.60 in 1834.[72] There is a corresponding increase in the production of spun silk during the same period—100,000 kilograms in 1810 and 206,000 in 1825, rising to 237,140 by 1834. Roger Dugrand argues that the introduction of a new technique for boiling the cocoons to release their silk thread—the *bassines à la Gensoul*—facilitated concentration of production in the silk-spinning industry. By 1842, the Gard would be producing 360,000 kilograms of spun silk. There would be 98 sizeable textile mills, some with 200 *bassines à la Gensoul*, to produce

---

[68] *AN* F12 2291, to the Minister of Commerce, 28 June 1828.
[69] Ibid.
[70] *AG* 6M 202, *situation morale et politique d'Alais*, 1818.
[71] Dugrand, *Villes et campagnes en Bas-Languedoc*, 389.
[72] *AN* F12 2291, *état comparatif des mûriers en France en 1820 et 1834*.

the original thread. We must note that Alès, rapidly becoming a centre of the coal and iron industry by this time, now had just 8 mills employing 828 workers; Anduze had 20 with 670 workers; Saint-Jean-du-Gard, 19 for 776 workers; Bagnols, 15 for 570; Uzès, 8 for 500.[73] No wonder the prefect of the Gard could announce proudly as early as 1828: 'Le mûrier est l'ornement et la richesse des ses contrées.'[74]

We have spent time providing the bare outlines, at least, of the political and socio-economic changes to affect our region because, as had been the case under the *ancien régime*, the fortunes of the coal industry during the Bourbon Restoration were to be inextricably linked to those determining the fate of viticulture and sericulture. In 1820, the subprefect of Alès, having established the fact that, so far as the local economy was concerned, the production of raw silk took pride of place, could now state that 'the production of coal comes second'.[75] There were, of course, many industries which provided a demand for coal—the iron industry, tanning, the production of lime, as well as the increased demand for domestic heating. Did the general increase in demand, particularly from the mechanization of the raw-silk indus-try, lead to profound changes in the coal industry? The simple answer is no. There were, as we shall see, important developments concerning the ownership of coal-mines, as well as a steady, but again hardly spectacular, increase in production, but any talk of 'revolution' or 'take-off' had to wait until after the Revolution of 1830 and the advent of the railway age.

So far as the coal industry was concerned, the early years of the Restoration were to be marked by the economic hangover inseparable from the collapse of the Napoleonic system and the end of protected markets, as well as by further clamour from a motley collection of would-be coal-owners for an even greater number of coal concessions from the government. Some, like the former noble Jacques Domergue, apparently thought that he could simply exchange the feudal dues which he had lost for sacks of coal, reflecting the widespread *ancien régime* conviction that coal was a 'crop' just like wheat or peas! Domergue thought that it would help his case if he pointed out that he had passed the period of the Jacobin Terror in prison.[76] But even

---

[73] Dugrand, *Villes et campagnes en Bas-Languedoc*, 389.

[74] *AN* F12 2292, to the Minister of Commerce, 14 Oct. 1828.

[75] *AG* 6M 202, *situation morale et politique d'Alais*, 1820.

[76] *AN* F14 7671, to the comte d'Artois, 22 Feb. 1815.

a government eager to reward *émigrés* could hardly fit a Domergue into the fairly tight provisions of the 1810 legislation, which required both money and mining expertise, neither of which this *ci-devant* possessed. However, someone with the name of Castries and the title of a duke was a very different matter. On 8 November 1815, the duc de Castries had written to the ultraroyalist Minister of the Interior, Vaublanc, asking if he could use his best offices at Court to ensure that the Abilon and Mas-Dieu mines were added to the prize he had secured in 1809, the Grand-Combe. The minister replied in the affirmative, saying that he would place the matter in the hands of the king himself.[77] The royal decree of 29 November 1815 duly incorporated Abilon and the Mas-Dieu into Castries's concession.

Louis XVIII's decree in 1815 actually created no fewer than eight concessions in the Basses-Cévennes—those belonging to Castries, Tubeuf, Puech and Goirand, Suffren, Serres, Méjean, Gilly, and the inhabitants of Champcloson. The case of the last-named concession reveals more of the *ancien régime* thinking which informed the decisions of the Catholic royalist administrations of the day. Champcloson was not a very productive mine; its coal had traditionally been used by the inhabitants of the Cévennes to dry chestnuts. It was this local function which had attracted the attention of the prefect of the Gard during the First Restoration when he suggested that all the mines in the Portes region should be integrated into the royal domain, thus protecting the interests of the local inhabitants from 'speculators' like Puech and Goirand. The rationale behind his argument was precisely that which Alexis de Trinquelaque had used to attack Tubeuf's 'monopoly' in the 1780s, namely, that local ownership would be more efficient and would keep prices down.[78]

All expert opinion in the region was agreed that the decision to divide the old Alès coal-basin into eight concessions proved to be a major mistake, preventing any single *concessionnaire*, or, indeed, two or three of them, from accumulating the necessary capital to invest in the modernization of the coalfield. The need to concentrate production into the hands of a small number of *concessionnaires* had been one of the key pieces of advice offered by two of the government's most experienced mining engineers during the late Napoleonic period—

---

[77] *AN* 306AP 498, *rapport sur les mines d'Abilon*, 15 Jan. 1816.

[78] *AN* F14 7677, letter to the *Directeur-général des mines*, 30 Dec. 1814. It is interesting and relevant to note that the royal *ordonnance* of 29 Nov. 1815 confirmed—although not definitively—the traditional rights of the inhabitants of the *forêt de Portes*.

Beaunier[79] and Lefebvre d'Hellancourt.[80] This point emphasizes one
of the major themes of this present study—the conflict of opinion
which separated the *fonctionnaire*, concerned, primarily, with the interests of the State, and the Court, whether under Louis XVI, Napoleon
Bonaparte, or Louis XVIII, confronted with a much wider brief,
including the interests of public order as well as those of its aristocratic élites. Let us see how the problems directly associated with too
much competition, insufficient capital investment, and insufficient
demand from industry in general, affected the two families who have
been our major concern in this study—the Castries and the Tubeufs.

When the duc de Castries assumed actual control of the Grand-
Combe at the end of the Napoleonic Empire, which he had bought
from his sister, the vicomtesse de Mailly, they were in an exceedingly
parlous state.[81] In the first place, as we have just established, it was
not until the government's decree of 29 November 1815 that the
Abilon and Mas-Dieu mines were added to the Grand-Combe. There
was also the constant economic and political uncertainty, culminating
in the White Terror of 1815. Castries's first *directeur des mines*, a
Protestant named Ango, was dismissed at the end of this turbulent
year, ostensibly on account of his 'political' (that is, religious) sym-
pathies. In fact, it seems that Ango had continued the time-honoured
Midi tradition of fleecing aristocratic and absentee mine-owners. His
reliable successor, Louis Lefebvre, a graduate of the École des mines,
suggested that Ango and his friends, like the Société des fermiers de
la Grand-Combe in the early 1780s, had pocketed the better part of
the profits made from the sale of coal; but, as Lefebvre put it
somewhat laconically, 'As the old proverb says, where there is nothing
at all to be gained, the king loses his rights'![82]

Equally depressing was the physical state of the mines: 'Roofs have
caved in and roadways have been flooded . . . the entrepreneurs, or,

---

[79] See *AN* F14 7684, Beaunier, *rapport général sur les mines d'Alais*, 18 June 1811.

[80] *AN* F14 7684, d'Hellancourt's report of 21 Oct. 1811.

[81] The mining legacy from the maréchal de Castries had been divided between
Armand-Charles-Augustin de Lacroix, the duc de Castries, his sister, the vicomtesse de
Mailly, and the duc's son, Eugène-Edmund-Hercule de Lacroix, the marquis de Castries.
The duc de Castries had received his ducal title after service in the American War of
Independence. Castries borrowed the money to buy out his sister and his son, and it
was the rising interest rate on this debt that finally drove him to sell the mines to
Barrot and Guiraudet in 1821, thus providing the cash to settle the debts he had incurred.
Castries, *Papiers de famille*, 309–10.

[82] *AN* 306AP 502, letter to Castries, 7 July 1816.

to put it another way, the pillagers, seeing that the water levels were getting the better of them and fearing the cost of dealing with the problem, just worked their way back to the mine-entrance, pulling down the pillars of coal used to prop up the roofs as they went'.[83] A government report for the spring of 1816 estimated that it would be all of three years, at a cost of over 12,000 francs, before the mines could be returned to good working order. The report concluded that 'it is only after the completion of this work that it will prove possible to extract coal on any major scale'.[84] However, another official report written two years later records the sad fact that of the ten known seams of coal in the Grand-Combe, only three were actually being worked.[85]

No engineering expert himself, the duc de Castries was not averse to the idea of improving his mine, although, from a technical standpoint, this seems to have involved little more than a return to the best pre-Revolution practices. The fundamental problem, as ever, was money, or, rather, the lack of it. As Castries explained to the Minister of the Interior in 1815 when he was pressing the government to give him the Abilon and Mas-Dieu mines: 'The entire loss of my fortune induces me to express, in the strongest possible terms, the wish that Your Excellency will deal with this matter as soon as it is convenient for you to do so.'[86] It is true that this kind of pressure brought its reward, but only at considerable cost. Castries was obliged to pay compensation to the Tubeufs for the excellent work which Renaux had master-minded at the Grand-Combe, compensation which amounted to no less than 50,000 francs.[87] Then there was the continous demand for money from his *directeur des mines*, Lefebvre, who was being besieged 'by demands for money from all sides; money to settle old debts, workers' wages to find every week, coal-heavers' wages every month, land taxes to meet in addition to the government's tax on the coal we extract'.[88]

But the duc de Castries himself wanted some profit from his mines; this was, after all, the main purpose of his interest in the Grand-Combe. Like the maréchal de Castries before him, he was not

---

[83] *AN* 306AP 501, Ango to Castries, 7 Sept. 1815.

[84] *AN* 306AP 495, *visite de l'ingénieur des mines*, 6 Mar. 1816.

[85] *AN* F14 4240, *p.v. de la visite aux mines de la Grand-Combe, Abilon, Mas-Dieu*, 16 Oct. 1818. In the Abilon mine, the most productive 6 ft. seam had been ravaged by fire.

[86] *AN* F14 7683, 8 Oct. 1815.

[87] *AN* 306AP 495, *pétition au Conseil des mines contre le sieur Barrot, 1816*.

[88] *AN* 306AP 501, Lefebvre to Castries, 10 Sept. 1815.

interested in long-term, fixed capital investment. As early as the beginning of 1816, he was pressing Lefebvre for a better return on the money he had already sent him,[89] only for his *directeur* to reply that, far from being able to send money to Paris, it might prove impossible for him to save the Grand-Combe 'given the fact that my resources do not amount to one-quarter of what they should be for so important an undertaking'.[90] It was not until the spring of the following year that Lefebvre was in a position to reopen the flooded Abilon mine,[91] prompting him to promise that, *in future*, Castries might count upon an annual revenue of 15,000–16,000 francs.[92] Unfortunately, 1817 marked the beginning of a pretty severe recession, following some poor harvests, and, on 22 June, Lefebvre reported gloomily that 'Hardly anything is being sold here.'[93] One year later, Castries was writing in some desperation to his *directeur*, seeking an answer to the time-honoured question 'When am I going to see some profit?', only for Lefebvre to reply that settling debts had eaten up a larger sum than he had actually received from Castries.[94] The sorely needed profits never materialized, at least, not on the scale envisaged by Castries. At the end of 1818, he wrote a long letter to Lefebvre which included a detailed list of his debts and obligations and which included the poignant, but profoundly revealing, remark, one that sums up the essential problem bedevilling the entire history of his family's involvement in coal-mining in the Basses-Cévennes: 'I have grasped the fact that if one does not possess considerable investment capital (*de grands fonds d'avance*) for such undertakings, one cannot realize their potential.' Borrowing, again precisely as his father had done before him, from local *hommes d'affaires* like Louis Dhombres at 6 per cent interest, plus brokerage charges, had only served to compound—almost literally—the duke's problems.[95]

---

[89] *AN* 306AP 501, Feb. 1816.

[90] *AN* 306AP 502, 16 June 1816.

[91] *AN* 306AP 502, 15 May 1817.

[92] *AN* 306AP 502, 10 Apr. 1817.

[93] *AN* 306AP 502, Lefebvre to Castries. Part of the problem, Lefebvre explained, lay in the fact that 'illicit mining' was continuing in Champcloson and other small mines in the *forêt de Portes*. As Pierre Tubeuf might have said: 'Plus ça change . . .'!

[94] *AN* 306AP 502, 12 Apr. 1818.

[95] *AN* 306AP 500, Castries to Lefebvre. Castries explained that he had already invested 30,000 francs without getting a penny in return. He added that he had taken out a loan of 65,000 francs to buy out the shares belonging to the vicomtesse de Mailly and the marquis de Castries, upon which he had been paying the annual interest over the past four years.

But even if Castries had been blessed with money and sound managerial expertise, substantial profit would still have been a pipe-dream: there was just too much competition. The maréchal de Castries had gained most from his mines only after Tubeuf had been defeated, reduced virtually to the Rochebelle mine near Alès; Tubeuf himself knew that, without the Grand-Combe, in addition to Rochebelle and a few other mines, his accounts would not show much of a profit. By 1815, given the continued protoindustrial structure of the economy and, in consequence, the continued fierce resistance of scores of local landowners, manufacturers, and colliers, there were far too many coal-owners chasing far too few industrial and large manufacturing customers. Lefebvre had made the position perfectly clear from the beginning. Prefacing his report with the comment that, during the 1780s, the coalfield around Alès had been divided between just two owners—Castries and Tubeuf—he explained that 'The considerable competition produced by eight concessions permits no hope of obtaining the kind of profit that, in earlier times, M. le maréchal de Castries enjoyed.'[96] Of these eight concessions, Serres's mine at Fe-nadou and Méjean's at la Tronche were relatively insignificant, output usually being recorded in hundreds rather than in thousands of tonnes. Gilly's Saint-Jean-de-Valériscle mine produced coal for the family's glassworks, in the main. So far as the Robiac–Meyrannes mines were concerned, the Suffren-Deveau family were only just beginning to exploit the considerable reserves of coal which would one day supply the Bessèges iron and steel works. Excluding these mines, which were situated in the Cèze valley and which supplied the old Bas-Vivarais region, competition in the Alès coalfield was reduced to a four-cornered fight featuring the Castries at the Grand-Combe, Abilon, and the Mas-Dieu, Puech and Goirand at Pradel and Trescol, the Tubeufs at Rochebelle, and the company with considerable local and Parisian clout Barrot and Guiraudet, who had fiddled the inhabitants around Champcloson out of their traditional rights.

During the difficult years—from a political and an economic standpoint—of the late 1810s, these coal-owners fought a continuous battle to weed out the more vulnerable of the eight *concessionnaires*, assisted by the economic recession of the period. Although they had already bought out the 'independent colliers' of Champcloson towards the end of the Napoleonic Empire, Barrot and Guiraudet did not obtain

---

[96] *AN* 306AP 501, letter headed January 1816.

legal possession without a much tougher fight. Eventually, however, on 17 September 1817, the two men were confirmed as the legal owners of the mine in the *forêt de Portes*.[97] The struggle was now on to eliminate the Levade mine belonging to the failed iron-master Jean Méjean, and the less important Fenadou, which had fallen into the hands of Stanislas Serres. Méjean had died in 1816, bequeathing Levade, plus its considerable debts, to a 13-year-old relative.[98] On receiving this fortuitous piece of information, Jacques Puech had actually offered to loan the duc de Castries the money to purchase the mine if Castries would use his 'good offices' to wrest Champcloson from the clutches of Barrot and Guiraudet. As we have seen, the move failed. In any case, as Lefebvre explained to the good duke, it was terribly important that 'this concession [Levade], situated so close to our own, does not pass into the hands of *étrangers*'.[99]

Throughout 1817 and the beginning of the following year, Castries, like the maréchal before him, found his Paris office besieged by coal-owners who had made the long trek from Alès to strike a deal favourable to all sides. Due to the intense mutual fear of one party emerging triumphant, no deal was forthcoming. Eventually, on 24 April 1818, the representatives of all the interested parties—Guiraudet, Puech, Lefebvre—crowded into the small courtroom of the *tribunal civil d'Alais* to agree a legal settlement. Lefebvre was obliged to accept a deal according to which Levade would be leased jointly by the three parties—Castries, Barrot and Guiraudet, and Puech and Goirand—for four years.[100] It was the only way that the three major coal-owners in the Alès region could prevent a new *concessionnaire* from entering the fray. Let us note the absence of the Suffrens, happy with their industrial 'fief' at Robiac and Meyrannes, but, more important, the Tubeufs, content now to engage in the wine trade and to supply their glassworks with coal from their own mine at Rochebelle.

The above arrangement proved to be no more than a stay of execution for Castries. With his competitors increasing their sales and undercutting his prices by up to one-fifth, the writing was very much

---

[97] *AN* F14 7677, *vente de Champcloson*, 21 Feb. 1818.

[98] *AN* 306AP 500, Castries to Lefebvre, 4 May 1816.

[99] Ibid. In this letter Castries agrees that it would be fatal to see the mine pass into the hands of 'les étrangers'.

[100] *AN* 306AP 500, Lefebvre to Castries, 26 Apr. 1818. The duc de Castries eventually agreed to this arrangement a week later. *AN* 306AP 500, Castries to Lefebvre, 4 May 1818.

on the mine wall.[101] Mounting debts and decreasing returns gradually eroded Castries's determination to fight on. Given his eighteenth-century approach to industry, added to the unnecessary degree of competition which the government's decisions on concessions in 1809 and 1815 had produced, his situation had been gloomy from the start, as, indeed, Lefebvre had told him. Although certainly not to the same degree as his father, the duc de Castries was still caught within the web of aristocratic patronage and *noblesse oblige*: whilst entrepreneurs like Guiraudet and Puech were ripping off the inhabitants of the region, Castries was pressed into defending their 'traditional rights'.[102] In June 1816, the Castries family had received a letter from 'un ancien serviteur' requesting a job in the Grand-Combe mine. The sender was a man named Puechlong, who, as he pointed out, had worked in the mine for the maréchal de Castries before the Revolution. The documentation does not enable us to say with certainty that his application was successful, but one's guess is that it was.[103]

All very noble, but not the kind of thing that would have worried the Guiraudets and the Puechs. Let us take another example. Whilst both Guiraudet and Puech were forcing their workers to spend at least part of their salary in their 'company stores', Castries was paying his men in hard cash. Article 4 of a price-fixing agreement which the duke felt obliged to sign with Puech and Goirand in 1817 had stipulated that Castries's workers would not be obliged to receive 'les denrées en échange de leurs salaires'.[104] Again, good, *ancien régime*, Catholic paternalism, but it did nothing to increase the duke's profits. And it is necessary to insist upon the *religious* aspect of Castries's industrial and business relations. Bas-Languedoc was still very much

[101] See *AN* 306AP 500, Lefebvre to Castries, 15 Apr. and 28 June 1818, which stress the financial difficulties associated with working the Grand-Combe mine.

[102] *AN* F14 7677, letter of the comte d'Auguesseau to the duc de Castries explaining that the tutor of his children, the abbé Ribot, wanted Castries to exercise his influence on the prefect of the Gard concerning the rights of the inhabitants of the *forêt de Portes*.

[103] *AN* 306AP 504, Puechlong to Mme de Mailly, 13 June 1816. See also the petition of François de Pantoustier, an inhabitant of the *forêt d'Abilon*, stating that his father and his brother had worked in the Grand-Combe during the period of conflict with Pierre-François Tubeuf, his brother having lost his life in a mining accident. François was also after a job. *AN* 306AP 504, letter to Castries, 27 Jan. 1816.

[104] Lefebvre explained that 'Dans ce pais-çi, les personnes qui font travailler aux mines, soit pour leur compte ou celui des autres, font un honteux trafic de denrées de première nécessité sur la sueur du malheureux, en le contraignant de prendre en échange de ses peines des denrées souvent très mauvais, toujours plus chères que le cours, et le poid manque souvent.' *AN* 306AP 502, to Castries, 15 Feb. 1817.

a *pays* where patronage was linked as much to the confession as to class. During the particularly difficult patch in 1818, when Lefebvre was using every device to shore up the confidence of his employer, Castries wrote: 'What really astonishes me is the fact that religion or political affiliation can have anything to do with selling coal. It's something completely new to me. However, continue to use all the tact you possess and, above all, do not show any party bias for one side or the other.'[105]

The umbilical social cord which really tied Castries to the *ancien régime* was his relationship with the local legal and business élite, the *gens d'affaires*, particularly his relationship with the powerful Dhombres family, which had exercised such a formative influence over the fate of the maréchal de Castries. At the beginning of 1816, Dhombres *fils*—describing himself as 'votre protégé'—had begged Castries to appoint him as the duke's agent, pointing out that his father and grandfather before him had acted in the same capacity. Stressing the exaggerated social significance of such appointments, another hangover from the *ancien régime*, Dhombres explained that if the position were to fall to the *homme d'affaires* of the marquis de Calvières, who had played such a significant role in the White Terror of 1815, he would feel 'almost ashamed'.[106] Dhombres got the job! Hence the old tripartite conflict of interests between the Castries family in Paris, their *directeur des mines* in Alès, and the local business mafia, whose overriding concern was the protection of their own and their clients' interests, began afresh. In the spring of 1817, Dhombres had dared to offer some mild criticism of the way Castries was pouring money into his coal-mines (shades of Louis Dhombres's criticisms of the maréchal de Castries's industrial ventures), provoking a stern rebuke from Castries: 'When one is operating a coal-mine, there are costs which, to someone not familiar with this type of work, must appear excessive.'[107] This comment contains a bitter irony, for whom do we find as one of the leading local investors in coal-mines in the Alès region after the Castries had been forced out? The Dhombres family!

The sale of Castries's mining interests is first recorded in the correspondence between the duc de Castries and his *directeur*, Lefebvre. The original offer for the Grand-Combe and Abilon mines was 80,000

---

[105] *AN* 306AP 500, Castries to Lefebvre, 20 Oct. 1818.
[106] *AN* 306AP 504, Dhombres to Castries, 25 Feb. 1816.
[107] *AN* 306AP 500, 15 Apr. 1817.

francs, prompting the remark from Lefebvre: 'Allez doucement.'[108] Good advice as it proved. The fierce competition between the Barrot–Guiraudet and the Puech–Goirand companies was bound to force the price up, particularly since the Méjean mine, having been 'farmed out' for four years, was also coming on to the market. A major redistribution of power was about to take place in the Alès coalfield: indeed, the future Grand-Combe mining company may rightly trace its nineteenth-century origins from the sale, officially recorded on 26 April 1821, between MM. Barrot, Guiraudet, and Deleuze, and the duc de Castries. The last representative of the Castries family to own important mining interests in Bas-Languedoc received 140,000 francs, 50,000 to be paid immediately, the rest in three instalments of 30,000 francs at 5 per cent interest.[109] According to their family papers, the duc de Castries sold out 'pour regler les droits de sa sœur, Mailly'. In fact, 110,000 francs went to his son, the marquis de Castries, and 30,000 to his sister, the comtesse de Mailly.[110] The sale of the Grand-Combe, which had always represented the 'jewel in the crown' for any Alèsian coal-owner, was an historic victory for the Protestant industrialists Barrot and Guiraudet, the latter having led the political fight against the maréchal de Castries in the Alès region during the pre-Revolutionary crisis. With so much emphasis currently being placed on sociological, linguistic, and semiotic *structures*, it is important to reveal the economic themes of continuity which link the origins of the French Revolution with the development of nineteenth-century French capitalism.

And what of the great rivals of the Castries family, the Tubeufs? The short answer is that they had lost the real battle in 1809 when their re-created coal empire had been divided into separate concessions. The sons had learned from the bitter experience of their father that without the rich seams of the Grand-Combe any attempt to dominate the Alèsian coalfield was doomed to failure. Rochebelle, which had been owned and worked by the Tubeufs from the 1770s, only produced second-grade coal, suitable for glass-making but not for the production of iron and steel, and the age of iron and steel had, somewhat tardily, arrived in France. What was needed now was

---

[108] *AN* 306AP 503, Lefebvre to Castries, 29 Mar. 1821.

[109] *AN* 306AP 497, *extrait de l'acte de vente faite par M. le duc de Castries*, 26 Apr. 1821.

[110] Castries, *Papiers de famille*, 310.

investment capital on a grand scale, and the Tubeufs, like the Castries, could not oblige.

In a major assessment of their financial situation, drawn up at the beginning of the Second Restoration, François Tubeuf explained to his brother that the loss of the Grand-Combe in 1809 had proved, in retrospect, to have been the mortal blow to their hopes. When he had left America in 1802, the only debts the brothers had incurred were those associated with their commercial interests in the Americas, principally the loss of the *Neptune*. These debts amounted to 160,000 francs, 'not a great deal compared with the restitution by the government of our property in Languedoc'. By the end of 1806, a year of rising expectations for the family, the Tubeufs had already paid off one-quarter of their total debts, but, according to François, the new division of the Alès coal-basin in 1809 deprived the family of three-quarters of what they had been provisionally awarded in 1802. 'As a result of this injustice, we found ourselves in the impossible position of trying to pay back the large sums which we had borrowed in France to invest in our business interests.' In 1811, the Tubeufs had been forced to mortgage these interests in Languedoc since their creditors were of the opinion that the value of their coal-mines and glassworks was entirely dependent 'upon our hard work'.[111] During a period of acute economic recession, industrial concerns were particularly vulnerable to the whims of individual investors. As had been the case with their father, the burden of debt was never lifted from the brothers' shoulders. In May 1823, we find the Tubeufs paying off 20,000 francs to Isaac-Marie Marette, representing the interest on a loan contracted in April 1814. Exactly one month later, the brothers were borrowing 24,000 francs from a *négociant* in Montpellier, Durand-Fajon, who was also a member of the Chambre des députés.[112] On 14 April 1828, in an out-of-court settlement, the Tubeufs paid M. de Montplanqua, who had been their mother's lawyer, 70,000 francs, representing the final payment of a debt contracted in the bad old days of 1811.[113] The expansion of the 1800s and the establishment of their glassworks at Rochebelle had been financed out of loans from family acquaintances like the Montplanquas. Such avenues of credit would be far too narrow for the industrial expansion of the 1830s.

---

[111] *AG* 58J 7, François Tubeuf to Alexandre Tubeuf, 10 Oct. 1816.

[112] *AG* 58J 8, entries for 19 May and 19 June 1823.

[113] *AG* 58J 8, *obligation de M. de Tubeuf à M. de Montplanqua*.

What emerges very clearly from an analysis of the annual profits made by the Tubeufs between 1813 and 1828 is the symbiotic relationship which continued to exist between viticulture, sericulture, and the coal industry (see Table 6.2). A glance at these figures will reveal the importance of the economic recessions which characterized the end of the Napoleonic Empire, the late 1810s, and the 1820s. However, it was not simply a matter of sales; investment in new machinery increasingly ate up profits in the 1820s. In June 1826, Alexandre Tubeuf decided to order a steam-engine to extract water from his Rochebelle mine; eighteen months later, trials with the steam-engine had only just begun![114] Again, a glance at the figures in Table 6.2 will explain, in large measure, why the Tubeufs decided to sell out in 1828.

Before looking at the details of the sale we should remind ourselves that the Tubeuf *fils*, in keeping with their American commercial experience, had never placed all their investment eggs in one industrial basket: their father had suffered too much as a result of his obsession with developing the Alès coal-basin; their mother had warned them of the dangers of risking too much capital in industry. Besides, in order to obtain credit in the first place it was important to be seen as a 'respectable' landowner or merchant, not (as the Tubeufs' father had appeared to too many local people) as an entrepreneurial gambler with other people's money. The conclusions reached by Pat Hudson in her study of the genesis of industrial capitalism in the West Riding during the same period may also be applied, with the appropriate qualifications, to the situation in Bas-Languedoc:

Contemporary business and bank records abound with assessments of the degree of 'respectability' of their clients. Being respectable had little to do with social morality but had everything to do with property and with a reputation for regularity in paying debts and avoiding speculation. . . . If a manufacturer gained respectable status he could be assured of continuing support from institutions of the capital market and from lenders or suppliers even in hard times.[115]

Alexander Tubeuf, by reason of his family history and personal career, was well aware of the dangers. During the Second Restoration, he would spend an increasing amount of time dealing with the family's

---

[114] *AG* 58J 8, entry in journal for 19 June 1826 and letter to Privat *aîné*, 2 Dec. 1827.
[115] P. Hudson, *The Genesis of Industrial Capitalism* (Cambridge, 1986), 269.

TABLE 6.2. *Annual profits*[a] *from the Tubeuf mines* (francs)

Year	Profit	Year	Profit
1813	4,155	1821	8,354
1814	8,626	1822	11,389
1815	16,527	1823	13,106
1816	22,084	1824	11,364
1817	19,156	1825	4,890
1818	12,612	1826	2,019
1819	8,106	1827	1,746
1820	3,475	1828	689

Note: Over 16 years the Tubeufs made an annual net profit of around 9,300 *livres*.

Source: AG 58J 7.

commercial interests as a bottler and shipper of wines and brandies, based, not in Alès, but in the port of Sète. By 1820, Alexandre Tubeuf, describing himself as a *négociant de Cette*, was acting as a commercial *vice-consul* for both Britain and Portugal.[116] The economic crisis of the late 1820s obliged him to close his commercial house in Sète and devote more time to his interests as a landowner and an *électeur*.[117] Alexandre Tubeuf, son of one of the most dynamic of eighteenth-century French industrialists, had finally achieved respectability, not as an industrialist, but as a provincial *notable*.

Lacking a strong financial base, and confronted with the prolonged economic crisis of the late Second Restoration, Alexandre and his brother got out just in time. Competition was becoming more intense, competition based ultimately upon Parisian capital. In the autumn of 1824, the subprefect of Alès, a pupil of the old Catholic royalist paternalist school, deplored the fact that whereas in 1815 there had been several coal companies in the region, 'today . . . as a result of the various sales and purchases which have taken place, we find the coalfield, as was the case in the days of Pierre Tubeuf, almost entirely in the hands of two companies, and even they have signed a price-fixing agreement'. The subprefect went on, in words which are remarkably similar to those adopted by the diocese of Alès fifty years

---

[116] See *AG* 58J 12, letter to Privat *aîné* reporting the closure of his business in Sète, July 1827.

[117] *AG* 58J 11, letter to same correspondent referring to his imminent trip to Nîmes to participate in the forthcoming elections.

earlier, to complain of 'the monopoly which is being re-established as each day passes, prompting one to appreciate, so far as the public good is concerned, the advantages of creating more competition by granting a few new concessions'.[118]

The opinions of the subprefect of Alès were received with some enthusiasm by the officers of Charles X's *ancien régime* administration. As had been the case in 1809 and 1815, concessions were frequently granted after 1824 to those who produced sound political, rather than industrial or entrepreneurial, pedigrees. Like Joseph Pagèze de Lavernède, who hailed from the Catholic royalist stamping-grounds of Malbosc in the old Bas-Vivarais. His request for a coal concession on his own estate near Villefort was founded upon the necessity—for the 'public good'—of providing competition against the Suffrens, who had 'monopolized' coal production in the Cèze valley. According to this former seigneur, the Suffrens had pushed up the price of coal from 35 to 60 *centimes le quintal* over the previous four years.[119] Two years later, Lavernède was granted the concession of the *mines de Villefort*.[120] Then there was the case of Nicolas *père et fils* of Saint-Ambroix, who appear to have been complete novices in the coal-mining field. None the less, the prefect of the Gard, the marquis de Lavalette, felt it was his duty to emphasize 'the services rendered to the Legitimist cause by these two men during the Dauphin's stay in the Gard at the time of the Hundred Days. Apparently, Nicolas *fils* had served 'under the marquis de Calvières and the comte de Vogüé in 1815'.[121] What these cases reveal is the *mentalité* of the ultraroyalist administrators determined to resist the growth of large industrial concerns and to defeat the challenge of 'des spéculateurs étrangers'.

But 'des spéculateurs étrangers' were not to be deterred. Between the latter years of the reign of Charles X and the early years of the July Monarchy, local sources of finance and of ultraroyalist political control were swept aside by Parisian money and a Parisian revolution. On 15 February 1828, an agreement was signed between the Société d'exploration des mines and the Tubeuf family for the sale of the latter's mining interests, lock, stock, and *baril*, for the sum of 630,000

---

[118] *AG* 8S 107, letter to prefect, 20 Sept. 1824.

[119] Ibid. The subprefect noted that it would be 'une très grande avantage pour la contrée d'établir une concurrence avec les concessionnaires de Meyrannes et Robiac', who were allegedly causing some discontent by pushing up the price of coal.

[120] *AG* 8S 107, Directeur-général des Ponts et Chaussées to prefect, 21 July 1827.

[121] *AG* 8S 106, *mémoire sur les mines de Lalle*, 29 Aug. 1827.

francs, a sum which finally transformed Alexandre Tubeuf into a *notable*. The Société d'exploration was managed by Auguste Bérard, a deputy, holder of the Légion d'honneur, and former *maître des requêtes*. Amongst the twenty-six leading shareholders of the new company formed by the take-over of the Tubeuf mines, destined to become the Société des fonderies et forges d'Alais, were Parisian bankers like Jacques Vassal, but also famous names like the comtesse du Cayla and Sosthène de La Rochefoucauld.[122] From this time forward, these 'spéculateurs étrangers' would struggle for control of the coal and iron-ore riches of the Alès coalfield with the locally based Société houillère de la Grand-Combe et autres mines réunis, formed from the successive take-overs by the Puechs and the Barrots of all the more important mines in the Alès coalfield since the 1790s, but particularly from the purchase of the Grand-Combe from the duc de Castries in 1821.[123] When, on 17 February 1833, the renamed Compagnie de la Grand-Combe decided to reorganize its finances we find that the Puech brothers and the Goirands *père et fils* held almost half the 800 shares of the company, with the Barrots, Jean-André and Odilon, owning over one-eighth.[124]

When, in 1828, these long-time enemies of the Tubeuf family had first confronted the challenge of the Parisian-based Bérard company, they had complained to the government about Bérard's 'projets gigantesques' and the 'ruinous competition' which followed his purchase of the Tubeuf mines.[125] 'Poachers turned gamekeepers', the Puechs and the Barrots reminded the government that

The number of concessions which the government fixed at seven [this excludes the Champcloson concession, which was not officially granted to the inhabitants of the *forêt de Portes*] was widely regarded as being too many and led, after 1815, to the ruin of several concessions, or to their neglect and subsequent sale. The petitioners then, at considerable personal sacrifice, set about purchasing, regrouping, and reactivating these mines.

[122] *AG* 58J 8, *liste des actionnaires*, n.d.

[123] For details and dates of take-overs see *AN* F14 7953, Société houillère de la Grand-Combe to the prefect, 5 Feb. 1836.

[124] *AN* F14 7953, *traité de la société houillère de la Grand-Combe, de Pluzor et autres concessions réunis*, 17 Feb. 1833.

[125] *AN* F14 7953, letter of the society to prefect, 26 July 1828. Puech complained that the Bérard company had boasted that it had 'les moyens de rendre plus promptement leur pays l'émule de Saint-Etienne'. In fact, Bérard was soon in deep financial trouble and would have to be bailed out by the government during the early 1830s.

Now, according to the major shareholders of the Grand-Combe company, the granting of new concessions threatened to provoke another 'disaster'.[126] This time, it was not just a matter of the price of coal to consumers or the lack of demand: coal and iron-ore would, in the opinion of Puech and Barrot, 'prove to be a certain source of prosperity for our region, for the department, and for France, which will now be in a position to free itself of the tribute which it is forced to pay to foreign countries'.[127]

If Alexandre Tubeuf had read the above petition it must have inspired a few bitter and ironic reflections. Had not his father, also an architect of 'des projets gigantesques' in the 1770s, begged the government of the day to limit competition in the region so that he might acquire sufficient capital from his profits to modernize the medieval mines of Alès, ship his coal along the Cèze to the Rhône, and hence to Marseille, in order to defeat the growing challenge of English imports? Lack of support, both local and national, had forced Pierre-François Tubeuf into a foreign grave. Louis-Philippe and the Revolution of 1830 were to succeed in delivering to the Grand-Combe coal company what Louis XVI and the Revolution of 1789 had manifestly failed to do for the man who had first brought the Alès coalfield into the modern age.

[126] *AN* F14 7953, letter to prefect, 26 Oct. 1828.

[127] Ibid. See also the opinions of Jules Renaux, son of Pierre-François Tubeuf's loyal director and engineer François Renaux, which included the conclusion that 'Le département du Gard renferme des richesses minérales immenses, et, jusqu'à présent, délaissées.' *AN* F14 7953, *Mémoire au roi*, n.d.

CONCLUSION: 1830: THE TAKE-OFF

ROGER PRICE writes: 'It was the complex of changes in the transport system associated with the development of the railway and its effects on market structures that finally brought the end of traditional French rural civilisation.'[1] Wherever the tracks marking the arrival of a new industrial era were laid, protoindustrial communities found themselves under threat. However, throughout Price's work there is the insistence on the interrelationship which exists between economic, political, social, and cultural changes, an approach which has also informed this study of 'the passage of a civilization founded upon wood and charcoal to one founded upon iron and coal', as Fernand Braudel phrased it.[2] Outside the recently renovated railway station in Nîmes, a statue has been erected to Paulin Talabot, marking the major contribution of this French Robert Stephenson to the construction, in 1837, of the railway—one of the earliest in France—linking the Grand-Combe to the port of Beaucaire: the modern meeting the medieval. There is no statue to Pierre-François Tubeuf in Alès. There should be. For it was Tubeuf who, more than any other single figure, endeavoured to bring the inhabitants of Bas-Languedoc into the age of coal and iron. But then it was these same inhabitants who, because they were only too aware of the fate that lay in store for their communities, treated him so miserably, driving this 'étranger' back to Normandy, and thence to Paris and, eventually, to Richmond, Virginia, where he was to meet an untimely death.

We have argued that no single factor explains the failure of Tubeuf's 'grand design'; certainly not the French Revolution, which, in the opinion of the new ideologues of the Right, was responsible for virtually all the 'economic disasters' that, it is argued—often speciously—afflicted France after 1815.[3] To understand the peculiar historical

---

[1] R. Price, *The Modernization of Rural France: Communications Networks and Agricultural Market Structures in Nineteenth-Century France* (London, 1983), 11.

[2] *Une Leçon d'histoire de Fernand Braudel* (Paris, 1986), 97.

[3] See e.g. F. Aftalion, *The French Revolution: An Economic Interpretation* (Cambridge, 1990), 195: 'How often has it happened, in recent history, that countries have fallen prey to totalitarian regimes through having accepted, albeit with a few minor variations, the same destructive cycle of crisis–inflation–price controls–nationalisations–Terror, set in motion in the name of the noble ideals of liberty, prosperity and social justice.' This is

gait of modern French capitalism, it is essential that one should retrace its early steps to those *longue durée*, protoindustrial structures which cover our entire period, structures which are inseparably linked to the origins, course, and consequences of the French Revolution itself. For many decades before Tubeuf's arrival, Bas-Languedoc had produced not for rustic, local peasants, but for consumers in Europe and the wider world. Set in international motion by wealthy *négociants*, the silks, woollens, and cottons of Anduze, Carcassonne, Clermont-de-Lodève, Sommières, and le Vigan had brought unknown prosperity to Bas-Languedoc, or at least, to its *bas-pays*, a region which 'attested to the existence of a very active local life; it assured the dissemination of bourgeois ideas, those of the small and middling bourgeoisie, artisans and traders, who lived not in the big cities, but who peopled the most modest *bourgs*'. The authors of this quotation, however, go on to stress the importance of Montpellier and Nîmes—'les deux grandes métro-poles'—representing as they did the twin centres of this economic system.[4] It was to be the strength and sophistication, the resilience and rootedness of this system which defeated Tubeuf, not its weak-ness. It could be argued that this 'civilization', with all its linguistic, socio-cultural, and *petit bourg* peculiarity, its antipathy to urban, indus-trial life, has shaped the contours of life in Bas-Languedoc to the present day.

Many recent historians have shared the antipathy of contemporaries to the social consequences of the transition to more modern forms of industrialization, to the attitudes of a Pierre-François Tubeuf, who proved to be 'too entrepreneurial' by half for some government ministers. At the end of their primarily quantitative analysis of con-trasting patterns of economic growth in France and Britain, O'Brien and Keyder call upon 'Morris Birkbeck, Samuel Cobbett, William Thornton and John Stuart Mill' as witnesses for the prosecution. It is an impressive quartet, although my choice would have included William Blake and Robert Owen, the latter only too conscious of the corrosive social and moral effects of industrialization but prepared none the less to understand that 'change with a human face' was worth contemplating. As someone who has frequently enjoyed the

the economic variant of the neo-Talmonic and anachronistic line which links Rousseau to Robespierre, to Lenin *et al.*

[4] R. Laurent and G. Gavignaud, *La Révolution française dans le Languedoc méditerranée* (Toulouse, 1987), 10.

very different, but not easily explicable, ambience of French life, particularly in the almost biblical hills of the Bas-Cévennes, I would be the last to defend the dehumanizing effects of the early factory system. However, I am not at all sure that it was all so prettily pastoral in France, as anyone acquainted with the harrowing accounts of life in the textile mills of Lille, Roubaix, and Tourcoing by the vicomte de Villeneuve-Bargemont will appreciate, to say nothing of Anzin or the Rive-de-Gier mining complexes. None the less, I rest part of my case upon O'Brien and Keyder's general conclusion that 'It is safer to assert that the French economy could have benefited from a more rapid rate of transformation between 1780 and 1914.'[5]

Without romanticizing his work—anyone who thought that all coal-miners should be integrated into the French army so that they could experience the 'benefits' of military life, acquiring the 'discipline' that the first wave of industrialists and entrepreneurs were keen to introduce, did not always have the best interests of his workers at heart—Tubeuf was one of those who also thought that the French economy could have 'benefited from a more rapid rate of transformation'. His arrival in the Alès region coincided with the beginning of the long depression in the Languedoc textile and wine industries which was to last, intermittently, until the Revolution. Our study has confirmed the conclusion reached by Ernest Labrousse in his *grande thèse* half a century ago: 'La régression couvre la fin de l'Ancien régime, s'étendant à peu près de 1778 à 1787.'[6] It was a decade which saw a marked increase in competition for the staple industries of Languedoc, textiles and wine, from inside and outside France. Competition was to increase throughout our period, even if the Continental Blockade was to shield some French producers from the worst onslaughts. The wars which punctuate our period are linked to changing patterns of trade and closing markets, particularly during the crucial decades of

---

[5] P. O'Brien and C. Keyder, *Economic Growth in Britain and France, 1780–1914* (London, 1978), 97. See also N. Crafts, 'Economic Growth in France and Britain, 1830–1910: A Review of the Evidence', *Journal of Economic History*, 44 (1984), 67, arguing that the revisionists have exaggerated French economic performance, which was, in Crafts' opinion 'respectable but certainly not outstanding'.

[6] C.-E. Labrousse, *La Crise de l'économie française à la fin de l'ancien régime et au début de la Révolution* (Paris, 1944), vol. i, p.xxii. In general, the economic history of Bas-Langue-doc mirrors, with some local distortions such as the closure of the Spanish markets after 1778, Labrousse's main conclusions: 'La crise n'est précisément qu'un accident du cycle, qu'un phénomène cyclique. Crises de 1770, de 1782–1784, de 1789–1790, crises de 1795, de 1802–1803, de 1812, de 1817, marquent les grands moments de l'histoire économique pré-révolutionnaire, révolutionnaire et post-révolutionnaire.' pp.ix–x.

the late eighteenth and early nineteenth centuries. It is not coincidental that the opposition .to Tubeuf grew more vociferous between 1778 and 1783, dates which cover the American War of Independence as well as the closure of Spanish and colonial markets, nor that this same period should have enclosed one of the worst popular rebellions in the history of Bas-Languedoc during the eighteenth century, the *masques armés* of 1783. The glad, confident morning of the mid-eighteenth century was never to be reached again. During the 1790s and 1800s, France would lose most of her traditional overseas trade, and, as François Crouzet has pointed out, 'foreign trade, and especially trade with the Americas, was the most dynamic sector of the whole economy'.[7] O'Brien and Keyder insist upon the importance of overseas trade when explaining the different pattern of economic growth in Britain, stressing the 'long-term advantages that the British economy enjoyed through trade and commerce with the rest of the world'.[8] Again, the personal history of the Tubeuf family may be woven, quite legitimately, into the general backcloth of French history at this point. The fortunes of Pierre-François's two sons, who had established themselves in the import and export business in the Americas, was sealed by war and the shift of economic power to Britain, just as the future of their coal concession in Alès was to be shaped by the consequences, internal and external, of the Napoleonic wars.

Increasing competition from Britain, Spain, Italy, Prussia, and Switzerland, as well as from other countries, forced protection upon the French. Although the occasional 'free trade' treaty was signed (the Eden Treaty of 1786 being a somewhat disastrous example), it is protection, not free-market competition, which characterizes our entire period. This applied, above all, to imports of coal and iron. It has been argued that the impact of the Napoleonic protectionist economic system upon the iron and silk industries was not particularly adverse. However, denied the assistance of English expertise, Jean Méjean's attempts at making saleable iron failed, whilst, so far as the Nîmes silk industry is concerned, the production of its cheap goods was especially prone to the closure of markets and changing fashions. One economic historian of our region concludes that: 'les dernières années de l'Empire furent catastrophiques pour les industries gardoises'.[9]

---

[7] Crouzet, 'Guerres, blocus et changement économique', 568.
[8] O'Brien and Keyder, *Economic Growth in Britain and France*, 98–9.
[9] Riou, 'La Terreur blanche dans le département du Gard', 388.

Other historians have stressed the link between the loss of overseas markets and the relative failure of the textile and metallurgical industries in France.[10]

After a brief period of experimentation with *laissez-faire* policies immediately after 1815, the Restoration government became one of the most protectionist in Europe, with the coal and iron industries amongst the most heavily protected sectors, although, according to one school of thought, it was not external factors but 'the deficiency of the internal market which retarded the modernisation of the French iron industry'.[11] The reasons that we have not dealt in any detail with the iron industry in this study is (1) that Denis Woronoff has already produced an exhaustive and scholarly work on the subject during the Revolutionary and Napoleonic period, and (2) the fact that, as Woronoff himself concludes, it was the 'question du bois [qui] domine l'industrie du fer', not 'la question du charbon de terre'.[12] Throughout our period, charcoal was used to smelt iron in preference to coal, which remained expensive, whether foreign or domestic in provenance. It can be argued that the high tariffs erected against foreign imports of iron in the 1823 (over 100 per cent) explains the original take-off in the iron industries, but, as we shall see, it was not until Staffordshire men and machinery arrived in the early 1830s that good-quality iron was to be successfully produced in Alès.

Textiles, coal, or iron, it would appear that real structural change, whether in the fields of finance, production, or industrial relations, was the exception rather than the rule, at least until the July Monarchy. This is Woronoff's final verdict on the iron industry, at least for the period up to 1815—some growth, but 'The prevailing conditions did not lend themselves to a revolution within the Revolution.'[13] Armand Cosson, the most recent and informed historian of the textile industry in Nîmes, reaches a very similar conclusion.[14] The first half of the

[10] C. Heywood, 'The Role of the Peasantry in French Industrialisation, 1815–1880', *Economic History Review*, 34 (1981), 363: 'On the demand side, the decisive lead in conquering overseas markets taken by the British during the Revolutionary and Napoleonic wars hampered French efforts to develop large-scale production in textiles and basic metallurgy.'

[11] Milward and Saul, *The Economic Development of Continental Europe*, 329.

[12] D. Woronoff, *L'Industrie sidérurgique en France pendant la Révolution et l'Empire* (Paris, 1984), 529.

[13] Ibid. 532.

[14] Cosson, 'L'Industrie textile à Nîmes: la fin d'une hégémonie, 1790–1850', *Mouvement social*, 133 (1985), 8–9: 'Les rapports de production entre main-d'œuvre, fabricants et négociants, restent dans l'ensemble permanents'.

nineteenth century in France, as well as in the majority of European textile regions, marked a period of expansion, not contraction, for protoindustrial forms of production. Christopher Johnson has noted that throughout most textile regions of France, the early decades of the nineteenth century 'witnessed a phenomenon that, at first glance, seems strange indeed for a country undergoing industrialisation—the massive development of rural outworking'.[15] The production and spinning of raw silk was the protoindustrial form of production *par excellence*. In Britain, the mechanization of the silk industry, centred around London, Manchester, and Coventry, proved just as difficult and protracted a process as in France. Here also merchant-manufacturers realized the advantages of the lower wages they could pay to rural workers as well as the flexibility of the system which could be programmed in accordance with fluctuating levels of demand.[16] In the southern Ardèche, sericulture was transforming the countryside as mulberry trees appeared on every hillside and highway: 'on assiste entre 1815 et 1855 à une frénésie de plantation'.[17] Production of raw and spun silk would continue in a few regions of the Ardèche until the Second World War! Peter Jones has shown how, in the region around le Puy, the silk, lace, and ribbon industry continued to develop 'along protoindustrial lines', employing around 50,000 workers in the countryside in 1789, but 130,000 by 1835.[18]

We need to introduce a note of caution, however, when applying these generalizations concerning the persistence of protoindustrialization, particularly when applied to the Basses-Cévennes region. Here, in and around Alès and the Gardon and Cèze valleys, the occasional silk-spinning factory, coal-mine, and iron foundry could be seen coexisting with 'domestic' forms of production even before the Revolution of 1830. Given the fact that the textile industry in the Gard, whether silk or cotton, aimed its products, primarily, at the cheaper end of the market, however, it generally attracted the cheapest form of technology. David Landes records 'instances of northern firms selling their discarded equipment to silk enterprises of Lyon, which,

---

[15] Johnson, 'The Revolution of 1830 in French Economic History', 144.

[16] See S. R. Jones, 'Technology, Transition Costs, and the Transition to Factory Production in the British Silk Industry, 1700–1870', *Journal of Economic History*, 47 (1987), 74.

[17] L. Cayrier-Gilliot, 'Discours pour vivre ou survivre: une histoire de la sériculture en Ardèche au XIXe siècle', *112e Congrès national des sociétés savantes* (Lyon, 1987), 10.

[18] P. Jones, *Politics and Rural Society*, 59.

after getting all possible use out of them, sold them in turn to mills in places like Nîmes, where the cotton manufacture was a generation behind the times'.[19] Cosson informs us that by the mid-nineteenth century these looms had been concentrated in the city of Nîmes rather than in its hinterland, whilst the gender division of labour had swung heavily in favour of the woman. A report of 1832 explains: 'In general, manufacturing industry is the preserve of women; a man's work is geared more to agriculture than to manufacturing.' Of the 1,000 workers mentioned as engaged upon the spinning of silk from June to September, the great majority were said to be women 'who devote themselves, at the same time, to their domestic chores'.[20] Increasingly after 1830, daughters who had learned their skills at their mothers' feet would be drawn, reluctantly in some cases, into the new spinning-mills set up in Anduze and Saint-Jean-du-Gard, whilst a few of their fathers and brothers, even more reluctantly, would descend the mines of the Grand-Combe or sweat for their daily *baguette* in the iron foundries of Alès and Bessèges. A new geographic and gender-orientated division of labour was operating. During the 1830s, the competition of Swiss and Italian raw silk and the threat from the nearby Saint-Étienne and Saint-Chamond silk factories (using Swiss raw silk) were forcing change upon the inhabitants of the Basses-Cévennes, long before the *pébrine* disease struck such a severe blow to the raw-silk industry in the 1850s. By this time, competition had spread as far as Japan.

The fundamental family unit upon which protoindustrialization in the Basses-Cévennes had prospered was the small property-owner. We have noted that protoindustrial forms of production were most commonly found in the poorer, mountainous regions, where the small property-owner was the norm. In the West Riding of Yorkshire, for example, the worsted branch of the woollen industry had found 'a propitious environment in an area of infertile upland and pasture where land was held in small farms and plots and where pools of labour were underemployed throughout the year'[21]; and in Piedmont and Lombardy protoindustrial forms of production were rooted in

[19] D. Landes, *The Unbound Prometheus: Technological Change and Development in Western Europe from 1750 to the Present* (Cambridge, 1969), 162–3.

[20] Cosson, 'L'Industrie textile à Nîmes', 9.

[21] Hudson, *The Genesis of Industrial Capital*, 67. See also Landes, *The Unbound Prometheus*, 189.

similar types of community.[22] From the beginning, Tubeuf had been confronted with the bitter opposition of *petits propriétaires* and petty seigneurs all involved, directly or indirectly, in farming, in craft trades, the growing or manufacture of silk, or the production of wine and brandies. During the Revolution, the 'Rights of Man' would become synonymous with the rights of property, at least, so far as the propertied class was concerned. But long before 1789, debate on the nature of property had raised explosive issues, linked as they had been to a crumbling, seigneurial structure, to the political independence of the provincial Estates, and, most of all, to a centralizing monarchy which could award huge concessions to entrepreneurs like Tubeuf. The agent of the Richard and Carrouge company in 1780 proffered the explanation that the Estates of Languedoc had rejected their historic agreement with Tubeuf 'because of the jealousy of landowners in and around Alès'.[23] Were the rights of property to be deemed as shallow as the topsoil? Or did they include the rich mineral deposits which lay beneath? A matter of some moment at a time when coal was beginning to replace wood as the energizing force of the Industrial Revolution.

The Revolution did not provide a satisfactory answer, at least, for *concessionnaires* like Tubeuf: for property-owners the legislation on mining passed in the summer of 1791 signalled an important victory, one which contradicted, in no small measure, the edict of 1744. It is no coincidence that Tubeuf emigrated in 1791. The French Revolution was, above all, a revolution of property-owners; every constitution bears witness to this cardinal fact; every speech by Robespierre, although concerned with the *distribution* of wealth, was informed by the concept that property was one of the foundations of the social order. The huge sale of land seized from the Church fuelled the debate. This spotlight, focused upon the rights and protection of property-owners, was to give an immense boost to the enemies of the Tubeuf family until the new legislation of 1810—at least. The Revolution, through its legitimization of property-rights and the massive transfer of land on to the open market, as well as through the successive political and economic crises which punctuated the entire period from 1789 to 1815, reinforced a 'back to the land' mentality. There were, after all, fortunes to be made in property. Florin

---

[22] Dewerpe, *L'Industrie aux champs*, 97.
[23] B. de N., MSS 496, Alles to Richard, 19 June 1780.

Aftalion, viewing events more from the standpoint of those 'who should have been protected from arbitrariness' (nobles and merchants, of course, not the poor), and convinced that the failure to adopt a more coherent 'free market' approach damned the Revolution as a vehicle for economic progress, believes that property-rights were, in fact, not as widely respected as they should have been in the early 1790s, failing to emphasize the point that no government in modern times which has been caught up in total war has avoided price controls and constraints on 'economic freedoms'. None the less, Aftalion concludes: 'the crucial consequence of the Revolution was the consolidation, for the next hundred and fifty years, of a regime of small farms and peasant smallholdings'.[24] This deep concern with property-rights was to queer the pitch for the ultras around Charles X in 1825 when it was decided to indemnify *émigrés* for their loss of property during the Revolution. The final decision, effectively to make the taxpayer pay yet again, was an important factor in Charles X's unpopularity with the property-owning and tax-paying bourgeoisie. Little wonder, then, that the Tubeufs, *père, mère, et fils*, should have wasted more of their time and energy on trying to defend the legal entitlement to their original concession than on any other single issue.

In order to challenge the conclusion that the Revolution was responsible for all France's ills, it is important to emphasize the point that as much of Tubeuf's time and energy was being expended on finding a solution to this problem before 1789 as after this date. Equally important to remind ourselves that the 'pull of the land' had exerted its powerful, if not magnetic, influence upon the French population long before the Revolution. Peasant 'individualism', their determination to defend, or to acquire, land, was most evident in the less fertile and mountainous regions where noble and bourgeois acquisitiveness had not made serious inroads.[25] There was a close relationship between terrain, types of peasant tenure, and protoindustrialization. If the peasant living on the edge of subsistence could not find extra money from spinning or weaving, then he would transfer his labour to other forms of activity which allowed him to stay on his *lopin de terre*. The origins of the shift away from manufacturing to the production of wine and raw silk are to be found at the beginning of the eighteenth century in some regions, prompted by the development

---

[24] Aftalion, *The French Revolution*, 193.
[25] P. Jones, *The Peasantry in the French Revolution*, 8.

of a more commercialized economy and the need for raw silk to further the expansion of the textile industry. Government edicts favoured the planting of mulberry trees after the 1750s, whilst Roger Dugrand informs us that the first 'modern' phase of the expansion of the wine industry covered the period from the 1670s to the 1780s.[26]

What the Revolution did is not only increase the attraction of land but make much more of it available, thus explaining what Roger Dugrand has described as a unique and persistent phenomenon—the increasing control of urban capital over the countryside in Bas-Langue-doc. Whereas, in most other regions of France, he argues, there is a shift of urban capital and ownership during the nineteenth century in the direction of industry, in our region, the reverse was to occur.[27] Throughout most of the first half of the nineteenth century, land continued to provide a living for thousands of cévenol *petits proprié-taires*, as well as for the landless who could purchase mulberry leaves and silkworms to produce the odd sack of raw silk, or work on the stepped hillsides of the northern Gard and the southern Ardèche—the lost 'département des Cévennes'. Clout stresses that there was a 'véritable révolution' in viticulture in the plains of Languedoc after 1820,[28] whilst the production of raw silk in the Gard shot up from 1 million kilograms in 1820 to 4 million by 1853.[29]

Another long-term factor inhibiting the growth of a modern coal industry in our region—as in most other industrial regions of France—one which certainly posed major problems for every promoter of *l'industrie en grand* in France, was the shortage of adequate long-term supplies of credit. For Pierre-François Tubeuf, the lack of a banking network which was flexible enough to finance his kind of work was unquestionably a major obstacle. Loans at high rates of interests were forthcoming from Jewish money-lenders as well as from a few land-owners who had made small fortunes out of textiles and/or wine. But for the massive amounts of capital that he needed, he was sent to Paris. We have seen how his mining ventures ruined the Chaulieus. Nor did his son fare a great deal better: both Alexandre Tubeuf, and his main rival, the duc de Castries, were continually on the look-out for substantial supplies of capital, loaned at reasonable rates of

---

[26] Dugrand describes the period as encompassing 'la première explosion du vignoble', *Villes et campagnes en Bas-Languedoc*, 356.

[27] Ibid. 539.

[28] H. Clout, *Agriculture in France on the Eve of the Railway Age* (London, 1980), 137.

[29] Dugrand, *Villes et campagnes en Bas-Languedoc*, 389.

interest. The duc de Castries was particularly critical of the financial activities of the Dhombres family, which *did* have a great deal of money, but which also knew, as a family whose history was rooted in the traditional socio-economy of Bas-Languedoc, what to do with it, which was certainly not to risk it in the bottomless pits of the Grand-Combe and Rochebelle, at least, not on behalf of other people!

Here again, the land settlement of the Revolution is important. Many historians have stressed that the Revolution, by offering huge tracts of land to investors, deprived industry of much-needed invest-ment funds.[30] However, O'Brien and Keyder approach the problem from a different angle: 'French retardation', they conclude, 'can cer-tainly be conceived in terms of an unrealised potential for economic growth derived from a failure to transfer labour from a low-produc-tivity agricultural sector into industry.'[31] Economic historians of the 'small is beautiful' tendency advise caution when dealing with this point, arguing that it was not so much the shortage of capital as the determination of investors to place their funds in concerns which were cost-effective, in contemporary market terms, that mattered most, concerns which were perfectly rational given the socio-economy of 'pre-industrial' woman and man. In any case, they argue, we are dealing more with Adam Smith's 'circulating' rather than Karl Marx's 'fixed' capital. For the cévenols, for example, textiles, leather, raw silk, wines, and brandies were tried and trusted commodities, and, even if official international markets closed, there was always the contraband trade, to say nothing of traditional regional markets.

However, the debate over cost-effectiveness or feasible and more humane alternatives to heavy industrialization rarely embraces the coal and iron industries. This crucial issue was raised—though hardly addressed directly—during the many conferences which popularized the concept of 'protoindustrialization' at the beginning of the 1980s.[32] Charles Tilly, whilst criticizing Marx's alleged overemphasis on the

[30] The most recent is Florin Aftalion, *The French Revolution*, 191–2, although the fact that he quotes François Crouzet in support of his argument emphasizes its long and honourable pedigree.

[31] O'Brien and Keyder, *Economic Growth in Britain and France*, 98.

[32] P. Deyon and F. Mendels in their contribution to the special issue of the *Revue du Nord*, 63(248) (1981) entitled 'La Proto-industrialisation: théorie et réalité, 17, posed the question: 'Dans quelle mesure le modèle de la proto-industrialisation s'applique-t-il également aux mines, aux industries du bois, de la métallurgie et aux industries textiles, ou prend-il au contraire un aspect différent pour chaque type d'industrie?' This study has been concerned, in the main, with finding the answer to such questions.

city and the factory as providing the necessary foundations for modern industrialization, did suggest a more dynamic and flexible model of protoindustrialization. Tilly none the less agreed that when one is talking about 'industrial revolution' one is talking about coal, iron, and large inputs of capital.[33] Protoindustrial forms of production *may* have been more cost-efficient and socially more acceptable for producing textile goods than the satanic mills of Lancashire or Tourcoing, but, so far as the business of producing coal was concerned, they were not. O'Brien and Keyder place some importance upon the coal industry when explaining Britain's advantage in labour productivity.[34] All of which is not the same as saying that developing countries are *obliged* by some iron law of economic history to adopt the same methods of production as those popularized by the British, and shared by a Pierre-François Tubeuf, in the late eighteenth century. Despite the politician and the businessman, modern technology is producing 'natural', as opposed to 'fossil' methods of producing energy; the microchip is replacing human muscle-power. None the less, the 'alternative' marvels of modern science are themselves founded upon the inventions of the 'first' and 'second' Industrial Revolutions. The Rance dam in Brittany is not made of mud and wattle. During the period we are discussing, coal and iron were prerequisites for launching what contemporaries referred to as 'l'industrie en grand'. As David Landes remarks, 'Coal and steam, therefore, did not make the Industrial Revolution, but they permitted its extraordinary development and diffusion.'[35] But, the sinking of pits and the construction of blast furnaces demanded considerable sums of capital, and, in France at least, these sums were very hard to come by. France simply did not have the banking and credit structures appropriate to an age of modern industrialization, in part, because the French bourgeoisie were not all convinced that 'where there's muck, there's brass', but also because, as Woronoff points out in his study of the iron industry, those that were did not believe that the times were propitious for risky industrial investments.[36] It was his debt, as much as his disappointment with the way things were going for *concessionnaires* by 1791, which finally convinced Tubeuf that his future lay where his creditors

[33] Tilly, 'Flows of Capital and Forms of Industry in Europe', 136.

[34] O'Brien and Keyder, *Economic Growth in Britain and France*, 158.

[35] Landes, *The Unbound Prometheus*, 99.

[36] Woronoff, *L'Industrie sidérurgique en France*, 331.

could not catch him. Unfortunately for our intrepid hero, the Indians of Virginia were even more wedded to a 'pre-industrial' ideology!

Finally, from the standpoint of long-term socio-economic and financial constraints on the emergence of heavy industry, and the *mentalités* which they produced, nothing is more indicative of the protoindustrial nature of production throughout our period than the widespread hostility to the idea of leaving the countryside for work in the factory or the mine. Pierre-François Tubeuf had been obliged to search for skilled labour in Germany and Belgium in the 1770s. This is not to say that there was no tradition of coal-mining or iron-smelting in the Basses-Cévennes; on the contrary, we have seen that many mining families were proud to trace their pedigree as 'independent colliers' back, at least, to the seventeenth century. It is all too easy to underestimate the importance of coal to the protoindustrial economy of eighteenth-century France, agricultural and industrial. In 1777, the abbé Perussis complained to the Estates of Languedoc that if Tubeuf's 'monopolistic' practices were not halted two thousand inhabitants would be reduced to abject misery, 'because those who are employed to extract coal possess no other skill than that which they currently exercise'.[37] But, not only did these old mining families reject the notion of working for a 'foreigner' like Tubeuf, reject, in fact, the same process of 'proletarianization' against which textile craftsmen throughout Bas-Languedoc had struggled, not entirely in vain, they simply did not possess the skills necessary for modern mining methods, something which John Harris considers to be of considerable importance when discussing the French road to industrialization. Professor Harris's conclusion confronts us again with the importance of the coal industry for modern industrialization: 'Perhaps the main point to be stressed is the long divergence in the technologies of the two nations, as England progressively concentrated upon, and specialized in, coal fuel.'[38] Throughout our period, men had to be drafted from the Lozère, the Forez, and the Saône-et-Loire, as well as from Piedmont, Germany, and Belgium. On the eve of 1830, the directors of the Société des fonderies et forges d'Alais felt obliged to send their chief engineer to Staffordshire to recruit workers for their brickworks and iron foundries, as well as to obtain the 'Boulton and Watt' steam-engines to produce the energy they needed. During the 1840s,

---

[37] *AG* C194, letter of 14 Aug. 1777.
[38] Harris, 'The Diffusion of English Metallurgical Methods', 38.

the Grand-Combe coal company would become one of the first in France to construct barracks to house its 'imported labour'. And the tradition lingered on. As late as 1945—not 1845—'foreigners' (that is foreign nationals) would still represent over 40 per cent of the work-force.[39]

No wonder there was little sense of a common working-class consciousness before 1848. If the working class had been 'made' by 1832 in Manchester and Merthyr, it was still in the process of being formed in Alès and Anduze as workers fought a losing, but lengthy, battle to remain above rather than below ground. To return to the developing world for a moment: it has been suggested that economists should pay far greater attention 'to the effects of local environment and culture when endeavouring to explain poor performance in textile mills' in the 'Third World'.[40] Tubeuf and his successors in the Basses-Cévenol region, including those responsible for attracting labour well into the twentieth century, were only too aware of this vitally important socio-cultural, indeed, 'eco-cultural' phenomenon. Bloody fights between rival associations of *compagnons*; occasional bouts of machine-breaking as urban and rural workers quarrelled over diminishing pools of work; tables overturned in *cabarets* as 'foreigners' stole their drink or their women: these were the customary problems for the local gendarmerie in the Basses-Cévennes—as well as for the forces of law and order in Coventry—until the 1840s.[41] In the south-east of France, however, the situation was aggravated by the religious divide which separated Catholic from Protestant. Only in periods of intense political debate would this atavistic tension be relaxed—1793, 1848. In the early 1830s, whilst the Lyon *canuts* were fighting what some historians have called the first modern struggles against their employers, Catholic and Protestants were killing each

[39] P. Joutard, 'Les Cévennes en difficulté', in Joutard (ed.), *Les Cévennes de la montagne à l'homme*, 285.

[40] See G. Clark, 'Why Isn't the Whole World Developed?', *Journal of Economic History*, 47 (1987), 172–87.

[41] See e.g. the report of a vicious fight between coal-miners working for the duc de Castries and foreign workers in 1815: 'les gens du pays se sont réunis en certain nombre pour attacquer les ouvriers étrangers'. *AN* 306AP 501, Ango to Castries, 16 Nov. 1815; and an official report drafted over 20 years later referring to the troubles being caused by 'L'augmentation des ouvriers étrangers', which prompted the prefect of the Gard to ask for regular troops to be sent to Alès. *AG* 6M 256, to General Suchères, 30 Jan. 1837. For Coventry, see the report of silk-workers accused of setting fire to a power-loom in 1831. S. R. Jones, 'Technology, Transition Costs, and the Transition to Factory Production', 85.

other again in the streets of Nîmes.[42] Coal-mining in the Basses-
Cévennes was to be, almost exclusively, a Catholic concern, and the
Grand-Combe company would exploit the fact, organizing a capitalist
theocracy, and thus perpetuating (for their own ends) the age-old
religious antagonisms which characterize the entire history of Bas-
Languedoc.[43]

If protoindustrial forms of production, linked to a seigneurial and
small property-owning society, formed major obstacles to the emergence of modern forms of industrialization in the Basses-Cévennes,
it should be remembered that their impact was not exercised *in vacuo*.
Rather late in the day, Engels admitted that he and Marx had
underemphasized the processes of interaction between the economic
and the political, insisting that it was vital to think in dialectical terms,
not in terms of linear arguments or polar opposites.[44] Michael Sonenscher, taking the current attack on unreconstructed Marxist analysis a
stage further, may also be right to stress that 'The identity of
modernity cannot be found, in other words, by extrapolating from
the labour process, or productive relations as such, towards political
action or institutional procedures.' One certainly needs a more sophisticated analysis, one that includes, as Sonenscher suggests, the altered
relationship of workers to the market, to law, and to government.[45]
One of the criticisms levelled against 'crude' Marxist determinists by
some economic historians, accused of producing teleological theses
charting the existence of a linear (economic–technological) path from
'pre-industrial' to industrial society, concerns the importance of legal
and political constraints. Such criticisms are legitimate and timely: we
are, after all, all 'pluralists' or 'post-modernists' now.

Pierre-François Tubeuf knew the importance of politics, how human
action and endeavour could challenge and give shape to 'la force des
choses'. Indeed, he must have regretted the unconscionable amount
of time he felt obliged to spend greasing the palms or bending the
ears of a succession of ministers, deputies, secretaries, clerks, and

---

[42] Fitzpatrick, *Catholic Royalism in the Department of the Gard*, 99–100.

[43] See e.g. the influence of confessional differences upon the course of the Revolution
of 1848. Huard, *Le Mouvement républicain en Bas-Languedoc*, 39.

[44] 'Marx and I are ourselves partly to blame for the fact that the younger people
sometimes lay more stress on the economic side than is due to it.' Engels to Joseph
Bloch, 21 Sept. 1890, in K. Marx and F. Engels, *Pre-capitalist Socio-economic Formations*,
(Moscow, 1979), 520–5.

[45] M. Sonenscher, *Work and Wages: Natural Law, Politics and the Eighteenth-Century French
Trades* (Cambridge, 1989), 375.

Court favourites. He also courted the bureaucrats attached to the
Estates General, with some success it must be noted, until the scale
of his operations began to disrupt the lives of the cévenol property-
owner, manufacturer, collier, lime-burner, and carter. The voices of
the latter were heard, via the clergy and the *assiettes des diocèses*, in the
council-rooms of the Estates of Languedoc. The members of this
prestigious body, whose livelihoods were bound up with the well-being
of their constituents, were wise not to turn a deaf ear. In the
eighteenth century, the collection of taxes depended as much upon
consent as coercion, and the right to collect taxes represented one of
the corner-stones of the political independence of provincial estates.
Another, linked, corner-stone—William Doyle would prefer the meta-
phor 'foundation stone'[46]—rested upon property-rights. The debate
over property-rights lay at the heart of the dilemma between Tubeuf
and his enemies. In Britain, there were frequent battles over the
ownership of mines and the types of lease granted, but there were
several important differences. In the first place, there was no argument
between the Crown and the landowner over who owned mineral
rights: in Britain, it was the owner of the surface, although some
friction existed over the rights of copyholders; secondly, leases were
invariably granted for twenty-one years or over (not five or nine as
was generally the case in Bas-Languedoc); and thirdly, there was 'a
general determination by Parliament to foster the development of the
[coal] industry'.[47] This is not to argue that these factors alone explain
the advanced state of the coal industry in Britain: the importance of
richer mineral reserves, a skilled labour force, wider avenues of capital,
and a far better transport system, for example, all played their part.
However, it seems evident that the attitude of Parliament, *unconstrained
by powerful provincial political bodies*, allied to the far broader acceptance
of the need for coal by 'maréchals and mine-owners' alike in Britain,
provides a central explanation. How many aristocrats in France could
say, as did the Earl of Crawford and Balcarres: 'Colliers we are and
colliers we must ever remain.'[48] The maréchal de Castries would have
been appalled at this fall from aristocratic grace: not so maréchal

---

[46] W. Doyle, 'The Parlements', in Baker (ed.), *The French Revolution and the Creation of
Modern Political Culture*, i. 164.

[47] Flinn and Stoker, *History of the British Coal Industry*, 281. In South Wales, the
customary term for a lease was between 40 and 60 years, and there was little problem
securing permission from landowners. See J. Morris and L. Williams, *The South Wales
Coal Industry, 1841–1875* (Cardiff, 1958), 117–21.

[48] Flinn and Stoker, 37.

Soult; but then his influence was at its peak *after* the Revolution of 1830, not before that of 1789.

It was the weight of a powerful aristocrat, locked into the socio-economic and political mechanisms of a decaying, but still functioning, feudal State, operating both through the Court and through the Estates of Languedoc, which crippled Tubeuf. He was doubly unfortunate in the fact that his success came just when the glory-days of the Bas-Languedoc silk industry were ending and when the political debate between central and provincial government was assuming troublesome proportions. It was in 1779 that the provincial assembly of Haut-Guienne was re-established: in the previous year, Tubeuf had made the decision to leave his home and family in Alès to reside in Paris in order that he could defend his rights against the Estates of Languedoc at Court.[49] Tubeuf's fortunes were inextricably bound up with the contemporary political scene in France. Under a Louis XIV, Tubeuf just might have won his case; under the pusillanimous Louis XVI his prospects were never bright.

There is a good case for arguing, however, that Tubeuf's fate was finally sealed not in Versailles but in Bas-Languedoc, when Castries bought the *comté d'Alais*. This purchase gave him considerable political leverage over the actions of the municipality of Alès (he had the right to confirm the choice of municipal *consuls*) as well as over the deliberations of the Estates themselves, as *premier Baron-né du Languedoc*. As we have noted, the Estates were not impervious to popular unrest—which Tubeuf's actions unquestionably provoked—as their fairly sensitive response to the *masques armés* rebellion of 1783 demonstrates. The Estates were also obliged to operate within the constraints of a seigneurial and protoindustrial society; workers articulated their grievances through their seigneurs, their clergy, and their courts of law, whether organized in guilds or not.

Much is made, quite rightly, of the cost and inadequacies of transport before the advent of the railway. We have noted how the cost of transporting coal from the Grand-Combe to the main manufacturing centres of Languedoc was unquestionably a major constraint upon production. The first task undertaken by the new breed of investors and entrepreneurs, led by maréchal Soult, responsible for the take-off of modern industry in Bas-Languedoc, was to oversee the construction of canals, although it is important to stress that they did

---

[49] *AG* 58J 2, entry in his Journal for 31 July 1777 recording his arrival in Paris.

subsequently organize the sinking of four new pits at the Rochebelle mine purchased from Alexandre Tubeuf in order to obtain good coking coal.

However, accepting that transport costs represented a major blockage on coal production until the age of the railway does not exhaust the problem. We need to dig a little deeper. Why was the river Cèze not improved for the transport of coal? Why was so little emphasis placed upon extending and improving the canal du Midi from Sète to the Rhône? Why, until the Tubeufs undertook the responsibility in the 1800s, were more roads not constructed between the Grand-Combe or Robiac to major loading-points, hence to Pont-Saint-Esprit, Saint-Ambroix, or Beaucaire? The reason, more often than not, had to do with the power of vested interests, noble and roturier, seeking to preserve lucrative, seigneurial rights of passage, traditional commercial networks involving old market towns, as well as the urgent need to protect the traditional transport mechanisms which ensured the exchange of food for coal, thus satisfying the powerful carters' association and anaesthetizing the very real fears of dearth haunting protoindustrial communities in particular. It is not coincidental that one of the most powerful coal-owners in the region by the 1830s was Pierre-Goirand, who had originally made his small fortune in the Alèsian transport industry.

1789 heralded the end of the Estates of Languedoc, as well as the end of many a seigneurial monopoly. It did not, however, mark the end of traditional 'restrictive practices'. If anything, the early years of the Revolution led to the erection of even higher political and popular barriers to the plans of Pierre-François Tubeuf. Apart from the brief and quite exceptional war cabinet of the Jacobins from 1793 to 1794, the 1790s saw power devolve from the State—without whose officials Tubeuf could never have operated in the first place—to those vital cogs in the machinery of modern French political and administrative history, the municipality. A recent general history of Bas-Languedoc informs us that the 'révolution municipale' of 1789 was to prove an 'event of truly revolutionary dimensions as a consequence of the subsequent extension of the powers of the municipal authorities through the policy of decentralization. Given the absence of grave disorders in the province, the "révolution municipale" proved to be the major political phenomenon, the event of the year 1789.'[50]

---

[50] Laurent and Gavignaud, *La Révolution française dans le Languedoc*, 57.

Once again, we note the interaction of economics and politics. The 'political economy' of the municipal authorities in the Basses-Cévennes was aimed at the reassertion of the rights of property-owners so far as control of coal-mines was concerned. Democracy in Bas-Languedoc in 1789 meant total freedom for the *propriétaire* as opposed to the *concessionnaire*. Whereas in Britain the trend was towards longer leases and more modern methods of extracting coal, in the Basses-Cévennes, as in other coal-mining regions of France including Anzin, it meant a return to shorter leases and 'medieval' mining practices. The economic clout of the municipality in France following the Revolution was to be considerably enhanced by the mining laws of 1791 as well as by the decision to confer upon the Régies de l'enregistrement the right to oversee the sale and management of 'national' property. Membership of the Régies tended to be drawn from the same local pool as for the municipalities. In fact—and this was to be a very significant factor in retarding the development of heavy industry in France—coal-mines were to be 'municipalized' rather than 'nationalized' during the French Revolution, the resources of the State, financial and administrative, being totally inadequate for the task until the twentieth century. Throughout our period, the municipalities of Alès, and the small mining villages of the Gardon and Cèze valleys, were to be the main source of opposition to the Tubeuf family.

Even before the Revolution, the State had failed to impose its will concerning regalian rights over mineral deposits and the legitimacy of the huge concessions it was increasingly prepared to grant to entre-preneurs like Tubeuf. For Bourbons or Jacobins, passing legislation was one thing, enforcing it quite another. The mining legislation of 1744 had been completely ignored in Languedoc, which helps to explain the caution and confusions of the legislators in 1791. Revolution compounded the problem of enforcing State legislation as the authority of the central government was further undermined. It is worth noting that the important decision to create a scientific structure for mining in France with the creation of the Agence des mines in 1794 was a product both of war and of Jacobin centralization. The exigencies of running a modern State were pushing Robespierre and his colleagues towards a more rational appraisal of the economy as well as a more rational response to the political and administrative chaos of the Year II. Robespierre's much debated 'totalitarianism' had more to do with the need to control the mines of France than with the desire to control the minds of his compatriots. In times of national crisis, politics and economics become increasingly indistinguishable. Robespierre signed the decree setting up the Agence des mines, together with its very influential in-house magazine, the *Journal des mines*, in the very same month that he was sent to meet the Supreme Being.

The debate over the respective virtues of so-called 'free markets' and State intervention is very relevant to the history of the struggle between the Tubeufs and the Castries. In France, it dates back at least to the days of Colbert. We have seen how, during the reign of Louis XVI, ministers like Bertin and bureaucrats like La Barberie had sided with Tubeuf and the principle of State intervention as a means of promoting heavy industry. During the Revolution and Empire, scientists like Hassenfratz (who, interestingly enough, was a member of the Jacobin insurrectional committee which organized the overthrow of the Girondins in June 1793) and Lefebvre d'Hellancourt, continued this *étatiste* tradition. The latter was primarily responsible for the legislation of 1810 which provided the legislative framework for mining in France until the present century. Members of the newly formed Ministère des ponts et chaussées et des mines during the Restoration would retain something more than a watching brief, although it would not be until after 1830 that their *étatiste* appetites were really to be fed. Christopher Johnson notes that from 1836 to 1840 'the administration [of the Ponts et chaussées] guided, cajoled, and sometimes bullied the Chambers through a stormy period during which both localist–traditionalist and excessive laissez-faire opinions were often undermined, and rational railroad policy, business law, and agricultural improvement orientations were forged'.[51] Johnson makes the valid point that there was nothing 'anti-capitalist' or retrograde about State intervention in France. Our study confirms this, as does the action of the French government under Napoleon III, as well as during the Fourth and Fifth Republics.

Although it would be totally wrong to identify 'maréchals' with the Legitimists after 1830 and 'mine-owners' with Orleanists, or even Republicans, 1830 does mark a very significant political and ideological fissure in the structure of modern French history: 'the attempt of the Bourbons to construct an aristocratic ruling elite was abandoned in a dramatic "émigration à l'intérieur"'.[52] It was not so much that the

[51] Johnson, 'The Révolution of 1830 in French Economic History', 159.
[52] P. Pilbeam, *The Middle Classes in Europe, 1789 to 1914* (London, 1990), 251.

new Legitimists hated all forms of industry; more that they were accustomed to the forms and practices of 'localist–traditionalist' proto-industry. In 1789, the local leader of the Catholic royalist counter-revolution in Bas-Languedoc, François Froment, had denounced the rich Protestant *négociants* not so much for prosecuting their commercial interests as for doing so unfairly. They were accused of fraud, of not paying their just share of taxes, of creating monopolies, of giving work to protoindustrial rural workers, not to urban artisans.[53] Under the July Monarchy, Legitimists, like the Calvières-Vézénobres family, would be caught in the same dilemma as the maréchal de Castries had been in the 1780s, torn between rationalizing their capitalist invest-ments 'and maintaining the loyalty of the peasantry . . . by permitting inefficient and unprofitable farming to continue'.[54] In the interim period, Joseph de Maistre and Louis de Bonald had given ideological form to these opinions. De Maistre 'consecrated an important part of his work to a violent critique of the materialist ethic'; De Bonald 'revealed his hostility against everything which was associated with production in the modern sense of the word'.[55] The Laffittes and the Périers lived in a totally different economic and ethical universe and, after 1830, would operate in a totally different economic and political universe, one in which the disciples of a de Maistre would feel excluded, at least on the national political stage.

This study has stressed the importance of socio-economic, political, and institutional factors in explaining the failure of industrialization in the Basses-Cévennes. We have emphasized the clash of interests between the Tubeuf family, whose more ambitious designs were thwarted by a protoindustrial society which, confronted by revolution, war, and changing, often shrinking, markets, chose to concentrate upon what it knew best, agriculture, the production of cheap textiles, raw silk, and wine. The father was driven into exile; his sons were forced to return home from America, ultimately to manage glassworks for their commercial business of selling wines and brandies. To have succeeded as industrialists during the traumatic, and decisive, decades of the 1790s and the 1800s, when Britain assumed control of the seas and the steam-engine, *père et fils* would both have required the

---

[53] F. Froment, *Charles Sincère à Pierre Romain* (Nîmes, 1790).

[54] Fitzpatrick, *Catholic Royalism in the Department of the Gard*, 124.

[55] L. Epsztein, *L'Économie et la morale aux débuts du capitalisme industriel en France et en Grande-Bretagne* (Paris, 1966), 106–7.

unequivocal support either of the State, or of the community in which they lived and worked, which, for a variety of reasons, was not forthcoming. The central importance of land and property-rights, allied to the uncertainties of revolution, war, and economic blockades, helps to explain why the revolutionary bourgeoisie in Bas-Languedoc, or, at least, the majority of them, failed to support any major move away from the land to industry. This provides the answer to the question posed by David Landes—why a country which had the 'technical competence' for growth was none the less 'slow to accomplish the transition' to modern forms of industrialization.[56]

Did the Revolution of 1830 accelerate the pace of change? The question has been debated and the differences of opinion, between 'Marxists', 'revisionists', and that more hybrid ideological species the 'post-revisionist', explained in Pamela Pilbeam's recent *The Middle Classes in Europe, 1789 to 1914*. It would be tiresome to repeat the points at issue: suffice it to note the author's ('post-revisionist'?) somewhat hesitant conclusion that *if* the governments of the July Monarchy were more 'constructive' in their attitude to capitalism, this may be explicable more in terms of 'evolutionary economic change than contrasting government preoccupations'.[57] Of course, no sensible historian has argued that modern industrial capitalism sprang, newly formed and fully fledged, from the Revolution of 1830. On the contrary, 'Marxist' arguments rested upon the premiss that 1830 marked an important stage, *particularly from a political and legal standpoint*, in the advance of modern capitalism in France. There is no question that, looking at our brief, which principally concerns the coal industry in the Basses-Cévennes, Christopher Johnson is absolutely right to conclude that the July Monarchy represented 'an era of economic progress and that state policy represented an advance over that of the Restoration'.[58] Since we have argued throughout that heavy industry in France, particularly given the peculiar circumstances of its history between the reigns of Louis XVI and Charles X, demanded unequivocal support from the State, the fact that State support was far more positive after 1830 may be considered to be of crucial importance. It is interesting from this standpoint that Donald Reid, in his study of Decazeville, notes that the coal industry there, which also took off

[56] Landes, *The Unbound Prometheus*, 216.
[57] Pilbeam, *The Middle Classes in Europe*, 253.
[58] Johnson, 'The Revolution of 1830 in French Economic History', 178.

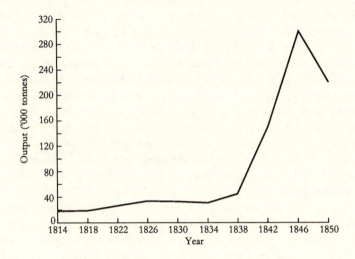

FIG C.1. Production in the Alès coal-basin, 1814–1850

after 1830, provides an excellent forum for discussing the wider involvement of the State in industrial development.[59]

To justify our application of the term 'take-off' to the 1830s, let us first of all examine the relevant statistics, recalling that from the 1780s to the late 1820s the production of coal from the Alès basin had only risen from around 15,000 to 30,000 tonnes, a miserable increase. The most striking statistic is a rise in production to 100,000 tonnes by 1840, which means that whereas coal production had only doubled in the previous forty years it would triple in just seven years after the Revolution of 1830. And this, with no meaningful technological change in the methods of production.[60] By 1845, this figure had increased to 300,000 tonnes; twenty years later to 1,250,000 tonnes. By 1914, production from the Alès coal-basin would rise to over 2 million tonnes, representing one-twentieth of total French production of coal.[61] Even more impressive is the take-off in the iron

[59] Reid, *The Miners of Decazeville*, p. xxxii. See also H. Sée, *Histoire économique de la France: les temps modernes, 1789–1914* (Paris, 1942), ii. 226: 'Dans l'ensemble, sous le règne de Louis-Philippe, se manifeste un grand essor économique, qui frappe tous les contemporains.'

[60] *Recherches historiques sur la ville d'Alais*, 656.

[61] *Nîmes et le Gard*, ii. 117.

and steel industry. From a negligible base in 1830, the production of iron and sheet metal from the Tamaris works in Alès rose to 6,000 tonnes by 1840, one-fifth of it being used locally, the rest being transported to Marseille. By 1885, the Tamaris works would be employing over 1,000 workers producing 18,000 tonnes of iron and 11,000 tonnes of track for the railways. It was just four years after the Revolution of 1830 that the Compagnie des fonderies et forges de Terrenoire opened its gates in Bessèges, producing steel using the coal of the Cèze valley, which Pierre-François Tubeuf had started to 'modernize' sixty years earlier. By the 1860s, it would house 4 blast-furnaces and 12 rolling and puddling mills, and employ over 800 workers.[62] The Basses-Cévennes region had well and truly entered the modern industrial era.

But the central question is: Did the policies of Soult, Périer, Laffitte, and Guizot create the framework for this undoubted take-off? The answer must be a qualified yes. The qualification concerns the fact that the Tubeufs and the Méjeans, the Soults and the Laffittes, had suggested what had to be done, and had gone some way towards the implementation of their ideas, before 1830: pits had been sunk, canals and roads had been constructed, banks had been opened before the last of the Bourbons left France. Our argument is not that modern forms of industrial capitalism only begin to take shape after 1830—which would be nonsense—but that a combination of forces and events, socio-economic, cultural, political, and revolutionary, prevented their expansion before 1830. In short, the political economy of protoindustrialization, refined by the exigencies of revolution and war, prevented a rapid transformation to modern forms of industrial capitalism. After all, Paulin Talabot's general plan for the region in the 1830s, which was to transport Grand-Combe coal to Marseille, was precisely the objective that Tubeuf had set himself during his first visit to Alès in the early 1770s.

It was to be during the 1830s that the nîmois textile industry went into terminal decline, despite its valiant attempt to keep ahead of market demand. It marked the end of an era for the inhabitants of the Basses-Cévennes, creating the space for new forms of industry.[63]

---

[62] Dugrand, *Villes et campagnes en Bas-Languedoc*, 392–4.

[63] 'Ainsi, la première moitié du XIXe siècle apparaît pour le textile nîmois comme un tournant. La ville n'a jamais pu retrouver l'apogée du XVIIIe siècle, parce que les fabricants n'ont su s'adapter à un environnement économique et politique différent'. Cosson, 'Industrie de la soie et population ouvrière à Nîmes', 212.

Creating more human space, too, marking the end of the demographic expansion of the majority of cévenol *bourgs* and villages. The depopulation of the old textile centres dates from the mid-nineteenth century. For example, the population of Saint-Jean-du-Gard, which rose from 3,755 to 4,128 between 1811 and 1831, had increased by only one soul by 1846; that of Anduze, which had risen from 5,451 to 5,554 between 1811 and 1831, had fallen to 5,306 by the same date. In the southern Ardèche, maximum population levels would be reached in the 1850s, when 'la sériculture est à son apogée'.[64] Population growth was now occurring in the industrial towns and villages of the region. The population of Nîmes increased by 50 per cent during the first four decades of the nineteenth century, but that of Alès *ville* shot up from 7,440 in 1809 to 18,871 by 1841. The future coal-mining village of Robiac had just 737 inhabitants at the end of the Napoleonic Empire, 1,379 by 1841. The centre of the new coal industry, the Grand-Combe, was given communal status in the 1840s reflecting its striking transformation from a cluster of small hamlets in the eighteenth century to a 'company town' of over 4,000 inhabitants.[65]

Secondly, there was a banking and investment 'revolution' in the 1830s, providing the capital that was vitally necessary for the industrial boom of the July Monarchy. The eminent historian of finance and industrial capitalism in France Bertrand Gille notes that: 'The years 1835 to 1838 . . . marked an appreciable modification of the economic structures of certain Western European countries. Private investment, "l'association" as it was called then, assumed a pre-eminent place.'[66] One could say that, from the standpoint of finance and share capital, French 'eighteenth-century capitalist man' died in the 1830s, and it was the State which organized the funeral. Some of the financial problems with which French industrialists like Tubeuf had been confronted had been overcome in Britain many decades before. However, recent work on this topic suggests that there is no direct link between the availability of massive sums of capital and industrialization; again, the links are far more complex and indirect, involving

---

[64] Cayrier-Gilliot, 'Discours pour vivre ou survivre', 13.

[65] Population figures above are taken from *AG* 6M 2, *tableau des mouvements de la population du Gard de 1800 à 1834*; *AG* 6M 102, *tableau des communes du Gard*; *AG* 6M 108, *dénombrement de la population du royaume, 1846*; *AG 6M* 651, *population du Gard entre 1789 et l'an XIII* (very detailed).

[66] B. Gille, *Histoire de la Maison Rothschild*, i: *Des origines à 1848* (Paris, 1965), 305.

social, legal, and institutional factors, as this study has suggested.[67] We must recall that Pierre-François Tubeuf had, in fact, obtained a relatively 'massive' sum of capital from the Chaulieus, though not at the requisite terms; but then we have not argued that credit facilities represented the *major* cause of Tubeuf's failure. Pat Hudson has noted that in Britain during the 1790s long-term credit was becoming easier to obtain and that a provincial and local banking system was providing capital for industrial development.[68] One can immediately appreciate the importance of this when one recalls that the 1790s in France was a decade of unparalleled upheaval and uncertainty, not the most propitious climate for large investors.

Some historians of Bas-Languedoc have blamed the bourgeoisie for not promoting modern industrialization, but, again, the charge is only partly valid.[69] During the eighteenth century, there had not been any shortage of money to oil the wheels of a world-wide manufacturing and commercial business. And we must recall that, until well into the nineteenth century, even the mighty Rothschilds had been very loath indeed to risk their millions in industrial ventures.[70] Finally, the great coal-and-railway boom of the 1830s *did* attract capital not only from Marseille but from Nîmes and Alès, with substantial sums being placed not only by the old coal-owners like Puech and Goirand, but by *négociants* like Veaute and Abric, as well by powerful local families like the Dhombres. Raymond Huard is surely right to conclude that the industrial take-off of the 1830s was a joint venture: 'Regional and national capital collaborated in these enterprises.'[71]

More to the point is the fact that the putative investors of Bas-Languedoc were not at all convinced, before 1830, that entrepreneurs and industrialists had conquered the problems associated with the mass production of coal or iron. Pierre-François Tubeuf had failed to win over the Estates of Languedoc, let alone defeat popular resistance to his grandiose schemes; Jean Méjean had not succeeded in producing good-quality iron. Could such men deliver the goods (and the profits)?

---

[67] See P. Mathias, 'Industrial Revolution: Concept and Reality', in Mathias and Davis (eds.), *The First Industrial Revolutions*, 4–5.

[68] Hudson, *The Genesis of Industrial Capital*, 262–8.

[69] Dugrand, *Villes et campagnes en Bas-Languedoc*, 398, noting that the Montpellier woolen industry had entered a phase of terminal decline before 1830, concludes that one is dealing with a commercial and manufacturing bourgeoisie which 'à l'avance [of foreign competition], avait accepté, voire même appelé, sa défaite'.

[70] Gille, *Histoire de la Maison Rothschild*, 193.

[71] Huard, *Le Mouvement républicain en Bas-Languedoc*, 29.

That was the question investors asked. Did they have the necessary political support as well as the technical know-how? As late as the summer of 1829, the directors of the 'Société des fonderies et forges d'Alais felt obliged to send their engineer, Communeau, on a prolonged visit to Belgium and England to obtain both workers and machinery, as well as a state-of-the-art report on the methods of making good iron and steel. He was successful on both counts, returning with skilled men and, to be delivered more than a year later, steam-engines (on the Boulton and Watt principle) manufactured in Staffordshire by Davies. In addition, Communeau managed to attract a Mr Potter to run the new brickworks in Alès (not an unmixed blessing, as it proved, since he ran off, leaving his wife and children, only a year later!).[72] Once again, the Tubeuf family's know-how is important here, for Alexandre Tubeuf knew Staffordshire well, whilst the first director of the ironworks at Alès, Bérard, had worked in Tubeuf's mines at Rochebelle. The evidence indicates that the French businessman reacted in a rational way to the circumstances he faced.[73]

We have stressed that one of the essential points distinguishing the Restoration from the July Monarchy concerns the attitude of the State. The industrial take-off of the 1830s in the Basses-Cévennes is inexplicable without the involvement of the State. It is true that maréchal Soult and his influential friends were busy on canals and ironworks before 1830, but it has to be noted that the first Alès railway company, formed to create the historic link with Beaucaire, as well as the first Alès ironworks, collapsed for a variety of reasons, political, technical, and financial. On 17 February 1833, the railway company headed by the Talabot brothers merged with the Grand-Combe coal company, creating a share capital (a *société en commandite par actions* had been formed) of 14 million francs.[74] It was Soult who had called in the Talabots, who had attracted Marseille bankers and industrialists.

And it was this same maréchal Soult who could be found at the heart of the government during these years, crushing the revolt of the lyonnais *canuts* in 1831, constructing the social, economic, and political ideology of the conservative Orleanist regime in the early

[72] R. Locke, *Les Fonderies et forges d'Alais à l'époque des premiers chemins de fer, 1829–1874* (Paris, 1978), 17–18.

[73] This is the main conclusion of R. Nye, 'Firm Size and Economic Backwardness: A New Look at the French Industrial Debate', *Journal of Economic History*, 47 (1987).

[74] Gaillard, 'La Naissance d'une entreprise industrielle au XIXe siècle: la compagnie des mines de la Grand-Combe', 192.

1830s, and sustaining it under Guizot in the following decade.[75] It was maréchal Soult who played a key role in putting together the final financial package which guaranteed the industrial 'take-off' in Bas-Languedoc. On 17 July 1837, the Grand-Combe company received a loan of 6 million *livres* from the State. It was not so much the size of the loan as the confidence such loans inspired in bankers, particularly the Rothschilds, who now invested several million francs of their own fortune. As the historian of the nineteenth-century Grand-Combe company writes: 'Thus, only the intervention of the State and of the Parisian *haute banque* had been able to provide the capital necessary for the take-off of this project.'[76] If only Tubeuf had enjoyed such a 'cast-iron' guarantee!

Many historians have pondered on the reasons for the 'de-industrialization' of Languedoc: Armand Cosson, referring to the final collapse of the old nîmois textile industry in the late 1830s, writes: 'the crucial question is posed—why, and how, did the industrial reconversion of Nîmes and, through its example, Languedoc itself, backfire?'[77] The first point to make, of course, is that Languedoc after 1830 hardly became an industrial desert. Again, the narrow focus upon the textile industry, or the constant inclination to compare French industrialization with the British example, seriously distorts the picture. The Alès region was to become one of the most industrialized regions in France; Decazeville, in the Aveyron, was also the site of important coal-mining and metallurgical works. Textile production in Languedoc, even in Bas-Languedoc, did not die out completely in the nineteenth century. When Roger Dugrand, at the beginning of his detailed study of Bas-Languedoc, poses the question concerning 'de-industrialization', he is talking about 1960, not 1860.[78] Many of the mining and metallurgical industries of Bas-Languedoc closed down after the Second World War, including those in the Basses-Cévennes.

None the less, Bas-Languedoc, as a region, never did become heavily industrialized, and Roger Dugrand offers some sound reasons why this should have been so, including the lack of relevant policies by the State, the 'égoïsme' of the port of Marseille, concerned above all

---

[75] See A. Jardin and A. J. Tudesq, *La France des notables* (Paris, 1973), i. 136–42; ii. 110.

[76] Gaillard, 'La Naissance d'une entreprise industrielle au XIXe siècle', 193.

[77] Cosson, 'Industrie de la soie et population ouvrière à Nîmes', 212.

[78] Dugrand, *Villes et campagnes en Bas-Languedoc*, p. 1–3.

about its own interests rather than those of the region, adding one point which is often ignored—the importance of urban geography. The vitality of the economic, cultural, and political life of the cévenol *bourg*—indeed, of the southern French 'village' in Maurice Agulhon's meaning of the word—was an essential ingredient of local democracy before the age of mass politics and the mass media. Life, economic, cultural, and political, revolved around the *hôtel de ville*, an entity which still commands greater respect and attention than our town hall. We have stressed the importance of the 'municipal revolution' in 1789–90, a revolution which facilitated the fusion of economic and political power. Is this one of the nodal points of French history, one which links the 'archaic' economic ideas of 'pre-industrial' communities with 'modern' political action? The mayors of the cévenol mining villages welcomed the 'modern' French Revolution precisely because it gave them the power to defend the 'archaic' rights and practices of their constituents. Hence, Maurice Agulhon can begin his study with the sentence 'The Republic and the village are closely linked in French history.'[79] Indeed they are. The Parisian sansculottes were to avail themselves of the new units of local administration to produce their unique mix of 'progressive' political and 'reactionary' economic ideas from 1792 to 1794.

But Roger Dugrand also accepts that, when analysing the resistance of the inhabitants to successive economic challenges in the eighteenth and nineteenth centuries—Tubeuf in the 1770s and 80s, the demise of the traditional nîmois textile industry by the 1830s, the disease which crippled the raw-silk industry in the 1850s, followed by the phylloxera disaster a generation later—one constant theme emerges: the vital importance of land. Throughout our period, the production of raw silk and the production of wine produced a certain culture, one might almost say, a cévenol civilization. Interesting that during a conference held only a decade or so ago which discussed, among other things, the possibility of substituting 'an intensive polyculture for the monoculture of the vine' (plus ça change . . . !) in Bas-Langue-doc, it was noted that 'Every reconversion is agonizing, forced to confront stubborn sociological obstacles.'[80] The sociology of resistance to rapid and brutal economic or political change helps to explain the

---

[79] M. Agulhon, *The Republic in the Village: The People of the Var from the French Revolution to the Second Republic* (Cambridge, 1982), 1.

[80] Laurent, 'Les Quatre Ages du vignoble du Bas-Languedoc et du Roussillon', 36.

bitter resistance to Pierre-François Tubeuf. Instructive to note that, following her husband's death, Mme Tubeuf became distinctly paranoic about over-rapid expansion, whilst her sons were obliged, after 1809, to accept the slower rhythms of the commercial, cévenol way of doing things.

Just after Christmas in 1786, a mining engineer named Dietrich, and a representative of one of the most influential bourgeois families in Alès Louis Dhombres, *procureur fiscal du comté d'Alais*, had accompanied no less grand a person than the maréchal de Castries on an inspection of the maréchal's new industrial property—the Grand-Combe mine. Emerging rather late from their underground tour, they discovered that it was too dark to make the journey home. Dhombres gathered some firewood 'and we ate a little by the light of the big fire that I had lit in the open air'.[81] It was a historic moment, *un Grand*, a *grand bourgeois*, and a mining engineer, standing on the threshold of modern industrialization. Over fifty years later, on 19 August 1840, an equally historic, but more publicized, event occurred in one of the Grand-Combe's main mining galleries. A buffet, complete with ice-cream, for guests invited to celebrate the opening of the Nîmes to Grand-Combe railway.[82] The threshold had been crossed. This study has endeavoured to explain why that crossing had taken over sixty years to complete.

[81] *AN* 306AP 487, Crozade to Castries, 27 Dec. 1786.

[82] 'Ce jour-là, un train de 26 wagons découverts, comme ils l'étaient tous dans les débuts, chargés de 700 invités, parmi lesquels de nombreuses dames, partit à 8 heures du matin et arriva à Nîmes à 9.15 heures. "Cette rapidité est presque féerique" dit un compte-rendu du temps.' Bruyère, *Alès, capitale des Cévennes*, 522.

BIBLIOGRAPHY

PRIMARY SOURCES

AN (Archives nationales)

Apart from the private papers of the Tubeuf family (see below), this *chartrier de Castries*, inventoried by M. Chassin du Guerny and available on microfiche, was the most important archival source for this study. It is a remarkably rich source for the study of the coal-mines of the Alès basin as well as for the landed estates of the maréchal de Castries covering the *comté d'Alais*.

3006AP 481 to 539

F14 (Travaux publics)

The relevant dossiers in this *série* proved to be the next most important source in the *archives nationales*, particularly:

F14 4240, *statistique des mines, 1740–1850.*

F14 4259, *exploitation des mines.*

F14 7670, *mines de Trouilhas, Saint-Jean-de-Valériscle, 1749–1814.*

F14 7671, covering most of the mines in the Alès coal-basin, year III-1822.

F14 7673, *renseignements sur les mines, year III–1834.*

F14 7677, *mines de Champcloson, year V–1831.*

F14 7682–88, *mines de la Grand-Combe, 1773–1888.*

F14 7912, *dossiers concernant plusieurs départements.*

F14 10291–9–1–49, and

F14 10363–4–1–5, contain a comprehensive collection of contemporary maps and drawings of the mines in the Alès basin.

F12 (Commerce et industrie)

Amongst the most important dossiers in this rich *série* were:

F12 235, *état des mines et usines.*

F12 502–18, *entrée des houilles étrangères.*

F12 611*a*, *situation commerciale, 1804–1819.*

F12 611*b*, *situation commerciale, 1820–1823.*

F12 618, *liste des fabricants du Gard.*

F12 652, *pétitions au Comité d'agriculture, 1789–an II.*

F12 780, Lansel to Saint-Priest, 20 Mar. 1783.
—— letter to the *Garde des Sceaux*, 4 Apr. 1771.
—— letters of Lansel to the *Garde des Sceaux*, 17 and 20 Mar. 1783.
—— *mémoire des maîtres-ouvriers à l'intendent*, 3 Mar. 1783.
—— *mémoire des négociants à l'intendant*, 28 Feb., Mar. 1783.
—— *observations et avis sur les contestations qui se sont élevées contre les frères Vidal, marchands juifs*, Feb. 1785.
F12 1228, *foire d'Alais*.
F12 1300, *forges, objets généraux, enquête sur les mines et forges. 1773–74*.
F12 1437, *manufactures, soieries*.
F12 1560/2 *coalitions, 1798–1810*.
F12 1569, *renseignements statistiques sur l'industrie et le commerce des départements de l'an IX à 1807*.
F12 1624, *statistique industrielle et manufacturière de 1811*.
F12 2291–2, *statistique de la soie*.
F12 2421, *mémoire sur les mines et les carrières, 1767–1858*.
F12 2713, *enquête sur le commerce et l'industrie, 1813*.
F12 4476a, *industrie dans le Gard, 1830*.

90AQ

Although the bulk of the material in 90AQ (Compagnie des mines de la Grand-Combe) relates to the post-1850 period, valuable information for the earlier period may be gleaned from:

90AQ-107–25, *dossiers d'études techniques, 1832–1944*.

100AQ

100AQ (Compagnie des mines, fonderies et forges d'Alais) contains some information (particularly 1–19, and 32–3); but again this collection is focused on the post-1830 period.

AG (Archives du Gard)

58J

Together with the Castries papers, the richest source-material for this work was undoubtedly 58J (les archives de Pierre-François Tubeuf). Details of the private journals, letters etc, contained in this archive are as follows:

58J 1, *Papiers de Pierre-François Tubeuf et de sa femme, 1771–1783*.
58J 2, *Journal des mines royales du bas-Languedoc, mars 1770–mai 1791*.
58J 3, *Journal du détail et menues dépenses de mes affaires domestiques et particulières*.
58J 4, *Livre de correspondance, novembre 1779–octobre 1791*.
58J 5, *Copies de lettres, entrées, notes, opérations, 1786–1791*.

58J 6 cover Tubeuf's operations in Normandy and the outskirts of Paris.

18J

18J 1, *pièces antérieures à la constitution de la société des mines et des chemins de fer du Gard, 1794–1835.*

18J 2, *mines de la Grand-Combe.*

18J 11–15, *comptabilité (commerce des houilles).*

22J

22J 4–5, *Deveau de Robiac, journal 1827–1836; 1823–39.*

22J 24, *Robiac: Registres des délibérations municipales, 1836–1846.*

22J 31, *chemins de fer, projets etc. 1835–1861.*

22J 40, *cartes et plans.*

This *série* would prove invaluable for anyone seeking to work upon the Deveau de Robiac family and their involvement in coal and steel-making during the nineteenth century.

C

For the pre-Revolutionary period see *série* C, in particular:

C186, *lettres du maréchal de Castries.*

C194, *lettres, mémoires . . . concernant les oppositions formées contre . . . M. de Tubeuf.*

C374, *réclamation du diocèse d'Alais contre . . . M. de Tubeuf.*

C430, *procès entre le diocèse (d'Alais) et le sieur Tubeuf.*

C431, *rapport du sieur de Camont* (against Tubeuf's concession).

C511, *état des contribuables sujets au payement au vingtième de l'industrie,* 1760.

IVE

IVE 22, *syndic de la fabrique de bas au Garde des Sceaux,* Jan. 1754.

IVE 23, letter to Vergennes, 25 Jan. 1787, 12 Mar. 1783.

—— *mémoire à M. Sartine,* 28 Dec. 1778.

—— *mémoire des marchands-fabricants de Nîmes,* 1778.

—— *mémoire des négociants de Nîmes à l'intendant,* 31 Jan. 1784.

—— *mémoire présenté sur les règlements du commerce,* 1780.

—— *mémoires à l'intendant,* 15 Feb. 1779, 24. Feb. 1780.

—— tableau de l'état annuel de la fabrique de bonneterie de Nîmes, 24 Feb. 1780.

IVE 31, *visite des syndics,* 1786.

IVE 139, letters to the Intendant, 6 May 1782, 19 Apr. 1788.

—— *mémoire des marchands-cardeurs de filoselle,* 31 Oct. 1789.

—— *mémoire des syndics de la communauté des cardeurs de la filoselle,* 17 Jan. 1785.

L

For the Revolutionary period, the following dossiers in *série* L proved most useful:

L421, *district d'Alais; troubles à Barjac et Saint-Ambroix.*
L488, *industrie et commerce; manufacture de soie et bourette.*
L767, *biens d'émigrés, Lacroix–Castries*
L770, *bois, mines et salins nationaux, 1790–an VIII.*
L912, *mines; tableaux de l'an II; divers, 1792–an VIII.*
L1048, *entretien des chemins, ponts, mines* . . . .
L3456–61, *canton d'Alès, justice de paix, an 111–VIII.*

8S

Série 8S (*Travaux publics et transports, an VIII–1940*) contains a variety of information on mines, accidents, etc. See, in particular:

8S 1, *lois, ordonnances, décrets, 1791–1853.*
8S 21, *exploitation: états et rapports, an IX–1900*
8S 22, *exploitations illicites, an XI–1870.*
8S 36, *accidents, procès-verbaux, 1825–1937.*
8S 46, *demandes, plaintes, pétitions, an IX–1941.*
8S 95, *pétitions, réclamations, communes d'Alès, Laval, Salles du Gard et autres, an IX–1812.*
8S 96, *avis du préfet du Gard,* Year XI; n.d. (1804).
——— Chabrol to prefect, 24 Mess. Year XIII.
——— prefect of the Gard to Minister of the Interior, n.d. (Year XI).
8S 97, *plan général des mines de houille comprises entre Alès et Portes.*
8S 98, *registres d'inscriptions de demandes en concessions de mines, 1810–1900.*
8S 104–8, *ordonnances et arrêtés de concession ou de rejet, an IX–1940.*

6M

The 6M *série* (*population, statistique*) contains very detailed information on population and social structures, particularly after 1800. The most relevant dossiers were:

6M 2, *tableau numérique, mariage, décès, an VIII–1840.*
6M 100–1, *état numérique de la population des communes des arrondissements d'Alès et de Nîmes.*
6M 102, *tableau numérique de la population des communes du département de plus de 1000 âmes.*
6M 103, *tableau numérique . . . mariage, culte, 1811–1820* . . . .
6M 104, *état numérique de la population, 1822–1830.*
6M 105, *communes des arrondissement d'Alès, le Vigan* . . . .
6M 106–8, dossiers containing very detailed breakdown of population by sex, marriage, etc.

6M 651, *de la vie familiale: mendiants* . . . .

6M 653, *statistique du département du Gard de M. Rivoire, 1827–1845.*

6M 665, *état numérique de la population des communes et répartition par hameaux, maisons* . . . .

6M 670, *statistique personelle.*

6M 671, *renseignements sur les principaux familles du département, 1809–13.*

6M 672, *états numériques des maisons, feux, familles du département*

6M 673, contains questionnaires on industry and commerce for 1838.

9M

The *série 9M* is indispensable for any social and economic study of the region. For this period, see:

9M 6–7, *renseignements sur la situation des fabriques, 1790–1806; 1807–1814.*

9M 8, *gives details of major industrial activities in each arrondissement of the Gard.*

9M 9–10, *tableaux des industries et manufactures, 1812–1813.*

9M 16–23, *états des fabriques et manufactures du Gard, 1808–1846.*

9M 24–41, *états de la situation industrielle et commerciale du Gard, 1810–1903.*

9M 44–47, *procédés pour l'amélioration de rendement des entreprises industrielles . . . an IX–1822.*

9M 48, *brevets d'invention, 1792–1837.*

AC Alès (archives communales d'Alès)

In the *archives du Gard.*

1D

1D 36–50, *délibérations du conseil municipal, 1781–1848.*

11D

11D 1–5, *actes de l'administration municipale, 1812–1838.*

11D 11–21, *correspondance, 1792–1838.*

AC Anduze (archives communales d'Anduze)

In the *archives du Gard.*

HH

HH 15–16, *jurandes, 1760–1789.*

2F

2F 3, *commerce, industrie, 1790–1813.*

3F

3F 1–2, *agriculture, 1790–1817.*

4F

4F 23, *travail, livres des apprentis, an XII–1821.*

AH (archives de l'Hérault)

C

The very rich *série* C in the *archives de l'Hérault* includes several important dossiers, particularly:

C1846, *role de répartition de la capitation des vigueries d'Alais et d'Anduze.*
C2250, *mémoire sur la culture de mûrier, 1743–1762.*
C4680, *mémoire* (on the shortage of wood).
C5602, *mémoire sur la filature de soie des Cévennes, 1744–1778.*
C5659–664, several very important dossiers on the coal-mines of the Alès basin and the struggle between Castries and Tubeuf.
C6547, *mémoire sur le diocèse d'Alais, 1761–1778*
C6689, *désordres aux mines de Saint-Sauveur, 1773–1780.*
C6690, *désordres aux mines de Tubeuf.*

AHC (archives des Houillères des Cévennes)

Fonds Tubeuf, Cajon to Tubeuf, 3 Oct. 1778.
—— *état des fonds que j'ai employé pour mon entreprise d'Alais.*
—— *mémoire que Tubeuf, Directeur des mines de Cransac, a l'honneur à présenter aux messieurs les intéressés aux mines, 29 février 1768.*
Ordonnance de M. l'Intendant, 15 July 1776.
Papiers de Tubeuf, Cambis to Tubeuf, 9 July 1784.

PRINTED SOURCES

Apart from the printed sources contained in the departmental archives, the Bibliothèque de Nîmes (B. de N.) and the Musée Calvet in Avignon house extensive collections of manuscript and printed works on the history of Bas-Languedoc and Provence.

Regional Works

AGULHON, M., *La Vie sociale en Provence intérieure* (Paris, 1970).
—— *The Republic in the Village: The People of the Var from the French Revolution to the Second Republic* (Cambridge, 1982).
ALLEN, E. A., 'Deforestation and Fuel Crisis in Pre-Revolutionary Languedoc', *French Historical Studies*, 13 (1984).
ARMOGATHE, J., and JOUTARD, P., 'Bâville et la guerre des Camisards', *Revue d'histoire moderne et contemporaine*, 19 (1972).
BARDON, A., *L'Exploitation du bassin houiller d'Alais sous l'ancien régime* (Nîmes, 1898).
BRUYÈRE, M., *Alès, capitale des Cévennes: vie politique, religieuse, intellectuelle, économique et sociale* (Nîmes, 1948).
CAVALIER, J., *Mémoires sur la guerre des Camisards* (Paris, 1979).
CAYRIER-GILLIOT, L., 'Discours pour vivre ou survivre: une histoire de la sériciculture en Ardèche au XIXe siècle', *112e Congrès national des sociétés savantes* (Lyon, 1987).
COSSON, A., 'Industrie de la soie et population ouvrière à Nîmes de 1815 à 1848', in *Économie et société en Languedoc-Roussillon de 1789 à nos jours* (Montpellier, 1978).
—— 'L'Industrie textile à Nîmes: la fin d'une hégémonie, 1790–1850', *Mouvement social*, 133 (1985).
DELORMEAU, C., 'L'Arrêt du Conseil du 14 janvier 1744 sur les mines de charbon et son application dans le diocèse d'Alès', in *Mines et mineurs en Languedoc-Roussillon et régions voisines de l'Antiquité à nos jours* (Montpellier, 1977).
DUCEL, A., 'Les Notables dans le Bas-Languedoc à l'époque napoléonienne', in *Économie et société en Languedoc-Roussillon de 1789 à nos jours* (Montpellier, 1978).
DUGRAND, R., *Villes et campagnes en Bas-Languedoc* (Paris, 1963).
DUPORT, A.-M., 'Le Fédéralisme gardois: de la théorie à la pratique', in *110e Congrès national des sciences sociales* (Montpellier, 1985), ii: *Histoire moderne*.
DUTIL, L., *L'État économique de Languedoc à la fin de l'ancien régime, 1750–1789* (Paris, 1911).
FARELLE, F. de la, *Étude historique sur le consulat et les institutions municipales de la ville de Nîmes, suivie d'un mémoire sur son passé industriel* (Nîmes, 1841).
FITZPATRICK, B., *Catholic Royalism in the Department of the Gard, 1814–1852* (Cambridge, 1983).
FROMENT, F., *Charles Sincère à Pierre Roman* (Nîmes, 1790).
GAILLARD, J.-M., 'La Naissance d'une entreprise industrielle au XIXe siècle: la compagnie des mines de la Grand-Combe', in *Mines et mineurs en Languedoc-Roussillon et régions voisines de l'Antiquité à nos jours* (Montpellier, 1977).
GALY, G.-R., 'L'Exploitation des houillères en Languedoc et le marché du charbon au XVIIIe siècle', *Annales du Midi*, 81 (1969).

GENSANNE, M., *Histoire naturelle de la province de Languedoc, publiée par ordre de NN. SS. des États de cette province*, 4 vols. (Montpellier, 1778).

GOIRAND, J. P., 'Documents historiques sur Alais pendant la Révolution', *Société scientifique et littéraire d'Alais*, 19 (1887).

——— 'Étude sur la ville d'Alais', *Société scientifique et littéraire d'Alais*, 26 (1891).

GUICHARD, P., 'D'une société repliée à une société ouverte: l'évolution socio-économique de la région d'Andance de la fin du XVIIe siècle à la Révolution', in P. Léon, *Structures économiques et problèmes sociaux du monde rural dans la France du sud-est* (Paris, 1966).

HOOD, J., 'Permanence des conflits traditionnels sous la Révolution: l'exemple du Gard', *Revue d'histoire moderne et contemporaine*, 24 (1977).

HUARD, R., *Le Mouvement républicain en Bas-Languedoc* (Paris, 1982).

JOHNSON, C., 'Artisans versus Fabricants: Urban Protoindustrialisation and the Evolution of Work Culture in Lodève and Bédarieux, 1740–1830', *European University Institute (Florence) Working Paper*, No. 85/137, n.d.

JONES, P., *Politics and Rural Society: The Southern Massif Central, 1750–1880* (Cambridge, 1985).

JOUTARD, P., *Les Camisards* (Paris, 1976).

——— (ed.), *Les Cévennes de la montagne à l'homme* (Toulouse, 1979).

LAFONT, R., *La Revendication occitane* (Paris, 1974).

LAURENT, R., 'Les Quatre Âges du vignoble du bas-Languedoc et du Roussillon', in *Économie et société en Languedoc-Roussillon de 1789 à nos jours* (Montpellier, 1978).

——— and GAVIGNAUD, G., *La Révolution française dans le Languedoc méditerranée* (Toulouse, 1987).

LEWIS, G., *The Second Vendée* (Oxford, 1978).

——— 'Political Brigandage and Popular Disaffection in the South-East of France, 1795–1804', in G. Lewis and C. Lucas (eds.), *Beyond the Terror: Essays in French Regional and Social History, 1794–1815* (Cambridge, 1983).

——— 'A Cévenol Community in Crisis: The Mystery of "L'Homme à Moustache" ', *Past and Present*, 109 (1985).

LOCKE, R., *Les Fonderies et forges d'Alais à l'époque des premiers chemins de fer, 1829–1874* (Paris, 1978).

MOLINIER, A., 'En Vivarais au XVIIIe siècle: une croissance démographique sans révolution agricole', *Annales du Midi*, 92 (1980).

MORINEAU, M., and CARRIÈRE, C., 'Draps de Languedoc et commerce du Levant au XVIIIe siècle', *Revue d'histoire économique et sociale*, 56 (1968).

PÉZERIL, C., *Ces mineurs de Littry: pionniers de l'ouest* (Bayeux, 1978).

Recherches historiques sur la ville d'Alais (Alès, 1860).

REID, D., *The Miners of Decazeville: A Genealogy of Deindustrialization* (Cambridge, Mass., 1985).

RIOU, M., 'La Terreur blanche dans le département du Gard: aspects économiques et sociaux', in *Économie et société en Languedoc-Roussillon de 1789 à nos jours* (Montpellier, 1978).

RIVIÈRE-DEJEAN, M., 'De l'émancipation de la bourgeoisie et des fonctions consulaires d'Alais', *Société scientifique et littéraire d'Alais*, 24 (1893).

RIVOIRE, J., *Statistique du département du Gard* (Nîmes, 1842).

ROUVIÈRE, F., *L'Exploitation des mines nationales du Gard, 1792–1810* (Nîmes, 1901).

—— *Mercredis révolutionnaires* (Nîmes, 1901).

SABATIER, G., 'De la révolte de Roure (1670) aux masques armés (1783): la mutation du phénomène contestataire en Vivarais', in J. Nicolas (ed.), *Mouvements populaires et conscience sociale, XVIᵉ–XIXᵉ siècles* (Paris, 1985).

SONENSCHER, M., 'Royalists and Patriots: Nîmes and its Hinterland in the Late-Eighteenth Century', Ph.D. thesis, Warwick, 1975.

THOMSON, J., *Clermont-de-Lodève, 1633–1789: Fluctuations in the Prosperity of a Languedocian Cloth-Making Town* (Cambridge, 1982).

—— 'Variations in Industrial Structures in Protoindustrial Languedoc', in Berg *et al.* (eds.), *Manufacture in Town and Country before the Factory Age*.

WOLFF, P., *Histoire du Languedoc* (Toulouse, 1967).

—— *Documents de l'histoire du Languedoc* (Toulouse, 1969).

General Works

AFTALION, F., *The French Revolution: An Economic Interpretation* (Cambridge, 1990).

AMINZADE, R., 'Re-interpreting Capital Industrialisation: A Study of Nineteenth-Century France', *Social History*, 9 (1984).

ASSELAIN, J.-C., *Histoire économique de la France du XVIIIᵉ siècle à nos jours*, i (Paris, 1984).

BAKER, K. (ed.), *The French Revolution and the Creation of Modern Political Culture*, i: *The Political Culture of the Old Regime* (Oxford, 1987).

BEREND, I., and RANKI, G., *The European Periphery and Industrialization* (Cambridge, 1982).

BERG, M., HUDSON, P., and SONENSCHER, M. (eds.), *Manufacture in Town and Country before the Factory Age* (Cambridge, 1983).

BONIN, H., 'La Révolution française, a-t-elle brisée l'esprit d'entreprise?', *Information historique*, 47 (1985).

BOSSENGA, G., 'City and State: An Urban Perspective on the Origins of the French Revolution', in Baker (ed.), *The Political Culture of the Old Regime*.

BRAUDEL, F., *Une Leçon d'histoire de Fernand Braudel* (Paris, 1986).

CASTRIES, DUC DE, *Papiers de famille* (Paris, 1977).

—— *Notice historique et descriptive* (Paris, n.d.).

CHAUSSINAND-NOGARET, G., *The French Nobility in the Eighteenth Century: From Feudalism to Enlightenment* (Cambridge, 1985).

CIRIACONO, S., 'Esquisse d'une histoire tripolaire: les soieries franco-italiennes et le marché allemand à l'époque moderne', *Études réunies en l'honneur du Doyen Georges Livet* (Strasbourg, 1986).

CLARK, G., 'Why Isn't the Whole World Developed?', *Journal of Economic History*, 47 (1987).

CLOUT, H., *Agriculture in France on the Eve of the Railway Age* (London, 1980).

COBBAN, A., *The Social Interpretation of the French Revolution* (Cambridge, 1964).

COLLINS, B., 'Protoindustrialisation and Pre-famine Emigration', *Social History*, 7 (1982).

CRAFTS, N., 'Economic Growth in France and Britain, 1830–1910: A Review of the Evidence', *Journal of Economic History*, 44 (1984).

CROUZET, F., 'Angleterre et France au XVIIIe siècle: essai d'analyse comparée de deux croissances', *Annales, Économie, Société, Civilisation*, 21 (1966).

—— *De la supériorité de l'Angleterre sur la France: l'économique et l'imaginaire, XVIIe–XXe siècles* (Paris, 1985).

—— 'Guerres, blocus et changement économique, 1792–1815', in *De la supériorité de l'Angleterre sur la France*.

DEWERPE, A., *L'Industrie aux champs* (Rome, 1985).

DEYON, P., and MENDELS, F., 'La Proto-industrialisation: théorie et réalité', *Revue du Nord*, 63(248) (1981).

DOYLE, W., *Origins of the French Revolution* (Oxford, 1980).

EPSZTEIN, L., *L'Économie et la morale aux débuts du capitalisme industriel en France et en Grande-Bretagne* (Paris, 1966).

FISHER, C., *Custom, Work and Market Capitalism: The Forest of Dean Colliers, 1788–1888* (London, 1981).

FLINN, M. and STOKER, D., *The History of the British Coal Industry, 1700–1830: The Industrial Revolution* (Oxford, 1984).

GARMY, R., *La Mine aux mineurs de Rancié, 1789–1848* (Paris, 1970).

GEIGER, R., *The Anzin Coal Company, 1800–1833* (Philadelphia, Pa., 1974).

GILLE, B., *Histoire de la Maison Rothschild*, i: *Des origines à 1848* (Paris, 1965).

GUTTON, J.-P., *Domestiques et serviteurs dans la France de l'ancien régime* (Paris, 1981).

HAMPSON, N., *A Social History of the French Revolution* (London, 1963).

HARDMAN, J. (ed.), *French Revolution Documents*, ii (Oxford, 1973).

HARRIS, J., 'The Diffusion of English Metallurgical Methods to Eighteenth-Century France', *French History*, 2 (1988).

—— 'Skills, Coal and British Industry in the Eighteenth Century', *History*, 52 (1967).

HARRISON, R. (ed.), *The Independent Collier* (London, 1977).

HEYWOOD, C., 'The Role of the Peasantry in French Industrialisation, 1815–1880', *Economic History Review*, 34 (1981).

HIGONNET, P., *Class, Ideology, and the Rights of Nobles during the French Revolution* (Oxford, 1981).

HUDSON, P., *The Genesis of Industrial Capitalism* (Cambridge, 1986).

—— 'Protoindustrialisation: The Case of the West Riding Wool Textile Industry in the Eighteenth and Nineteenth Century', *History Workshop*, 12 (1981).

HUNT, L., *Politics, Culture and Class in the French Revolution* (London, 1986).

HUTT, M. *Chouannerie and Counter-Revolution: Puisaye, the Princes and the British Government in the 1790s* (Cambridge, 1983).

JAMES, C. L., *The Black Jacobins: Toussaint L'Ouverture and the San Domingo Revolution* (London, 1982).

JARDIN, A., and TUDESQ, A. J. *La France des notables*, i: *L'Évolution générale, 1815–1848*, and ii: *La Vie de la nation, 1815–1848* (Paris, 1973).

JOHNSON, C., 'The Revolution of 1830 in French Economic History', in J. Merriman (ed.), *1830 in France* (New York, 1975).

JONES, E. L., 'The Agricultural Origins of Industry', *Past and Present*, 40 (1968).

—— 'Environment, Agriculture and Industrialization', *Agricultural History*, 51 (1977).

JONES, P., *The Peasantry in the French Revolution* (Cambridge, 1988).

JONES, S. R., 'Technology, Transition Costs, and the Transition to Factory Production in the British Silk Industry, 1700–1870', *Journal of Economic History*, 47 (1987).

Journal des mines, publié par l'Agence des mines de la République (Paris, 1794–). A major source of government information on all aspects of mining in France. (Becomes the *Annales des mines* during the Restoration.)

KRIEDTE, P., 'The Origins, the Agrarian Economy and the World Market', in *Industrialization before Industrialization* (Cambridge, 1981).

LABROUSSE, C.-E., *La Crise de l'économie française à la fin de l'ancien régime et au début de la Révolution*, i (Paris, 1944).

LANDES, D., *The Unbound Prometheus: Technological Change and Development in Western Europe from 1750 to the Present* (Cambridge, 1969).

LEFEBVRE, G., *La Grande Peur de 1789* (Paris, 1932).

—— 'Les Mines de Littry, 1744–an VIII', in *Études sur la Révolution française* (Paris, 1963).

LEMARCHAND, G., 'La Féodalité et la Révolution: seigneurie et communauté paysanne', *Annales historiques de la Révolution française*, 52 (1980).

LE ROY LADURIE, E., *Montaillou: The Promised Land of Error* (New York, 1979).

—— *The Mind and Method of the Historian* (Chicago, Ill., 1981).

LEWIS, E. D., *The Rhondda Valleys: A Study in Industrial Development, 1800 to the Present Day* (London, 1959).

MACKRELL, J. Q., *The Attack on 'Feudalism' in Eighteenth-Century France* (London, 1973).

MAGRAW, R., *France 1815–1914: The Bourgeois Century* (London, 1983).

MARION, M., *Le Brigandage pendant la Révolution* (Paris, 1934).

MARX K., and ENGELS, F., *Pre-capitalist Socio-Economic Formations* (Moscow, 1979).

MATHIAS, P., and DAVIS, J. (eds.), *The First Industrial Revolution* (London, 1990).

MENDELS, F., 'Protoindustrialization: The First Phase of the Industrialization Process', *Journal of Economic History*, 32 (1972).

—— 'Seasons and Regions in Agriculture and Industry during the Process of Industrialization', in S. Pollard (ed.), *Region und Industrialisierung* (Göttingen, 1980).

MILWARD, A., and SAUL, S., *The Economic Development of Continental Europe, 1780–1870* (London, 1973).

MORRIS, J., and WILLIAMS, L., *The South Wales Coal Industry, 1841–1875* (Cardiff, 1958).

MOUGEL, F. C., 'La Fortune des princes de Bourbon-Conty: revenus et gestion, 1655–1791', *Revue d'histoire moderne et contemporaine*, 18 (1971).

NYE, R., 'Firm Size and Economic Backwardness: A New Look at the French Industrial Debate', *Journal of Economic History*, 47 (1987).

O'BRIEN, P., and KEYDER, C., *Economic Growth in Britain and France, 1780–1914* (London, 1978).

PARISOT, E., *Les Industries de la soie* (Lyon, 1890).

PILBEAM, P., *The Middle Classes in Europe, 1789–1914* (London, 1990).

POLLARD, S., *Peaceful Conquest and the Industrialization of Europe, 1760–1970* (London, 1981).

PRICE, R., *The Modernization of Rural France: Communications Networks and Agricultural Market Structures in Nineteenth-Century France* (London, 1983).

ROCHE, D., *The People of Paris: An Essay in Popular Culture in the Eighteenth Century* (Leamington Spa, 1987).

ROEHL, R., 'French Industrialization: A Reconsideration', *Explorations in Economic History*, 13 (1976).

ROOT, H. L., *Peasants and King in Burgundy: Agrarian Foundations of French Absolutism*. (Berkeley, Calif., 1987).

ROUFF, M., *Les Mines de charbon en France au XVIIIe siècle, 1744–1791* (Paris, 1922).

—— *Tubeuf: un grand industriel français du XVIIIe siècle, 1744–1791* (Paris, 1922).

RULE, J., *The Experience of Labour in Eighteenth-Century Industry* (London, 1981).

SABEL, C., and ZEITLIN, J., 'Historical Alternatives to Mass Production: Markets and Technology in Nineteenth Century Industrialization', *Past and Present*, 108 (1985).

SÉE, H., *Histoire économique de la France: les temps modernes, 1789–1914*, ii (Paris, 1942).

SOBOUL, A., *Précis d'histoire de la Révolution française* (Paris, 1962).

SONENSCHER, M., *The Hatters of Eighteenth Century France* (London, 1987).

—— *Work and Wages: Natural Law, Politics and the Eighteenth-Century French Trades* (Cambridge, 1989).

STEIN, R. C., *Léger-Félicité Sonthonax* (Cranbury, NJ, 1985).

SUTHERLAND, D., *France, 1789–1815: Revolution and Counterrevolution* (London, 1985).

TARLÉ, E., *L'Industrie dans les campagnes en France à la fin de l'ancien régime* (Paris, 1910).

THOMPSON, E. P., 'Time, Work-Discipline, and Industrial Capitalism', *Past and Present*, 38 (1967).

—— *The Making of the English Working Class* (London, 1970).

TILLY, C., 'Flows of Capital and Forms of Industry in Europe, 1500–1800', *Theory and Society*, 12 (1983).

TULARD, J., *Napoleon: The Myth of the Saviour* (London, 1984).

WOOLF, S., *The Poor in Western Europe in the Eighteenth and Nineteenth Centuries* (London, 1986).

WORONOFF, D., *L'Industrie sidérurgique en France pendant la Révolution et l'Empire* (Paris, 1984).

—— *The Thermidorean Regime and the Directory* (Cambridge, 1984).

YOUNG, A., *Travels in France during the Years 1787, 1788 and 1789* (Cambridge, 1950).

INDEX

Abilon, mines 1, 31, 81, 103, 110,
131–2, 142, 146–7, 178, 180–3,
190–1, 200, 211, 215, 240–1,
244–6, 249, 262, 266, 274–8
Abric 314
Aftalion, Florin 296–7
Agence des mines 184–5, 190–1, 242,
307–8
Agulhon, Maurice 15, 227, 317
Aigoin et Delord 223
Aiguesvives 230, 271
Airebeaudouze, brothers 14
Alais-Montalet, vicomte d' 126
Alès, municipal revolution 118–26
Allen, E. A. 21 n.
Alles, Louis 29, 38–9, 46, 76, 91, 97,
99, 107, 111, 131
Alphonse, baron 214, 269
Alzon, Daudé d' 83
Aminzade, R. 67
Amsterdam 161, 219–20
Andance 71
Anduze 2, 5, 8–9, 26, 56–7, 59–60, 68,
70–1, 75–7, 101, 118, 216, 218–19,
226–8, 253, 258–9, 270, 273, 290,
295, 302, 313
    seigneurie d' 14
    viguerie d' 16
Ango 275
Antoinette, Marie 63, 82, 155
Anzin, mines 24, 31, 34, 82, 171, 197,
240, 291, 307
Arbaud Jouques, marquis d' 253
Arbousset, Jean 79
Argenson, André 250–1
Arles 139
Artois comte d' 255
Asselain, Jean-Charles 184
Assembly of Notables 118
assignats 168–9
Aubenas 3, 26, 70, 76, 101
Aubin 25
Aubrespin, Jacques 90, 181, 206, 263,
266
Aulas 225
Auzonnet, valley 31

Avignon 26, 228

bagarre de Nîmes 117, 147, 150–5, 165–8,
171, 184, 212, 216, 252
Bagnols 17, 59, 144, 218, 273
Baker, Keith 115 n.
Ballainvilliers 9, 67–8, 72, 94, 178
Balleroy, marquis de 24
Balore, Courtois de 110–11
Baltimore 234
Banne, mine 27, 31, 33–4, 43, 46, 84,
91, 109, 149, 194
Bardon, Achille 23, 36, 100, 138,
144–5, 163, 174, 176
bassines à la Gensoul 272–3
Bastide, Louis-Joseph 148
Barbut, Jean 176
Barjac 26–7, 182
Barrot, Jean-André 287
    and Guiraudet 278–82, 287–8
    Odilon 213, 264, 267, 287
Barruel, abbé de 154
Barthélemy 44
Bausset, Monseigneur de 111
Bâville 6, 12
Bayeux 19
Beaucaire 1, 3, 89, 96, 99, 123, 203,
220–1, 306, 315
Beaunier, Ingénieur-en-chef 240–2,
245–6, 275
Beauteville, de 84–5
Bellegarde 271
Bénezet 59
Berg, Maxine 99
Bertin, Henri 18, 20, 24, 26, 51–3, 85,
101–5 passim 111, 132, 163, 173,
208, 220, 308
Bessèges 2, 31, 246, 278, 295, 312
Birkbeck, M. 290
Blacas, duc de 252
Blaenant, mine 264–5
Blake, William 290
Blancher 183
Boncerf 145
Bonald, Louis de 309
Bonin, H. 184